THE CLUB

Also by Stephen Brook

The Double Eagle (1988)
Liquid Gold: dessert wines of the world (1987)
Maple Leaf Rag: Travels Across Canada (1987)
The Dordogne (1986)
Honkytonk Gelato: Travels Through Texas (1985)
New York Days, New York Nights (1984)

STEPHEN BROOK

✤ THE CLUB ✤

The Jews
of modern Britain

CONSTABLE · LONDON

First published in Great Britain 1989
by Constable and Company Limited
10 Orange Street London WC2H 7EG
Copyright © 1989 Stephen Brook
Set in Linotron Ehrhardt 11pt by
Rowland Phototypesetting Limited
Bury St Edmunds, Suffolk
Printed in Great Britain by
St Edmundsbury Press Limited
Bury St Edmunds, Suffolk

British Library CIP data
Brook, Stephen
The club: Anglo-Jewry observed.
1. Great Britain. Jewish communities. Social
life.
I. Title
305.8′924′041

ISBN 0 09 467340 3

Contents

Contents

Acknowledgements

No book of this kind could ever be written without the generosity and help of a large number of people. I owe a great debt of gratitude to the many people who gave me access to their time and knowledge and experience. I particularly wish to thank:

Leo Abse; Bella Aronovitch; Sir Isaiah Berlin; Sidney Bloch; Anthony Blond; Rabbi Barbara Borts; Rabbi B. Berkovits; Leon Brittan; Michael and Kitty Brod; Helene Bromnick; Simon Caplan; Melvyn Carlowe; Rita Christie; Michael Codron; Shimon Cohen; David Collins; Dr Kenneth Collins; Morton Creeger; Rabbi A. B. David; Eva Figes; Sir Monty Finniston; William Frankel; Steven Fruhman; Tony and Marion Godfrey; Rabbi David Goldberg; Mark Goldberg; Raymond Goldman; Ezra Golombok; Lord Goodman; Alan Greenbat; Henry Guterman; Sir Sidney Hamburger; Arieh Handler; Rabbi Dr Louis Jacobs; Chief Rabbi Lord Jakobovits; Hon. Greville Janner; Stanley Kalms; Melvyn Kaufman; R. B. Kitaj; Nick Kochan; Dr Lionel Kopelowitz; Dr John Launer; Ivan Lawrence; Tony Lerman; Dr S. S. Levenberg; Rabbi Shlomo Levin; Rabbi Dr Abraham Levy; Jonathan Lew; Rabbi Jonathan Magonet; Rabbi Rodney Mariner; Dennis Marks; Ian Mikardo; Dr Jack Miller; Dr Jonathan Miller; Dr Maurice Miller; Sir Alan Mocatta; Marjorie Moos; Sir Claus Moser; Rabbi Julia Neuberger; Geoffrey Paul; Manny Penner; Hayim Pinner; Rabbi Avraham Pinter; Rabbi Alan Plancey; Dame Simone Prendergast; Frederic Raphael; Monty Richardson; Margaret Rigal; Rabbi Michael Rosen; Jack Rosenthal; Rabbi Michael Rosin; Evelyn de Rothschild; Ann Salingar; Trudy Schama; Rebbetzin Judith Schlesinger; Colin Shindler; Lois Sieff; Anthony Simmons; Ita Simons; Clive Sinclair; Dr Walter Sneader; Professor George Steiner; Deborah

Stuart; Arthur Sunderland; Dr Henry and Mrs Judith Tankel; Rabbi S. F. Vogel; Lord Weidenfeld; Esther Whitby; Dianna Wolfson. I also thank those few who assisted me but did not wish to be named in the book.

Rabbi Dr Isaac Levy was kind enough to cast his expert eye over some of my writings on Jewish belief and expunged errors. Any that remain should be blamed on me. I am also grateful to the staff of the Mocatta Library at University College, London. And finally, I must express great gratitude to my wife Maria, who must, as the deadline approached, have thought she was living with a zombie.

S. B.
1988

Author's Note

In writing this book I have made the hopeful assumption that its readership will not be confined to British Jews. It has therefore seemed important to say something about the history and beliefs of Jews, both traditional and Progressive. Those readers already well versed in these matters may wish to skip lightly through some of the opening chapters. On the other hand, it has become clear to me in the course of my researches that the ignorance of one group about the tenets and attitudes of various others is astonishing. I hope to have shed light on these different religious groupings in a reasonably dispassionate way.

Jews not only have very different ways of worshipping and observing their religion, but they also have different ways of pronouncing Hebrew. The Ashkenazi pronunciation, which held sway in most British synagogues until quite recently, is gradually giving way to the Sephardim pronunciation, since the latter is much closer to modern Hebrew or Ivrit. The principal difference between the two systems is that many s's are turned into t's, and o's into a's. Thus the Ashkenazi sound *hot* would be rendered as *hut* by an Ivrit speaker. I have not tried to be consistent. Many older Jews cling to Ashkenazi pronunciation, and it seemed cavalier on my part to transcribe, say, the 'Shabbos' they spoke into the 'Shabbat' they should have spoken. Readers who enjoy picking out inconsistencies will therefore have a field day.

Foreword

There is, in Britain, as in most nations of the Western world, a club known as the Jewish community. Its most curious feature is that new members are not elected but born. Membership, like an ancient title of nobility, is inherited. Some find the inheritance a joy, others a burden, and others are indifferent. The club is difficult for outsiders to join, and new applications are not sought, despite declining membership. Once you are in the club, it is, as George Steiner once remarked to a colleague who disclosed he was 'no longer Jewish', almost impossible to resign from it. Resignations do occur, and at a rate that alarms the club's directors, but in times of stress the non-Jewish community has been known to fail to distinguish between active and former members. Although club activists scorn those who disregard the club's strict rules, the outside world finds little to choose between observant and non-observant members. Fidelity to the rulebook is an internal matter.

On any Saturday morning, some members observe certain rituals unique to the club. Others ignore them. In a converted Edwardian house in a Manchester suburb, a young man dressed in a frock-coat from which his white stockinged legs protrude like sticks is immersed in prayer. His bearded head is covered in a white and black shawl as he sways forward and back, and from side to side, murmuring and occasionally shouting a word or phrase for emphasis. Behind him sit two of his small sons, little boys with closely cropped hair and light whiskery side curls framing their pale faces. They too are praying, but with less concentration, for they are nudging each other and whispering admonishments in Yiddish.

Meanwhile in London, in a more elegant house in a more elegant suburb, a long-faced man is deep in thought. He is not praying. He has

11

never prayed. Instead, he is working, mapping out the framework of a new theatrical production. He too is a member of the club, though he has never been known to attend a meeting. He is a busy and inventive man, and is simply not interested in the club's innumerable activities. He does not conceal his Jewishness, but finds that it plays no part in his life. Yet, despite himself, it does, for there is something about his brilliance and intellectual fertility that is recognizable as peculiarly if indefinably Jewish.

South of the Thames, a teenage girl is gazing into a full-length mirror. She is admiring her appearance, and with good reason. On most Saturday mornings, she would be scampering about in jeans and a T-shirt, but today she is wearing a new frock, tied prettily around the waist with a bright sash. Her hair, normally curly and unruly, has been laced with ribbons. In a few minutes, her parents will drive her to a local synagogue, where she will participate in one of the rituals that play so important a part among the activities of the club. She and a few other girls of a similar age will confirm their allegiance to the club. There is a fly in the ointment. Her father is Jewish, her mother is not. Consequently, in the eyes of those who guard the rulebook, she is not a Jew. But she thinks she is, and so does her rabbi. Indeed, those who guard the rulebook don't think her rabbi is entitled to call herself a rabbi, for this rabbi is female. But she thinks she's a rabbi, and that's good enough for her and for her congregation.

I too am a member of the club, and I have spent the past year touring the membership. Because we are born and not elected, we are a diverse bunch of people, almost as chaotic and uncategorizable as the society within which we happen to find ourselves living. Tucked into a pluralist society, we flourish by being pluralistic ourselves. Despite the strictures of those who wave the rulebook, few sanctions are applied to those who ignore the rituals and ceremonies of the club. Whether we follow the rules or ignore them, we are still members. We are British Jews, and the subject of this book.

✤ A BRIEF HISTORY ✤

– 1 –

Laying the foundations

FOR almost 2,000 years dispersal has been the constant condition of the Jewish people. With the destruction of the Second Temple in Jerusalem in 70 AD and the doomed revolt of Bar Kochba against the Romans some seventy-five years later, the Jews found themselves better able to flourish out of Palestine than within it. The diaspora was established, and communities, often small, sprang up all over Europe, the Mediterranean, the Middle East, and Asia. England was no exception, and in the twelfth century there were Jewish settlements in York, Oxford, Winchester, and other towns. Norwich, with 200 Jews, was the largest centre of Jewish population, which in medieval Britain never exceeded 5,000. Although the Jews were well established in the community, and some had achieved wealth and influence, they learnt to live with derision and slander. Accused of ritual murder and other offences, though there was little evidence to support the accusations, they became targets of anti-Semitic fury that even took the form of massacres. Many Jews were moneylenders, and though their dealings provided much revenue to the monarchy, the complexity of their operations prompted much resentment among poorer borrowers. This resentment, together with the anti-Jewish decrees promulgated by Pope Innocent III in 1216, served to justify the increasing restrictions, including the seizure of assets, that hemmed in those English Jews who survived the executions and massacres. Towards the end of the thirteenth century, only 2,500 Jews remained in England, and in 1290 they were expelled by Edward I.

Although a handful of Jews came to London at the end of the fifteenth century after their expulsion from Spain, there was no significant return of Jews to England until the seventeenth century. With the establishment of the Commonwealth, an opportunity arose to argue to the puritanical masters of Britain on strictly biblical grounds that Jews should be readmitted. And in 1656, after much haggling, they were, largely thanks to the efforts of Menasseh ben Israel of Amsterdam. Nor did the restoration of the monarchy in 1660 affect the agreement. In many other parts of Europe, Jewish communities eked out an existence, some more successfully than others, but were invariably handcuffed by petty restrictions, frequent threats of expulsion, and even massacres. In England they were free of such restrictions, and so it was to remain. Not, of course, that Jews were regarded as first-class citizens of the nation, but then neither were Catholics or Nonconformists. Since no specific legislation curtailed the economic or social activities of the newly arrived Jews, they soon made their mark in English life, just as they had done in previous decades in the flourishing communities of Germany and Holland, from which many of the new immigrants had come. There would be no such thing as the ghetto in the history of Anglo-Jewry. The Jews adapted with remarkably little effort to their new circumstances. Some arrived in London with proven financial skills; others mastered the ways of the City until they too attained a measure of prosperity.

The dispersal of the Jews over the previous 1,500 years had resulted in the gradual development of two distinct groupings: the Sephardim and the Ashkenazim. They differed in matters of liturgy and ritual, although there was no doctrinal antagonism between the groups. Their difference is cultural. The Sephardim were, in the main, Spanish and Portuguese Jews who had enjoyed five centuries of cultural and intellectual splendour, religious and secular, until the rigours of the Inquisition and the edicts of Ferdinand and Isabella brought it all to an end. Many Spanish Jews converted to Catholicism in order to retain their homes and livelihoods; about 100,000 fled to Portugal, while the remaining 50,000 fanned out to safer havens in Holland, Greece, Egypt, and Turkey. The Ashkenazim, on the other hand, were concentrated in central and eastern Europe. To put the distinction crudely, the Sephardim were Mediterranean Jews, the Ashkenazim North European Jews.

The first Jewish families to come to London after Menasseh ben Israel's triumph were Sephardim. They set up a congregation of Spanish and Portuguese Jews in Creechurch Lane in 1657, and moved in 1701 to more capacious premises at Bevis Marks, which remains in active use as the oldest synagogue in Britain. The Sephardim were attracted not only by the religious freedom London offered, but by the economic opportu-

Commons voted repeatedly to admit Jewish MPs, but the legislation was repeatedly blocked by the House of Lords, until that bastion of reaction was persuaded, after a quarter century of intransigence, to change its mind. By 1855 there was a Jewish Lord Mayor of London, Sir David Salomons. The first Jewish peer, Lord Rothschild, was seated in the Lords in 1885. Jews were no longer second-class citizens.

This slow march towards full civil rights met the aspirations of the Jewish middle classes, but for many Jews, notably those who lived in the East End of London, it was of less immediate concern. Those Jews who had grown rich were mostly merchants or brokers or bankers; by the mid-nineteenth century a handful were gaining a foothold in the legal profession, since they had been admitted to practise at the bar in 1833. Many other Jews earned their living, both in London and in provincial cities, as manufacturers; others set up as retailers, especially in the jewellery business. Henry Mayhew, who reported on Jewish life in the East End in 1851, ascertained that certain wholesale trades, dealing in such commodities as citrus fruits, birds, cigars, and dried fruit, were dominated by Jews. In the sea-ports Jews flourished as chandlers. Lower down the social scale were the artisans, the tailors and watchmakers, and beneath them the pedlars and street traders. There were no formal obstacles to upward mobility, and many street traders later succeeded in opening retail businesses, though few could emulate the progress of the Marks and Sieff families in Manchester, or Sir John Cohen. The criminal class that had undoubtedly existed among Anglo-Jewry in the eighteenth century remained active in Victorian times, and more than 1,000 Jews, mostly poor Ashkenazim, found themselves setting off for a new life in Australia with free passage on a convict ship.

With Jewish communities thoroughly rooted in London and the provinces, it was necessary to provide the institutional support required to sustain them. The central institution was the Chief Rabbinate. There is no Jewish tradition of a Chief Rabbinate. In Poland and Russia each community would adhere to its own rabbi. Some notably learned or charismatic rabbis would attract pupils and disciples from other parts of the country, but there was no such thing as a rabbinical hierarchy. Among Anglo-Jewry, however, a need was clearly felt for a single figure in whom religious authority could be vested. The Chief Rabbi would be, as it were, an intermediary between the demands of religious Orthodoxy and the need to live within the norms of British society. In the late eighteenth and early nineteenth century, the rabbi of the Great Synagogue was regarded as the senior British rabbi, until in 1845 Nathan Adler, who came originally from Hanover, was appointed the first Chief Rabbi. Adler and his successors also exercised authority over Ashkenazi congregations throughout what was then the Empire and is now the Commonwealth. The Sephardim, of course, did not recognize the authority of the Chief Rabbi, and took their orders from a religious leader they call the Haham.

The lay leadership of Anglo-Jewry was expressed through a body known as the Board of Deputies of British Jews – deputies being an anglicization of the Portuguese *deputados*. Although founded in 1760 as a joint committee of Ashkenazi and Sephardi community leaders, it was not formally recognized as a representative body until 1836, when it was empowered by statute to register Jewish marriages. Other institutions developed throughout the Victorian era. The Jews' Free School opened in Bell Lane in 1817, and by 1850 had almost 1,200 pupils. If the Jewish vice, then and now, is gambling, the Jewish virtue was a thirst for self-improvement. In addition to the various schools, London Jews also had access to supplementary education in the form of courses and lectures on Jewish religious and cultural matters, as well as on completely secular subjects. The aim of such education, even if not consciously expressed, was twofold: to ensure that children and adults retained their religious background, and to enable them at the same time to survive and prosper in a society where the arcana of Jewish religious observance could be regarded as an impediment to worldly success. The community was unified further by the publication of a national newspaper, the *Jewish Chronicle*, which was founded in 1841.

Jewish religious law requires wage-earners to give a tenth of their income to charity. How many Jews ever obeyed this law strictly is impossible to ascertain, but it is clear that from the time of its resettlement in Britain, the Jewish community did care for its poor and indigent. Its schools were funded by donations from rich families such as the Rothschilds, and these grandees were also the mainstay of the voluntary and welfare organizations. A Jewish Board of Guardians was founded in 1859 and assisted the destitute with allowances and clothing. Similar bodies were established in all the major communities of Britain, and many still exist, providing old people's homes and other services to an increasingly elderly Jewish population. The 1850s saw a burgeoning of religious and charitable institutions because the community was then beginning to be augmented by a new wave of immigration. In an article printed in the *Morning Post* in 1849, Henry Mayhew quotes a Hungarian-Jewish tailor in the East End, who remarks that many Polish Jews are beginning to come to London in search of work. They had intended to return home after a while, but most stayed put; those that did leave Britain travelled on to America, not back to Poland or Russia and the conscription they had fled in the first place.

Many of the early nineteenth-century immigrants were from northern Germany and Austria. They were not impoverished tradesmen or ped-lars, but well-to-do young men hoping to expand their family businesses. Many of them prospered, not only financially but socially. Some, such as Sir Ernest Cassel, formed the Prince of Wales's extensive circle of Jewish friends and advisers. One can point to the achievements of Nathan Mayer Rothschild, who came to Manchester in 1799, and Ludwig Mond, who founded one of the largest companies in the world, Imperial Chemical Industries, and was ennobled as Lord Melchett. Other German Jews, such as the Rothensteins, achieved prominence as artists and adminis-trators. By the 1870s the immigrants were arriving at British ports in a steady stream. In 1850 the Jewish population had been no more than 30,000 but by 1871 there were 35,000 Jews in London alone. Ten years later the Jewish population of Britain had risen to 60,000. Most were Ashkenazi Jews from Russia and Poland, though others from Germany and Holland continued to emigrate to Britain. Sephardi merchants, mostly from North Africa, were drawn to cities such as Manchester, where overseas trade supported the local economy. But it was London, in particular the East End, that remained the magnet for the majority of immigrants. The population of the West End, home to many successful Jewish bourgeois families, had increased only slightly by the 1880s, while the immigrants poured into Spitalfields and Whitechapel, crowded dis-tricts where they at least stood a chance of finding a relative or *landsman* who could help them settle in.

Political emancipation inevitably opened up many previously barred professions to Anglo-Jewry, though most successful Jews continued to earn their fortunes as financiers or brokers, or as manufacturers. Boot-making, clothing and tailoring, and the fur and diamond trades were all attractive to Jewish businessmen. In the last quarter of the century, many of these middle-class Jews moved out of central London to the developing suburbs. The St John's Wood Synagogue was in operation by 1882, and there were growing Jewish communities in Islington and Dalston. The historian V. D. Lipman maintains that by the early 1880s, '14.6 per cent of the Jewish population of London were upper or upper-middle class with family incomes of £1,000 or over; 42.2 per cent were middle class with family incomes in the £200 to £1,000 bracket; and 19.5 per cent "lower" class with family incomes of about £100 per year . . . In addition there were no less than 23.6 per cent of the population in receipt of at least casual relief, on poor lists and in institutions.'[1]

Russian Jews came flooding into Britain, not to mention other refuges such as the United States, because they were pushed. Life in Russia for its five million Jews had always been restrictive and circumscribed by rules and regulations. They were, for instance, subject to conscription but any rank higher than that of private was closed to them. The emancipation that liberated the Jews of western Europe found no echo in the governments of the Tsars. Conditions had certainly been improving under the relatively liberal regime of Alexander II, and some Jews were allowed to settle in areas outside the Pale of Settlement in western Russia to which they had previously been confined. Unfortunately Alexander was assassinated in March 1881. Soon there were anti-Jewish riots and massacres not only in parts of Russia but in Poland too. A series of laws enacted in 1882 expelled many Jewish communities – the same orders Jews throughout the diaspora had been receiving from an assortment of regimes for a thousand years and more. Jews, the lucky ones who had not perished in the pogroms, left in droves. Still the repressive measures continued. In 1891 they were expelled from Moscow, and those that remained in the country were hindered from earning a living by an ever-growing list of economic prohibitions. As late as 1903 there were brutal pogroms. Between 1881 and 1905 a million Jews left Russia and Poland, and one tenth of their number came to Britain.

By this time a large section of Anglo-Jewry had become, in manners and appearance and aspirations, thoroughly anglicized. Throughout the course of the century the Jews had tapped gently on the doors that were still closed to them, until gradually they were all opened and they entered, with their dignity intact, into the formal fray of Victorian social and professional life. Their religion remained their own, but their mores were those of the host society. A remark that would have brought a blush to the cheek of a Young Person in Mr Podsnap's household would have had the same effect in the drawing-rooms of the Mocattas or Montefiores or any of the other Jewish grandees of the time. Wealthy Jews, such as Baron Worms and Sir George Jessel, were hobnobbing with the Prince of Wales, no less. It does not take a great deal of imagination to realize that the sudden influx of destitute fellow Jews, arriving by the boatload in their

hundreds of thousands, unable to speak English, utterly untutored in embroidery or the singing of part-songs or other social graces, would be greeted with, at best, mixed feelings.

The Anglo-Jewish Establishment did its best to keep the problem at bay. Jewish newspapers in eastern Europe ran advertisements from the Board of Guardians seeking to dissuade refugees from settling in Britain. More subtle pressure was directed at community leaders in Russia and Poland with the same intention. And still they came. Some merely paused for breath before changing ships and proceeding to New York, but many stayed here, too weary or impoverished to continue. The influx offered a golden opportunity for demagogues, and they took it. Organizations such as the British Brothers' League rented halls in Mile End and Stepney to warn against the hordes from the East who would rob decent English men and women of their livelihoods by taking their jobs at low wages and crowding into their houses and driving up the rents. The meetings attracted large crowds, who may have been puzzled to spot on the platform not only rabble-rousers, whose dire warnings were tinged with anti-Semitic rhetoric, but pillars of the Anglo-Jewish community, including Jewish Members of Parliament, who keenly feared that any sudden disturbance of the status quo – and Jewish history is woefully short of status quos to be squandered – might revive anti-Semitism. They and their forebears had struggled for generations to build up their lives and their businesses in this hospitable land, and the last thing they wanted was to have their equanimity and good name smeared by the uncouth habits of their co-religionists from eastern Europe. Indeed, the Board of Guardians actually persuaded tens of thousands of immigrants to return to eastern Europe. It was not a noble performance, but it was an understandable one.

It was undeniable, of course, that the demographic impact of well over 100,000 Yiddish-speaking Jews on the already crowded and bustling East End of London would be immense. When the immigrant disembarked, he carried with him, in addition to his bundles of precious possessions, two handicaps. In the first place he was a foreigner, ill equipped to find employment in a strange land. Secondly, he was an Orthodox Jew, which imposed constraints on his adaptability. Being unwilling – or in his own terms, unable – to work on the Sabbath, he could not expect regular employment from a non-Jewish boss. Only a Jewish employer could guarantee him work that would be harmonized with the strict requirements of his religion. Consequently the new arrival would inevitably find

himself at the mercy of Jewish employers, who, in the East End in the late nineteenth century, were as likely as not sweatshop owners. The immigrant was willing to accept the abysmal conditions of sweated labour in the hope that, with diligence and application, he too could one day rise from the ranks of the underpaid employee to the modest liberty of the employer. Not that the running of a sweatshop was an ideal path to riches. Locked into a system of high productivity and small margins of profit, few sweatshop owners could expect to enrich themselves hugely by their labours or by those of their wretched employees. Moreover, many bosses could not afford to rent business premises, and had to make space for their workforce within their lodgings. But at least it was better to be the employer than the employed, and to this day British Jews, to a disproportionate extent, favour self-employment.

Despite the inauspicious circumstances in which the newcomers found themselves, the worst fears of the Anglo-Jewish Establishment were not realized. The immigrants were desperately eager to succeed, and were not a conspicuous burden on the community. Only an infinitesimal proportion of immigrant Jews were registered as paupers, and relatively few turned to crime or prostitution. Hopeless destitution was rare, and the Anglo-Jewish charities were able to alleviate the worst cases. Nevertheless, the rapid swelling of the East End population did pose problems that seemed to confirm some of the warnings of the British Brothers' League and its allies. Accommodation was so scarce that there was no alternative to sub-letting. Rents rose alarmingly, and more and more people were crammed into smaller and smaller spaces. By the end of the century the population of some parts of the East End, such as Whitechapel, was one-third immigrant. In Spitalfields alone, according to Lipman, there were some 15,000 Jews. This state of affairs increased the pressure on the government to act on the vexed issue of immigration controls, and in 1902 A. J. Balfour set up a Royal Commission to investigate the possibilities. The outcome was the Aliens Act of 1905, which empowered immigration officers to turn back 'undesirable immigrants', although the rejected refugees did have the right to appeal and the legislation did preserve the right to asylum. Soon after the act became law the government was defeated and the incoming Liberal government enforced the act in a lackadaisical manner: about 5,000 Jewish immigrants continued to arrive each year. This marked a decrease on earlier rates of immigration, but fears of a complete halt proved unfounded.

In the meantime the immigrants were preparing themselves, and their

children, to master the opacities of British life. The children proved astonishingly quick to learn. They may have come from homes where Yiddish was the only language, but school inspectors often remarked on the eagerness and rapidity with which the Jewish pupils absorbed their lessons. At the turn of the century about 6,000 children were attending the six Jewish schools in the East End; many more children attended local authority schools, some of which were, for obvious demographic reasons, dominated by Jewish children. While their offspring were learning to be good young Britons, the parents too were learning the ropes. Adult education classes helped many immigrants to master the English language. Trade-union organization made some headway even into trades such as tailoring, and regulated the exploitation. It did not prove easy to organize so intensified a workforce, and at times there must have seemed to be almost as many unions as workers, but eventually work practices and conditions began to improve.

The overcrowding which had been the subject of so many complaints also began to ease. The United Synagogue and other Anglo-Jewish bodies established dispersal committees to persuade immigrants to move out of the East End and into the expanding London suburbs or, better yet, into provincial communities. The approach was reasonably successful. The Jewish population of Leeds, for example, trebled between 1888 and 1902. Before the First World War, there were about 120,000 Jews living in the provinces. Even within the East End, serious efforts were made by the community to improve housing conditions. The Rothschilds organized the Four Per Cent Industrial Dwellings Company, which erected cheap but adequate blocks of flats that accommodated many thousands of immigrant families not only in the East End but in outlying areas such as Camberwell and Stoke Newington. Friendly Societies mushroomed, enabling even the poorest members of the community to ensure that they would not be deprived of the proper rituals of a Jewish funeral.

Synagogal organization, however, proved almost as intractable a problem as trade union organization. The principal synagogal group, the United Synagogue, must have seemed as alien to an immigrant Jew from Poland as that Jew would have seemed to an Anglo-Jewish banker. The cathedral-like size and atmosphere of the major London synagogues bore no resemblance to the small crowded rooms in which the Orthodox Jews of Eastern Europe liked to gather. Consequently the immigrants set up their own houses of worship (*shtieblach*) modelled on what they had been used to. Anglo-Jewish worthies were not overly impressed by these dingy, crowded and often dirty prayer halls, and it was Samuel Montagu who came up with a solution in 1887. Aware that the formal atmosphere of the United Synagogue deterred the immigrants, he established small independent synagogues in the East End by amalgamating some of the *shtieblach*. Within these decently maintained buildings, congregations were able to preserve their own mode of worship while enjoying a reasonable standard of comfort and sanitation. Although most of these early Federation synagogues in the East End are no longer in existence, the Federation itself still supports religiously conservative congregations in many London suburbs. Its foundation was a typical, and in this instance very sensible and successful, Anglo-Jewish compromise which sought neither to absorb the new immigrants *en bloc* into an English society with which they had nothing in common, nor encouraged the newcomers to recreate without adaptation the institutions and practices of their former homeland. Similarly, the majority of the immigrants' children were attending local authority schools where they received a completely secular education; but after school hours most of the children would attend religious instruction classes organized either by the Jewish Religious Education Board or by individual synagogues and rabbis.

By the outbreak of the First World War, there were some 300,000 Jews in Britain (of whom 180,000 lived in London), but the demographic pattern was changing. It was no longer possible to assess the Jewish community in Britain by looking solely at the colourful East End. Jews had fanned out into the suburbs and provinces. Manchester, Leeds, Glasgow all had large and vibrant Jewish communities, complete with the institutional support system to sustain them, and smaller communities flourished in industrial regions such as South Wales and the North-east: neighbouring towns such as Newcastle, Sunderland, Gateshead, and South Shields may individually have had rather small Jewish communities, but, taken as a group, the numbers added up. In London, the small congregations founded in the 1890s in Maida Vale, Hampstead, and Hammersmith had grown steadily, as had the suburban communities favoured by a slightly earlier generation of upwardly mobile immigrants: Dalston, Stoke Newington, and Hackney. The East End was about to begin its long slow period of decline. Its remaining population tended to be working class; successful immigrants and their better educated children had begun to move not only to more spacious suburbs but into the middle-class professions. The stereotype of the elderly Jewish tailor or pawnbroker or scrap merchant in his dingy shop or yard may have remained accurate enough in Whitechapel or Manchester's Cheetham Hill, but it was no longer a typical or adequate image of Anglo-Jewry in the twentieth century.

By the end of the war, over 40,000 British Jews had joined the armed forces, although some Russian-born immigrants had been reluctant to volunteer. They had, they argued, endured considerable hardships, not to mention deracination, in order to escape from the very real persecutions of the Tsarist regime, and they didn't see why they should now sign up to fight side by side with their former oppressors. Not only were the British authorities unsympathetic to this lack of proper patriotism, but so were the Anglo-Jewish leaders, who fully supported legislation passed in July 1917 that required the deportation of unnaturalized Russian-born immigrants who refused service with the British armed forces. A few months later the issue fizzled out as the Bolsheviks came to power in Russia. The great majority of Jews, of course, were willing to fight for their new country. They contributed not only to the war effort but to the literature of war: both Isaac Rosenberg and Siegfried Sassoon left vivid accounts of their experiences.

It had been a war between nations, and Jew had fought Jew, according to which nation he was attached to. The experience consolidated national, even patriotic, feeling. Jews who survived the trenches and the battles returned with impeccable credentials as Britons. With the waves of immigration halted, Jews no longer felt themselves compelled by bullying organizations such as the British Brothers' League to justify their existence. Much more widely dispersed than they had been thirty years earlier, they were also less conspicuous as a minority group than when they had been crowded into Mile End and Whitechapel. During the inter-war years, British Jews, like the rest of the population, devoted themselves to their businesses, their careers, their domestic lives, their pleasures. Those with Zionist aspirations had been greatly heartened by the Balfour Declaration of 1917, but that story will be told in more detail later in this book. Even their religion had taken on a placid English style, nominally Orthodox, full of gravitas. Reform Judaism had won over few of the East European Jews, who were far more likely to adhere to the Federation or to the United Synagogue. Rabbis were called reverends and wore clerical bands. The anglicization of British Jewry must have seemed almost complete. And then, in the early 1930s, Anglo-Jewry became aware of a new and most terrible threat.

– 2 –

The 'Thirties and after

W HILE the Jews of Britain were unstitching the political disabilities that hemmed them in, and while the Jews of Russia were
dodging punitive legislation on the one hand and vicious
pogroms on the other, the Jews of Germany were doing just fine. True,
from time to time in the eighteenth century the occasional princeling
or grand duke would adopt a current fashion and expel the Jewish
community, but Germany was still the sole country in Europe from which
Jews had never been expelled *in toto*. Even before the formal emancipation
of the community, gifted Jews in Austria and Germany had risen to
positions of great influence. Their financial sagacity was highly respected,
and their advice sought by half the courts of Europe. Indeed, the term
Hofjude (Court Jew) was coined to describe these privileged men, some of
whom functioned as unofficial prime ministers. The Habsburgs turned to
Jewish contractors both to supply their armies in times of war and to
finance the construction of their palaces in times of peace. They had their
counterparts in England – men like the Goldsmids and the Rothschilds –
but it was financial expertise rather than political nous that was in demand.

With the unification of Germany in 1871, the process of emancipation
that was already well under way on a more *ad hoc* basis was completed.
Jews could live where they wished, marry whom they wished, work as they
wished, and vote as they wished. Whereas in England the delay in
achieving emancipation had little effect on the piety of many British Jews,
this was not the case in Germany. There arguments for full emancipation
had been pressed from as early as the 1780s, and the expectations of
German Jewry were very high. The failure to achieve full emancipation
rapidly led many German Jews to abandon Judaism and convert, so as to

28

be able to put the whole miserable struggle behind them by means of a mere sprinkle of water. In the 1820s half the Jews of Berlin had converted. Some of the great figures of German Jewry, such as Heinrich Heine and Karl Marx, were in fact baptized. It was no accident that Reform Judaism was born in Germany, as was a compromise brand that within an Orthodox format of worship permitted a more enlightened interpretation of the faith.

German Jews were thoroughly at home within the host culture. Just as successful Victorian Jews tended to ape the philistinism and country pursuits of the native gentry, so in Germany the Jews felt thoroughly attuned to the works of Goethe and Schiller, Beethoven and Brahms. They were far more assimilated than their British counterparts, almost more German than the Germans. They shared the values of the culture in which they were embedded. And, like Jews elsewhere in Europe, they fought for their country in the First World War. After the war German Jews aided the reconstruction of their country, notably the highly cultivated industrialist Walther Rathenau, who acted as foreign minister of the Weimar Republic until his assassination in 1922. Most German political parties had been founded by Jews, who were also highly successful in the arts and in academic and professional life. Being so thoroughly rooted in German *Kultur*, it was difficult for the Jews to conceive of any serious threat to their continuing wellbeing. True, there were anti-Semitic rumblings from time to time, but they could look to the Dreyfus Affair in France and the passage of the Aliens Act in Britain to demonstrate that hostility to Jews was not unique to Germany. Some were made uneasy by the arrival in Germany of Polish Jews, who tended to be deeply religious, unworldly, and conspicuous in their garb, gesture, and manner of speech. The Germans' own sense of cultural superiority was transmitted to the Jewish community, who exhibited the same kind of snobbery and xenophobia shown by some of the Anglo-Jewish grandees. Clearly the bearded *Ostjuden* from Poland conformed far more closely to the anti-Semites' caricature of the grasping Jew than did the urbane bankers, lawyers, and university professors who dominated German Jewry. They may only have constituted 1 per cent of the population, but Jews had succeeded in mopping up one quarter of the Nobel Prizes awarded to German citizens.

It is easy with hindsight to marvel at German Jewry's false sense of security. But if Jews can never feel fully at home in any country, the Jews of Germany had stronger grounds for feeling rooted than any other national

29

grouping in Europe. That in the middle of the twentieth century they could actually be expelled, or worse, seemed at the very least improbable. The Nazis fired warning shots as soon as they came to power, and passed a law that barred Jews and other non-Aryans from State employment. Two years later, in 1935, the Nuremberg Laws were passed, depriving Jews of citizenship of the Third Reich and placing all kinds of restrictions and prohibitions on Jews pursuing professional careers. There is no need here to document the tightening of the screws. Some Jews had the foresight to leave soon after Hitler came to power. Others hung on, incapable of realizing the extremity of their peril.

Some came to England, but it was not made easy for them. Anti-alien legislation was still on the statute book, and officials could reject would-be immigrants without explanation. The British governments of the 1930s were on reasonably good terms with Chancellor Hitler and were usually disposed to give him the benefit of the doubt as he set about expanding the frontiers of his Reich; so there was no reason for the Home Office or for immigration officials to go out of their way to admit refugees from the Nazi regime. The authorities, like immigration authorities in all countries, were better disposed towards refugees who arrived with a bagful of money or jewels, or had some other way of guaranteeing that they would not become a burden on the nation. The difficulty was that while the Nazis were, in the spring of their persecution, willing to allow fearful Jews to leave, they at the same time felt it would be wasteful in the extreme to allow the fugitives to take their money and worldly goods with them. A good deal of asset-stripping went on before Jews were allowed to emigrate, and this compounded the difficulties of obtaining an entry visa for another country.

By April 1934 just under 3,000 German Jews had managed to find refuge in Britain. During the same period the United States took in 6,500 refugees, and the French 30,000. Other German Jews took thankful advantage of the willingness of many South American consular officials to be corrupted; bribery flourished, but at least they obtained their visas and got out of the country. Anglo-Jewry set up organizations such as the Central British Fund for World Jewish Relief, both to provide financial assistance to refugees and to help them find employment. Although many of the would-be refugees were men and women of great eminence within their professions, this did not make the task of resettling them any easier. The British government, to its credit, was prepared to admit a substantial number of German doctors, but caved in under intense pressure from the

British Medical Association, which reduced the number to a handful. Lawyers, unfamiliar with the British legal system, found themselves unable to pursue their careers and had to take jobs for which they were clearly overqualified. Jews with commercial experience were in the most fortunate position, as their managerial and entrepreneurial skills could be put to good use. Other refugees, especially women, accepted positions as cooks and maids. Many had come from privileged backgrounds and had never boiled an egg in their lives, so one must applaud the generosity of those English families who were willing to have their household routines disrupted by Germans who didn't speak the language and had never laid eyes on a mop.

When war broke out, some 50,000 German and Austrian refugees and 6,000 Czechs had found refuge in Britain. Of these, 10,000 were children. Many of the refugees who arrived in the late 1930s were not from Germany, but from Austria and Czechoslovakia, the latest victims of Hitler's expansionism. When anti-Semitic atrocities began to occur in Germany, many Jews had been slow to realize their danger. After the Anschluss in March 1938, however, few Austrians paused to give the Nazis the benefit of the doubt. So ferocious was the anti-Semitism unleashed by the Viennese that thousands of Jews made rapid preparations for their departure. In the year that followed about half of Vienna's 200,000 Jews made their escape, and some found their way to England. Unlike the earlier waves of immigrants from Russia and Poland, these refugees were overwhelmingly middle class; they brought their culture, and their cultural snobbery, with them, and never considered moving in to the traditional Jewish areas of the East End. Instead they made straight for north-west London, to Kilburn, Hampstead, and Swiss Cottage. In provincial communities, too, such as Glasgow and Manchester, there was a tendency for the refugees to keep to themselves.

Once Germany became the official enemy, the refugees were once again robbed of their status as free men and women. They were classified as 'enemy aliens', which must have struck most of them as, at the very least, highly ironic. Tribunals classified them into various categories. Those in Category A were interned; those in Category C endured no restrictions other than those that applied to all foreigners in wartime. Those in Category B were not interned but were subject to irksome restrictions. Only 600 refugees were interned initially, though the situation deteriorated after the German victories of June 1940. The popular press, whose role during the 1930s had been thoroughly ignoble, stayed

31

true to form by seeking to identify Jews as Fifth Columnists. How much influence such xenophobic absurdities had on government actions it is hard to say, but it was at this time that a policy of mass internment was first adopted. By the summer of 1940 11,000 men and women had been rounded up and dispatched to internment camps. Later that year the process was reversed, and many men and women were released, especially those anxious to join the armed forces. Thousands joined the Pioneer Corps, where they performed the most menial tasks connected with the military life, but at least it was an improvement on the tedium of internment and they could at last contribute to the fight against Nazi Germany.

After the war the process of integration into British life continued. Refugees were naturalized in their thousands. Many established businesses, notably in the clothing, textile, and fur trades. Expertise gained before the war – a gift for languages or a network of rusty business contacts in various parts of Europe – proved invaluable. Others resumed academic careers. Not all chose to remain in Britain. Some made their way to America or to Palestine; a handful returned to the land of their birth. For those who remained, it was not an easy time. Their European accents made them painfully conscious of the difficulty many Britons found in distinguishing between German nationals and German refugees. Many were unsettled by the obduracy of the postwar Labour government, which did all it could to prevent Jewish refugees, 100,000 of whom were languishing in displaced persons camps in Europe, from making their way to Palestine. Some refugees, especially the elderly ones, tried to recreate the quiet, enclosed, comfortable world they had known in Hamburg or Vienna. Others put the past behind them and rebuilt their lives by playing down their backgrounds. Some succeeded in doing so while retaining, even proclaiming, their Jewishness, their foreignness; others went to great lengths to minimize their exotic background, even to the extent of denying that they were Jewish. I shall take a closer look at the refugee community, which numbered about 40–50,000 in the 1950s, in a later chapter.

The arrival of so many German and central European Jews made a considerable impact not only on Jewish life in Britain but on British life as a whole. Many publishers, impresarios, and academics who were later to make a profound contribution to the nation's cultural life were refugees. The Warburg Institute soon became a mainstay of the academic research establishment. The riches of the Wiener Library were brought to London from Amsterdam in 1939, and another seat of Jewish learning, Leo Baeck

College, was founded in 1956 and staffed by a number of distinguished European rabbis. Although some of the refugees were Orthodox Jews, the majority were either marginally religious or adherents of the German variety of Reform Judaism. Their influx into Britain gave a badly needed shot in the arm to British Reform Judaism, which was revitalized by the foundation of Leo Baeck College and its facilities for rabbinical training.

Although some sections of the refugee population have retained a separate identity, or seem unable or unwilling to forsake their original identity, many have integrated both with the Jewish community of longer standing in Britain and with the native community as a whole. Other smaller waves of immigration have brought slight additions to the numbers of Anglo-Jewry. The failure of the Hungarian revolution in 1956 brought some Hungarian Jews to Britain. The rise of Islamic fundamentalism in the Middle East persuaded many Jews resident for generations in Arab societies to take their leave. There is now a sizeable community of Jews from Iran and Iraq, as well as small numbers from Egypt and Syria, resident in Britain. Unlike the refugees from Nazism, those who came here from the Middle East were usually able to bring some or all of their assets with them. Less dependent on the community for financial or other forms of support, they too have tended to keep to themselves rather than participate in Anglo-Jewish communal life. Lastly, the urgent appeals of Zionist emissaries to British Jews to emigrate to Israel have been somewhat undermined by the continuing stream of Israelis who have made their home here.

Since 1945 the community has gone through enormous transformations. It has, along with much of the rest of the British population, grown richer and more conservative but its numbers have dwindled. There has also been a marked change within the power structure that dominated Anglo-Jewry for centuries. The families that achieved wealth and worldly success from the seventeenth to the nineteenth centuries were relatively few: the Mocattas, the Goldsmids, the Samuels, the Montagus, the Franklins, and the Montefiores are the best known. Intermarriage was so common among these families that they became known as the Cousinhood. It was members of this closely knit group who founded and dominated all the institutions of Anglo-Jewry until well into this century.

Many of those families still exist, but few retain any connection with the community they once led. Some are no longer identifiably Jewish. The first Viscount Bearsted was Marcus Samuel, a banker and founder of Shell Oil. His descendants have no connection with Jewish life and the

Jewish community. Neither do the Melchetts and the descendants of Rufus Isaacs, Marquis of Reading. With the recent death of Major-General Sir James d'Avigdor-Goldsmid, what is left of the Goldsmid clan will probably cease to have any formal association with the community. There are still Montefiores who are nominally Jewish, but the most famous current Montefiore, Hugh, is an Anglican bishop. Chaim Bermant, in his exemplary study *The Cousinhood*, observes that the Jewish house at Clifton College was founded to cater for the education of the grandees' children, combining the virtues and severities of the British public school with a Jewish environment; yet nowadays, there is not a Montefiore or a Waley-Cohen or a Franklin to be found at Clifton. As Frederic Raphael, himself the scion of an old Anglo-Jewish family, remarks: 'It's not surprising that such families don't take on the allure of a new society when they are firmly embedded in an old one. There is no real reason why such Jews should be obstreperous in their innovations. They are much more likely to be ingenious in their infiltrations. My father genuinely believed that American Jews were Jews but British Jews were British. Nowadays American Jews have become much more American, and British Jews have become much more Jewish.'

A few members of the old clans still assume the kinds of responsibilities their grandparents assumed as a matter of right. Sir Alan Mocatta, whose forebears founded the oldest bullion broking business in Britain, is an Elder of the Spanish and Portuguese Synagogue. A former barrister specializing in shipping law and, until 1981, a High Court judge, Sir Alan gives, with his tall lean figure and quiet careful speech, every appearance of being a typical English gentleman of the old school, which is exactly what he is. Yet his commitment to Judaism is strong indeed, and his four children have all remained within the faith. The grandest family of them all, the Rothschilds, no longer seek to be the spokesmen for Anglo-Jewry that they were a century ago; their influence is exerted very much behind the scenes. Victor Rothschild, the present Lord Rothschild, is not an observant Jew; yet, while neither of his wives was of Jewish birth, his first wife did convert, and their eldest son maintains, like many of the Rothschilds, an interest in major Israeli institutions such as the Weizmann Institute. Jacob de Rothschild also married out, and although he takes very little part in Anglo-Jewish affairs, he too takes a keen interest in Israeli matters. Evelyn de Rothschild recalls crisis meetings at the bank whenever Israel was endangered, but clearly feels less compulsion to intervene in Jewish affairs in Britain. With the Jewish community thoroughly settled in and partially assimilated, there are few obvious threats to British Jews and thus no need for overt leadership from the top, as it were.

And so the leadership of Anglo-Jewry has passed to the descendants of the Polish and Russian, and to a lesser extent German and Austrian, immigrants. It was the opposition of the Cousinhood, and of the Jewish Establishment with which it was almost synonymous, that paved the way for the new wave of leaders. Apart from the private observance of Jewish ritual and a public espousal of the civic rights of the Jewish population, the Cousinhood were in manners and ideas indistinguishable from upper-middle-class Britons. They feared that any espousal of Zionism would lead to charges of dual loyalty and thus undermine the social position that had been secured after two centuries of decorous struggle. The less genteel immigrants had no such reservations. When in 1962 Ewen Montagu, Lord Swathyling's nephew, passed the baton of the presidency of the Board of Deputies to the Glaswegian Sir Isaac Wolfson, the abdication of the Cousinhood from community leadership was more or less complete. As William Frankel, a former editor of the *Jewish Chronicle*, remarked: 'There were no Rothschilds or Montagus who were interested in taking on the job. The older families found their interests had moved outside the community. They had joined the fox-hunting set. Their preoccupations were incompatible with great personal involvement in the Jewish community.' Or as Jonathan Lew, the chief executive of the United Synagogue, put it: 'Perhaps their desire to assimilate into British society was greater than their desire to retain their identification with the Jewish community.' Of course the retreat of the grandees also reflects the general fading of the aristocracy from positions of political power. The days when the likes of Lord Salisbury, Lord Curzon, and the Duke of Devonshire were powers in the land have also gone for ever.

It would be satisfying to be able to conclude this brief historical survey with some incontrovertible facts and figures about the state of the Jewish community in the late 1980s. This too is difficult, as there is no foolproof method for ascertaining the size of the Jewish community in this country. Census returns do not state the religion of respondents. Jews are substantially a self-identifying community. Ceremonial milestones, such as Jewish weddings and funerals, are undertaken as a matter of personal choice. Many Jews affiliate to the community by joining a synagogue or Zionist organizations; others play no active part or disclaim their Jewish identity. Intermarriage with the non-Jewish community results in offspring who, even if they identify with their Jewish heritage, may not be acknowledged as Jews by the religious authorities.

The skilled statisticians of the Research Unit of the Board of Deputies of British Jews have grappled with this demographic nightmare and estimate the Jewish population in the late 1980s at no more than 330,000. If this figure is correct, then Anglo-Jewry has lost a quarter of its population in thirty years. About a third of Britain's Jewish population lives in north-west London, and half of those who live in north-west London live in the borough of Barnet, which includes the suburbs of Hendon, Golders Green, Finchley, and Edgware. As many Jews again are dispersed through Hampstead, Swiss Cottage, Hackney, St John's Wood, and the north-eastern suburbs of Ilford, Southgate, Redbridge, and Gants Hill. The United Synagogue still attracts over half the synagogue membership. Reform and Liberal congregations enjoy large followings in the London suburbs and in the newer Jewish communities in south-east England such as Brighton, but have made little impact on older provincial communities, where mainstream Orthodoxy of various degrees of severity prevails. Nevertheless, both the ultra-Orthodox and Reform movements appear to be gaining strength at the expense of mainstream Orthodoxy. Inner-city congregations have become extinct as an ever more affluent community moves into the suburbs, where many congregations report growing membership figures. In London's outer suburbs, to which many first-time buyers or parents with young families have been driven because of the high cost of housing in more traditional Jewish suburbs, new congregations appear to be attracting members at a satisfying rate. Synagogue membership bears no relation to synagogue attendance; most rabbis, except for those ministering to ultra-Orthodox congregations, calculate that only one-tenth of their membership will make regular appearances at services.

Anglo-Jewry, like the waters of an estuary, is tugging in innumerable directions simultaneously. While declining in numbers, it is growing in Jewish awareness. Its religious structure is becoming increasingly polarized, as the various synagogal bodies adopt irreconcilable positions on interpretations of Jewish law and on such crucial matters as Jewish status. Loyalties to Zionist principles and causes that twenty years ago seemed unproblematic to most diaspora Jews are now under severe strain. Religious authoritarianism is on the increase while the rate of assimilation into the non-Jewish community continues unabated. The placid forward movement of this historical account has opened into this swirling estuary of conflicting movement, as will become painfully apparent in the chapters that follow.

✤ THE RELIGIOUS COMMUNITY ✤

– 3 –

The ground rules

Ａ LTHOUGH Judaism is a marvellously wordy and bookish religion, and every phrase of every injunction or parable can be haggled over for hours, its joyous disputatiousness has led to sectarianism, caused as much by geographical dispersal and isolation as by theological debate. Judaism, moreover, is relatively unstructured. No figure of papal authority oversees the Jewish community. Most British Jews wouldn't be able to name the Chief Rabbi of Israel, for he has no authority over them and his rulings are of limited concern to the diaspora. In this country too the Chief Rabbi is not the head of the Anglo-Jewish community but of the United Synagogue and its affiliates in the Commonwealth. In rural Poland or the German principalities or small Turkish sea-ports, the rabbi of any community might command the allegiance of a majority of observant Jews in the area, but then again he might not. A rabbi, after all, is a religious teacher rather than a figure of authority.

The differences between various Jewish sects derives from the manner in which they interpret Jewish law, the Halachah. The more rigid the observance, the more Orthodox the Jew. It is also a question of emphasis. Some Jews play down the messianic aspect and emphasize the ethical – or vice versa. The British Jew has a full menu to choose from, from ultra-Orthodox groups modelled on Chasidic sects that thrived in eighteenth-century Poland, to synagogues so unconcerned with ritual Judaism that males attend services with their heads uncovered and not even the rabbis eat kosher food. Anglo-Jewry has adopted the terminology of modern politics to describe the spectrum of belief: the ultra-Orthodox are referred to as the Far Right, the Liberals as the Far Left. I shall try to avoid these misleading terms. Only about 4 per cent of British Jews could

41

be described as ultra-Orthodox, but they are important because they set standards of observance from which, in their view, other Jews deviate. This is not to say that an ultra-Orthodox Jew is a 'better' Jew. But if one can come to grips with the passionate religious feelings that inspire the ultra-Orthodox, it will be easier to understand and assess the less demanding forms of Jewish observance to which the overwhelming majority of British Jews subscribe.

The primary belief of all Jews is in monotheism. The first declaration taught to a Jewish child, and the valediction made by a dying Jew, are one and the same: *'Hear O Israel, the Lord is our God, the Lord is One.'* God is unified, indivisible, omnipotent, omniscient, eternal. God is spirit, not the elderly gentleman of much Christian iconography. In its early formulations the doctrine was revolutionary, for the ancient world, whether Egyptian or Greek or Canaanite, was prolifically polytheistic. Even Catholicism flirts with idolatry by pulling out of its bag of hagiographical lore a saint for every day of the week and for every need and supplication. In the face of such a multiplicity of available gods and handy manifestations of the Godhead, the Jewish insistence on the unity and indivisibility of God was and still is momentous, unshakeable, galvanizing. God is utterly transcendent, yet not beyond reach. God, to put the matter in terms familiar to every Briton in the 1980s, is not a free marketeer but an interventionist. Being omniscient, He is not slow to judge. Jewish liturgy and lore are replete with such terms as 'righteous', 'merciful', 'just', 'vengeful', 'repentant'. His Covenant with the Jewish people is an ethical one. God expects his 'chosen people' to measure up; His mercy and favour are not unconditional.

Consequently, how Jews behave is in a very real sense more important than what they believe. For Jews there is no catechism. Judaism is a disputatious religion, but not a conceptualizing one. Its rules and formulations seek to regulate behaviour, not exercise the mind. It is easy to be left with the impression that certain rabbis couldn't care less if you believe in pixies and elves, so long as you do not neglect to light candles on the eve of the Sabbath. Or to put it another way: Jews have beliefs, but lack a theology. It is this absence of a code of belief, as opposed to a code of laws, that makes it difficult to communicate the religious – as opposed to the national or cultural or behavioural – flavour of Judaism. Jewish beliefs have to be teased from the rambling and often contradictory texts that lie at the heart of Jewish understanding. God's immanence in the world permits man to enjoy a personal relationship with Him. Thus the devout

Jew prays three times a day, with additional services on the Sabbath and festivals. Jewish liturgy is rich and complex, and is not confined to defined times of prayer, since the liturgy offers the religious Jew an abundance of prayers and blessings with which the most mundane acts can be sanctified and for which God can be thanked and praised.

Judaism doesn't have much time for determinism. Man, being created in the divine image, has the moral consciousness of his creator, and it is up to him to exercise it. God will mete out the rewards accordingly. Chasidic teachings regard evil as a veiled path to an ultimate good – a cunning but unsatisfactory formulation. Jewish sages, like Christian theologians, are incapable of resolving the problem of evil, and in the post-Holocaust world the problem seems more intractable than ever. If God is truly omniscient and omnipotent, as the Mosaic code uncompromisingly insists, than He cannot be let off the hook by even the most deft and heartfelt sophistry. Thus any post-Holocaust Jewish theology has to reconcile the wilful destruction of one third of His people with the crucial notion not only of God's omnipotence but of His righteousness and passion for justice.

God is not, for all His chastizing and smiting, draconian. God allows enormous scope for repentance and atonement, for return to the fold. The most solemn day of the year is the Day of Atonement, but repentance and prayer alone are insufficient to cancel out the offence; in Jewish law, reparation should be made whenever possible. Judaism is a tolerant religion. In the Middle Ages some Jews were excommunicated by their peers, and the same fate befell the philosopher Spinoza, but in general it is hard to fling a Jew out of the Jewish community against his will. God would rather see the repentance of the sinner than his punishment or destruction. There is no damnation or hell to which the unrepentant sinner will be confined for all eternity. Even the notion of an afterlife is hazy in Jewish lore.

It is the Mosaic code – the Torah, the Pentateuch, the first five books of the Old Testament – which lays down the rules for Jewish observance. Torah, which means 'teaching' rather than, as many suppose, 'law', is not restricted to the Pentateuch, but includes the Oral Law, the entire body of commentary and tradition that the wisdom of the ages has appended to the Mosaic code. Nevertheless, the specific religious commandments and injunctions of the Pentateuch are at the core of Jewish religious observance, and cannot be down-played. There is a fundamental division between Orthodox Jews, who regard the Torah as having been dictated directly to Moses as part of God's revelation to the Jews, and the Progressive branches of Judaism, which merely maintain that the Torah is divinely inspired. This formidable document, which embraces ritual law, dietary law, criminal law, and family law, still regulates the daily lives of a substantial number of Jews. Yet immersion in the Torah was not intended to be restricted to rabbis alone. Each Jew was to be a scholar, to the best of his abilities, and the only distinction in earlier times between a devout Jew and a rabbi was that the rabbi was ordained by having the title conferred upon him by other rabbis, thus authorizing him to give religious rulings.

A commandment laid down in the Torah is known as a *mitzvah* (plural: *mitzvot*). There is no single translation of the term, which can mean 'commandment' or, less rigorously, 'religious obligation'. By performing *mitzvot*, the Jew, as it were, earns religious credit, though they are undertaken not with the aim of winning applause but in order to carry out the will of God. The Torah stipulates no fewer than 613 *mitzvot*: 248 are positive injunctions, and the remaining 365 are prohibitions. Many relate to social and environmental conditions that no longer obtain in western societies. The obligation to perform them, Orthodox Jews maintain, has not been dropped but merely put in abeyance. Reform Jews, on the other hand, discard those religious obligations they consider irrelevant to modern conditions. Rabbinic teachers laid down further rules and regulations derived from and intended to supplement and protect the commandments of the Pentateuch. They adopted two methods of textual exposition and commentary: Midrash, a line-by-line examination of the Torah; and Mishnah, a more legalistic study of specific issues of Jewish obligation and conduct. Midrash was first transmitted orally at least 2,500 years ago, and only after hundreds of years of this oral tradition was Midrash transcribed and codified. The Mishnah was transcribed towards the end of the second century AD. The Mishnah and Midrash were not restricted exclusively to legal argument and judgment. Anecdotal, moralistic, historical and other speculative excursions were also included, and these became known as Aggadah, which stood in contrast to Halachah, which related solely to statements of the law. These early codifications were hardly the end of the line as far as rabbinical commentators were concerned. Academies in Palestine and Babylon studied the Mishnah exhaustively and appended further amplifications, ranging from scrupulous textual analysis to legend and parable. This additional layer of commentary, often bewilderingly digressive, is known as the Gemara, and the Mishnah and Gemara conbined form the Talmud. Completed in about AD 500, the Talmud still forms the basis of Jewish study.

Before they received God's revelation to Moses on Mount Sinai, the Jews' special sense of identity derived from the Covenant made between God and the patriarch Abraham countless generations earlier. Through Moses the Covenant was renewed and the code of Jewish law promulgated and codified. For as long as the Jews undertook to keep those laws, which were binding on all future generations as well, God would offer them protection and favour. But the Covenant was not to be regarded as a free ride. Election to this kind of spiritual aristocracy placed enormous obligations, of obedience and conduct, on the people He had chosen. The reward for keeping His laws would be not only a form of redemption, but a return to the Land of Israel. For as long as Jews were scattered in the diaspora, as they still are, they were consoled by the promise that they would one day return to Zion, as indeed they have done.

It is this expectation, amply reflected in the traditional liturgy, that sustained the Jewish spirit even during times of greatest torment and uncertainty. Moreover, Jews believe they have been chosen by God as the means by which His revelation would be made not only to Jews but to all mankind. Jews are required to elevate mankind by the force of their example; they are to be a light unto all nations. The supreme Jewish values of justice and equality are to be practised and demonstrated, so that their moral force shall be felt by all. To enjoy a special relationship with God may be a privilege, but it is also a responsibility; and the Covenant could be imperilled and even revoked through neglect of God's laws. Such responsibility has confirmed the necessity of transmitting a sense of religious obligation and performance from generation to generation. Just as Jews can imaginatively gaze back over 4,000 years in collating their religious tradition, so too they can project forward to the culmination of God's redemptive plan: the messianic age, or the Kingdom of God. The term Messiah is derived from the Hebrew word *mashiach*, which means 'anointed'. The reign of the Anointed One, to which Jews look forward with considerable fervour, is envisaged as a kind of Utopia, in which everything implicit in God's revelation – justice, truth, spiritual purity – will be granted not only to Jews but to all mankind. The messianic age is the fulfilment of the Covenant, the conclusive triumph of good over evil.

Regular prayer and the observance of the Sabbath and the Jewish festivals are intrinsic to the Jewish way of life. (Sadly, Woody Allen's 'sacred Jewish holiday commemorating God's reneging on every promise', is only his invention.) Even Jews who completely ignore the laws and rituals of their religion will often put in an appearance at synagogue on a High Holyday. The Reform rabbi Jonathan Magonet is well aware of the 'vast majority of people for whom the synagogue represents Jewish identity in a very nebulous sort of way. It's a way of combating a certain sense of isolation or peculiarness in the secular world. Why do people come on Yom Kippur? That's the great riddle. A lot of people come because they feel they're doing the right thing somehow, so it's their one *mitzvah* of the year. A lot of people who come regularly resent this. It's peer pressure, it's identifying, it's checking up on a base. It's as if a lot of Jews wander around with the security of knowing that institutions exist even if they don't want them. It's as if there are unconscious threads of connection.'

Orthodox Jews pray three times a day; great value is also placed on additional study of the Torah. On the Sabbath, which commences at sundown on Friday and ends at sundown the following evening, all work ceases. No activity of a creative nature may be undertaken. This includes riding or driving or being driven; writing; picking flowers; switching on or off any electrical appliance such as a light switch or telephone; handling money; carrying objects outside the home. The Sabbath, in other words, is intended to be a complete day of rest, to be devoted to prayer, study, and a sense of joy and wonder at the completion of God's creation of the universe and the continuing presence of divine grace. 'To observe the Sabbath,' Gerda Charles wrote in her novel *The Crossing Point*, 'is to fall into the harmonious rhythm of the universe.' Nevertheless the Sabbath laws may be broken if it is necessary to save life by doing so, for human life is the highest value of all. There is a tendency among the ultra-pious to allow the prohibitions to count for more than the social and festive aspects of Sabbath observance. The Sabbath should also be an occasion for families to gather and observe together the rituals that mark its arrival: the lighting of candles, and the blessings over bread and wine, and a good meal to follow. The same prohibitions apply to the festivals, most of which commemorate crucial events in the history of the Jews, such as Passover, which celebrates the delivery of the Jewish people from slavery in Egypt.

Orthodox Jews will observe the stringent dietary laws known as *kashrut*. These forbid the consumption of animals that do not chew the cud and have cloven hooves; hence pork and horsemeat are not kosher, but *trefah* (non-kosher). Only fish with scales and fins may be eaten, which rules out such delicacies as prawns and lobsters and caviar. Even those animals which are kosher must be slaughtered according to religious law. Such slaughter, which is a complex procedure, is known as *shechita* and is undertaken by a *shochet*. Moreover, milk may not be eaten after meat, or not until at least three hours have elapsed. Orthodox homes will keep separate sets of crockery according to whether they will be used for dishes containing milk (and its by-products) or meat. Other commandments, such as those governing the fabrics to be used in clothing or the strict separation of the sexes and the covering or shaving of women's heads, are only obeyed by ultra-Orthodox Jews.

An example of the intricacies and burdens of religious observance was provided, in satirical form, by a correspondence that appeared in the *Jewish Chronicle* in April 1988 during the Passover season. During the eight days of Passover not only is it forbidden to consume leavened bread, but all traces of *chametz* (leaven), such as breadcrumbs, must be eradicated from the home. This requirement supplies the pretext for an orgy of house-cleaning. The first letter in the series sternly declared: 'No one has made any attempt to encourage the meticulous cleaning of teeth and gums as a preparation for Pesach [Passover]. Normal tooth-cleaning methods cannot eliminate all the minute traces of *chametz* which are bound to be present between the teeth and in the pocketing around the gums.' Since this letter appeared on April Fool's Day, it was tempting to assume it was a jape, but the name and address were genuine. A reply followed from a Harley Street doctor: 'For years some of the Orthodox have maintained a second set of dentures rather than rely on soaking them in boiling water. A more difficult practice is to have all one's fillings changed. The problem is the short changeover period. By erev Pesach [Passover eve] all Jewish dentists are in Netanya or Miami and non-Jewish practitioners may not realize the importance of using only substances with a certificate of *kashrut* from the correct Beth Din.' The following week a correspondent from Stamford Hill declared that the doctor evidently 'has no idea about Jewish laws. Dental fillings fitted more than 30 days before Pesach (similar to *chametz* glue behind wallpaper) do not require to be changed, even if they are made of pure *chametz*. People with such problems should consult an authorized rabbi. But our Jewish laws should not be made fun of, as it is in very bad taste for your readers who respect our old Jewish traditions.' Point taken. Oddly, the writer realized the doctor's letter was in jest, yet was sufficiently exercised to want to correct the fabricated exposition of Jewish law elaborated by the doctor.

The fantastical complexity of the rules of Jewish observance clearly constitutes part of their appeal to those who adhere to them, while at the same time they appear to justify the charges of anachronism and legalistic nitpicking that Progressive Jews level at those who insist on the centrality of rigid observance. Fortunately, the great majority of Jews, whatever their synagogal allegiance, would stress that Judaism is more than a collection of *mitzvot*. The ethical content of Judaism and the infusion of daily life with the high principles of Jewish conduct are equally essential to a full Jewish existence.

Holier than thou: the ultra-Orthodox

O N any Saturday morning the undistinguished suburban pave-
ments of Stamford Hill are paced by a strange group of people.
Two men have emerged from a small detached house, followed
by four scampering small boys, all identically dressed in black peaked
caps. The men, with long bearded faces partly concealed by broad fur
hats, could be thirty-five years old, perhaps older. They, together with
innumerable other small groups also wearing eighteenth-century costume, are on their way to one of dozens of synagogues in the district. The
synagogue itself is unlikely to be one of the large neo-Byzantine structures
found in many inner London suburbs. Instead, it is probably located in a
house hardly distinguishable from the suburban houses in which the
worshippers dwell.

There are thought to be up to 15,000 ultra-Orthodox Jews in the
Stamford Hill and Clapton areas. Not all, like the bearded men on their
way to synagogue, are Chasidic Jews, faithful to a way of life that
flourished two centuries ago in Poland, but a great many, possibly the
majority, are. Although many of the pious Jews are working-class, a
handful are very rich indeed, but even they do not live in the more
spacious suburbs favoured by London Jews with plenty of money. They
remain in these graceless Edwardian streets because they need the
resources of the Orthodox community if they are to maintain their
peculiar and very demanding way of life. A kosher butcher acceptable to
the average Jewish family in Edgware or Leeds may not be up to scratch as
far as a Chasidic Jew is concerned. Nor can his children receive elsewhere
the kind of Jewish education he insists upon. There are so many
ultra-Orthodox Jews in this part of London that they have become part of

the landscape, and nobody gives them a second glance. They can walk to synagogue without being stared at or laughed at – well, hardly ever. They have, in a sense, established their own ghetto, allowing them to preserve their values intact.

One morning I approached a large house on Stamford Hill itself. I had noticed a number of Chasidim making their way towards it, and I followed them in. A group of boys and two older men were standing about in the hallway, glancing at communal notices in Hebrew and Yiddish. From the pegs hung long and heavy black coats, for it was a cold day. I felt conspicuous wearing clothes that were, if not exactly modern, at least based on designs considered dashing in 1955. I had brought my own bodyguard with me, an old friend called John, who was tall and bearded and almost as rabbinic in appearance as our hosts. Unfortunately his knowledge of Hebrew did not match the authenticity of his physical appearance.

The synagogue itself consisted of two rooms that had been broken through. At the far end, near the windows overlooking the forecourt, stood the ark that contains the scrolls of the Law, and half-way down the room someone – it was impossible to see who – was declaiming in Hebrew at breakneck speed from a reading desk. The brightly lit room was filled with long tables covered with a kind of white oilcloth, and men at prayer sat or stood behind these tables, poring over their prayer-books. An elderly man, scarcely visible beneath his *tallit* (prayer shawl), pushed two books towards us, and with great difficulty I managed to find the place, but I soon lost it again. There are great local variations in Jewish liturgy. I can recognize the major markers, the beginnings and sometimes the ends of a sequence of prayers, but in this tiny synagogue we were cast adrift on a continuous blur of shimmering prayer, a hum of supplication scarcely interrupted by paragraphing let alone by the dramatic ritual that punctuates the more formal services of mainstream Orthodoxy.

The men – there were perhaps forty of all ages, plus innumerable small boys – were uniform in appearance. They had hung their lovely shallow fur hats, a foot or more across, from a row of pegs, and their heads were covered by *kippot* (skullcaps) and by voluminous woollen prayer shawls. The standard outer garment was a long black coat (*bekescher*), made of gaberdine or silk, that fell in a straight line from shoulder to knee. Their legs were encased in white stockings (*zocken*) that made them appear even more spindly than they were, and it seemed scarcely possible that such delicate pins could support the weight of hat and *tallit*. Some of the men sported sidelocks as well as beards. The boys, beardless as yet, had to make to do with wispy sidelocks alone. On their heads they wore caps with peaks that dipped down over their foreheads. If their fathers and uncles were dressed as Polish merchants of the eighteenth century, then their offspring were clad, I assumed, as military cadets of a later era. Some of them had very closely cropped hair, partly covered by their *kippot*. They were unruly, like small boys everywhere, and when they whispered among themselves, as they did all too frequently despite the frenzied prayer all around them, they did so in Yiddish. These were not immigrants, recent arrivals from some miserable peasant *dorf* in the Ukraine, but London-born children, many of whose parents were born here too. Despite their vivacity, some of the children did not seem in exemplary health. Eczema marched across their faces, and blotched the hairy cheeks of their elders too. John whispered to me that if he had only brought along his doctor's bag he could have performed medical wonders.

We were inevitably regarded with considerable curiosity, though not hostility. It's not every Sabbath that Jews of no demonstrable piety walk in and sit down at the Ahavat Israel Synagogue D'Chasidey Vishnitz, for that, I soon learnt, was where we were, among the followers of the Vishnitzer Rebbe. If the rabbi who guides the London Vishnitzers, Rabbi Schneebalg, was in attendance that morning, it was impossible to tell, for there was no way to distinguish a rabbi from any other member of the congregation. The Sabbath service takes at least three hours. The liturgy is divided into certain sections, and within each section the worshipper proceeds as slowly or as rapidly as he wishes, rather like a jazz musician let loose on a chorus. As long as he gets through the notes and reaches the end of the passage at roughly the same time as everybody else, it doesn't matter much what he gets up to in between. This explains the constant babble that assaults the ears on entering an ultra-Orthodox synagogue. The services do lack decorum. In the course of three hours of prayer, it is not considered lacking in reverence to switch off for a few minutes, either by chatting to a neighbour or by wandering around or even leaving the room for a few minutes. There will be plenty of time to catch up on your prayers after your return. Although much of the recitation appears to be mindless mumbling, individual worshippers mark their progress through the liturgy by giving emphasis to those prayers or phrases that in their view require it. This is achieved either by standing up – though many ultra-Orthodox Jews pray on their feet as a matter of course – or by shouting, swaying, jabbing a finger in the air, or swishing the air with a flattened palm. You can make as much noise as you like; nobody will stare or make you feel out of place. A measure of ecstasy is not only tolerated but encouraged within Chasidic communities at prayer, which they are much of the time. Boys too, with their unbroken voices, attain exceptionally high decibel ratings with the greatest of ease.

After an hour, a smooth-shaven man of about sixty walked in, wearing conventional dress. I had by this time grown so accustomed to the living anachronisms all around me that his suit and tie struck me as intrusive. He donned his *tallit*, intoning the appropriate blessing that accompanies the act, then walked over. I explained that we were mere visitors; he shook hands, said we were very welcome, then returned to his prayers. A short while after, he returned. 'Why don't you boys go out and have a cup of coffee next door? You don't want to sit here all the time. It must be difficult for you to follow.' An excellent idea: John and I made for the hallway outside. No coffee in sight. I asked a passing Chasid where the coffee room was, and he told us to follow him. We passed through a passage into what was clearly the adjoining house, then climbed the stairs to a kitchen. The Chasid prepared some instant coffee, then asked us to take our mugs back downstairs with us, as we were now in the room adjoining the women's synagogue, and our presence might disturb their devotions. There didn't appear to be many women in the room designated for their use. Jewish women are not obliged to attend synagogue services, as it is recognized that they have domestic responsibilities that keep them within the house.

While we were sipping our Vishnitzer coffee, another worshipper emerged from the synagogue, in search of his three tubby little sons. 'This must be boring for you. Why don't you go up the road to the Lubavitch synagogue? It's much bigger, and they have better facilities for visitors. Prayer-books with English translations. You'll find it more interesting, I'm sure.' We took his advice, but not before quizzing him about the Vishnitzers. This community consists of some fifty families, many of which have come from other countries. He himself was Belgian. Almost the entire congregation spoke Yiddish as a first language, though most spoke English too.

Up the road at Lubavitch the ambience was less exotic, though I happened to find myself sitting next to a man whose bilingual prayer-book had translations not into English but into Russian, which he also spoke to his neighbour. There was a family resemblance between the two congregations: the long tables, the scattered books, the gabbled prayers, the absence of formality and ritual.

It is believed by many that Chasidism developed in eighteenth-century Poland and the Ukraine as a reaction against a lack of religious commitment among the population as a whole. Nothing could be further from the truth. Chasidism was a reaction against a dry-as-dust scholasticism that seemed out of touch with popular piety. The movement was founded by Rabbi Israel ben Eliezer, who became known as the Ba'al Shem Tov (the Master of the Good Name). The Chasidic masters placed great emphasis on the power of prayer, the aim of which, they argued, was to attain an annihilation of self-consciousness, an ecstatic closeness to God. Unlike the tradition of rabbinical exegesis, Chasidism was not a movement restricted to the scholar and the bibliophile. It affirmed that any Jew had the capacity to pray, however poor he might be, however limited his mental agility, however weak his Talmudic learning. The capacity for prayer was seen as a force for equality; you didn't need to attach yourself to a rabbinical academy to be a pious Jew. Through prayer alone the most humble Jew could draw closer to God. Chasidism proved a resounding success. By the early nineteenth century, it had won over half the Jews of eastern Europe. Its emotional charge engendered a human warmth lacking in the scholastic tradition of the day. A Chasidic meeting, religious or social, bears some resemblance to Christian revivalism. Although there were ascetic strains in some branches of Chasidism, it was essentially a life-affirming movement, infused with joy and enthusiasm, and those elements are still strikingly present today. Chasidic prayer could appear almost reckless in its physicality, although the Lubavitchers prefer greater decorum and conduct themselves in a more stately manner. Some Chasidic groups embraced a kind of mysticism not unrelated to cabbalistic mysticism, with its emphasis on disclosing symbolic meanings and intimations of the supernatural hidden within the configurations of Hebrew letters and quasi-mathematical conjunctions within holy texts.

The other major innovation of Chasidism was the veneration of the *tzaddik*, a holy man who acted almost as an intermediary between God and the members of a Chasidic community. Any Chasid, vexed by a religious or domestic problem, could consult his *tzaddik*, who would pray on his behalf and offer advice. Like great rabbis, *tzaddikim* were regarded with awe by their followers, who would often travel for hundreds of miles to visit and perhaps dwell within his 'court'. Unlike a devout and scholarly rabbi immersed in his studies and commentaries, the *tzaddik* had a pastoral as well as a spiritual role. More curiously, his qualities were thought to be genetically transmissible, and the early *tzaddikim* became founders of religious dynasties. Sometimes the mantle fell on a son, sometimes on a son-in-law. For an ambitious Chasid, it was a shrewd move to wed the *tzaddik*'s daughter. Despite the decimation of European Jewry, many of these rabbinical dynasties have survived. Each of the major Chasidic movements – Lubavitch, Belz, Vishnitz, Satmar, and many more – pays homage to its own *tzaddik*, nowadays known as the Rebbe.

Chasidim wield the cutting edge of ultra-Orthodoxy, but there are many ultra-Orthodox Jews who are not Chasidim. Among the Sephardim, for instance, Chasidism made no impression. As Chasidism spread through eastern Europe, there was tremendous opposition from Lithuanian rabbis, notably Elijah ben Solomon, known as the Vilna Gaon. He inveighed against the irrationality that he perceived at the heart of Chasidism. He scorned the appeal to emotion over reason and to mass hysteria over scholarly application, and the over-familiarity of their desired relationship with the Almighty. He was equally scathing about the veneration of *tzaddikim*, which in his view verged on idolatry, and made moves to excommunicate Chasidic leaders. The primary duty of the pious Jew was to reach God through constant prayer, declared the Chasidim. Not so, replied the Vilna Gaon: his primary duty is to study the Torah so as to live in accord with God's law. By the late eighteenth century the argument was becoming increasingly academic, as the ideas of the Enlightenment began to invade even the closed world of Orthodox communities, and young Jews became tempted to pursue more worldly ambitions away from the Jewish community, free from the constraints of the Torah. Faced with the threat of the Enlightenment, or Maskalah, the Orthodox, whether scholarly or pietistic, began to combine and close ranks. Even so, it is still possible to find in Stamford Hill small groups of *mitnaggedim*, traditionalists who follow the line originally propounded by the Vilna Gaon. Although resolutely opposed to many Chasidic ideas, and less committed to antique costume, the piety and social and religious values of the *mitnaggedim* are every bit as fervent as those of the Chasidim.

In the 1980s Chasidism is on the increase. This is an astonishing state of affairs. An Orthodox Jew such as Ephraim Margulies, the immensely rich chairman of the commodity brokers S & W Berisford, does not feel that his religiosity is diminished by his personal preference for shaven cheeks over bearded, but his many children are all Chasidim. In a rambling house on Stamford Hill that is the British headquarters of the ultra-Orthodox Agudas Israel movement, a charming grandmother of ferocious energy called Ita Simons runs a housing association for the Orthodox. One of her charms is that she isn't in the slightest bit fazed by aggressive questions, and didn't take it amiss when I suggested that it was simply perverse to aspire in the late twentieth century to return to the remote and relatively backward eighteenth.

'You ask why there is this need to retreat? It's because of this extreme freedom and tolerance which we experience in the present moment. The more tolerance and freedom there is, the easier it is to become assimilated. One has to become more extreme to keep the religion undiluted. Otherwise it's very difficult. I once told someone who came to see me: What Hitler did with his gas ovens, you people are doing by becoming assimilated and marrying out and breaking the chains of Judaism.' The metaphor is revealing, for it should not be necessary to be fettered in order to be a Jew. Nor, I imagine, would non-Orthodox Jews take kindly to the suggestion that their inability to dedicate their lives to 'Torah-true' Judaism is in any sense comparable to genocide. But a siege mentality, as I expect she would concede, is part of the ultra-Orthodox outlook. I asked her to characterize 'the religion undiluted' that was under such grave threat.

'The philosophy of an undiluted Jew', she replied, 'is that he was brought into this world because it's a *mitzvah* to be born and to serve his Creator. To serve his Creator he has to have a healthy body, and to have a healthy body you have to eat and sleep, and to eat and sleep well you have to go out to work. But it's all a means to an end, not an end in itself. Our kind of Judaism is not the kind where we just want our children to eat kosher. Our aim in life is not to make a good living, it's not to lead a comfortable life and be religious. First and foremost, from the time a child is born to the time he dies our basic aim in life is to serve our Creator and to develop our potential to lead the most pure and spiritual life we can. So that when we go back to our Creator, to the world after, we are in a good condition to do so. In order to achieve this aim, we can't lead a life of compromise. We have to take a very extreme attitude in order to preserve our aim of leading spiritual lives.'

That extreme attitude consists primarily in shutting out the rest of the world, in keeping its corrupt and corrupting values at bay. 'The ultra-Orthodox community sees the modern world – although it's very free and very democratic and very beautiful and wonderfully modern and clever – as a time of Sodom and Gomorrah. There's murder and every kind of permissiveness and perversion being actively promoted and given status.

The time we're living in is one of terrible spiritual degradation, a total breakdown of everything ethical, everything decent. Fifty years ago there was this glitter of Zionism and Communism that grabbed youngsters away from traditional Chasidic and Orthodox backgrounds – because young people want something definite, and Jewish people particularly so, because Jewish people are thinkers. Now the only definite things in society – the way we interpret it – are drugs, permissiveness. There's no idealism. I think this view is shared not only by ultra-Orthodox people but by ordinary English people too. Unless we go to the extremes that we do, we feel there's a danger we'll be contaminated. I come from a Chasidic background, but my father was very broad-minded and we always had a newspaper in the house. My husband has had to say no, we can't have a newspaper in the house at all because of all the filth. You can't subject children to that kind of literature when you want them to be spiritual.'

The Chasidim may have battened down the hatches, but they are not unsophisticated in terms of their relations with the rest of the community, Jewish or non-Jewish. Agudas publishes a newspaper, the *Jewish Tribune*, which is the principal source of news and information for many ultra-Orthodox households. Assisted by Hackney Council, Agudas runs a crèche, an advice centre, and an employment service for those requiring jobs that do not involve working on the Sabbath. Its housing association helps those who want to live among a community that caters for ultra-Orthodox practice, but who may not qualify for assistance from the local authority or other housing associations. All the more curious, then, is the wish to don white stockings and fur hats. Not that Mrs Simons sees it that way: 'Our menfolk don't feel different being dressed the way they are. They just dress Jewish, that's what they feel. In Stamford Hill there are many punks around with violet hair – so we feel our mode of dress is very tame and ordinary compared with what goes on around here. Maybe we would feel more out of place in a more exclusive area.' Many non-Chasidic Orthodox, however, feel too much importance is placed on such matters by some sects. They suspect costume is used as a method of social control, since it could be tricky walking into a discotheque or strip joint in Chasidic garb. There may also be a pride in outlandishness for its own sake, as though dress were a measure of Orthodoxy.

With the Chasidic movement so fragmented (as it has always been) it is hard to gauge the cohesiveness of ultra-Orthodoxy, which is divided not only on grounds of dogma or even practice, but according to the personalities of individual religious leaders. The rabbi is not only the focus of all religious life but of much social life too. Prayer and study take place in the Beth Hamedrash (study house), which also functions as a community centre and club house. Some rabbis, such as the Sassover Rabbi, Simcha Rubin, have a reputation for discreet good works within the community, often supplying its poorer members with financial help. A social worker who knows the ultra-Orthodox community well claimed that each Chasidic group is very much under the thumb of its religious leader. 'The authority of the rabbi is absolute. Before you move house or change job, you will consult him and he will tell you whether or not that's a good thing. Many of the rebbes live in New York now, and sometimes Chasidic groups charter a plane so they can go off and see their rebbe. I once travelled on the celebrated occasion when the plane was shared by Lubavitch and Satmar Chasidim – that was not exactly a harmonious trip. There's a Satmar school in Stamford Hill, and some of the little girls who go there come from other Chasidic groups. They study together, but during breaks they split up into their different groups. You do what your rabbi tells you to do.' Ita Simons disagreed: 'We're not a very coherent community. There are so many different rabbis, so many different ideas, that everybody is really their own rabbi. Everybody does exactly what they want. The rebbes live in Israel or America, so the people here do what they like. Of course there are standards we try to live up to. The whole idea of religion is to harness human nature and bring out the best in us, to behave like a human being rather than an animal. But some people are born with more difficult characters than others.'

Her insistence that Orthodoxy safeguards high ethical standards that are a cornerstone of the Jewish heritage is shared by Rabbi Abraham David, who nurtures a small but growing congregation in the London suburb of Hendon. Although a Sephardi, and thus not a Chasid, he is as rigid in his religious observance as any Ashkenazi Chasid. 'In the east', he points out, 'there was no other form of Judaism, no such thing as Reform.' Rabbi David has his origins in Baghdad, and members of his congregation come from India, Iran, Iraq, and other parts of the Orient. Not that his synagogue is restricted to Sephardim; Ashkenazim worship there too, if only because it's convenient. Like many ultra-Orthodox clerics, he holds Progressive Judaism in low esteem. 'Before the recent period everybody was within the community. There was no Reform, no Liberal, just the community. You were Orthodox, and that's all. Reform rabbis think you can tell people: "If you can't keep to the standard, you can still call yourself a Reform Jew. Carry on as you are, just give us your signature or come once a month, and that's enough. We don't require anything more." For people who want to take it easy, that's fine. But what have you done for them? What have you given them? You haven't given them anything! We've got a standard, we've got a Torah, a set of laws worth keeping. Reform is bending the rules because of convenience. If someone comes to our *shul* in a car, we try to convince him he shouldn't. But sometimes he doesn't want to make any effort. He says: "Why should I walk? I'll go to a *shul* where they allow me to park my car." He's not being asked to make any effort. But we will try and convince him.

'There is so much in the Torah, especially for the intellectual. It can hold a man's mind more completely than anything else. Orthodox Jews are committed in their life: they've got patterns and aims you won't find elsewhere. In our homes you'll find that three generations can think together and work together and find an interest together. Our children have the same interests as their parents, and the same is true of their grandparents. You won't find this outside an Orthodox community. I know people who are not Orthodox. They sit in front of the television, there's no conversation, there's no contact between people. In an Orthodox home it's not like that. We have Shabbat together, at the table we talk about things of common interest. A boy of twelve, an old man of eighty, they can learn the same thing from the Gemara, and it keeps your mind fresh and agile. God is controlling the world, so we have faith in the future, and we have a way of life that's been successful through all time. Our way of life has kept the Jews together, it's kept us at home.'

It is precisely this unchanging aspect of Orthodoxy that Progressive Jews find troubling. Both Orthodox and Reform Jews acknowledge that Halachah has to be interpreted, but Reform Jews resent the way their critique of Jewish law is blithely dismissed by their Orthodox counterparts. The Reform rabbi Colin Eimer has written of Progressive attempts to criticize Orthodox interpretations of Halachah that they tend to be declared inadmissible on the grounds that they demonstrate 'some deficiency on the part of the critic, rather than the system. If the critic only had more knowledge, better understanding, or the right disposition, he would come to see how wrong and misguided he is.'[1] Moreover, the certainties of ultra-Orthodox belief make rational argument very difficult. The pious Jew who believes that the Torah is a divinely inspired code given by God to Moses on Mount Sinai is inevitably going to run into trouble when called upon to consider the theory of evolution and historical and archaeological evidence that challenges a literalist, or fundamentalist, reading of the Pentateuch. Some ultra-Orthodox Jews, such as the following correspondent to the *Jewish Chronicle*, deny the possibility of alternative cosmologies: 'Science tries to make us believe in millions of years of our planet's existence, whereas one who believes in God knows that there is a definite plan from the beginning of creation until the appearance of man six days later and up to this day . . . Only by subordinating science and technology to the supremacy of the Torah shall we continue to exist. All other attempts and isms have failed.'[2] A more sophisticated ultra-Orthodox Jew will often play down the role of the intellect and point to other means of apprehending the truth. An argument along these lines was made to me by Shlomo Levin, an intelligent and charismatic Lubavitch-trained rabbi:

'The question is, does intellect question belief, or is belief higher than intellect and thus unquestionable? I'll tell you how I think the issue is resolved. There are two ways to look at a circle. One is to stand on the circumference and try to find the centre. From the circumference you hit off in all different directions in the hope that you'll find the centre point. That's the secular approach. Judaism starts off with the belief, and that belief is at the very centre of the circle, the belief that we were given a Torah which is the Torah of truth. From that belief there's a sense of radiating out to embrace the entire circle and moving out to the circumference. The rabbis who compiled the Talmud left no secular stone unturned: they were astronomers, mathematicians, doctors, but they all started from one very strong belief in one God and the creation of the world as described in the Torah.'

Thus belief takes precedence over intellect, it would seem. 'Intellect builds on belief. Intellect on its own is a very slippery kind of thing; it can lead you to tremendous confusion. A person needs an anchor, a solid base on which one's intellect can grow, a recognition that truth is not necessarily grasped exclusively by intellect. There are other ways to grasp truth. There's emotion, there's soul. Perhaps one of the problems of our society is that we are living at the tail end of a rationalist age. It's been assumed that all the truth of the world would flow from our intellectual grasp. Orthodox Judaism would say that intellect is a powerful tool and has to be exercised to the utmost, but it's not the exclusive tool for finding truth.'

It is this bit part offered to intellect by ultra-Orthodox Jews that most other Jews, including religious ones, find unrealistic and unacceptable. Rabbi Levin offered his argument with some elegance and sophistication, but it does not differ in its import from the rebuffs I experienced as a child

when I questioned my religious teachers about the essentially fundamentalist presentation of biblical history they were dishing out to me.
Shlomo Levin would never, I am sure, dismiss such questioning by his
students and would at least give them the intellectual courtesy of a
considered reply. But the message is much the same. Or consider the
breathtaking demotion of the inquiring mind implicit in the following
passage written by Britain's senior Sephardi rabbi, Dr Abraham Levy:
'For the traditional Jew all explanations are unnecessary, interesting
though they may be. The laws were given by God to the Jewish people to
live by . . . Jews are encouraged to discuss their laws and to study them:
ultimately, though, the laws exist to be accepted and obeyed. Man will
never understand God's purposes and ways: attempts to find satisfying
rational explanations for his commandments are secondary, and in most
cases futile.'[3] In which case God must have had a pretty low opinion of His
most sublime creation: mankind.

Perhaps it is this rigidity that many of those who have succumbed to the
lure of ultra-Orthodoxy find so appealing. Talmudic disputation and
rabbinic study juggle with the incidentals almost as a means of affirming
the inviolability of the central core of belief, the Torah. If you accept the
literal truth of the Torah, then you are at liberty to discuss the fine print –
up to a point. Undoubting belief, after all, is very reassuring: it provides all
the answers. Because the Gemara does indeed contain much secular
learning and debate, it becomes easy for ultra-Orthodox rabbis to present
their faith as more open than it in fact is. For behind the apparent
suppleness of mind exhibited by sophisticated modern rabbis lies an
intellectual intransigence that rejoices in supposed certainties. Other
brands of Judaism, uncomfortable with such rigidities, have played down
the centrality of conformity to religious law while highlighting other
aspects of Jewish tradition, be they ritualistic, ethical, Zionist, or whatever. The considerable numbers of those who find this more questioning,
less dogmatic approach unsatisfying, wishy-washy, and lacking in authenticity are among the people who are embracing ultra-Orthodoxy. Some
are also drawn by the idealism – reinforced by its very lack of practicality
and worldliness – of passionately messianic Judaism.

This rush to Torah-true Orthodoxy is encouraged by many rabbis as a
form of *teshuvah*, or return. Ita Simons confirms that more people are
joining ultra-Orthodox communities than leaving them. I met two young
women, sisters, who live comfortably enough in a council flat in the East
End but are determined to move to Stamford Hill so that they can

participate more actively in Jewish communal life. One of them has found work teaching at the Lubavitch school. There is no council accommodation for them in Stamford Hill, so they must rent a private flat, which will be more costly and less spacious than their council flat. The expense, even for two working-class girls, is a minor consideration compared to the positive benefits they hope to derive from living among like-minded Jews. It was Mrs Simons, naturally, who found a flat for them, though she was self-deprecating about her efforts: 'I spent a long time helping them, though I'm not interested in having them move to the area – it's another headache for me. We're not missionaries.'

But many ultra-Orthodox Jews are indeed missionaries. The Lubavitch Foundation openly seeks to bring Jews back to a greater sense of their Jewishness and thus, they hope, to greater observance. Rabbi David takes a similar line: 'We're getting our people back to the fold. People come to our *shul*, they feel comfortable, we go out of our way to make them comfortable, and they get drawn in. We don't force them into anything, we just try to attract them, by showing them that Judaism is attractive if you keep it properly, keep it fully. If a person looks at Shabbat and hears you mustn't go out, you mustn't do this, you mustn't do that, it becomes a burden. But if he comes into a home and sees what Shabbat can give, the atmosphere and the beauty of Shabbat, he enjoys it. A lot of people don't know what Shabbat is like. So we give them an opportunity to see and feel what it is, and to appreciate the knowledge behind it, the meaning. That comes through studies, through *shiurim*. And that's how we get a lot of people to come back. They are mostly younger people, from fifteen to thirty-five. Orthodoxy is very vibrant today. We are going out to get people, to get people to our standard, which is the standard that has been accepted for generations. When we started here three and a half years ago, we couldn't get a *minyan*. Today on Shabbat we get a hundred people. People are committing themselves more because they realize the beauty of Orthodoxy. We demand something, we demand a standard. We didn't invent it. It's there. We can't change the rules. The rules are there.'

Many Jews regard the *teshuvah* movement as an unwelcome retreat into authoritarianism and obscurantism. Even a distinguished Reform rabbi such as Dow Marmur cannot avoid a tone of distinct disdain when he remarks on 'the regimentation and ostensible certainty of Orthodoxy. Its noisy piety and aggressive religiosity is attractive to those who wish to tell the whole world that they have at last found a spiritual haven.'[4] Many young men and women, often highly educated and with excellent career prospects, have suddenly abandoned their secular life and disappeared into *yeshivot* and seminaries to emerge soon after with all the trappings of the ultra-Orthodox Jew. This can lead to heartbreak within families, as parents and children find they no longer share common ground, and the demands of strict *kashrut* often persuade the born-again Jew that he or she can no longer live among a less observant family. Rodney Mariner, a Reform rabbi yet himself no slouch when it comes to religious observance, is candid in his dislike of the crusading rabbis. 'The growth of ultra-Orthodoxy frightens the hell out of me. At the end of the day it divides one Jew from another. It divides families. If Jews can't sit at the same table as their own family, then the heart goes out of it.'

Such estrangement is not inevitable, but it is a likely consequence of *teshuvah*. The demands of daily life among the ultra-Orthodox are such that contact with those who do not share their beliefs and customs is not possible on anything more than the most superficial level. This is even more true of Chasidim, who keep very much to themselves. 'You can be friends with your neighbours,' says Rabbi David, 'even though they do not belong to the same group or community. That's normal. We do business with people from other communities, other backgrounds – that makes no difference. But a person usually socializes with those he feels comfortable with. I think it's like that in any community. People who meet regularly in *shul* tend to live nearby. I don't associate socially with non-Jews, because we haven't got a lot in common, and I don't want my children to be with their children. I don't think it's just Orthodox Jews who feel like that, it's most Jews, except those who want to forget their identity. Sometimes we have to take a business associate to dinner – so we make it a kosher restaurant. There's no shortage of kosher restaurants. Or I might invite him home for a meal. There's nothing wrong with that. As a rabbi, I can invite people who are not so Orthodox as well, because we want to influence them, we want them to become more Orthodox.'

There is a strong streak of puritanism in ultra-Orthodoxy that seems out of tune with Jewish tradition, for Judaism is not an ascetic religion; self-denial and penitential scourgings play no part in Jewish practice. Celibacy is not a Jewish value, and neither is monastic withdrawal. Yet the ultra-Orthodox go to extraordinary lengths to protect their young people, in particular, from corrupting influences. I asked Rabbi David whether he disapproved, for example, of cinema-going. Not in itself, he replied, though in practice, because of the low standards of the medium, he would not wish to encourage it. 'Today there are *shuls* where you have music or singing. Today it's Jewish entertainment. We give them discourses and debates.' Football too. And when all else fails, he can bring out the books. 'We can show them fantastic things in the Torah!'

Orthodox women are protected from worldly contamination even more than men. From an early age the sexes are kept apart, and in most Orthodox schools even children of kindergarten age are educated separately. Dating is unknown and social contact between people of the opposite sex – even mature adults – is frowned upon. Mrs Simons suggested that, in order to gain more information about the ultra-Orthodox community, I should contact a friend of hers. 'Try,' she said, 'but I don't think she'll see you. Her husband probably won't let.' She was right. The woman replied to my inquiry saying that it would not be possible to meet me, though she would be glad to answer my questions in writing. Her husband, in other words, wouldn't let. If it's very difficult for adults of different sexes to meet, it's even harder for younger people. Their marriages are invariably arranged, and even during wedding festivities men and women are divided by a high curtain. Men will dance with men, women with women.

Ita Simons finds the term 'arranged marriages' too fusty. She is, by her own account, a dab hand at matchmaking herself. 'There's a better word for it: blind dates. Somebody thinks of somebody and somebody else thinks of somebody and they get together and think about it, and the parents think about it. Are they suitable, is the background similar, what are the aspirations of the young man, what are the aspirations of the girl? We'd never put the two people together where the girl perhaps is flighty and the young man is very serious, or the other way round. The boy and the girl have a choice. If they don't like each other, they just say so.' The ultra-Orthodox, Chasidim in particular, very rarely marry outside their own community. 'A man would only marry outside the Chasidic community if the girl wished to follow a Chasidic way of life. Otherwise how would they identify with one another? How could he identify with a United Synagogue girl that wants him to take her out twice a week? A United Synagogue person understands Judaism, will keep kosher, do this, do that – but that's it. It's not body and soul.'

Halachah requires the young persons themselves to agree to the match and they may meet, suitably chaperoned, as often as they wish while making up their minds. By the fourth or fifth meeting, however, they are usually ready to come to a decision. If the marriage takes place but goes wrong, the couple can always divorce, which the ultra-Orthodox regard as an acceptable solution if a couple prove clearly incompatible. Not that Ita Simons is terribly happy about this kind of solution. 'The light-headedness of our permissive society, the breakdown of all values, have reached our community, too – but only in the matter of divorce. Instead of couples putting up with one another as they did in the old days when one was used to struggle and to suffer, now they have an easy life. If they're not comfortable with each other, they divorce.'

The primary responsibility of an ultra-Orthodox woman is to marry – it would be considered calamitous if a healthy young woman failed to find a husband – and once she is married she is expected to be fruitful. Marriage was considered so crucial to Jewish life that in biblical times the High Priest of the Temple was not only married, but required to be married. Judaism exalts marriage because it offers human companionship and is a necessary precondition of the founding of the family on which Judaism places such stress. A fulfilling sexual relationship is considered intrinsic to any Jewish marriage. On the other hand, Orthodox Jews place great stress on the laws of purity, which forbid sexual relations between husband and wife during and for some days after the menstrual period and childbirth. Women are also required to attend a *mikveh* or ritual bath to purify themselves before resuming their sex life. Extra-marital and homosexual relationships are regarded with horror. Rabbinic law suggests that the woman's role is fulfilled after she has borne one son and one daughter, though of course there is no prohibition on having more children. In practice, ultra-Orthodox families are encouraged to produce as many children as possible, partly to satisfy biblical injunctions that laud fecundity, partly to increase the numbers within the community. Birth control and abortion are firmly discouraged by their rabbis. Rebbetzin Judith Schlesinger, a formidable and very acute woman married to the learned Rabbi Elyakim Schlesinger, has nine children, and one of her daughters-in-law has recently given birth to her thirteenth child, which hasn't prevented her from running a school in Stamford Hill. Mrs Simons, though she has a responsible job within the community, took the trouble before working for Agudas to bear seven children. 'It's a very typical set-up. Except I'm not typical. Most women stay at home. Some do a bit of teaching or help their husbands in business.' There is an intricate mutual support system within the community. Parents and in-laws help with child-minding, and even take in children for weeks at a time if their mother needs some peace and quiet – usually because she's about to go into labour once again. If in an emergency someone requires a flat or a car in a hurry, it will be provided, and on such occasions factional differences between the sects are forgotten.

There are some more disquieting aspects of the Orthodox marriage system. Constant inbreeding, hard to avoid among small Chasidic groups, leads to the widespread occurrence of hereditary diseases that are virtually exclusive to Ashkenazi Jews. A social worker brought to my attention the case of a Chasidic family with a daughter who carried an obscure hereditary disease that is only suffered by males. Her family were desperate to conceal the information that she was a carrier, since if it became public knowledge the girl would be unmarriageable. Poverty is another problem within the community. Even a man with a reasonably high income could find himself strapped if, as is likely, he has eight or even twelve mouths to feed. At the Vishnitz synagogue, Mrs Simons assured me, I was breathing the same air as two multi-millionaires. 'But there would also have been families who rarely eat meat and never go on a holiday. Even some of the children may not be properly fed.' Moreover, inbreeding has resulted not only in the spread of some hereditary diseases but in a higher-than-average incidence of mental and physical handicap. The director of a large Jewish welfare agency believes many of the women carry intolerable burdens: 'If you've got a girl that's been married at sixteen and will carry on producing children till she is no longer capable of doing so, she'll have had no opportunity for any emotional or other kind of development. She's totally drained just by producing kids. There are problems of child abuse, when mothers no longer capable of coping are beating their children. That community places more emphasis on Jewish education than on the physical and mental well-being of their children, and there's a good deal of malnutrition. When a rabbi tells you there are no problems in the community, it means he's sitting very firmly on the lid. That community is absolutely rife with problems.'

Another experienced social worker agreed, with qualifications. 'From our enlightened viewpoint, the women get a hard time. But I don't think they see it that way themselves. Because a woman has nine children doesn't necessarily mean she has nine times the maternal supervision that a mother with one child would have. They are trained to look after one another all the way down the line, and the big children will look after the little ones.' Nevertheless he agreed there were problems of neglect and abuse. Nor is the situation eased by the reluctance of the ultra-Orthodox to seek help from outside their immediate community. The Jewish community's principal child care agency, Norwood Child Care, considers the problems grave enough to justify placing a social worker within the ultra-Orthodox community. They found it difficult to locate that social worker, since it had to be in a place where Chasidim, who are not exactly inconspicuous, can avoid being observed by their neighbours should they seek such help.

The situation is gradually improving. There is now an old people's home for the ultra-Orthodox and a school for handicapped children in Golders Green. Ita Simons is trying to set up a home for the mentally ill. There are many such facilities in north London specifically for the Jewish community, but the ultra-Orthodox won't use them, since the religious supervision of such homes is not up to their exacting standards. Mrs Simons suspected the problems of the community were exaggerated by Jewish social workers who were not part of it. 'We are very health-conscious. There is no difficulty getting dispensation from a rabbi not to have any more children if things go badly and the mother can't cope.' Mental illness used to be brushed under the carpet, she told me, but nowadays attempts were being made within the community to discuss it and treat it.

No community, however strict the code that regulates its everyday existence, can shut out the wider world completely. Chasidic Jews have to work like everybody else. Financially successful Chasidic Jews – such as those who run some of London's property empires – often find or create jobs for their numerous relatives. A few, a very few, Chasidim are even active in local politics. Rabbi Avraham Pinter, who directs the largest ultra-Orthodox school in London, is also a Labour councillor in Hackney. Older Orthodox Jews, in his experience, tend to be apolitical, but this is less true of the younger generation, such as himself. 'It's paramount for us to retain our culture and education, but that's no reason not to participate in the community. You can be part of the community without compromising your integrity.' There is little evidence that the ultra-Orthodox community is politically left-wing – indeed, the evidence points the other way – so it seems possible that Rabbi Pinter is a Labour councillor not out of deep socialist conviction but because it is the only way he can secure a position of influence on the council and thus represent the interests of his community. Reciprocally, the Labour Party can enjoy access to the large ultra-Orthodox community. Of course his religious beliefs can be a constraint. Rabbi Pinter has had to absent himself from meetings at which gay rights have been discussed, as his Orthodox viewpoint would conflict with the views of his political colleagues. Nevertheless, his participation represents one of the few institutional contacts between the ultra-Orthodox and the community among whom they must live.

– 5 –

The Lubavitch movement

THE followers of the Lubavitcher Rebbe have assumed such an important role among world Jewry that we should take a closer look at them than at the other Chasidic sects. The Lubavitch sect was founded in the eighteenth century by Rabbi Schneur Zalman, whose peculiar brand of Chasidism became known as Chabad Chasidism, encapsulated in a volume known as the Tanya. Lubavitch is a dynastic sect, and its leadership has passed down through the generations. The predecessor to the present Rebbe was born in Lubavitch, Russia, in 1880. Arrested and sentenced to death in the late 1920s, he was eventually released after pressure was brought to bear on the Soviet government by foreign politicians. He then emigrated to the United States but travelled to Poland in 1934 to be closer to his flock and stayed there until 1940, when he escaped to the United States once again. He died in Brooklyn in 1950, and was succeeded by the present Rebbe, Menachem Schneerson, who, although in his late eighties, still leads the movement.

Lubavitch is an extraordinary success story. While other Chasidic groups lead sequestered lives in ghettos of their own making in Jerusalem or London or Brooklyn, the Lubavitchers see themselves as a worldwide missionary movement, carrying their mission not of course to the *goyim* but to other Jews. Lubavitch established a presence in England in 1960, and grew very rapidly indeed. Schools and seminaries and community centres have been set up not only in London but in provincial cities. The fashionable word 'outreach' could have been coined for Lubavitch, for it defines their approach of striving to bring Jews, whatever their state of religious consciousness or observance, back to their religious roots. It seeks to awaken a sense of Jewishness even among those in whom that awareness has been deeply buried or almost obliterated. It does so by any feasible means, from buttonholing passers-by in Jewish districts, to dispatching missionaries to schools and counsellors to universities, to founding youth clubs and libraries and *yeshivot*, to driving around north London in a converted ambulance known as a Mitzvah Tank, kitted up as though it were designed to attract voters in a general election. There are visitation programmes and adult education courses, and a 'small communities division' to bring religious services to towns where the Jewish population is minute. *Lubavitch News* advertises not only 'New Wigs for Yom Tov!' but a 'Dial-a-Jewish-Story' service with phone numbers in London, Manchester and Glasgow. Rabbi Zvi Telsner, who ministers to university students, declares: 'For us, every Jewish student who performs a *mitzvah* has tipped the scales in the right direction. We'll use any techniques that we can. If you can use advertising to sell deodorant, you can use it to push Judaism.' The approach is overtly emotional, as Telsner's colleague Rabbi Gershon Overlander makes clear: 'We're not out to make people religious. Our main aim is that people should realize the tremendous warmth and heritage of Judaism.'[1]

The Lubavitchers may lack subtlety, but not fervour. A Lubavitch publication states with typical overkill: 'Torah and *mitzvot* are the only authentic life of the Jew . . . It is only a concerted, whole-hearted devotion to Torah that enables one to achieve ascendancy of the soul, which is the sway of the spirit and holiness over the forces of egoism and selfishness which are the source of evil.'[2] Yet for all the activism of the Lubavitchers, their life is based on a complete acquiescence to the will of God: 'God's reason for issuing *mitzvot* is beyond our powers of divination . . . Our observance is based completely on accepting them as God's teachings, as the will and understanding of His mind.'[3] Translated into practice on the streets of British cities, the benign aggression that marks the Lubavitch method has led to accusations of brainwashing. While Lubavitch counsellors participate in 'deprogramming' sessions for young people who have come under the malignant influence of sects such as the Moonies, there are many who believe that a course of deprogramming would not come amiss for many of those who have fallen under the spell of Lubavitch.

To promote the return to the faith of wayward souls, Lubavitch, despite its roots in eighteenth-century eastern Europe, will use all the resources of modern technology. The exceedingly long discourses of the Rebbe are relayed to his followers throughout the world by live satellite or by videotape recording. There is nothing abstruse about the message of the

Lubavitchers, who have no more subtlety than an American TV evangelist. The following passage from a Lubavitch publication corresponds exactly in spirit and tone to some of the fervent declarations to be heard on any of fifteen Kentucky television stations on any Sunday morning: 'A Jew must be "plugged in" before he can start functioning. Regardless of his complexity and sophistication . . . he must take the first step and connect himself to the Power Supply with the inexpensive plug – his *Tefillin* . . . he is not "operational" until he has dedicated his heart, mind and hand to his Creator.'[4] Other sources of power include 'first class, kosher, and cost price' *mezuzot*[5] – which Lubavitch counsellors will not only supply but will afix to your doorpost in the approved manner – and giving the religiously uncertain the opportunity to spend a Sabbath in the warmth of a Lubavitch household. Lubavitch stresses the breadth of its embrace: nothing is beyond the divine grasp or outside the divine interest, and no one need feel excluded from the full appreciation of the wonder of God's continuous creation. The Jew, who acts as an agent of his Creator, is enjoined by Lubavitch doctrine to see every obstacle not as a challenge but as an opportunity. There is no difficulty that cannot be turned to advantage. Lubavitch proclaims a kind of positive thinking, except that its goal is not the vulgar one of self-enrichment or professional self-aggrandizement, but that of expressing God's purpose in this world.

Any legal means can and should be used to further the goal of bringing wayward Jews back to their faith. In the words of Rabbi Shraga Faivish Vogel, who directs the Lubavitch Foundation in Britain from their headquarters on Stamford Hill: 'We want to bring the message of Judaism to more Jews, irrespective of background, commitment, or label. There are pockets of intensely Orthodox Jews who see their purpose in life as survival by locking the world out and creating a milieu of a very intense defensive position against the encroachment of the secular permissive world. But the unique distinction of Lubavitch is that it does not see that as an end in itself at all. The whole orientation of our education systems and the pride that we give to our young people is the ability to take our religious message to the outside secular world. Take, for example, the tremendous explosion of communications there is today. These are seen not as negative forces but rather as opportunities.'

At the head of this international movement is the aged bearded figure of the Rebbe. Despite his impeccably rabbinic mien, the Rebbe is a man of considerable sophistication, complete with a degree in science from the Sorbonne. His teachings, according to Rabbi Vogel, 'are authoritative in the sense that he has acquired a total knowledge of Jewish law. He was a child prodigy and has never stopped studying. Every week he holds gatherings for three or four hours at which he expounds Jewish law. His teachings are authoritative because they are reasoned and argued and presented in the tradition of Jewish exposition, based on precedence and previous guides to Jewish teachings. Nuances are created and insights developed. The major rabbinical authorities in the world have a deep respect for the Rebbe's knowledge and learning.' (It is hard not to be reminded of Woody Allen's Rabbi Zwi Chaim Yisroel, an Orthodox scholar who 'was unanimously hailed as the wisest man of the Renaissance by his fellow Hebrews, who totalled a sixteenth of one per cent of the population.'[6]) But, like the head of any major corporation, he is more concerned with policy direction than with nuts-and-bolts administration. 'He restricts himself to giving directions to leaders of the community, heads of organizations. Equally, he expects local initiative to take place, so as to apply those truths in the local circumstances. In each of the five continents where we have representation the flavour might come across slightly differently.'

Yet, stresses Rabbi Vogel, the Rebbe is not a remote unapproachable figure to his followers. 'He maintains personal relationships with thousands of people. He will give them advice on their most difficult personal problems, in the spirit that if any person comes to you for advice, you're not entitled to refuse. He has instituted over the past five or ten years a whole hierarchy of teachers, people who are spiritually charged enough for ordinary people to talk to them.' The head of an Anglo-Jewish welfare agency told me that when he was a student, a friend wrote to the Lubavitcher Rebbe to say he was about to take an examination and would the Rebbe say a *brocha* (blessing) for him. 'That was the ultimate in faith, though it doesn't sound very Jewish to me. I was delighted when I learnt that the Rebbe had replied: "Thank you for your letter. I must point out that examinations are passed by hard work, not *brochas*." That's the answer of a man who's knocked about and sat examinations himself.'

The venerable Rebbe is childless, and it is unclear who his successor will be. No doubt he will in due course indicate which of his followers is worthy of the succession, and should he fail to do so the Chasidim themselves will appoint a new Rebbe. Because the leadership of a Chasidic movement is a burden as well as an honour, a certain coyness is advisable on the part of those elevated to the highest office. Rabbi Schneerson himself displayed unparalleled modesty. When, after the death of his predecessor in 1950, he was asked to become Rebbe, he cited innumerable references from the mystical work known as the Zohar to suggest that the former Rebbe, appearances notwithstanding, was still alive. When that argument, not surprisingly, failed to sway his fellow rabbis, he adopted a more subtle approach, conceding that while the former Rebbe might have passed away in a physical sense, his spirit was still very much present and therefore it would not be appropriate for his humble self to take his place. Eventually the Lubavitchers laid it on the line: All this spiritual speculation is delightful, but the plain fact is we need a new Rebbe and you're our man. After suitable hesitancies, Schneerson gave in, and ever since has led the movement with relish and aplomb. Indeed, to the astonishment and even dismay of other Jews, including Orthodox Jews, the Lubavitch movement has encouraged the notion that the Rebbe is none other than the Messiah, though he is at present constrained from revealing himself as such.

Lubavitch's non-exclusivity is its greatest strength. 'We pride ourselves', says Rabbi Vogel, 'on not having a membership or party card. We see every Jew as a member, because we believe in the potential of every Jew to ascend this ladder of awareness and commitment, so that eventually there will be this full achievement – maybe not in his own life, but in his offspring's life. There are hundreds of thousands of Jews around the world who are keenly sympathetic to the Lubavitch movement, but sense that they cannot fully participate. Our response to them is that that's fine, as long as they are moving in a certain direction and as long as their commitment doesn't just remain intellectual but finds response in practice. Even a minor change in their daily lives is wholly positive and wholly acceptable within the criteria of spiritual self-development. That is why Lubavitch is able to embrace all Jews, or certainly most Jews. People may take up certain practices and observances which are wholly desirable, but then feel they can't handle them, so they backslide marginally. That doesn't mean you're out. You're never in or out. You are part of the process of searching, creating, and moving forward. We're keen to see a Jew perform even one *mitzvah* if it will sow the seeds. Other Orthodox people often don't understand this: they value the purpose and function of *mitzvot* but can't see the value of one *mitzvah* in isolation.' Every occupation gives opportunities, insists Rabbi Vogel, 'for the expression of the knowledge of God in the world. Therefore the more apparently contradictory that profession would be in Jewish eyes, there – the Rebbe would insist – lies the greater opportunity for the sanctification of God's name within that purpose. We want that essential divine quality to percolate through not just our own little enclave but into the wider Jewish community and even beyond that.' Unlike other Chasidic groups, Lubavitch does not recoil in horror from the prospect of university education for its adherents, provided they pursue their studies within the framework of Jewish law.

Shlomo Levin, the Lubavitch-trained rabbi of South Hampstead United synagogue, explained how he incorporates his religious feelings into his daily life, for he is a businessman as well as a rabbi. He makes no distinction between the religious and the secular: 'In Judaism the person is seen in holistic terms. You're the same person in synagogue as you are in business. Whatever values you have in the religious environment, those same values have to be carried through and implemented in the secular environment. That doesn't mean to say you go round quoting verses from the Bible. You just lead an ordinary life, but your morality is guided by the Torah. But there are tremendous pressures. Other people wake up in the morning, snatch a bit of breakfast, and rush off to work. If you're a committed Jew, you have to get up earlier than anybody else because you've got to pack in a great deal more before you can get anywhere near the office. You've got your davening [praying], your learning, and of course there's the family. In the evening, instead of coming home with masses of work to plough through, you have other learning obligations. You're left with less time each day to pack in what other people are doing in a larger amount of time.'

The seeming open-mindedness of the Lubavitch movement has drawn thousands of Jews back from the brink of assimilation to the rigours of Orthodox observance. 'If you broaden the terms of reference,' says Rabbi Vogel with undisguised pride, 'and talk about people who have been touched, moved, and inspired to regenerate their own lives at a less dramatic pace, or even in private so that we're not even aware of it, then it's my guess that this runs into many tens of thousands in this country alone.' Conversion experiences, however, can have unfortunate social consequences. A young man or woman living with his assimilated parents may, on discerning the true path as illuminated by Lubavitch, find it impossible to remain at home. But Rabbi Vogel denies that this is a major problem 'if one puts the right amount of effort into it. We've seen how parents, who have initially been very tormented by this split in their family, have eventually come round to it, even though it's taken many years. And the only reason why they have come round to it is because of the enormous amount of time and effort made by our counsellors in relating to these parents.' Clearly this effort is directed at persuading the parents to meet Lubavitch halfway, if not further.

Lubavitch, he insists, should not be confused with other missionary movements within Judaism that are less sensitive to the problem of divided families. 'You may "save the child" and bring him back to Judaism but you create an awful amount of hostility on the other side. The Lubavitch effort has always been to forgo victories of this sort when we see that the down-side effect on a family would be so negative as to offset the value, in the global sense, of this one returnee to Judaism.' Every rabbi has a tale to tell of Lubavitch seduction. David Goldberg, a minister at the Liberal synagogue in St John's Wood, remembers 'a classic German-Liberal refugee family, twice-a-year Jews, whose son, a very dynamic computer expert, came home, announced he was joining Lubavitch and could no longer eat at home, though he lived at home. He couldn't have food on unkosher plates. He was a fellow in his thirties, obviously very lonely, never married, spent his life in his career. He found something that gave him an intellectual and emotional point of contact. My mediation involved using paper plates and his bringing in kosher food.'

Lubavitch has the advantage over most other religious movements within Anglo-Jewry of being generously funded. Make a single phone call to Lubavitch expressing interest in their mission, and you will be deluged with books and pamphlets and invitations. The British branch of Lubavitch alone has a budget of about £1.3 million. Some funds are raised by school fees and local authority grants tied to the provision of social services, but about 65 per cent is raised from private contributions. What is extraordinary is that a substantial proportion of those funds are donated by Jews who are not themselves Lubavitcher Chasidim. Cyril Stein, chairman of the Ladbroke Group, is a prominent supporter. This is the true significance of Lubavitch, that it has the support, if not always the whole-hearted support, of large sections of the Anglo-Jewish Establishment. 'Some of our supporters are Orthodox Jews,' according to Rabbi Vogel, 'some of them are non-practising, but nevertheless they all recognize that we provide a very vital ingredient in the community. The Jewish Establishment recognizes us as specialists in a crucial field. They know that the more successful we are, the more likely they are to be successful. We look to the Lubavitcher Rebbe as the repository of authentic Jewish tradition, but we are bound by the rulings of local Orthodox rabbis in this country, as long as they rule according to Jewish law. We have very good relationships with the Chief Rabbi and other Orthodox groups, and we often go to them for rabbinical guidance in the field of halachic rulings. The Rebbe himself doesn't give halachic guidance; he guides in matters of life and death and the wider areas of Jewish concern. Within the Jewish community in Britain we regard the Chief Rabbi and other Orthodox leaders as our allies.'

The willingness of the Lubavitchers, unlike their *confrères* in the Chasidic movement, to play a full part within mainstream Anglo-Jewry has given them enormous influence. Many rabbis, Hebrew teachers, and Jewish social workers, all trained by Lubavitch, are active within mainstream Orthodoxy. They have penetrated the Anglo-Jewish Establishment with all the energy of American entrepreneurialism. Where British Jews tend to be decorous, the Lubavitchers are raucous. Many United Synagogue pulpits are now filled by rabbis trained at Lubavitch *yeshivot*. Rabbi Shlomo Levin told me of his first encounter with a Lubavitcher Chasid in his native South Africa: 'My family was warmly Jewish but not observant. I grew up in a perfectly normal environment, dating girls, having fun, studying at university. One day I went to hear a Lubavitch rabbi who was visiting South Africa give a talk. That was the first time I encountered an Orthodox Jew who actually seemed to enjoy being Jewish. He just exuded a kind of vitality and a sense of enjoyment, which made me feel a bit uncomfortable, because he very subtly turned the tables on my conventional way of thinking. It wasn't easy to be observant in my community because there wasn't a format within which one could express it comfortably. We always had the feeling that if you were going to be *frum* [pious], you were bound to be a little bit boring, somewhat dowdy, musty, and old-fashioned. Then all of a sudden, this young man comes on the scene, full of vitality, full of excitement, and that was very attractive. For the first time I felt here was a person who seemed to be getting much more out of life being religious than I was getting out of life being irreligious.' Under the influence of the rabbi, Levin completed his university degree, then went to a Lubavitcher *yeshiva* in Israel and emerged as a rabbi.

The brashness of the Lubavitchers has, not surprisingly, earned them the disdain of many other Chasidic groups. Some resent the eagerness of Lubavitch to make and maintain contact with the wider world; the eagerness to drag back to Judaism those who have allowed their commitment, if they ever had any, to lapse is seen as somehow undignified. Other Chasidic groups are content to survive by the more private method of frenzied procreation (though *Lubavitch News* urges its readers not to be slack in this regard either: 'As survivors – and each one of us in our generation is a "survivor" – we have a moral duty to make good that devastating loss . . . One father of eight was recently challenged by a cynic, "When are you going to stop already?" His reply? "When I hit six million!" '[7]). The Lubavitch movement also recognizes the State of Israel, which sets them apart from Satmar and other Chasidic groups that are implacably opposed. Some ultra-Orthodox observers report that the animus comes from Lubavitchers themselves. According to Rebbetzin Schlesinger: 'The only ones who don't tolerate any other movement are Lubavitch. They do tolerate people who are not Orthodox, but they put being a Lubavitcher Chasid before being an Orthodox Jew. They are very fanatical, very convinced that theirs is the right way for Judaism. They don't mix at all, and live separately from the rest of us.'

Yet one should be in no doubt that, for all their sophistication and delight in electronic gadgetry and hi-tech jargon, the Lubavitchers are religious fundamentalists. They may have the sense and tact not to expect those they woo to become strictly observant Jews overnight, but their values do not differ from those of other ultra-Orthodox Jews. When I asked Rabbi Vogel whether the Lubavitcher Chasidim accepted the theory of evolution, he referred me to the writings of the Rebbe, who twenty-five years ago 'explained in very simple terms why he did not accept the evolutionary theory. He suggested that this was all hypothesis, because all science is based on hypothesis, and scientists extrapolate from known knowledge to the unknown. Consequently at best evolution is a theory. To be fair to the scientists, they don't say it's more than a theory. Science is not contradictory to faith, because it's axiomatic that nothing in this world can be a contradiction to God and his faith. The question is: have you got your faith right?' As a response to a simple question, that just won't wash. The Reform rabbi Rodney Mariner is highly suspicious of the movement. 'Lubavitch are very very clever. They have tremendous PR, but at the end of the day there's not a lot of difference between them and the ultra-Orthodox. They are just as ruthless but they do it with a smile. They're quite seductive, because they produce superb material and appear to be very open-minded. Lubavitch offers a very comfortable safe world, but a dangerous one.'

– 6 –

The burgeoning of ultra-Orthodoxy

A striking change within Anglo-Jewry over the past thirty years has been the growing provision of Jewish education, especially at the primary school level. At these schools, secular education is supplemented by classes in religious knowledge, Jewish history, modern and ancient Hebrew, and so forth. Such schools are, of course, unacceptable to the ultra-Orthodox, who maintain their own schools. Most Jewish primary schools are co-educational, and this in itself is anathema to the ultra-Orthodox, who maintain a strict separation of the sexes. To complicate the matter further, not all ultra-Orthodox schools are acceptable to all ultra-Orthodox Jews. Almost every Chasidic sect runs its own private school, and in addition there are larger schools such as Lubavitch and Yesodey Hatorah. It is estimated that over 5,000 children attend Chasidic schools in north London.

Yesodey Hatorah in Stamford Hill draws its pupils from all sections of the ultra-Orthodox community. When I arrived to visit the school, I spotted a suitably rabbinic figure, in a long black coat and sporting a splendid white beard, standing in the forecourt. I recognized him as Rabbi Shmuel Pinter, the founder of the school, which is now run by his son Avraham. When I asked him where his son was, he pointed to a car edging into a vacant space: 'He's parking my car.' Avraham emerged from the car and dashed into his basement office. I pursued him. It is not easy to talk to Avraham Pinter, who finds it hard to concentrate not only on what is being said to him but on what he is saying in reply. How this nervous man manages to sit through marathon sessions on Hackney Council and run a large school is something of a mystery. Untidy, disorganized, scraggily bearded, and occasionally incoherent, he appealed to me immediately.

When, in the middle of our talk, the leader of the Labour group on the council walked in to discuss their strategy at a forthcoming meeting, much of the diffidence vanished, and the rabbi actually managed to conclude the occasional sentence.

By asking the same question two or three times, I was gradually able to piece together the story of Yesodey Hatorah. The school was founded in 1942 with only six pupils. Ultra-Orthodoxy had been no more than a tiny remnant within Anglo-Jewry between the wars, but the arrival of pious Jewish refugees from various parts of Europe added to their numbers. Rabbi Shmuel Pinter arrived in 1939 and opened a series of establishments: a synagogue on Heathland Road in Stamford Hill, a *kollel* (an academy where married men could pursue advanced religious studies), and Yesodey Hatorah. The students are drawn from about twenty sects, ranging from extreme Chasidic groups to more recent immigrants from Hungary in 1956 and from Aden and Iraq in the 1970s. Most of the children live within a mile of the school, which occupies a series of buildings on Amhurst Park. In terms of its religious ideology, Yesodey Hatorah is, if you will excuse the absurd formulation, middle-of-the-road ultra-Orthodox, for there are many Chasidic establishments which regard both Yesodey Hatorah and the nearby Lubavitch school as dangerously assimilationist, if only because they make extensive use of the English language. Avraham Pinter estimates that out of the 12,000 or so ultra-Orthodox in this part of London (his estimate of numbers is lower than Mrs Simons', but nobody knows for sure), there are 3,600 children of school age, of whom 1,000 attend the Yesodey Hatorah complex, which includes a kindergarten, a primary school for boys and girls, and a grammar school for boys and girls.

The children are separated according to gender at the age of three. Nor is the education they receive identical. The boys receive a more extensive religious education, while the girls benefit from a wider secular education. Half the curriculum is devoted to religious studies, but there are also classes in computer studies and English literature and history. Since few of the children come from homes with a television set, classes in current affairs keep them in touch with the political and social events that take place outside N.16. Not all the teachers are Jewish, for there is a lack of trained Jewish teachers throughout the country. Rabbi Pinter is dissatisfied with the physical state of the school, its undoubted shabbiness and overcrowding and its lack of certain equipment and facilities. At present the school is community-funded, though Rabbi Pinter has been fighting vigorously for voluntary-aided status which would make it eligible for grants from the Inner London Educational Authority. The proposed abolition of ILEA will complicate the task further. Other ultra-Orthodox schools are in the same position, and complain bitterly that ILEA's intransigence is in fact discriminatory, and that they should be regarded in the same light as Roman Catholic and Church of England schools that do have this status. The two primary schools in Stamford Hill that do receive ILEA funding, Simon Marks and Avigdor, are shunned by many local parents as insufficiently Orthodox.

Children leave Yesodey Hatorah at the age of fifteen. The boys will pursue further religious studies at a *yeshiva*, and some of the girls will receive further education at seminaries. Some students will undergo secular training in fields such as law and accountancy, but it is almost unheard of for an ultra-Orthodox student to pursue studies at a British university, since, with the exception of the Lubavitchers, the community considers such institutions suspect because the sexes are mixed. With half the timetable devoted to religious or Hebrew studies, it is not surprising that schools such as Yesodey Hatorah, not to mention *yeshivot* where the proportion is even higher, are sometimes charged with failing to provide an adequate secular education. Rabbi Pinter insists that Jewish studies are very broadening.

The entire range of human knowledge (as comprehended in AD 500) is alluded to in the Gemara: astronomy, medicine, civil law, business practice, as well as exposition of religious law. The Talmud resembles a roomy old mansion, in which every parlour and attic is stuffed with chests and heirlooms, some priceless, others of mere curiosity value; within this mansion the pious Jew wanders at leisure through the course of a lifetime, admiring the view from this window or that, conversing with the other inhabitants, or borrowing from the library, always with the prospect that he might leave his own personal traces in the mansion – a footnote, a thought, a speculation, an example – after he had walked out of the door for the last time.

Over a thousand years of Talmudic study and disputation have resulted in further commentaries and codifications, of which the most important is the *Shulchan Aruch* (The Prepared Table), compiled by the Sephardi sage Joseph Caro and first printed in 1565. The Ashkenazi rabbi, Moses Isserles of Cracow, was not entirely happy with the opinions cited by Caro, and prepared an additional gloss called the *Mappah* (Tablecloth), which the Ashkenazi community placed on Caro's prepared table. The two texts, customarily printed side by side, are the most widely accepted authorities for the niceties of religious practice and observance. Alongside the formal codifications of the law is a network of Responsa, which consist of the replies of individual rabbis to questions submitted to them. Thus the study of rabbinic law encompasses such matters as commercial and matrimonial law, as well as the dos and don'ts of Jewish ritual and observance. Study of the Talmud develops the ability to argue for or against different points of view. Such training, in Rabbi Pinter's eyes, enables children to develop all kinds of problem-solving skills. Somehow a proportion of the children must manage to muddle through, for there are Chasidic and other ultra-Orthodox Jews employed in a variety of professions, some of which require high levels of skill and training.

Nobody in this community sends their children to State schools, which are tainted by mixed classes and overt secularism. This imposes an additional burden on many families, who must somehow come up with the school fees for as many as half a dozen children simultaneously. Some schools draw on charitable contributions to subsidize children whose parents simply can't afford the fees. Just as Chasidic groups have grown in north London, so too have their schools. Consequently, most of the younger generations have become even more extreme than their ultra-Orthodox parents and grandparents. I met a bewigged woman of about sixty who came from a background that was strictly Orthodox but not Chasidic. Her grandchildren all attend Chasidic *chedorim* and she has learnt Yiddish not from her parents but from her grandchildren.

Ita Simons' youngest son, who is nine, attends the *cheder* run by the Belz Chasidim, a community of about 130 families. This school acquired some notoriety a few years ago. School inspectors declared that the education it provided was unsatisfactory. Much of their dissatisfaction stemmed from the fact that many of the children lacked a good command of English, since Yiddish is the principal language of instruction and is also the language spoken in their homes. The *cheder* responded that the inspectors were in a poor position to judge the standard of education, since on their own admission they are unable to understand Yiddish or Hebrew. The challenge to the inspectors proved successful in the courts, though the *cheder* has since made provision for English-language lessons in mathematics, history and geography. Nevertheless most of the school day is devoted to Hebrew and religious studies, which mostly consist of chanting and learning by heart large chunks of the Torah and Mishnah. Talmudic studies begin at the tender age of eight. Because religious studies are so much more important for boys than for girls, and because the language of translation and discussion has traditionally been Yiddish rather than Polish or, now, English, many Chasidic boys grow up with Yiddish as their first language.

Mrs Simons' child is, by her own account, contemptuous of the minimal secular education he receives. 'All day the children study the Talmud and other Jewish texts and they learn these highly intellectual and spiritual subjects. Of course they find it very difficult to respect the secular textbooks because the content is so banal. He finds their approach insulting to his intelligence.' Although her son appears to thrive at the Belz *cheder*, she does have some doubts about this kind of education. 'I'm not sure what the repercussions of these schools is going to be. It's all very well for my young one, who's obviously cut out to be a rabbi and to have a comfortable position in Talmudic circles, but most children aren't like that. Those who aren't academic, what are they going to do? It's fine when their fathers are terribly well off and can provide for them – you don't need to be very educated to get into the property field – and not everybody has got a very good position in Hatton Gardens either. So we have yet to see how things are going to work out for the average and below-average child that is poorly prepared in his secular education.'

After they leave the *cheder*, usually at thirteen, these children will almost without exception join a *yeshiva*. 'From your point of view,' said Mrs Simons, aware of my lack of enthusiasm for this pattern of education, 'things get dramatically worse. At the *yeshiva* their secular education comes to an abrupt halt.' Moreover, since the children come from homes where television is banned and where in many cases newspapers are too, they become increasingly isolated, kept in ignorance of the world beyond the streets they inhabit. Even the *Jewish Chronicle* is insufficiently purist for the ultra-Orthodox, who have to rely instead on the narrow-minded *Jewish Tribune*. Girls are luckier: they may live in even greater isolation than their brothers, but they receive a broader secular education. This is less because of a passionate belief in the value of such education for girls, and more because of a reluctance to teach Torah to ultra-Orthodox Jewish women. When I suggested to Rebbetzin Schlesinger that this must be very frustrating for intelligent women in the community, she replied: 'It's not a question of intelligence. To study Torah you need firmness and concentration, great concentration. My husband can open the Talmud and be carried away for eleven hours without his realizing the time is passing. A woman has to be within call of her children, so she can't study.

It can be frustrating, yes. But once her children are grown up, some women start to learn again. There are books now in every language and it is not so difficult as it used to be.'

The new generation of boys, who will one day have to support families of their own, are emerging from *chedorim* and *yeshivot* with an inadequate secular education, and this worries Mrs Simons greatly. 'We are living in a very affluent society where there are lots of opportunities, but I don't know what would happen if things really tightened up. Today we can help one another and the youngsters get taken into businesses. But if a lot of the wealth were to disappear, what would happen to all these youngsters who are so poorly equipped to deal with making a living?' Rebbetzin Schlesinger was less concerned. In her view it mattered little that most *cheder* children receive no more than two hours' secular education each day. Simple experience of life would make up for it. The ultra-Orthodox rejection of worldliness extends to their homes. In the Schlesingers' house in Stamford Hill no great attention has been lavished on the décor. The only pictures on the wall were Israeli roofscapes and calligraphic diplomas. Wallpaper gently peeled. Wine beakers and goblets were ranked behind glass-doored cabinets. And while we spoke, her front door was left ajar, for it is contrary to Jewish law for an Orthodox wife to be alone in the same room with a man not related to her; the open door transformed her living room into an extension of the street, where no such prohibition applies.

She told me about some of her eight sons, who were educated at *chedorim* and *yeshivot* and are nevertheless well informed and literate. She admitted that the ultra-Orthodox community is woefully ignorant about many aspects of culture and science. Nor are Chasidim particularly well informed about other aspects of Jewish studies, such as history. Torah is the basis of all education. 'What people learn as young children impresses them more than what they learn when they're older. Whatever a boy learns when young will last. So the basis is Torah, Torah, Torah. They believe this is the foundation, and if you have a strong foundation, you can build and build and it stays. Some will pursue more studies after *yeshiva* – take A levels or a course in accountancy. You don't need much to go into business. Mr M.' – she mentioned a prominent property developer – 'is a multi-millionaire but can't write his name.'

To see what happens next to the best students, I had hoped to visit the *yeshiva* at Gateshead, which has been for some time the leading academy for rabbinical training. Unfortunately the directors of Gateshead were in a paranoid mood when I asked for permission to visit the *yeshiva*, and invented so many difficulties that I felt I had to call off my proposed visit. However, Rabbi Abraham David, himself a Gateshead graduate, offered to take me to his own *yeshiva*, Od Yosef Hai. He welcomed me into his Hendon house. He amplified his rabbinic splendour by wearing a dashing black and white dressing-gown, which he later discarded in favour of a more severe black frock-coat. While we talked, his teenage son brought me tea, and also, on a signal from his father, a *kippah*. Although I dislike covering my head as though I were devout, I have no wish to offend rabbis with my bare head. Consequently, I usually keep a *kippah* stuffed into a pocket for use on such occasions, and just as the rabbi's son was about to hand me one of his, I whipped out my own and placed it on my head. Religious decorum was satisfied and our conversation continued.

The *yeshiva* fulfils two purposes. Its primary role is as an academy for the young men, aged from nineteen to twenty-five, who study there full-time. It also functions as a study house, attended by pious members of Rabbi David's congregation at various times of the day, when they supplement their prayers with further study of the Torah. Many people come to the *yeshiva* at seven for morning prayers before going to work. After the service, the fifteen full-time students have their breakfast and then study all morning, instructed by Rabbi David and other teachers. (Although Rabbi David and most of his congregation are Sephardim, some of the other teachers are Ashkenazim. 'When it comes to the study of the Torah,' observes Rabbi David, 'there's no difference. Each respects the other.') After lunch and *minchah* (the afternoon service) the students have a break before resuming their studies from 4 until 6.30. Some of those who attended the morning service will return to the *yeshiva* on their way home from work. Rabbi David will join those present in the evening prayers and then conduct *shiurim* (study sessions) until 9.30 or 10 in the evening. The *yeshiva* occupies the upper storey of two adjoining suburban houses on Hendon Way. The principal room was furnished with a scattering of rickety chairs which looked as though they had been acquired twentieth-hand from a defunct primary school. Bookcases contained leaning rows of religious texts, some in gilt-stamped bindings. The usual long tables at which the students sat straddled a grubby carpet. Prayer desks and a small ark completed the furnishings. Another small room was empty when I was there, but on the Sabbath the womenfolk congregate there.

When I arrived with Rabbi David shortly after seven in the evening, there were about ten boys and men in the room. Some, including a midget, were swaying back and forth as they davened behind their desks. As soon as the rabbi walked in the door, those young men not immersed in their prayers crowded rounded their spiritual leader. The rabbi and I sat at a table with two young men: a handsome youth who had left Iran in 1980 and a swarthy bearded Israeli who had lived in Britain for two years. The Iranian asked the rabbi who was his favourite character in the commentaries. Was it not Rabbi Akiva? No, speculated the Israeli, it was King David, surely. It was neither. The rabbi then admonished his students on the grounds that the Torah was not a story book but contained lessons we had to learn. A few minutes later everybody rose to participate in the evening prayers. One of the students led the service from the main desk, though as in most Orthodox services, the reader does little more than place vocal markers so that every few minutes there is at least a fighting chance that the congregation will be at roughly the same place in the proceedings. After the service, the *shiurim* began and I left. As I was making my way down the steps that led to the street, a man following me observed me removing my *kippah*.

'You don't have to take it off,' he said. 'It's all right to keep it on.' He was using that coercive tone that comes naturally to religious zealots, of whatever persuasion. I ignored him. Nor was I any more responsive when he suggested that I should return another evening and attend a *shiur*. Perhaps he was one of the born-again Jews that were drawn to such *yeshivot*. The rabbi had told me with pride that many of his students had rediscovered their Judaism after a lapse of faith. 'We support the full-time students, the ones who live in. We want to give them an opportunity to catch up on what they missed earlier in their lives. The people in the community support them, though if parents can afford to pay for their children to study, they pay, as in any *yeshiva*. We have young men who are dedicated to becoming rabbis. Others want a few years of concentrated study. Then when they feel they can stand on their own two feet, they go back to whatever they were doing before.'

The traffic seems to be unbelievably one-way: young Jews are gently persuaded to take up or resume a strictly Orthodox way of life and abandon careers and families in order to do so. Yet where were the disenchanted Chasidim, lured away from the community by beautiful Gentile women or the taste of lobster? Or, as a non-Orthodox friend put it to me: 'What do they put in their teenagers' tea to keep them from breaking out?' Yet that phenomenon appears to be virtually unknown.

Rabbi Pinter said his family numbers about one hundred, and hardly any of them have opted out. And Rabbi David agreed: 'That happens very seldom. If you live in the same place and have a communal life, then these things don't happen. When there's change – you move to a different area, say – children may be affected. But the situation shouldn't arise.' Alan Greenbat, the executive director of the Association for Jewish Youth, speculates: 'It may be too early in the intense Chasidic life of the Anglo-Jewish community for those traits to evolve. If we look back to my generation's grandparents, they came from this intense life and were suddenly thrown into the open society, and the reaction was like giving a child a pot of jam. But today if you want to rebel, what do you step out of line into? The Chasidim have come to terms with being able to remain in the ghetto while earning their living in the big wide world.'

The spirit of adolescent rebellion is not entirely extinguished within the ultra-Orthodox community. The kids do rebel. Rabbi Pinter claims that some of his pupils complain that 'English literature isn't kosher enough.' Ita Simons confirms this: 'How do kids rebel? They become more *frum*. My nine-year-old is rebelling against the few English lessons he gets. But breaking away from the community? It just doesn't exist. When I grew up, I looked with envy at some of the other children, the convent girls and the ones who went on to university. Our children, they look at all these things with disgust. The youngsters from the ordinary schools, they yell and scream – in my day the ordinary kids behaved nicely and were interested in education and so on. I'm not saying all our children grow up to be upright and normal and noble. We get odd behaviour and personality problems. But there's no interest in dropping out of the community. I don't know a single one.'

The ultra-Orthodox tug me in two conflicting directions. Part of me says, 'This is the authentic voice of traditional Judaism, unshakeable in its integrity, faithful in its dissemination of Torah, the guardians not only of ancient law but of the long-term health of the Jewish religion.' And another part of me says, 'These people are nuts.'

My two responses echo those I hear from all sections of the community. Mainstream Orthodox rabbis worry that the piety of the Chasidim can degenerate into religion by rote, that an obsession with ritual and rule can blind the practitioners to spiritual values. Others discern parallels between Jewish fundamentalism on the one hand and Islamic fundamentalism and born-again evangelism on the other. Yet others value the curatorial function performed by the ultra-Orthodox – so long as they stay in their place. The Reform rabbi Barbara Borts put it this way: 'I'm not disturbed by the ultras. I think they're necessary. I think it's important to leave some Jews like that around. But I don't like them to have power over the destiny of Judaism.' The former president of the Board of Deputies, Greville Janner, is both blunt and conciliatory: 'I'm very happy to have actively involved Orthodox Jews, provided they leave me alone to get on with what I do. In many ways they are the repositories. If it weren't for them, we'd be in a very bad way. As long as they are prepared to offer the same tolerance to me as I have for them, I'm happy. I find that on the whole they are.'

Reform theologians, who of course have an axe to grind, have taken a sterner view. Ignaz Maybaum has written: 'The graduates of a *yeshiva* have a characteristic which . . . is rather unexpected. It is a lack of knowledge of the Bible. Their concentration on the legal treatises of the Talmud is one reason . . . What is in the mind of those who offer a Talmud-Shiur as religious food to Jews of today, or read a treatise on a legal code as an act of worship? It can only be primitivity or hypocrisy.'[1] Dow Marmur is more polite but equally wary: 'Much of Jewish life today systematically confuses religion with tradition and nostalgia with faith . . . It is taken for granted that the past is better than the present, because those who have lived before us were closer to the Revelation of Sinai on which Orthodoxy rests.' He goes on to compare ultra-Orthodoxy with a totalitarianism in which 'to show dissent is to be labelled ignorant and feeble-minded.'[2] The totalitarianism consists in Orthodoxy's obsessive legalism, its claim, as Reform Jews see it, to be the sole guardians, the principal repositories, and thus the most authentic guarantors, of Jewish values.

Mainstream Orthodoxy also tends to view the ultra-Orthodox as opponents in a power struggle for the soul of Judaism. Stanley Kalms, who when he is not running the retailing chain Dixons is chairman of Jews' College, pulled no punches: 'What we are fighting against is those rabbis who are moving towards fundamentalism. Right-wing Judaism is a complete, rather self-sealing culture, very comforting, very warm. It's easier for a young rabbi who needs a career in Judaism to become extreme. Those of us in the centre are fighting a much harder battle because we're arguing for greater flexibility, less certainty.' Rabbi Jonathan Sacks, in talks broadcast on the BBC in December 1988, cautioned listeners against confusing the extreme with the authentic, and argued against private piety and in favour of the mediation of Jews in the wider world.

For William Frankel, the thoughtful former editor of the *Jewish Chronicle*, it is the anti-intellectualism of the ultra-Orthodox that disturbs him most. 'Their view appeals to people whose approach to religion is emotion. Personally, I don't think that's a good basis for survival, because the emotion is less transmissible than something which is more thoughtful and intellectual, and this is in a sense an abandonment of the intellectual element. For all these groups, attending university is a heresy. They are attractive as persons but the doctrines they advocate are baneful. You don't open your mind to outside civilization. Our Jewish civilization has everything, they say; you don't have to go any further. It's a very damaging element for the future of Jewish life.' The emotion that Frankel finds suspect in ultra-Orthodoxy is one of the elements that another Jewish intellectual, George Steiner, finds slightly sympathetic: 'I have some respect for those who have returned to Orthodoxy. They express a deep fear of losing their identity, now that we live in a country where assimilation is easy and safety seems to be within sight. Orthodoxy expresses a joyous coherence, a re-entry into the womb. It offers the pleasures of competition, as there's always the possibility of being more Orthodox than your neighbours. On the other hand, Orthodoxy has sacrificed those other Jewish traits of irony, scepticism, and the willingness to borrow from other cultures.' I suspect I caught Professor Steiner in a moment of indulgence, for there is a small-mindedness and narrowness of vision common to large sections of the ultra-Orthodox community that Jews with access to the cultural traditions that have enriched not only Judaism but all of Western civilization must surely find depressing.

Let us consider the case of the *eruv*. The Torah forbids Jews to carry on the Sabbath in a public place. You may carry objects within the private domain, such as within your own home, but not in the public domain, such as the streets of a city. This has practical consequences, since a woman may not carry a child or wheel a pram on the Sabbath through the public domain, and thus she may be unable to attend synagogue. The public domain is now defined by rabbinic law as anything outside what is unequivocally perceived as the private domain, namely, your own house or flat. Thus an observant Jew may not carry anything outside his house. Later rabbis, feeling that this requirement of Halachah was excessively restrictive, hit on the idea of an *eruv*. This is a string or wire placed in symbolic fashion around a particular area, so long as no more than

600,000 people move through that area on any day. This has the effect of extending the private domain, while at the same time reminding those who enter it that a special rabbinic dispensation has been given to alter the status of the space. Thus if a district composed of streets inhabited almost exclusively by ultra-Orthodox Jews together with their synagogues were to be designated an *eruv*, then the inhabitants would be permitted to carry within it. Are you still with me?

There is a problem. Even though the *eruv* only defines a specific area, rabbis requested to rule on the eligibility of a space to be so designated are concerned that the beneficiaries may not realize where the *eruv* ends, and thus may carry beyond the limits of the *eruv* and so break the religious law. Some Orthodox rabbis in Golders Green and Hendon established the feasibility of an *eruv* in their area so as to enable women with children to attend synagogue, the short-sighted to carry their spectacles, and so forth. *Eruvs* have been permitted in American and Israeli cities with large Orthodox communities, and it seemed reasonable that an Orthodox suburb of London should have one too, since that appears to be the wish of its residents. The Chief Rabbi agreed. Of course the Chief Rabbi has no authority within the ultra-Orthodox community, and five rabbis who do exercise authority decreed after lengthy cogitation: No. No *eruv*. Not only was there a danger that Jews might carry beyond its boundaries, but if the string that defined those boundaries were to be inadvertently broken, then Jews would be violating religious law without realizing it. One rabbi who ruled on the matter, Simcha Rubin, the Sassover Rabbi, conceded: 'It is undeniable that it would make life more comfortable on the Sabbath, especially for mothers with small children, the elderly and the infirm.' However, he added, 'in the life of a believing Jew, religion takes priority over ease and comfort.' An *eruv* in a London suburb is apparently too complex a project to be undertaken with confidence, and the followers of those rabbis who ruled against the *eruv* must, if their leaders' arguments are to be taken seriously, be a feeble-minded bunch.

For myself, I don't care greatly either way, since the terms of the debate don't engage me. It strikes me as absurd that grown men and women, including some leading rabbis, can actually expend so much energy arguing about a piece of string and an imaginary boundary. It also seems extraordinary that a few ultra-Orthodox rabbis can block a measure openly favoured by the majority of devout Jews within mainstream Orthodoxy, the Chief Rabbi included. Rabbi Shlomo Levin gently rebuked me when I accused those conducting the argument of the legalism that so many Jews find baffling and trivializing about ultra-Orthodoxy. 'There are subtle workings here,' he told me. 'It may sound legalistic, but it's soundly legalistic as opposed to nitpicking. There are sound concepts which rely on learning and understanding. You're looking at a vast legal system.' Alan Greenbat of the Association for Jewish Youth agreed that the whole issue was legalistic but was untroubled by that. 'It's no more unreasonable if you are legalistically minded than to find loopholes in the Chancellor of the Exchequer's budget. A number of people will use great ingenuity to ensure that they can evade their tax – legally. Jews are technically legal-minded: they will look for that sort of let-out.'

This also explains the ingenuity exercised by nominally pious Jews to evade Sabbath prohibitions without contravening Jewish law. You may not activate an electrical switch on the Sabbath, but it's acceptable to install a time switch to ensure that the television set or the oven turns on or off as required. Prohibited from carrying keys on the Sabbath, other Orthodox Jews will wear a belt buckle (not an example of carrying, since a belt is an essential garment) to which the front door key is attached. And so forth. What is puzzling to the non-Orthodox is why there should be a qualitative difference between slipping a key into one's pocket and attaching it to a buckle. If the law can be justifiably evaded, with the approval of the highest rabbinic authorities, then how much weight should be given to the law in the first place?

Strict Orthodoxy is marvellously excluding as well as exclusive. Those who plunge into the thickets of the Talmud can find copious nourishment, a labyrinth of highways and byways, a culture based on observance and disputation, on conformity and challenge. If many Chasidim take comfort in their certainties, the dismissal of questions and doubts, and the legalistic subtleties, there are others who, without appearing to compromise their sincerity or depth of belief, have more open minds. And among some very Orthodox Jews there is a feeling that the Chasidic groups in particular have hijacked Orthodoxy and infused it with an intolerance and pettiness and narrow-mindedness that are not, or should not be, identified with Jewish tradition. Rabbi Louis Jacobs observes that it is often not the learned Orthodox rabbis but their lay followers who are the most coercive zealots. 'The result has been a constant looking over the right shoulder by all but the most intrepid Orthodox rabbis anxious not to be accused by extremist followers of indifference or worse.'[3]

I also discern a repugnant element of moral blackmail in some Ortho-dox discourse. There are Jews who claim that God inflicted the Holocaust on the Jewish people to punish them for their failure to keep His laws. Various letters to the *Jewish Chronicle* have stated the argument as follows: 'What distinguishes the last 150 years from the past is the organized ideological mass rebellion that originated in Continental Europe against the hitherto unchallenged rule of the Torah as the supreme force in the life of the Jewish people ... To say we have sinned is certainly no "affront" to the victims, who included some of our greatest and holiest. On the contrary, they are the kedoshim [holy ones] who have paid the price for all of us.' Or, more crudely, from another letter in the same issue: 'In Russia, the three million Jews had succumbed almost entirely to ... Communism. In Poland, Lithuania, Rumania, and Hungary, the masses were imbued by virulent Yiddishism, Bundism and atheistic Zionism, with an intense hatred towards Judaism, and declared that no belief in God and Torah was necessary to be a genuine Jew. The Orthodox had become a small minority.'[4] This repulsively coercive argument, quite apart from its inaccuracies and distortions, ignores the fact that the highly assimilated Jews of North America, against whom one might have expected God's wrath to have been most powerfully directed, survived the war intact, while the Chasidic communities of Europe, which followed and obeyed Jewish law with passionate fervour, were virtually eliminated. (To which our second correspondent replies: 'The extenuation for Anglo-American Jewry, in their exemption from such a visitation [by the Angel of Death], is that they did not rebel, but were swept along on a wave of ignorance.' Gosh, that was a lucky break. Presumably, if the Jews of Chicago hadn't been so dumb they too would have been shipped to Treblinka.) It seems astonishing that many ultra-Orthodox not only hold this view but clearly continue to worship a God who not only destroys a third of his people within the course of a few years, but does so in such a capricious manner. The danger of the ultra-Orthodox position is the ease with which dogma can fly in the face of reality and the most basic human values.

The United Synagogue

B Y far the largest synagogal group in Britain is the United Synagogue, a federation of nominally Orthodox synagogues, despite
the fact that only a modest proportion of its members is Orthodox
in the sense of being thoroughly observant in their religious practice. The
United Synagogue was founded in 1870 with the intention of 'maintaining, erecting, founding and carrying on in London and its neighbourhood,
places of worship for persons of the Jewish religion, who conform to the
Polish or German ritual'. Sephardi and Reform congregations have never
played any part in the United Synagogue. From its inception it was a
curiously formal body, laden with committees and procedures. Originally
established by the three major Ashkenazi synagogues of London, it
carefully preserved the independence of its constituent synagogues,
which led to a certain passivity. As the Jewish population of London began
to penetrate the suburbs, the United Synagogue, instead of initiating the
construction of new synagogues, preferred to wait until approached by
growing congregations that wished to join the organization. Nor were
such applications always accepted, for a new congregation had to be able
to afford its dues to the umbrella organization. For the first half century
after its foundation, the officers of the United Synagogue were invariably
patrician Jews from the Cousinhood. The Rothschilds were prominent in
the organization and various members of the family acted as presidents
over some seventy years, even though they were more conspicuous on the
letterhead than in the boardroom. The rabbinate, an underpaid profession, attracted few of the learned and charismatic figures so common
among the Chasidic rabbis of Europe.

The United Synagogue also concerned itself with the provision of burial grounds and of assistance to the needy; it supervised *shechita*, and provided *matzoh* to Jews languishing in prison. Such everyday concerns seemed trifling in comparison with the difficulties faced by the Anglo-Jewish Establishment in responding to the influx of Russian and Polish immigrants during the late nineteenth century. The formality of United Synagogue congregations was quite alien to Jews from the East, and ambitious United Synagogue schemes to provide large houses of worship in the East End never got off the ground. Samuel Montagu's Federation of Synagogues provided the middle way, cutting the immigrants loose from the *chevras* and *shtieblach* they had imported from Poland and Russia, while providing them with a modest synagogal structure and organization that would oversee such matters as burial. Many congregations that initially wished to join the United Synagogue were deterred by lengthy procedural delays and turned instead to the more welcoming Federation. In the United States, many immigrants drifted towards Progressive synagogues, notably Reform, whereas in Britain mainstream Orthodoxy, as represented by both the United Synagogue and the Federation, retained the allegiance of most of the new arrivals. Very few were drawn towards Reform, which in Victorian Britain was a thoroughly upper-middle-class congregation. Samuel Montagu, himself a respected member of the United Synagogue, did not intend that the Federation should become a separate synagogal organization. But a succession of quarrels with the United Synagogue has kept the two organizations estranged, with often ludicrous consequences, which we shall assess later.

In this century the United Synagogue has played a growing and important role in the provision of Jewish education, and it is also responsible for maintaining the Chief Rabbinate, an institution that predates the founding of the United Synagogue. The two Adlers, father and son, Nathan and Hermann, who held the office from 1845 to 1911, were pillars of Anglo-Jewry, but the appointment of Dr Joseph Hertz as successor to the distinctly episcopal Hermann Adler in 1913 brought a very different kind of rabbi to the post. Hertz took a much broader view of his role and gave the office the great status it still enjoys among the Jews of Britain and the Commonwealth. Until the election of Hertz the Federation had contributed to the Chief Rabbinate fund, but after 1913 it withdrew its funding and still refuses to recognize the authority of the Chief Rabbi. The relationship between the United Synagogue and the Chief Rabbi, while inevitably close, has not always been smooth, for while the former is occupied with community organization and management and the latter with religious matters, such boundaries are not always clear-cut.

The lay leaders of mainstream Orthodoxy tended to be less rigorous in their observance than the spiritual leaders. Most British Jews, while nominally Orthodox, were probably even less pious than they are today, and the same was true of the men who ran the United Synagogue. They may have paid lip service to Orthodoxy, but they were also men of the world who were unlikely to get too steamed up about, say, *chametz* between your teeth. The election of Sir Isaac Wolfson, the Glasgow-born son of immigrants, to the presidency of the United Synagogue in 1962, a post he held for eleven years, initiated a profound change in two respects. It reflected the relinquishing of overt influence by the Cousinhood, who had been generous with time and money but often patrician in attitude. Secondly, it heralded the gradual shift to more Orthodox positions. The days when rabbis of the United Synagogue were addressed as 'Reverend' and habitually wore dog-collars and bands were numbered.

While Jews continued to move to the London suburbs in the postwar years, the shrinking city congregations remained in buildings far too large for their purpose. The United Synagogue was dogged by financial difficulties exacerbated by the high cost of building and maintenance, and the slow but inexorable shrinkage of Anglo-Jewry as a whole has added to those problems, since the United Synagogue depends for much of its income on levies paid by individual members. Many believe that the constituent synagogues are losing members to the ultra-Orthodox congregations on the one hand, and to the Progressives on the other, though Jonathan Lew, the current executive director of the United Synagogue, denies that this is occurring to any significant, let alone alarming, degree. If Reform synagogues are attracting new members in suburbs on the fringes of London, such as Borehamwood, so too are United synagogues. It is clear to even the casual observer that the enthusiasm and commitment of those who do participate in the religious life of the community have never been more intense.

This shift towards Orthodoxy has not been welcomed by all. A retired United Synagogue rabbi who is widely esteemed is dismayed by the trend. When he first became a minister in the 1930s, his synagogue was thoroughly representative of middle-of-the-road Anglo-Jewry. He recalls how Chief Rabbi Hertz used to speak of 'progressive conservatism'. 'That was a lovely expression, and it covered a great deal. In those days people observed *kashrut*, they came to synagogues, because it was the mode of the

93

period. Christians went to church, so Jews went to synagogue. Christians dressed up for the occasion, and Jews wore top hats. After the war things changed, largely as a result of the Holocaust and of a peculiar ambivalence inside the Jewish community. People began to look for a new form of salvation.' University-educated rabbis such as himself began to be replaced by *yeshiva*-trained rabbis, who may have been more single-minded but were less worldly and less in tune with their communities. United Synagogue Jews make a greater show of their Jewishness than they used to. The silk *kippot* and *tallit* with which I grew up are now outmoded, and have been replaced by skimpy knitted *kippot* (an Israeli fashion) and heavy woollen *tallit* of a type formerly worn mostly by rabbis. *Kippot* are no longer stuffed into a pocket on leaving the synagogue after a service, but are proudly worn in the street.

If the retired rabbi is wary of this modish flaunting of greater Orthodoxy, interpreting it as a new brand of conformity rather than as a measure of observance, younger rabbis positively welcome it. Alan Plancey, who is chairman of the rabbinical council of the United Synagogue and leads a rapidly expanding congregation in Borehamwood, is proud of the commitment demonstrated by his flock. 'The young marrieds who are moving in to my area are far more committed than their parents ever were. There is a revival going on, and we have to nurture it, otherwise we'll lose it. In 1967 we had a revival after the Six Day War, when everything was running in our favour, but we lost it and we were back at square one again. We have to make sure that doesn't happen again. I've been in the ministry for twenty-three years and I've never seen a revival like this one. Even laws of family purity are coming back in, and I know many young wives who use the *mikveh* regularly. If we can keep this impetus, then we have a tremendous future. It's becoming the in thing, the trend, to come to *shul*, to keep the same laws as your friends, and have a home that will be suitable to invite your friends into.' In these new suburbs religious commitment goes hand in hand with social life, if only because the temptations and facilities of central London are less accessible.

The retired rabbi is wary of the growing cult of the *kippah*, but Jonathan Lew sees it as a positive sign: 'If you come to a council meeting of the United Synagogue today, you will see more people sitting in *kippot* than there has ever been in the past. We have a more Jewishly educated leadership.' But the rabbi sees it differently: 'When I think of past presidents of the United Synagogue – Robert Waley-Cohen, Ewen Montagu, Frank Samuel – they weren't particularly observant but they were desperately devoted to the United Synagogue. Nowadays it's expected that members of the council come to a meeting all wearing their *kippah*. This is a new development. This is a symbol, a badge of our tribe. You're discussing synagogue finances, and you need to wear a hat? There is this tendency to regard middle-of-the-road Orthodoxy with disdain. The Chief Rabbi once said: "Only horses walk in the middle of the road." That was something I took great exception to.' (The Chief Rabbi did indeed make the remark, but was quoting an earlier commentator.)

Despite this tendency towards stricter observance, services and their accompanying rituals remain unaltered. Strictly Orthodox synagogues treat one part of the service much like any other, but the United service is more structured. The high point is the removal of the scroll of the Law from the ark. Cradling a scroll under one arm, the *chazan* intones the *Shema*, the basic declaration of the Jewish faith, and the congregation responds. The rabbi, *chazan*, and those members of the congregation honoured with the *mitzvah* of opening the doors of the ark then process around the synagogue carrying the scrolls. The congregation face the scrolls as they are circulated, and those close enough press the fringes of their *tallit* against the velvet covering over the scrolls or against the silver breastplate laid over the velvet, and press the fringes to their lips. The scrolls are then taken up on to the *bima*, the elevated reading desk in the centre of the synagogue hall. There the breastplate and coverings are removed, the scrolls are placed on the desk and the readings from the Torah begin. Later, the scrolls are returned to the ark with similar pomp.

Visitors to United synagogues often remark on the lack of decorum. Even during supposedly solemn moments in the service, you will find men in a huddle swopping stock-market tips or boasts about their favourite football teams. Progressive synagogues are far more orderly, for they are modelled on church services, and that means good behaviour. In a Progressive synagogue, where services rarely last more than ninety minutes, you do not wander out during a dull bit, but in United synagogues there is a fair amount of traffic throughout the three-hour service. Only during certain parts of the service, such as the sermon and the recitation of the *Amidah* (a lengthy prayer recited *sotto voce* and standing), does the congregation stay put and stay silent. The wardens try to shush the congregation, especially when there is an unseemly burst of laughter or noisy disputation from frequent offenders at the back. The congregation is better behaved now than it used to be, but the atmosphere remains relaxed and pleasantly informal.

Reform congregants speak with pride of the exquisite manners of their congregations, their attentiveness and Germanic sense of decorum, while deriding the hubbub of an average Saturday morning at the United. The decorum of Reform is exactly what I dislike about it, and the seeming casualness of United is precisely what I enjoy. For many Reform Jews, the Sabbath service is weekly worship, God's due out of the week. For the mainstream Orthodox Jews of the United, God is omnipresent and will not object too strenuously if, for a few minutes on Saturday morning, Mr Berg and Mr Lucas nip out into the forecourt for a chat about mortgages. Not that members of the United Synagogue are all devout Jews. Far from it. The majority are nothing of the kind. Those, however, who go to synagogue regularly on the Sabbath are likely to be reasonably observant. A few may drive to synagogue, but most will walk; they probably observe the dietary laws and will almost certainly maintain the ceremonies of Friday night.

Moreover, as in all other synagogues, the barmitzvah, a rite of passage for boys at the age of thirteen, is a crucial ceremony. Curiously, given its social importance, the ceremony is not required by Jewish law and only came into existence in the Middle Ages. The religious maturity it celebrates may be assumed by Jewish males at thirteen even if they bypass the ceremony itself. These days its religious import is intermeshed with its social significance, and even boys from non-religious backgrounds often have their barmitzvah. Peer pressure has much to do with it, as does the prospect of a splendid and lavish party thrown by the parents and the cascade of gifts from all those invited to attend. Chaim Bermant, in waggish mood, has written: 'When a boy is barmitzvah, he becomes a man. What does his father become? A bankrupt ... The cost of hiring a synagogue hall these days would have paid for a synagogue when I was a boy.'[1] A company called David Michaels in Ilford even offers a barmitzvah plan to help parents spread the costs over ten years. On the occasion of his barmitzvah a boy will be called up for the first time to read from the Torah, and he will, like the rabbi, chant the portion directly from the Scroll of the Law.

As a boy I enjoyed the United service, but once my barmitzvah was behind me, I, like thousands before me, allowed my visits to synagogue to lapse. Of the richness of Jewish tradition and culture, religious and secular, I had been taught next to nothing, and my legacy from years of dutiful religious study was a familiarity with the service of the synagogue and a list of rules I could no longer be bothered to obey. Over the decades since my lapse, the religious temperature of the United Synagogue has risen several degrees, yet the organization is still worrying over the correct balance between the demands of Torah and the necessity, for those of us who are not rabbis, to live in the modern world. Stanley Kalms is the chairman of Dixons and thus one of the most successful retailers in Britain. Also chairman of Jews' College, he takes his responsibilities to the United Synagogue very seriously. In an interview published in the *Jewish Chronicle* in late 1987 he declared: 'We have to find out how we perpetuate Judaism, stop assimilation and yet take part in society.' A tall order! He recognizes that although the rabbinate has to endorse a fairly high level of religious observance, it must also acknowledge in turn that even an active synagogue member is not necessarily devout. 'The vast majority of those in the United Synagogue go for reassurance, comfort, friendship, a sense of identity . . . You don't influence people by telling them not to switch the light on or watch football on TV when they get home from the synagogue. If a rabbi's best message is, "You are doing wrong," he should ask himself whether he should be in the pulpit.' Predictably, a correspondent attacked him in the following terms: 'If Mr Kalms were marketing Torah and not cameras, he would surely call an immediate board meeting. With "sales" down throughout the year, how can the chairman sit idly by?'[2]

'I'm an Orthodox Jew,' Kalms told me unequivocally. 'I keep kosher, I keep Shabbos, I keep a whole range of the conventional and traditional customs. What I'm arguing is that you don't have to keep these consistently to be a practising member of the tribe. I haven't always been Orthodox. I've gone through phases. I don't find myself apologizing for them, but I need to explain that because you can't keep Shabbos to start with, doesn't mean you can't be a strong and active Jew. Keep what you can. Don't feel that by not keeping everything you should keep nothing.'

'Surely that's not a view one would hear a rabbi express?'

'The rabbi is there to teach Halachah and to represent the continuity of Orthodox Judaism. His environment is the synagogue and *cheder*. I live in a pluralistic world. I'll look to the rabbi for purity but not necessarily as my model. If you can find an Orthodox lifestyle that suits you and fits, good. My argument is that not everybody can find that lifestyle. Those who don't or can't commit themselves to that lifestyle should not feel excluded from the body of sensible, responsible, committed Judaism. The door should be wider open. Don't freeze them out and tell them their lifestyle is wrong. Don't ask them to do something they cannot do. If you work on a Saturday and you're a small-time retailer, you stay closed Shabbos and you're dead.'

'What would you say to rabbis who take a very different approach and urge their congregations to toe the line?'

'That's just a third-rate rabbi,' replied the chairman of Jews' College, with the candour of someone who doesn't need the job. 'I would argue that rabbis like that should be thrown out and there's no place for them in the United Synagogue. What you need in the United Synagogue are modern rabbis who understand modern society.' Most of them, of course, do acknowledge, in private if not in public, that few of their congregants can practise the same pure Judaism that they do. The danger of Kalms's view, for all its flexibility and pragmatism, is that it turns the rabbinate into surrogate Orthodox. A United Synagogue member can go to a football match on Saturday afternoon without fearing that he is 'diluting' Judaism, because he knows his rabbi is carrying the torch of traditional Judaism on his behalf. Why be devout when you have an Orthodox rabbi to do it for you?

Rabbis are also well aware that if they harangue their congregation in an effort to spur them on to greater observance, they could deter their members from coming to synagogue at all. What, I asked the retired rabbi, did he do to dissuade his members from driving to synagogue on the Sabbath? 'I looked the other way. What else can one do? I'm not going to say categorically that it's better to ride to *shul* than not come to *shul* at all. But if I were to say to people, "If you can't walk to *shul*, don't come," then it's good-bye to their membership. In parts of London where people live close to the synagogue, there's no question of not walking. It's a question of locality. I don't think one can lay down any hard and fast rules about this. But today there is this tendency among younger rabbis to be much stricter in their approach. My generation, we knew how to look the other way and make compromises.'

There seems to be an element of hypocrisy in this need for rabbis to preach a code when they know perfectly well that most of the congregation isn't going to pay the slightest attention. Is there not a case for acknowledging the constraints of modern urban life and – gasp – changing the rules? Shimon Cohen, the executive officer of the Chief Rabbi's Office, thinks not. 'Many people think the driver who parks around the corner and walks the last block is a hypocrite. But the one who does that knows he's doing wrong, and therefore there's a chance that one day he might do right. The driver who parks smack bang outside the synagogue knows he's doing wrong and couldn't really care about it. He's a lost cause. The Reform people have come along to change the rules and allow that sort of thing. But once you change the rules for that, you change the rules for everything else. There's a very great difference between being open to interpretation and open to change. Halachah is divinely inspired and cannot be changed, but it has been interpreted in many different ways. But we draw the line when it comes to changing it. Our philosophy is the synthesis between an Orthodox Jewish life and the modern world. It becomes a totality of life. I do observe *kashrut*, but I don't consider it in that way. It's part of my life. I don't have tears in my eyes when someone near me is eating a prawn cocktail. It never registers on my mind that this is something I could be involved in.'

A sophisticated Orthodox observer such as Rabbi Michael Rosen is not dismayed by the United Synagogue because it appears to support a religion of compromise, a religion that declares: Our rules are strict and immutable, but don't worry if you can't see your way to obeying them. His complaint is more to do with mediocrity and mundanity: 'You go to your local synagogue and the minister is going to preach and you know that if you just keep your head down, eventually he's going to stop. One goes out the way one went in. Your average United Synagogue – and it's not just the United Synagogue, only it's easier to make fun of the United Synagogue – is like a pub without beer. It provides an occasion for men to meet. If one actually started talking there in terms of inner spiritual life, somebody would probably turn round and ask you if you're feeling all right.'

There is an element of truth in this. In many of the more stolid United synagogues the service has become a routine, and attendance less an expression of religious belief than an opportunity to catch up on the week's gossip. For others going to synagogue is simply the done thing, and has nothing to do with spiritual needs. William Frankel suspects that if you asked most United Synagogue members, including rabbis, whether they believed that God dictated the Pentateuch to Moses on Mount Sinai on a particular day, 'no intelligent person could honestly say they believed that. But that's the party line. These people haven't abdicated their intellect. It's a kind of schizophrenia. They belong to synagogues, but to say the majority of them are Orthodox would be patently absurd. For the majority, they remain members because, as an old friend put it, it doesn't matter to them which synagogue they don't go to. They might as well belong to the synagogues their fathers went to. There's a certain filial piety attached to it.'

The lack of decorum in United synagogues that I rather relish can indeed easily deteriorate into chumminess. The reason for going to synagogue becomes going to synagogue. This doesn't bother the rabbi of Borehamwood, Alan Plancey: 'I love to see a full *shul*, even if they come just to have a chat. They haven't written themselves off. Even if they're cynical and there's no depth – perhaps they've come to criticize the sermon or the *chazan* – the fact is they've come to *shul*. It's up to their rabbi or their friends to convince them that there is something to be gained from religion.' But are United Synagogue rabbis that interested in spiritual leadership? They are not, like Chasidic rabbis, the leaders of small, like-minded congregations. The rabbi of a large London congregation must be, as Alan Plancey points out, a marriage counsellor, a student counsellor, an administrator, and a welfare and education officer. He must preside at barmitzvahs and weddings and funerals. And on top of all that you want a sage and a saint? Good rabbis, or potential rabbis, are thin on the ground. The United Synagogue estimates that thirty-eight major appointments will need to be filled in the course of the next decade. Shimon Cohen believes those posts will be filled without too much difficulty, but admits that most of those appointed may be trained abroad. Jews' College simply isn't producing a sufficient number of rabbis to meet the demand. The debt-ridden college has only managed to produce a tiny number over the past decade.

Of course there are other routes to the rabbinate. It is perfectly possible for a would-be rabbi to head off to a *yeshiva* in Israel, study for a few years and obtain a rabbinical diploma, and then scour Britain for a vacant position. But as Cohen readily admits, 'There's a very great difference between a rabbi who holds a rabbinic diploma and a rabbi who becomes the rabbi of a congregation.' Jews' College has in recent years taken a leaf from the Progressives' book, and requires trainee rabbis to take a course in 'practical rabbinics', those aspects of rabbinical life that have to do with pastoral matters such as bereavement counselling that occupy the greatest part of a rabbi's time. Even rabbis who graduated before the programme was instituted are expected to return and take the course. Shimon Cohen suggests that the Progressives' superior practical training is not unrelated to the fact that a Reform rabbi has a much lighter liturgical workload than the average United Synagogue rabbi: 'They don't have to deal with *kashrut* supervision or *shiva* work; they don't have to go to *shul* every morning at seven.' When a vacancy occurs, the United Synagogue placements committee will do its best to offer a candidate in tune with the needs of that particular congregation. The synagogue members will then vote, and if the vote is positive, the new rabbi is appointed and offered a contract. Sometimes the congregation asks to see another candidate; in other cases the rabbi doesn't find the congregation to his liking. For example, if the rabbi has small children, he will not be anxious to join a provincial community where there is no Jewish school. The system is not unlike a dating agency, and seems to work reasonably well. Rifts do occur between rabbis and the lay leadership of the congregation, but they are infrequent. Salaries used to be low, but nowadays the salary structure and conditions of employment and benefits are more in line with modern expectations.

Jews' College is at last getting itself organized. Even though enrolment has increased, there are still only seven rabbinical students at the college. Scholarships are being offered to attract students not only to rabbinical training but to some of its educational courses. A typical rabbinical student might leave school at eighteen, spend a year or two at a *yeshiva*, take an academic degree at Jews' College, and then spend a further three years at the college completing the rabbinical programme. Israel, with its huge *yeshivot*, continues to attract many would-be rabbis. Simon Caplan, the director of Jews' College, observes: 'An institution with forty or fifty students, however good the teachers are, can't compete with an environment of several hundred people studying together, nor with the kinds of dynamism developed by a whole society in Jerusalem committed to this process. So many of the brightest people want to do their rabbinical training in Israel. We provide scholarships for a small number that allows them to do that but commits them to coming back to this country.' In the meantime Lubavitch, with its belief in 'outreach', has placed its own Chasidic-trained rabbis among United Synagogue congregations. Because their outlook differs considerably from that of their easy-going flock, some of these appointments have been disastrous, but others have been very successful. Lubavitch are, as it were, the evangelists of Orthodox Judaism.

I paid Saturday morning visits to two United Synagogue services, one in the thriving suburb of Stanmore, the other in South Hampstead, a congregation that has recently been galvanized by a Lubavitch-trained rabbi. Stanmore was packed for the annual youth service, though the gentleman sitting next to me with the military moustache and the grey bowler hat assured me that the turnout was almost as impressive on an ordinary Shabbos. The congregation looked sleek with prosperity, the men in smart suits and the womenfolk in the ladies' gallery squeezed into well-tailored two-piece outfits. From my seat it was hard to get a good view of the ladies' gallery, but I could glimpse a froth of millinery. On this occasion the entire service, including the readings from the Torah, was conducted by boys. This would have been inconceivable thirty years ago, but today such proficiency is routine. One portion was sung by a small lad with cerebral palsy, which must have taken great courage and determination, for the boy clearly had to struggle mightily to produce the sound. He took his time, and did it beautifully. Another portion was read by one of the four sons of the robust gentleman seated next to me. I mentioned to him that I was amazed by the liturgical command of the boys clustered around the scrolls.

'It's the Jewish day schools that have done it. My boy goes to Hasmonean. Some of the other boys go to schools such as Haberdashers', but they still know their stuff. Let me tell you, I come from an Orthodox background and I went to *yeshiva*, but my youngest boy is far more *frum* than me.'

Since Stanmore is typical in its neglect of decorum, I was able to enjoy a pleasant chat with my neighbour, and I remarked on the air of prosperity among the congregation.

'Let me tell you something. There are more millionaires in this hall than in all the other congregations around us.'

Since the children were running the show, the rabbi took a back seat and didn't open his mouth. Dr Jeffrey Cohen had only been at Stanmore for a year, and my neighbour was not sure what to make of him. 'He uses Shakespearean terms and long words. Listening to him is sometimes like being at a lecture. But who am I to say? I wish I had his learning.' At the end of a Jewish service it is customary to shake hands with one's neighbours and greet them with the words 'Good Shabbos' or 'Shabbat Shalom'. As the service ended, the elderly gentleman rose, whipped off his *tallit*, and grasped my hand: 'You're welcome here any time. Shabbat Shalom, and God bless.'

South Hampstead synagogue is very different. Although located in the inner London suburb of Chalk Farm and an easy walk from both Camden Town and Belsize Park, which must have reasonably high Jewish populations, the congregation had been moribund until 1985 when a Lubavitcher rabbi, Shlomo Levin, had been invited to take over the synagogue. Although Levin had obtained his rabbinical diploma after studies at *yeshivot* in Israel and elsewhere, he had not practised as a rabbi for many years. 'I think the United Synagogue allowed me to take the job because the *shul* at South Hampstead was so dead that they thought even a Lubavitcher couldn't revive it. But it has taken off.' When I asked him how the congregation reacted on seeing their new rabbi with his striking beard and long black coat, he replied: 'There wasn't that much of a congregation to react. On my first Shabbos, they pulled out all the stops and pulled in all the people who hadn't been to *shul* for years. I stood up and said: "Look here, folks, I'm telling you now that in a few years' time, please God, people will not be able to get into this place." I came out fighting, telling them we were going to make things happen. And nobody can say this place is dead now. We have nearly three hundred families, one of the fastest-growing memberships of any inner London *shul*.' Rabbi Levin is unusual in that he has not relinquished his business career, and combines the demands of the rabbinate with a heavy workload in the City. 'There are many bright people in this congregation. They demand the real thing. They want substance, and in order to provide substance you have to work very hard indeed. Whatever you do, it has to be good. In order to come up with the goods time and time again, you've got to be growing yourself. You've got to study, you've got to be involved, and whereas other colleagues might have the whole day to do what rabbis are supposed to do, I have much less time.'

The South Hampstead synagogue resembles a lecture hall at a 1960s university, but its gently raked seating on either side of the hall gives everyone a view not only of the ark and the *bima*, but of each other. It's a medium-sized synagogue, less cathedral-like than most synagogues in inner London suburbs. The morning I looked in there was a larger than usual congregation, perhaps two hundred, celebrating a barmitzvah. Rabbi Levin did not participate in the service until after the scrolls had been removed from the ark. He then mounted the *bima* and did something I'd never heard a rabbi do before. Levin gave a brief summary of each portion of the Torah to the congregation before it was chanted in Hebrew. Telling the congregation what it was all about! Such an extraordinary thing to do!

Rabbi Levin was clearly going to have a field day, because the readings dealt with the Exodus from Egypt, that marvellous account of early Jewish triumphalism. 'This portion', began the rabbi, 'is full of blood and thunder, for it begins the account of the ten plagues.' Or later: 'At the end of this chapter Pharaoh has hardened his heart against the people of Israel and will not listen unto them.' He paused, raised a finger in the air, grinned, and went on in a stage whisper: 'But *we* will listen.' And we did. The barmitzvah boy was not content with chanting a single portion from the Torah, but helped himself to a couple more for good measure. Then the boy's father was called up to intone the blessings over the next portion, and after that was over I saw, to my surprise, the boy climbing the steps of the *bima* once again. 'Now,' declared Rabbi Levin, 'by popular demand the barmitzvah boy returns to read a further portion.' As the boy completed that final portion, the rabbi launched into a jaunty song with the congratulatory refrain of '*Mazeltov, mazeltov*'. Many of the congregation joined in, singing and clapping their hands to the rhythm. It was vulgar, perhaps, but it was also very warm, and the boy certainly deserved all that praise. In my youth, barmitzvah boys had quaked with nervous terror for fear of making mistakes or bungling the coloratura and thus bringing dishonour on the family name. That, fortunately, seems to be a thing of the past, for most of the barmitzvahs I've inadvertently attended while touring the synagogues of Greater London have shown the boys to be in complete command of the situation.

Later in the service, the rabbi wandered slowly round the synagogue, talking briefly to almost every member of the congregation. That too would have been inconceivable at most other synagogues, where the rabbis are still remote figures of authority, proclaiming from on high. On another visit to South Hampstead, while members of the congregation were taking the service, both chanting the prayers and reading from the Torah, Rabbi Levin was leaning against the reading desk keeping a benevolent eye on the proceedings, and perched against his shoulder and resting on his arm was his small daughter. Other small children, mostly well behaved, scampered about or sat on the steps of the *bima*. Such informality would have been unthinkable a decade or two ago, but here it seemed perfectly natural.

If the United Synagogue can continue to attract rabbis as idiosyncratic yet charismatic as Shlomo Levin, the future cannot be too bleak. Dr Isaac Levy, a United Synagogue rabbi from a very different mould, expresses his admiration of Levin by referring to him as the Pied Piper of the rabbinate. He also warns, however, that 'to show our Orthodoxy by a reversion to earlier forms is quite contrary to the whole ethos of the United Synagogue'. Indeed, it must be recalled that for all his charm and rapport with his congregation, Levin's sympathies lie with ultra-Orthodoxy. As Simon Caplan put it: 'He's highly successful with his congregation, very creative and dynamic, yet when push comes to shove, philosophically he is not at one with his congregation.'

There is no single perfect model for the rabbi, just as there is none for any other cleric. For Stanley Kalms, a model rabbi is someone like Jonathan Sacks, the present head of Jews' College, Orthodox in outlook yet Cambridge-educated and widely read, with none of the blinkered ignorance found among many of the ultra-Orthodox. Kalms also stresses that modern rabbis must be not only well educated but interested in education itself. Alan Plancey, a *yeshiva*-trained rabbi, agrees that rabbis should not be monastic figures: 'The rabbi needs to be a worldly person, someone not only able to give a *shiur* but able to talk about cricket or football or whatever, and keep up with the news.' Dr Isaac Levy wishes that rabbis were trained to be worldly in another sense too: 'Many young Orthodox rabbis don't touch inter-faith work at all. They can't discuss religious philosophy or theology with a Christian clergyman of equal status, because they haven't got the equipment. There's a gap there which is not being filled. From what I've seen of the younger rabbinate in the United Synagogue, I don't think we speak the same language, and I think it's a great pity.'

Once rabbis are appointed, they enjoy considerable independence. There is no institution in Judaism comparable to the papacy. When the Chief Rabbi offers his views on theological or social issues in the light of Jewish law, his fellow United Synagogue rabbis are not obliged to parrot those views. 'There is no party line,' declares Rabbi Plancey. 'On the issue of Israel, for instance, there is great diversity. But we're entitled to our opinions. The Chief Rabbi does not speak on behalf of the Anglo-Jewish community. He speaks for himself. I happen to agree with ninety or ninety-five per cent of what he does, but I'm not a puppet. We're not stifled in any way. We're free to use our initiative in the community, and on political issues we're also entitled to our views. We're individuals, although we would never dictate politics in the community.'

It is difficult to predict the future for the United Synagogue. Its membership is shrinking, but no more than the rest of Anglo-Jewry – and, if Jonathan Lew has got his figures right, rather less. The effects of the re-vitalization of Jews' College will not be apparent for some years to come. In the late 1980s there are eight to ten vacancies among the rabbinate at any time; by the early 1990s, it is hoped to reduce that number to two or three. This may be partly the result not only of a greater intake of rabbinical students, but of demographic changes: many provincial communities are on their last legs; whatever the growth rate in the London suburbs, there are many imminent closures in the north and west of the country. The United Synagogue is more than an umbrella organization for a group of mainstream Orthodox synagogues. It is also responsible for such matters as prison and hospital visits, welfare and educational work, and the funding of the Chief Rabbinate and the Beth Din. The president of the United Synagogue, Sidney Frosh, believes the major efforts of the organization should be chanelled into education at all levels and the development of synagogues into community centres, thus strengthening the links between religious and secular life. For years to come, it is inevitable that, as the largest synagogal group in Britain, the United Synagogue will continue to play a pivotal role in Jewish communal life.

– 8 –

The Beth Din

JEWISH law may be immutable, but it does require to be interpreted. With 613 *mitzvot*, not to mention the accretions of rabbinical law over 3,000 years, Judaism is a thoroughly legalistic religion. What is permitted and what is forbidden? And even more importantly, who is a Jew? The Liberal Synagogue will accept, as Jewish, persons that both Reform and Orthodox Jews could not. Conversions that are valid within one group may be unacceptable to another. To interpret the law, each synagogal group (except for the Liberals, who don't see the need for such a body) has established a Beth Din or rabbinical court. A Beth Din only has jurisdiction within its own area, so, for example, the Beth Din of Greater Manchester has no sway over Jews outside that area. The leading Beth Din, that of London, is the court of the Chief Rabbi, and is funded by the United Synagogue. In recent years it has become a pillar of Orthodoxy and probably the most prestigious Beth Din outside Israel; consequently it is on the receiving end of a deluge of bouquets and brickbats. The court itself consists of three judges or *dayanim*, senior rabbis of great erudition who are appointed by the honorary officers of the United Synagogue in consultation with the Chief Rabbi. Its work is regulated by the registrar, Rabbi Berel Berkovits, the descendant of a long line of rabbis. He studied at Gateshead *yeshiva* and subsequently in Israel. He also has a law degree from the London School of Economics and lectured in law for seven years before coming to the Beth Din as its registrar.

Berkovits is a nimble-minded man, quick in manner, thoroughly committed to his work. I asked him, as we sat in his office at Woburn House, the shabby Bloomsbury headquarters of the United Synagogue, how he spent his day. He whipped out a notebook, in which, for the hell of it, he had one day jotted down how the hours had passed. In the course of three hours one morning, he had read twenty letters and dictated replies, signed the post from the previous day, had a discussion with various authorities about *shechita*, written to a leading opponent of *shechita*, taken a phone call from a radio station, spoken to the police about an unidentified corpse they believed might be Jewish, taken another call from a school principal regarding the Jewish status of a candidate for admission, written part of a guide for nurses and doctors on dealing with Jewish patients, used the library, and, over lunch, read a paper about *shechita*. At least half of his time is spent on work relating to Jewish divorce or problems of Jewish status, which includes dealing with conversion and adoption. He also tries to arbitrate between Jews quarrelling over defaulted loans or other financial matters.

I was anxious to discuss the whole matter of flexibility within Jewish law. It seemed reasonable to question the claims of the ultra-Orthodox to be the standard-bearers of Jewish values, since nobody obeyed all the *mitzvot*. You don't see anybody in Stamford Hill being stoned to death for having committed adultery. I knew the articulate Rabbi Berkovits would have an answer, if not the answer, so I put the question to him. It is not true, he told me, that the penalties under Jewish law have changed with the passing of time. 'They're just not enforced. There are various penalties which were designed to be deterrents, but which in practice were almost never enforced. For example, the death penalty for murder or adultery. You have to have two eligible witnesses who saw the act, whose testimony corresponds in every detail, and who warned the person immediately before that what he was about to do was a capital offence and that they would testify against him and that he would be put to death. The idea is to rule out crimes of passion. So in practice it was almost impossible to actually execute somebody. And adultery doesn't often happen in public.'

'So why bother to have all these draconian penalties that are never enforced?'

'They express moral disapproval. And as an ultimate deterrent a person should know that there are circumstances where the death penalty will be applied.'

Of course a diaspora Beth Din has no authority when it comes to such matters as murder. Its sole jurisdiction lies in problems of religious law; all other matters are covered by the laws of the host nation, which Judaism insists its adherents must obey. Even in matters of religious law, however, there seems little room for flexibility, given the immense body of law subscribed to by traditional Jews.

'No, that's not true,' replied Berkovits. 'Inflexibility is the main charge brought against us by the non-Orthodox community. It's true that any biblical law, as such, is binding. The Torah says that certain foods are not permissible. There is no way that any rabbinic authority could ever say that pig's meat is permitted. You might one day breed a new creature which isn't a pig. That would be an issue that would lead to Responsa. Genetic engineering, for instance, allows you to put in chromosomes of other creatures, and you could end up with a new creature which is an improved sort of pig. Is that a pig or is that not a pig? That's the sort of issue we'd take to a leading rabbi and he might well decide this is not a pig. That's the area of flexibility. There was an issue recently in Israel, about a kind of carp. Carp is a kosher fish. But they managed to breed a carp which doesn't have scales. Is it a carp or is it not a carp?'

'That's nitpicking stuff!'

'It's true that much of Jewish law appears to deal with unimportant issues, but that's true of every legal system. In English law burglary is defined as entering a building with intent to steal. But what is a building? Is a caravan a building or not? A non-lawyer would say that this is petty. But it does matter, because you have to understand what a rule includes and what it excludes.'

Fortunately the Beth Din does not have to spend much, or any, of its time assessing the status of new breeds of fish. It is the question of divorce that both takes up most time and generates the greatest heat in the community. In theory, a Jewish divorce is beautifully simple. The parties are not required to give the grounds for divorce; mutual consent is all that's required. Only in one or two cases, such as the husband finding his wife committing adultery, is he required under Jewish law to divorce her. In almost all other cases, mutual consent is sufficient. It is with the ceremony itself that difficulties are likely to arise: in the presence of the judges of the Beth Din, the husband writes out a *get* or bill of divorce (or rather a scribe prepares the document, since it has to be written in Aramaic). If the wife accepts the *get*, that's the end of the matter, and both parties are thenceforward divorced and free to remarry under Jewish law. Should she refuse to accept it, the problems begin. There are more intractable problems if the husband refuses to grant the divorce, since he cannot be forced to do so. Should he persist in his refusal, his wife may not remarry under Jewish law. The giving and accepting of the *get* is not a judgment of the rabbinical court; it is a voluntary transaction between husband and wife which the court will witness and validate.

'The common misconception', according to Berkovits, 'is that it's only the wife who suffers, because the husband has the power to give the *get* unilaterally. But this is just not so. It is true that the document is written on his instructions and handed by him to her. But she can apply to us for a *get*, just as he can. If they both agree, fine. If the husband refuses to give his wife a *get*, then until they've sorted out their differences we can't do anything about it, and she is stuck. But equally, if she refuses him a *get*, we also can't do anything about it and he is stuck. It works both ways.

'I'm constantly telling people: Don't refuse a *get*. Yesterday I spoke to a wife who didn't want to agree to a *get*. I told her that was her prerogative and if she wouldn't agree, then her husband wouldn't be able to remarry. But if in two years' time she was the one who wanted to remarry, she would have to come to us and we would go back to her husband. And if he said: "You didn't help me two years ago, and I'm not going to help you now. Go to hell," – there's nothing we can do about it. It's entirely reciprocal. People think the main problem is with husbands refusing their wives a *get*. In fact, for every such case, I have two cases of wives refusing their husband. And I can't say that in all cases when somebody is refusing their consent, that they are being unreasonable. Very often the wives feel hard done by. Perhaps the husband has run off with his secretary and not provided for his wife and children. She's not going to accept the *get* until that's sorted out. So a lot of my work consists of negotiating between the two parties and trying to get them to come to agreement. It's only in very rare and exceptional cases that the consent of the wife can be dispensed with. That's where to some extent the husband has a slight advantage.'

Even the Beth Din wishes to see a reform of English divorce law so as to assist in obtaining a *get* without difficulty. This has to take the form of an amendment to an Act of Parliament, since it involves the British legal system. The aim of such reform is that no decree absolute should be granted in the civil courts until the marriage has also been terminated under Jewish law. This will encourage a husband and wife who intend to divorce under British law to do so under Jewish law as well, so that neither is prohibited from remarrying in a Jewish ceremony. This reform is intended to deter either party from unreasonably refusing to grant or accept a *get*. In Israel it's much simpler, for there Jewish and civil law overlap. Under Israeli law, a refusal to give a *get* can be regarded as contempt of court and you can be hustled off to prison until you change your mind. Clearly, this simple procedure is a non-starter in the diaspora. The reform proposed by the Beth Din has the support of all sections of the Anglo-Jewish community and all those involved are confident that, in time, it will become law.

A more picturesque aspect of Jewish legal practice is provided by the ancient ceremony of *chalitsa*. Under Jewish law, if a wife is left a childless widow and her deceased husband has an unmarried brother, she is required to marry him. Fortunately for both parties, the brother-in-law can absolve her from this requirement by means of the ceremony of *chalitsa*. Rabbi Berkovits explains. 'The idea is that the brother-in-law has set obligations towards his sister-in-law. He is supposed to marry her and look after her. If he fails to do that, then we have to remind him of his failure. He wears a shoe on his foot, similar to a Roman slipper. She takes off this shoe and throws it away. Then she asks him whether he is prepared to marry her. He says no, and then she spits in his presence – not at him. People think it's he who spits at her, but it's the other way round. It's a symbolic way of saying that you haven't fulfilled your obligations. And that's it. Of all our procedures at the Beth Din, it's the one that arouses the most hostility from the outside world. It's not as unpleasant as people imagine. In any case, it's extremely rare. In the four years I've been here we've had only two cases.' Unless the brother-in-law agrees to this ceremony, the poor woman may not, under Jewish law, remarry. This gives him leverage over her, which can be used unscrupulously, though Rabbi Berkovits recalls no instance when this abuse actually occurred. And if the brother-in-law is a minor, he may not participate in the ceremony, and she may not remarry, until he has attained his majority.

Far more important is the matter of conversion. Jewish parents who adopt children often wish those infants, whatever their true parentage, to be formally converted to Judaism. Because the conversion is usually imposed on the child at a very young age, he or she is given the opportunity to opt out at the age of barmitzvah or batmitzvah, as the case may be. The procedure may seem a meaningless formality, but Berkovits claims that 'it solves a lot of problems. If people adopt a non-Jewish child and don't have that child converted as a baby and don't tell the child he or she was adopted, twenty years later I may have a young man or girl in my office who's just about to get married and has discovered that their natural mother was not Jewish, and that therefore in the eyes of Jewish law they are not Jewish either. It's a tremendous shock to be told you're not Jewish when you've thought you were Jewish all your life. Then we have to do the conversion at that stage, and it's much more difficult.'

The conversion of adopted infants is not especially contentious. Adult conversion, on the other hand, can be a very contentious matter indeed. Judaism is not a proselytizing religion: it does not go out of its way to persuade non-Jews to join the faith. Those who express a wish to convert often do so because they are contemplating marriage to a Jew and wish to be able to participate in Jewish life to the full. This, however, is not a satisfactory reason to proceed with a conversion in the eyes of the Beth Din. Says Berkovits: 'The requirements in Jewish law for conversion are that the applicant who wants to embrace Judaism does so sincerely out of love of Judaism, for no ulterior motive. We have to establish that that is the case.' How the Beth Din can distinguish between a motive and an ulterior motive is unclear. The Chief Rabbi made the same point to me in a less legalistic way: 'The Beth Din wants to ensure that if a person wants to be Jewish, it's not just that they've fallen in love with a Jew but have fallen in love with Judaism. If the two converge, well and good. I accept annually a considerable number of people for conversion, provided that proof can be given that the conversion goes on in the heart of the person, and is not just a formality, a convenience. The Beth Din merely testifies to the fact that from what we know of this person, he or she thinks Jewishly, acts Jewishly, has no reservations about accepting the burdens of Jewish life and passing it on to his or her children. Once we're convinced that these conditions are met, we carry out the conversion.'

But even if the motive is acceptable, there are more difficulties ahead. Rabbi Berkovits explains: 'We also have to establish that the person concerned is going to live a Jewish life. Therefore we try to assess the person's sincerity and commitment, and also we will monitor their standard of knowledge. If you have someone who is intelligent and motivated, the process will go very quickly. I had a case which took only nine months. Other people take two or three years or whatever. There's no minimum and no maximum. We probably have about a hundred applications a year, of which not more than ten per cent are people who just happen to like Judaism. Sometimes we have people coming off the street who say they are interested in Judaism, and we very soon discover a girlfriend or boyfriend lurking in the background.'

The rigour of the London Beth Din is decried by many. A leading Manchester rabbi, no radical, considers it the most rigid in the world. 'Standards for conversion have been raised to ridiculous levels. Halachah does indeed say that one must query motives for conversion, but everyone knows that there is usually a marriage in the offing. After all, anyone who converts for any other reasons is almost certainly a crank! Before a conversion takes place, the Beth Din will ensure that the Jewish partner, if he's male, is laying *tefillin* and behaving in a scrupulously religious way. Then after a year of this, the girl will be put through the same kind of drill. But none of this is required by Halachah! The upshot is that many people decide to give the Beth Din a miss and marry outside the religion.'

I discussed this matter with Rabbi Plancey, who enjoys a good scrap. When I said the London Beth Din had the reputation of being the most rigorous in Europe, he stopped me. 'Why do you say rigorous? The London Beth Din is the most efficient and best renowned Beth Din in the world. If you get a conversion from them, you're Jewish. They're not ogres, because I've dealt with them.'

'Isn't it obvious that most people who wish to convert do so because they wish to marry a Jew? What's so terrible about that?'

'It's fine, as long as the partner is prepared to toe the party line. Judaism is not a religion of conversions. Some rabbis say people who want to convert should be able to do so, keep what they want, and that's enough. But is that enough? If it's a woman, for example, and she's going to bear children, and they're going to keep nothing – so what have we accomplished? We've done a big disservice. We've made somebody Jewish, but the children don't know anything about Judaism. It's not fair to the next generation.'

'But let's take the case of a middle-of-the-road Jew, who may keep *kashrut*, doesn't lay *tefillin*, occasionally goes to synagogue. Not wonderfully observant, but Jewish in consciousness and to some degree in practice. He wants to marry a non-Jew. Why not make it easy rather than an obstacle race? Why impose standards of observance far higher than those of most United Synagogue Jews?'

'If he wants to marry somebody outside, he has the option of coming back in completely.'

'But he's already in! He's Jewish!'

'But if he wants to bring somebody else in with him, he's got to be of a certain standard. Because you were born Jewish doesn't mean you are completely Jewish. If you don't keep anything, so what are you?'

'So by denying the conversion, you're prepared to see that middle-of-the-road Jew marry out, with the consequence that his children certainly won't be Jewish, rather than accept the conversion of his wife which would at least give the children the option of being Jewish?'

'Those children wouldn't be brought up as Jewish anyway, unless the parents converted properly. A Jew is somebody born of a Jewish mother, or somebody who converts according to Halachah, which means that you accept completely the yoke of all the laws of Torah and you dispense with all your previous ways. Unless you're prepared to accept the yoke, you're not converting.'

'But most born Jews don't accept that yoke either. They're not meticulously observant.'

'They don't keep. Yes, that's fair enough. That's our job as rabbis, to try to get them to keep more. But if somebody wants to get into the game, then they've got to aim for the top. If a person doesn't keep very much and someone converts, I'll guarantee you that both of them will keep nothing by the time they've finished. I have a lot of sympathy for such people, but there's sympathy and there's Halachah. There's a responsibility placed on our shoulders, and I think all my colleagues would agree with me. If somebody's genuine, we will help them, but if it's just a case of convenience, well, Judaism is not a religion of convenience. Judaism is a way of life.'

Many older rabbis, such as the Manchester minister, dislike what they see happening at the London Beth Din because they recall a time when the rabbinical court was not seen as primarily obstructive in its role. Converts were always expected to take their new religion seriously, to study it and satisfy the *dayanim* that their commitment was genuine. But all this talk of 'yokes' and 'letting people in' is abhorrent to many rabbis of the old school, as well as to a large segment of mainstream Jews. If a committed but middle-of-the-road Jew chooses that ambling path rather than the rigours of full Orthodox observance, that does seem insufficient reason to refuse his or her would-be partner the opportunity to convert. Since the consequence of such refusals is that such men and women have no choice but to marry outside the faith, the attitude seems akin to cutting off one's nose to spite one's face.

But let us conclude on a merrier note. A Beth Din also issues rulings on *kashrut*. Here too the tendency is to be as rigorous as possible. To my knowledge, there is no halachic prohibition on munching parsley. But in some Beth Din somewhere there is bound to be a *dayan* who can find a good reason to ban anything. Some authorities allow their flock to use butter, any old butter. Others say, no, the butter must have been prepared under the supervision of the *kashrut* authorities. It all depends where you live. It is pleasant to reflect that although these elderly gentlemen can issue their edicts, they cannot compel their flock to obey. Even that scourge of the half-hearted, Rabbi Alan Plancey, acknowledges that such matters can be taken to extremes. 'My daughter came home from seminary the other day and said you can't have parsley or strawberries unless you wash them in Fairy Liquid first.' And why? It appears to have something to do with micro-organisms that are in themselves *trefah* and that may not be shaken loose by mere washing in water. 'So my daughter doesn't eat strawberries. We do.'

Reform Judaism

R EFORM Judaism in Britain began life as a German import, though it has been greatly modified subsequently. It originated in about 1810 as an attempt to adapt a religion that seemed increasingly anachronistic. As long as Jews lived in the ghetto or the *shtetl*, it did not matter how arcane or obscurantist their religion appeared to others. But once Jews tasted the sweetness of the Enlightenment and emancipation, and directed their energies and intellects not to studying the Torah but to making their way in the wider world, the all-inclusive and inward-looking dictates of Torah began to seem outdated and irrelevant. This is not to say that Jews who participated in such worldly activities as stockbroking or international trade automatically became more secularist in outlook. In Britain, where most Jews were integrated into society from the eighteenth century onwards, Reform Judaism would make little headway for about a hundred years.

The original goals of Reform were modest, and consisted mostly of liturgical modifications. Services were shortened but also supplemented with a sermon, some prayers were said in the vernacular, a few vernacular hymns were added, and a choir and organ were introduced in some congregations. Over the next twenty years, however, a more radical theology developed, and changes took place that were more than cosmetic. Early Reform leaders argued that references in the traditional liturgy to the sacrificial cult, to the personal Messiah, and to the return to Zion were no longer acceptable in the modern world. The sacrificial cult was a relic of primitive times, the belief in the Messiah was rationally untenable, and the return to Zion was an irrelevance to a community attuned to living in the diaspora. Much greater weight was given to the Prophetic Books of

116

the Bible, with their explicit and implicit appeals for social justice and compassion. This rationalist and humanist trend was bolstered by the development of *Wissenschaft des Judentums*, 'Jewish Science', which beamed the light of modern scholarship on to Jewish belief and practice. Not surprisingly, its practitioners deduced that Jewish law was far more flexible than the Orthodox would have us believe, and that certain changes were well within the parameters of Jewish tradition. Judaism, the science sought to show, was not just a collection of outdated laws and rites, but a rich cultural and ethical tradition that still had much to teach its followers. There was also a strategy to Reform. For those Jews, and they had always existed, who could not or did not accept Orthodox Judaism, the only alternative hitherto had been assimilation leading, in some cases, to baptism. The modifications of Reform Judaism at least offered another possibility, allowing Jews who could not conform to the rigours of Orthodoxy an opportunity to maintain their links with the more palatable elements of their religion.

The difficulty was that Reform Judaism was thus in many respects a negative reaction to Orthodoxy. It was easy enough for its early leaders to decide that certain parts of the liturgy and certain concepts were no longer relevant. It was far more difficult to pin down which aspects of Torah were either immutable or at least binding on all Jews. Nor did theological matters have much to do with the founding of Reform Judaism in Britain, where, typically, it was a question of practicality rather than conviction. Prosperity prompted many Jews of the early nineteenth century to move from their traditional quarters in the City of London to the more fashionable West End. The City synagogues, however, notably the Sephardi synagogue of Bevis Marks, sought to enforce a rule of theirs that forbade the founding of new synagogues. For those who lived in the West End, the Saturday morning hike to the City was an excessive demand and they saw no reason why they could not worship closer to their homes. Their requests were repeatedly rejected by Bevis Marks, and on 15 April 1840 twenty-four prominent Jews, eighteen Sephardim and six Ashkenazim, founded a new congregation. Not only were the twenty-four West Enders defying the Establishment, but they were agreeing to ignore the traditional differences – admittedly more form than substance – between Sephardim and Ashkenazim. Fifteen of the twenty-four came from three of the most prominent Anglo-Jewish families: the Mocattas, the Montefiores, and the Henriques. It is perhaps not surprising, therefore, that the new congregation, instead of becoming a trail-blazing band of pioneers, had more the air of a very select gentlemen's club. Apart from an offshoot congregation in Manchester and a short-lived Reform community in Hull, the movement made virtually no impact on Anglo-Jewry as a whole. The social exclusivity of the West End congregation deterred working-class Jews and the new immigrants from even considering whether or not they should join it. Nor, despite the wealth of the individual membership of the West End synagogue, was any attempt made to establish institutions to match those of the United Synagogue.

The British Reformers were not especially reform-minded. True, the service was shortened and the second days of certain Jewish festivals were not observed, but men and women were seated separately until after the First World War. 'Jewish Science' had little appeal to the pragmatists of Anglo-Jewry. The new congregation sprang from convenience more than intellectual conviction. Its early leaders occasionally muttered about reconciling faith and reason, but this was woolly stuff, reassuring but bland. Orthodox Judaism did not need a theology because it had Torah, in its broadest sense of 'teaching'. Reform Judaism did have need of a theology because of its rejection of the centrality of Torah, but had no means of agreeing on how to arrive at such a theology. Having raised the anchor of Torah, the Reformers were theologically adrift. The German Reformers, with their love of philosophy and abstraction, certainly tried, but the more empirical British, for the most part, gave the whole problem a miss. It was not until the 1930s and 1940s that British Reform Judaism was given a long overdue shot in the arm by immigrants from Germany and central Europe. In Europe, Reform had developed, in the century since its founding, various traditions of its own, both liturgical and theological, and these were able to enrich the undernourished British branch. The European Jewish middle classes were the mainstay of the Reform movement, while impoverished Eastern Europe clung to the certainties of Orthodoxy. The largest proportion of Anglo-Jewry in the early twentieth century had either come from Eastern Europe or was directly descended from those immigrants, and to them the bland refinements of Reform were completely alien. For many of the refugees in the 1930s, however, Reform was the norm. The German Reform Jews called themselves Liberals, but had little in common with the English Liberals, who were an offshoot of Reform and the closest thing in Judaism to Unitarianism.

After the Second World War, British Reform began to grow and attract new adherents. It was not only a result of the influx of European refugees but also a reaction to what many perceived as the hypocrisy that infuses many United congregations. If you're not going to keep kosher and if you have every intention of driving on the Sabbath, then it's far better, in their view, to admit it and call yourself a Progressive Jew than perpetuate the hypocrisy of paying lip service to practices you prefer to ignore. Moreover, Reform Jews are not necessarily slack in their religious observance: they may not observe every law of *kashrut*, but some attend Sabbath services regularly, celebrate all the festivals, keep Friday night, and maintain the Jewish atmosphere of their homes. In recent years Reform Judaism has abandoned some of its former radicalism and lessened the gap between its practices and those of mainstream Orthodoxy. Thirty years ago Reform services were conducted mostly in the vernacular. Today more prayers are recited in Hebrew. Modern Reform rabbis are well trained and often deeply interested in Jewish history and tradition. Raymond Goldman, the executive director of the Reform Synagogues of Great Britain, stresses both tradition and an accommodation to contemporary circumstances: 'In the great majority of Orthodox communities, the rabbi is out of touch with his community. Of course he has to set standards and be a role model. The crux of the Reform position is that we do want to maintain the tradition and utilize it to the greatest extent possible to enhance the Jewish living of our members. We give rabbinic law a strong vote but we don't allow it a veto. The business of saying that people in the past were very much greater than we were and therefore we have no right to change their decisions – well, there was change, and that process of change became fossilized in the Middle Ages. The ghetto preserved Jewish life, but religion must be prepared to change.'

There is no more uniformity of liturgical style within Reform Judaism than within mainstream Orthodoxy. Reform at its most ossified may be sampled at the West London Synagogue near Marble Arch, which first opened its doors in 1870 and is the oldest of the thirty or so Reform congregations in Britain. The interior of the synagogue is undeniably splendid, vaguely Moorish in style, with cupolas and arches and grilles. The *bima* used to stand in the centre, but has been moved to the front so as to provide more seating. All eyes now face the front. The worshippers drift in and take their seats quietly as the organ plays softly in the background. Most of the men, but by no means all, wear a *tallit*. On this typical Saturday morning, there were about 150 people in the congregation, not a particularly strong showing given that the membership of West London is about 2,500 families. But then West London has always been the most fashionable Reform congregation, and many people join for that reason. The Reform liturgy relies on formal prayer and response: the rabbi reads, and the congregation responds with a set line or two, as written in the prayer-book, either in Hebrew or English. But religious fervour is not a characteristic of this congregation, and the responses were mumbled. Often lips were moving but no sound was being emitted. The Reformers not only deleted vast sections of the liturgy, but added some of their own for good measure. Thus the prayer-book includes a 'study anthology', and on this particular Sabbath the passage we were directed to read in the middle of the service was a one-liner about preparing for death written by that well-known militant atheist, Sigmund Freud.

There is music at West London, but no chanting. A hidden mixed choir, accompanied by that soporific organ, provided all the music, with the exception of some concluding hymns in which the congregation participated. The sexes are mixed, of course, and a woman seated in the wardens' box alongside two top-hatted gentlemen processed with the scrolls. The principal rabbi at West London is Hugo Gryn, an Auschwitz survivor and one of the most respected rabbis in Britain. He combines warmth and dignity and conviction in an impressive way, and exudes authority without being authoritarian. It was he who read from the Torah and translated each verse as he went along, an eminently sensible procedure. This particular service included a memorial to the war dead, and a scroll of honour was read out. A uniformed bugler then appeared, and he bugled. The National Anthem was then sung. By now I was aching to leave. From the front of the congregation, Rabbi Gryn spoke directly to his flock, but there seemed to be no real communication. I cannot recall a more dust-laden atmosphere at any religious service. The congregation was both impeccably dressed and impeccably behaved. There was no flicker of spontaneity at any time. It was not just the formality of West London that I found off-putting, but the tedium. Orthodox services, despite their inordinate length, at least require the congregation to take an active part.

(Rabbi Jonathan Magonet, the principal of Leo Baeck College and one of those who redrafted the current Reform prayer-book, applauds the didacticism of the service. 'When we put together the new prayer-book about ten years ago, it seemed to us very important to bring in a dimension of education in the synagogue. Traditional things that spoke clearly to today were worth having. Among the moderns our own personal teachers, in terms of those who gave us contemporary religious insight, tended to be people like Kafka and Freud. The fact that some of them were secularists did not deter us, because there was obviously a quest for truth, which is a religious vocation in a way. The study material is neutral. It's there for study purposes if you want it.')

West London, it must be stressed, is not a typical Reform synagogue, any more than the Brompton Oratory is a standard Catholic church. To find a Reform congregation with a stronger bite, I visited the outer London congregation at Radlett and Bushey, which occupies a converted aisle-less chapel on the High Street next to a Chinese restaurant. The east window of the chapel had been filled with simple stained glass. There was no *bima*, of course, and the ark and desks were placed on the raised chancel area. If I had experienced religious culture shock on seeing a woman carrying the Torah at West London, I was in for a deeper disturbance here, where the rabbi was then a woman. Until she stepped down as rabbi in October 1988, Barbara Borts, an American with strong feminist convictions, led her congregation with cheerful authority. Gifted with a fine voice, her singing held the service together by inspiring the rather small congregation – fifty or so – to participate. There was an abundance of small children, for the congregation is largely composed of young couples who have moved out to the very edge of the city. The congregation here was informally dressed; few of the men were wearing a tie. Yet the *tallit* on display were of the heavy woollen kind – like those commonly worn in Orthodox circles – not the skimpy silk scarves of twenty years ago. Apart from Rabbi Borts, there was even a woman wearing a *tallit*, which surprised me.

Rabbi Borts defended both the clarity and informality of her service. 'You can't claim that it's more spiritual to mumble through prayer at breakneck speed. An Orthodox service goes on for three hours, and it's hard to sustain concentration for three hours. There's a lot more thought content to a Reform service than an Orthodox one, and a lot more flexibility. I don't think the synagogue is a place for talking about your business. Sephardi synagogues are not like that. It's an Ashkenazi thing: you come in and you talk. Many people from Orthodox backgrounds complain that they didn't understand their services, they seemed strict and inflexible, and the prayers were mumbled through at such a pace that they couldn't keep up. So they felt totally turned off. If you can have a shorter service, with a slower pace, something people feel comfortable with, then we can move towards greater informality without making the travesty that some Ashkenazi synagogues have made of the service. I'm not in favour of the pious churchlike atmosphere either. I like informality.'

Flexibility is crucial to the Reform outlook. Orthodox critics of Reform regard this flexibility as a pandering to convenience at best, and a renunciation of seminal Jewish values at worst. Reform Jews reject the concept of Halachah as a monolithic and immutable body of law. Orthodox Jews see their religion as timeless and hence unchanging and unchangeable, whereas Reform Jews place a positive value on adaptibility and a willingness to make changes. The Reform theologian Ignaz Maybaum goes so far as to declare: 'The concept of an immutable historical law is alien to Judaism . . . The Torah has a history, and one which is not yet closed.'[1] Rabbi Colin Eimer has written sternly: 'God's revelation comes in many different ways and it is not for any person or group to say which is the more authentic.'[2] Revelation, in other words, is continuous, and is more than the sum of Jewish law. The injunction on Jews to study the Torah is another way of indicating that the law is not immutable but is always open to reconsideration and reinterpretation. This willingness to re-evaluate Jewish tradition does give Reform Judaism a degree of intellectual vitality less commonly encountered among the more scholastic debates within Orthodoxy. It also scatters its net more widely than Orthodox Judaism. Non-fundamentalist Jews, write Liberal Rabbis John Rayner and David Goldberg, 'will recognize as Torah not only the legislation of Moses but also the visions of the prophets, the commentary of the rabbis, the insights of the mystics and all wise and noble guidance in the way of holiness. For him, the Torah has never ceased to grow'.[3]

Rabbi Magonet told me: 'There is really no part of Jewish tradition that we are not open to either ransacking or imbuing with new meaning. In the pre-Holocaust Reform and Liberal world we were the great intellectual rationalists and universalists, and we explored as far as one could the limits of rationality and reason. The Holocaust brought to our lives the eruption of unreason. The awareness that superficial intellectualism or rationality only skated over the darker side of human beings was something we had not taken seriously. In the post-Holocaust world, we are intuitively fighting a battle on two fronts. One is to preserve reason and rationality and liberalism at a time of increasing irrationality and a retreat from rationalism. Secondly, in order to do this legitimately, we have to explore those other dimensions of life which had been rather neglected.'

This openness to recent historical experience, as well as to the

122

implanted communal memory of Jewish experience in biblical times, is admirable, but its very open-endedness poses a problem for Reform Judaism. Just as there is no agreement among Reform Jews about which *mitzvot* are essential there is also no agreement on what should constitute a modern Reform theology. Maybaum has written: 'The task of Jewish theology is to give guidance in the change in which the westernization of our lives involves us.' Really? Is that all? Jewish life, even Reform theologians usually agree, has as much to do with conduct and behaviour as with adherence to codes of law, so surely a modern theology must concern itself with more than mere guidance. 'Once modern Jewish theology is established, and has done its work,' he continues, 'Halachah, guidance through codes, may reappear. But it will be a new Halachah, a law which guides and organizes Jewish life under modern conditions.' But Reform theologians have long ago disposed of what they see as anachronisms in Jewish law; since Progressive Judaism gives Halachah no binding authority, it can't make much sense to speak of 'new Halachah'. To do so plays into the hands of those critics of Reform Judaism who regard its tinkerings with Halachah as no more than a capitulation to convenience. The intellectual barrenness of Maybaum's approach is summed up in his own tautological declaration that 'Jewish theology will start with the intellectual approach and convince modern Jewry of their absolute need of Jewish life'.[4]

John Rayner, a Liberal rabbi, has taken up Maybaum's challenge. He admonishes those Progressive Jews who have tended to dismiss the value of Halachah altogether: 'Any modern Judaism which ignores the Halachah exposes itself to the danger of losing in some measure these precious characteristics – practicality, comprehensiveness, specificity and intellectuality.' On the other hand, Reform Judaism came into existence precisely because emancipated Jews could not accept the rigours of Halachah. But it's hard to have it both ways, to respect it as the foundation of Jewish observance and culture and at the same time to declare it outdated. To maintain such a position, Rabbi Rayner has to squirm in the following way: 'To us, the fact that a law is biblical does not *ipso facto* make it valid. It has, in some sense, to validate itself.' Rabbi Rayner's 'new modern Halachah' is to be based on a re-examination of the old one 'with respect but not with subservience. It will ascribe to it only a presumptive, never a conclusive, authority.' That's a handy phrase, no different in its logic from declaring that one respects the law of the land, expect in those instances when one doesn't agree with it and is thus at liberty to break it.

The new Halachah will call on the skill of doctors and sociologists and psychologists as well as rabbinical scholars; it will emphasize moral rather than ritual law. Yet when all this has been done 'it will not claim *finality* in any of these areas . . . In matters of personal and domestic observance, it will offer guidance rather than legislation.'[5] Such wishy-washy stuff as this would seem to justify the disdain which many Orthodox feel towards the evasive tacking of Reform Judaism. Even some Reform rabbis recognize the intellectual dishonesty of much Progressive cogitation. Dow Marmur has written of non-Orthodox movements that 'they seem to attract those who want the comforts of tradition without being burdened by the guilty conscience that may result from its unheeded demands. What goes under the name of honesty and integrity is often a mere camouflage for convenience.'[6]

The arrival of refugees from Nazi Europe gingered up the bland provincial universalism of the British congregations, and injected a note of greater sophistication, both in theological and liturgical terms. But that welcome infusion was a one-off benefit, and facilities had to be provided to train the next generation of rabbis. Leo Baeck College was founded in 1956, and has subsequently trained more than eighty rabbis. Eighty per cent of Progressive rabbis with British congregations were trained at Leo Baeck, and many of its graduates minister to non-Orthodox communities abroad. Not all trainee rabbis come from religious backgrounds. Some arrive at the college with only the most rudimentary knowledge of Hebrew. Once enrolled, however, the students receive a long and sophisticated course that includes not only standard rabbinic studies, but seminars in comparative religion, counselling, and management, all skills deemed essential for a modern rabbinate. Half the current enrolment is female. Rabbinical students spend a year in Israel, where they often experience a religious intensity that is not always in harmony with the relatively laid-back Progressive outlook. Rabbi Magonet admits that Leo Baeck students returning from Israel 'often have re-entry problems coming back here into the Anglo-Jewish scene. They receive a broad experience which on the whole tends to move them more to the right than to the left.'

After graduation, rabbis file off into the Reform or Liberal community, depending both on their personal convictions and on where suitable vacancies happen to arise. Individual communities enjoy even greater autonomy than in the United Synagogue, and rabbis are hired on open-ended contracts and paid directly by their community. This is a mixed blessing. 'You can have problems with your community,' says Rabbi Borts, 'but communities that fire rabbis don't get a very good reputation. It's not easy to speak out on issues, and you can't offend people, but not because people are going to hold over you the threat of firing you. The real problem with being paid by your community is that it messes up the relationship a bit. You have a fight with somebody, and then they become the treasurer, and it can get messy all round. And demeaning. On the other hand, we're not dependent on tips. You go to an Orthodox wedding or funeral and they've got their hands out. I personally favour central payment with some restrictions on how it's to be administered. But I'm in a minority.'

Reform rabbis are organized into the Ministers' Assembly, and they form a back-up team for the Beth Din. The ministers discuss such issues as birth control and conversion, hoping to arrive at a common approach that can guide those who serve on the Beth Din, which the rabbis do by rota. The Beth Din has retained many of the formalities that characterize the Orthodox rabbinical courts. The Reform Beth Din, for example, also tries to arrange for religious divorce in addition to civil divorce in the event of a breakdown of marriage. Of course the procedure is very different, which is one of many reasons why the Reform Beth Din is regarded as beyond the pale by the Orthodox. Whereas the London Beth Din of the United Synagogue has no authority to force a husband to issue a *get* against his will, the Reform Beth Din will intervene if, in its judgement, a husband withholds a *get* on unreasonable grounds. In such cases, the Beth Din will issue a document dissolving the marriage and freeing the wife to marry again without fear that any children from her subsequent marriage will be regarded as *mamzerim* (bastards), as would be the case were she to remarry without having accepted a *get* in an Orthodox Beth Din. It is also easier for a non-Jew to convert to Reform Judaism. The Beth Din requires a knowledge of Hebrew and a minimum of one year's religious instruction, though often that period of instruction can last two or three years. Male converts must be circumcised, and female converts must attend the *mikveh*.

Just as Reform Judaism always claims that its flexible approach to Jewish observance has lessened the rate of assimilation, so too its more hospitable attitude towards conversion bolsters its claim to lessen the deleterious effects of out-marriage on the Jewish community. Whereas the London Beth Din reacts with horror to the suggestion that someone might wish to convert because they wish to marry a Jew, the Reform community welcomes sincere converts, arguing, persuasively, that it's better to keep Jews within the fold than force them out of it. Many converts later become stalwarts of the Reform movement. Naturally, such conversions are not recognized as valid by the London Beth Din.

The Reform movement has about 42,000 members, and is thus twice as strong as the Liberals. The demographic distribution of its membership corresponds to the dispersal of British Jewry in general, and about 80 per cent of Reform Jews live in Greater London, with particular areas of strength in such suburbs as Hendon and Edgware and Golders Green. Some of the outer suburban congregations, such as Barbara Borts's, and the community at Hatch End, also show a healthy growth rate. Small Reform congregations flourish elsewhere in south-east England, in Cambridge and Milton Keynes and Brighton. Some years ago the Reform movement pitched its tents in suburban Finchley at the Sternberg Centre for Judaism, more widely known as the Manor House, which is now the headquarters of the Reform Synagogues of Great Britain and also houses Leo Baeck College, a Jewish museum, and Akiva, the only Reform primary school in Britain. The Centre also provides a venue for lectures and adult education courses and cultural events, and thus offers a focus to the Reform community of north London, the largest outside North America. Manor House has given the movement greater visibility than ever before. 'We're listened to,' says Jonathan Magonet, 'and our representatives are listened to. We're moving into the Establishment. We're the loyal opposition, almost.'

The two Progressive organizations account for no more than about 22 per cent of synagogue membership in Great Britain. This doesn't prevent the Orthodox Establishment from expressing great wrath at what they see as the disproportionate prominence of Progressive religious leaders on the media. Although the Chief Rabbi is regarded as the senior religious leader in the country, few other Orthodox figures have attained the popularity of the likes of Rabbis Julia Neuberger, Lionel Blue, and Hugo Gryn. Not that the various broadcasting authorities are closet Reform or Liberal Jews, rather that many Orthodox rabbis lack the breadth of vision and intellectual sophistication of their Progressive counterparts. Nonetheless, to hear a United Synagogue rabbi inveighing against Lionel Blue or Julia Neuberger – who is invariably referred to simply as 'that woman' – is a treat for students of invective. Rabbi Alan Plancey, for instance, objects to their prominence on the airwaves not necessarily because of the views they present, but because they often claim to be speaking from a Jewish point of view. Rabbi Plancey, and many others, regard Reform Judaism as a curious religious lagoon, isolated from the main flow of the majestic tides of traditional Judaism, and therefore not even entitled to use the word 'Judaism' in connection with their beliefs.

If Reform Jews find it hard to respect nominally Orthodox Jews who either break the laws they claim to uphold (such as by driving on the Sabbath) or devise ingenious ways to circumvent them, Orthodox Jews deplore the laxity of their Reform brethren. Many are dismayed by the Progressives' choosiness when it comes to *mitzvot*. Others dislike the liturgical changes, the operatic choirs, the excessive decorum. A more profound objection to Reform Judaism comes from those who see in it the first stage of an ever greater dilution of the faith. 'Reform doesn't last,' an Orthodox teacher insisted to me. 'The children of those who are Reform may be Jews, but the grandchildren are Christians. It's a step down, a lowering of standards. It's better to aim higher than lower.'

This argument is, predictably, dismissed by Reform leaders. Dow Marmur has written: 'Reform Judaism is almost invariably attacked, not on account of its teachings, but because it is seen as a threat to Jewish survival. And Reform demands itself not by means of scholarship seeking to demonstrate its case but with statistics, showing that it preserves more and more Jews for Judaism.'[7] Barbara Borts remarks: 'The only ones who could say with more certainty than anyone else that their grandchildren will be Jewish are the extreme ultra-Orthodox. No United person can say that about their kids. By and large, United Synagogue kids marry out more often than Reform. Just because somebody is a bit more formal in their ritual isn't a guarantee that their children will marry in. I don't believe there's much correlation at all. The only ones sure of survival are those who live in the ghetto.'

Rabbi Borts is not interested in jockeying for position with the United Synagogue. 'Reform has been waging this war with United over who is to be the mainstream Jewish community. I'm not interested in that battle. The Orthodox don't impinge on me. Unfortunately there are more of them and they have more power. This means that if I wanted to do hospital visiting, I'd be blocked because the United Synagogue wouldn't be happy. The answer is to have more Reform synagogues, simply so that we don't find ourselves being pushed out of doing work in the community. If we need more power to achieve that, okay, but not because we want to appeal to the masses. We're definitely setting the lead over the United Synagogue in many respects. We're much better at handling bereavement. Some

Orthodox rabbis are incredibly insensitive to that. We instituted pastoral and management training for the rabbinate, and all of a sudden the Orthodox rabbis are getting the same training. I don't think rabbis should be Jewish social workers, but certainly we're better trained.' Even in ritual matters, the United Synagogue has borrowed from the Reform. The *bat chayil* ceremony for girls clearly reflects the wish for greater equality between the sexes that Progressive Judaism so easily satisfied. Just as the Orthodox have borrowed some ideas from the Progressives, so Reform has not hesitated to wrap its shoulders not only in woollen *tallit* but in some of the other customs of Orthodoxy. At the Manor House it is now possible to attend weekly *shiurim*, even though their content would be unlikely to find favour in Stamford Hill.

Reform Judaism continues to hold enormous appeal to the many thoughtful Jews who are dismayed by the growing stridency of the Orthodox. Every Reform congregation has its handful of defectors. A London solicitor told me he had always been a loyal United Synagogue member until he moved to a different suburb and was told by the rabbi there that the congregation would have little use for him and his wife unless they were more demonstrably devout. Not surprisingly, the lawyer told the rabbi to get stuffed and promptly joined the local Reform synagogue. For others, it is the values, humane and urbane, represented by Reform that constitute the appeal. Sir Claus Moser reflected: 'I'm terribly put off by a lot of the traditions of Orthodoxy. I'm much more drawn to the liberal outlook, and I think the greatest hope for the survival of Judaism might lie in the Reform movement. The extremities of Orthodoxy may have seen their day. They're not concordant with modern ways of thinking. But the reason I'm very pessimistic on this subject is because I meet a lot of Orthodox Jews in high positions and the intolerance towards the Reform movement is a great danger. It's not mutual. Hugo Gryn will speak with much more understanding and respect about the Orthodox than they will about him. There's a very prominent Jew in this country – not the Chief Rabbi – who told me not very long ago that he didn't consider Reform Jews real Jews. I blew my top and told him that's why we may not have a future. I would put any money on the proposition that if all that's accepted as Judaism is going to be Orthodoxy, then we're really for the birds. In Berlin, when I was a boy growing up there, a more effective opposition to the Nazis came from the Reform Jews, who actually engaged in the fight, than from the Orthodox, who went on praying.'

– 10 –

Liberal Judaism

ICONOCLASTIC movements often contain the seeds of their own enfeeblement. Orthodoxy tolerates no radical probing; you either love it or leave it. But Reform Judaism, having questioned the tenets of traditional Judaism, found itself in due course subject to heretical defiance from within its own circle. In the early years of this century Claude Montefiore, a biblical scholar, and Lily Montagu, whose father had been president of the United Synagogue, were at the hub of a study circle that met regularly at West London Synagogue. Their discussions were free and wide-ranging, so much so that they found themselves drifting towards a theological position that was out of harmony with the Reform movement to which they belonged. They formed themselves into the group that soon after founded the Liberal Synagogue. In 1912 they acquired the site in St John's Wood of what was to become the principal Liberal synagogue in the country, under the spiritual leadership of the American rabbi, Dr Mattuck.

Miss Marjorie Moos, now ninety-four, remembers the day she and Claude Montefiore and Lily Montagu dug up the first turf at the site of the new synagogue. 'There were only seven of us there, and I'm the only one still alive.' She came from a nominally Orthodox home, and attended Hampstead Synagogue, and even taught at the *cheder* there. She was drawn to the new offshoot of Liberal Judaism by its rationalism. 'The appeal of Liberal Judaism was that I understood the services from A to Z. Parents and children all sat together. The service was very largely in English, though the most important prayers were still in Hebrew. The whole feel of the service was much more friendly, much more a family thing. I couldn't stand sitting up in the ladies' gallery – the women up

129

there were so uneducated. I wanted to be in a synagogue where I could worship. The other great appeal of the Liberal movement was that there was no barmitzvah. At sixteen you had to take a confirmation exam. It was at that age that children were considered old enough to understand enough of their religion to really be able to carry it on into future generations. The teaching was very high class. We made no difference between the boys and the girls, and expected our youngsters to understand what their faith was about, to know their history and their Hebrew.'

One of Miss Moos's pupils at the St John's Wood synagogue was Julia Neuberger, now the rabbi of the South London synagogue in Streatham. When I suggested to her that Liberal Judaism sprang from the same rejection of Jewish law that motivated the Reform movement, she corrected me. 'No, no, none of that's right. What the founders actually said in the early days was that most of it was irrational. Looking back at it from the 'eighties, you could say that religion isn't about rationality. But you can see why they did it: it was a huge reaction to what was going on in so-called Orthodoxy, which was ritual but nothing else. I think they stripped away far too much of the ritual and I don't think they recognized the human need for ritual. For the older diehard members of my congregation, for whom I have a great respect though I don't always agree with them, Liberal Judaism is the Judaism of the prophets and not about what you do in the home. It's not about how you practise it, it's about a series of beliefs which should motivate you to do things in this world. Liberal Judaism stresses individual conscience rather than obedience to a set of rules. The original Liberals actually did what they talked about. They really did go out and work in the East End. The involvement of Liberal Jews in all the social welfare issues of the 'twenties and 'thirties was phenomenal, given their small numbers in comparison with the rest of the community. Services in those days were very crowded too. For people who are younger, or who come from a slightly different tradition, while they have enormous respect for that strong ethical sense, they also say that they have other needs too. There's been a conflict between the two which in my congregation we're just beginning to resolve.'

David Goldberg is a rabbi at the St John's Wood synagogue, and he is also a historian. He has a somewhat ponderous, grave manner, as soothing as an anaesthetist. His father was a Reform rabbi in Manchester, so he has been imbued since childhood with the values of Progressive Judaism. He has little patience with the standard Orthodox attack on Progressive Judaism. 'It has an internal logic,' he concedes, 'but it just won't wash.

Historically, it's a nonsense because it posits a historical assumption that Judaism is a monolith, a static, undynamic series of traditions that have remained unchanged throughout the centuries. That's cobblers. Anyone with one iota of knowledge of Jewish history from the time of the Babylonian exile onwards must realize there has been the most astonishing variety of local examples of Jewish practice. And also there was far greater freedom in the ancient world, which was religiously chaotic anyway, than there is today in welcoming half-Jews who didn't accept all the rites and rituals. Philo, one of the revered philosophers of Judaism, didn't know a word of Hebrew, and he allegorized the Torah according to modes of Aristotelian thought to make it acceptable to his compatriots in Alexandria and to the wider public. In Ethiopia you have something entirely different. There's a Chinese Jewish community which is largely Muslim by now but still has strange adherences to Jewish tradition. Ashkenazi Jewry is entirely different from Sephardi Jewry. Venice Jewry in its acculturation and tolerance and mixing with gentile society was entirely different from what went on in, say, Poland. The Essenes were part of Judaism, the Rabbinites were part of Judaism, the Chasidim were part of Judaism. It's always been the reaction of those who think they are the Torah-true guardians of the tradition to want to say of other kinds of Judaism that they are not authentic. They'd have cast out Philo and the Ba'al Shem Tov, given half a chance. Unfortunately the ancient rabbis were great guys but they were ignoramuses; they were not widely cultured men.

'Orthodoxy presupposes that there is such a thing that can be encapsulated as Judaism; Progressive Judaism affirms God's rule in the world. It affirms a value system based on the Law; it gives a presumptive authority to Halachah. A magnificent voluminous system of Halachah developed to tell a Jew at every waking moment what God required of him. It is an extraordinarily strong, valuable, comprehensive value system. If you come to me and say what is the Jewish view on abortion, my first automatic response is to go and look up these sources. However, because I am, for better or worse, a product of Western civilization, I find it a little difficult to accept wholeheartedly an insistence on a miraculous divine descent on Mount Sinai, a once-and-for-all divine appearance until the coming of Jesus, that said: "Here, this is it. It may not be added to or detracted from one jot or tittle. This is it, boys, for all time." This I find a little hard to swallow intellectually.

'I do take the right to make use of scholarship, reason, and, most of all,

131

informed conscience in order to look where tradition does not accord with what I, as a very fallible twentieth-century human being, would nevertheless consider to be divine justice. Take the treatment of women. It must surely be generally accepted that however reverential, respectful, and thoughtful Halachah is towards women, it patently did not accord them equality, legal or religious. Of course the Halachah was compiled in a patriarchal era. However, it seems to me fairly generally understood in the Western world in the twentieth century that equality of the sexes is a definite advance on biblical legislation.' Similarly, Rabbi Goldberg has little patience with stern pronouncements from the Orthodox rabbinate on sexual morality. 'Despite the Chief Rabbi's desire to restore homosexuality to the legal code, it seems to me an undoubted advance that many of us are ready to be a lot more sympathetic and understanding of homosexuality as an expression of sexual orientation, whether approving of it or not.' Most other Progressive rabbis take a similar line; Hugo Gryn argues that sexual morality is a private matter, which is emphatically not the Orthodox view.

Yet Rabbi Goldberg, for all his liberal social attitudes, is not what Julia Neuberger calls diehard in his religious Liberalism. Just as Reform Judaism, in its liturgical and ritual practice, has edged towards more traditional observance, so a comparable swing can be discerned among Liberal congregations. At St John's Wood, says David Goldberg, 'I have discreetly moved to encourage people to wear head coverings and *tallit* when they come to worship. This community used to take a positive pride in not wearing a *kippah* or *tallit*. Now we offer them to worshippers when they arrive. We have processions with the scrolls, which would have been unthinkable fifty years ago. The way we celebrate Simchat Torah [the festival that marks the conclusion of the reading of the Pentateuch], the jollity, the exuberance – that was absolutely undreamt of by our founders, who had a very austere, ethical, rather Quaker kind of Judaism. We and the other Liberal congregations introduced barmitzvah a few years ago – we never had that before. Previously we only had confirmation.'

Helene Bromnick attributes the change to the influence of Continental rabbis, such as John Rayner, the senior minister at St John's Wood. This influence duplicates that made on Reform congregations by German and Czech rabbis. 'They brought a much more Orthodox version of Liberalism with them into this very English 1930s form of Liberalism, which was very much like Christianity with Jesus taken out. Liberals have become very much more mainline in their services. I remember going to St John's

Wood as a child, and the main thing was English hymns, of the kind where Jesus is not mentioned. "All things bright and beautiful" and "Oh God our help in ages past" – that kind of thing.'

Marjorie Moos, as a founder member, takes a dimmer view of these changes. 'I don't like them, because I don't feel we think in Hebrew. To go back to Hebrew prayers doesn't make the services more reverent, not from my point of view. Also we don't get as much singing as we used to in the days when we sang English songs and hymns.' Julia Neuberger has mixed feelings: 'There are some rituals which make one feel extremely silly. I do find waving a *lulav* at Succoth [the harvest festival] a very difficult thing to do because I feel like a complete idiot waving a palm branch in the middle of Streatham. On one level it's totally absurd. At the same time there are lots of things I'd like to do and I think there are new rituals which could be created to help people identify with that side of themselves. One Liberal introduction that's worked immensely well is the baby-naming service at the end of a Shabbat service. Both parents come and stand in front of the open ark and say something, and it's much better than the old traditional calling up of the father. What did the father have to do with it? Precious little. I feel strongly that processing the scrolls is a very nice thing to do. If you're going to read the thing, you might as well process it and give it some ceremony. The old diehards say, "But that's Torah worship!" and I say, "Don't be ridiculous, are you worshipping it because you're reading it?"'

Torah worship, indeed, seems just about the last thing of which one could accuse Liberal Jews. At the St John's Wood synagogue one Sabbath morning, I watched Rabbi Goldberg raise the scroll and declare, 'Render honour unto the Torah,' but the service as a whole does nothing of the kind. For Liberal Jews, Torah is a source of tales rather than prescriptions. I attended a barmitzvah at this synagogue and a more lacklustre procedure it would be hard to imagine. As at West London, the atmosphere was churchy and stiff. The sheer size of the galleried synagogue militates against intimacy, communion, spirituality. Despite the rabbis' prodding, few of the male members of the congregation wore *tallit*, and some were bare-headed. A lusty choir, accompanied by an organ, took care of the responses, though there were some desultory communal readings, emitted in an embarrassed drone, from the prayer-book, which is gummily known as Service of the Heart. The barmitzvah boy read rather than chanted his portion from the Torah in Hebrew and then translated it. The Haftorah was read by his father, in English. How this dreary ceremony, so perfunctory, so trite, could have any spiritual or ritual significance is puzzling.

Nor was I able to derive much spiritual nourishment from the Sabbath service at Julia Neuberger's congregation in Streatham. Although half the men were bare-headed, the woman – not Rabbi Neuberger, who was absent – who read from the Torah did wear a *kippah*. As she read she not only translated but gave a fairly detailed commentary after each couple of verses, a useful exercise. However she omitted to read the first half of the final portion on the grounds that the previous year she had read that half and, besides, she 'preferred' the second half, as though unwelcome parts of the Torah could be discarded according to the reader's whim. I imagine non-Jewish visitors being brought proudly to a Liberal service and being deluded into thinking that what they are witnessing has much to do with Judaism. The ethical content of the service may be beyond reproach, but all the other aspects of worship, in particular the sheer warmth you can find even in the most rundown Chasidic *shtiebl* in north London, are missing. Even the rabbi of this congregation couldn't work up much enthusiasm for her services: 'I always find our services terribly bare, though I don't think they lack gravity. Gravity is precisely what they do have. It's everything else they don't have. They're immensely serious, but to my mind they don't satisfy that part of one that responds to ritual and to action that doesn't have a rational meaning.' (No one could have accused Clifford Cohen of excessive gravity. Rabbi of Southgate Progressive Synagogue until 1984, he was sacked for spicing his sermons with risqué jokes. He took his jokes to an industrial tribunal, but remains an ex-rabbi.)

Not surprisingly, Liberal Jews attach little importance to such matters as *kashrut*, though a few try to restrain themselves when offered bacon or prawns. 'On the other hand,' according to Rabbi Goldberg, 'we're very strong on Shabbat observance, and I take much pleasure in the fact that our youngsters coming up to confirmation are much more familiar with Hebrew and such things as grace after meals. Our youth networks are flourishing, many kids have been to Israel on youth schemes and return with a familiarity with traditional rituals that would amaze their parents or grandparents. There's an awareness generally that the pioneering proselytizing movement that this was seventy years ago may, in rejecting the past, have thrown the baby out with the bathwater. Some of us are beginning to realize that perhaps there was value, after all, in the traditions and the customs. So we're by no means the congregation that we were forty years ago or even twenty years ago.' Julia Neuberger, however, notes an even more marked increase in traditional observance. 'We have a few who keep strict *kashrut*. Most will do something at home on Erev Shabbat and a lot come to synagogue as well. You'd find relatively few who celebrate the last day of festivals, but almost everybody would have a Seder.'

Although some Liberals clearly have a deep commitment to their somewhat pragmatic form of religion, the spiritually anaemic quality of Liberalism may be impeding any growth in membership. Reform Judaism is flexible enough to offer a degree of ritual observance for those who value such things, and an intellectual athleticism that will justify the abstentions of those for whom ritual and observance are unimportant. It is thus not surprising that the market share of the Liberal brand is declining. Over the past decade the St John's Wood membership has declined from 3,000 to 2,300. This is not only the result of the flight to the suburbs, for many members have always lived far from the synagogue, to which they maintain a sentimental attachment either because their grandparents were founders, or because it is considered chic to belong to the grandest of all the Liberal synagogues. Nevertheless, the majority of those who attend services with any regularity live in St John's Wood or Hampstead. Attendance is seasonal, admits Goldberg: 'Shortly after the High Holy-days it goes down. And during Harrods sale . . .' Jews have always been relatively thin on the ground in south London, so it is not surprising that the catchment area of Rabbi Neuberger's congregation is considerable, ranging from Surrey to Kent. There are even some members who live just north of the river, 'though most people in Fulham and Chelsea go to smarter synagogues. We are a bit trendy now, but we're definitely not smart. We have about 600 members. Membership went through a terrible decline after the Brixton riots. Now it's beginning to pick up again. We don't lose people because they get cheesed off with us. We lose people because they move away. But the synagogue has bred an extraordinary loyalty and people continue to come to it from a long way away.'

Although Liberal Judaism is at the opposite end of the religious spectrum from ultra-Orthodoxy and its diehards would hold views that might make even a Reform rabbi blanch, nevertheless there is far more that unites the two branches of Progressive Judaism than divides them. There are differences in the liturgy, and differences in the approach to prayer and tradition, but their fundamental attitude to Halachah is more or less the

135

same. If there is diversity among the ranks of Progressive Jews, it cannot be any greater than that which pervades mainstream Orthodoxy. In recent years there has been talk of merging the Reform and Liberal organizations. Since 1969 their rabbis have nearly all been trained at the same college and they join forces on many communal matters, so it seems strange that the congregations they serve should remain divided. The difference between them tends to be one of emphasis, rather than dogma. Raymond Goldman of the RSGB puts it this way: 'We would tend to say that tradition is innocent until proved guilty. The Liberals come from the other direction and say of tradition: Okay, persuade us. It's a difference of feel, and something difficult to analyse clearly.' Liberal rabbis have no Beth Din to offer halachic guidelines, and have greater freedom to formulate their own religious views and positions than their Reform colleagues.

One issue, however, does divide the two organizations: the familiar yet fundamental question of Jewish status. Just as the London Beth Din will deny Jewish status to those deemed Jewish by the Reform Beth Din, so too the Reform Beth Din does not recognize as Jewish all those admitted into the ranks of Liberal Judaism. Reform Judaism may not subscribe to Halachah in all its Byzantine intricacies, but it does accept many of its basic rulings, even while it chooses to ignore others. The child of a Jewish mother is Jewish, according to Halachah. Consequently, if a Jewish male marries a non-Jewish female, their offspring will not be Jewish unless their mother converts, and even then a Reform conversion is dismissed as invalid by the Orthodox. The Liberals, however, will accept as Jewish the children of a non-Jewish mother if they have been brought up as Jewish, received some Jewish education and undergone bar- or batmitzvah and confirmation. The leading Liberal Rabbi Sidney Brichto makes the case sharply: 'Whatever the Torah or Talmud says, a modern Jew cannot accept that a child automatically be considered as Jewish if the mother is Jewish, although it was raised as a Catholic in a convent, but automatically not Jewish when only the father was Jewish and it was raised as a Jew.'[1] In practice, this distinction between Reform and Liberal is more blurred, and although they don't publicize the fact too loudly, there are Reform rabbis who take an indulgent attitude towards children who have been brought up as Jews even though they may not be halachically admissible.

Despite this one major difference between the two movements, attempts to merge them have been made. Jonathan Magonet agrees that 'it is totally illogical to have two non-Orthodox movements in this country, because we're in the same camp and involved in the same business and there is some overlap. Logically, logistically, financially, bureaucratically, it's crazy to have two organizations when one would do. What stands in the way is as much the bureaucratic realities, because there's a reluctance on the part of institutions to disappear, which is then rationalized in terms of theology.' Many of the Liberals, perhaps aware of their weakening position as an independent body, were strongly in favour, and the most heated objections came from those whom David Goldberg describes as 'neo-Orthodox Reform rabbis', some of whom threatened to resign if merger took place. 'It foundered', says Goldberg, 'on the objection that a merger would be a dilution of classic principles. Those of us who wanted merger obviously did not want it powerfully enough to overcome the objections. Personalities became involved as well, inevitably. There were too many bureaucrats in both organizations who were obviously very worried about their positions and fought very skilfully. I think in the minds of some Reform people there was a fear of being tainted by excessive Liberalism, and in certain Liberal minds a fear of being tainted by quasi-Orthodoxy. I find it very regrettable personally because we could merge with West London very easily. We have very close cordial relations, the rabbis are personally friendly, the congregants intermarry. But we don't have the power. We have the numbers, but the power now lies in the suburbs.'

According to Rabbi Magonet, 'Merger also didn't work because it bumped into personal issues of Jewish status and conversion. It's also a question of style. Reform is a bit more middle-of-the-road, while the Liberals look back to a time of greater radicalism. In their prayer-books they like to spell out where they stand and we tend to fudge the issue by using traditional forms and fudging the translation a little bit. The Liberals include in the prayer-book new pieces which are more overtly universalist in their sentiments. They don't like the messianic stuff and replace "the Redeemer" with "redemption". They don't like the concept of the resurrection of the dead. They like to be consistent and logical. They don't feel they have to look like they're antique when they're not. If they are going to break with a traditional view, they feel it should be straight up. They also have a shorter service, which is to some extent a blessing. Reform, on the other hand, has tended wherever possible to stick to the traditional formulations and use the translation to indicate alternative options. We retain the language about resurrecting the dead but speak about life beyond death, so we don't pin it down too much. We haven't changed the messianic references. Our styles are dependent on what a previous generation decided. Who knows how they will evolve in the years ahead?'

Rather than merge formally, the two movements decided to work even more closely together. They teamed up their education departments to form the Centre for Jewish Education. A liaison body for students was set up jointly. The lay and religious leaders of both bodies meet formally twice a year, and such contacts may draw them closer together. The latest proposal is for a 'federation'. On both sides there is a recognition that a failure to merge is a confirmation of the increasing fragmentation that riddles Anglo-Jewry. Reform and Liberal decry factionalism, yet cannot free themselves of it. The pressure is on the Liberals more than Reform, for over the past decade liberal membership has remained static at 12,000, while RSGB membership has risen from 33,000 to 42,000.[2]

The fragmentation has been intensified by the decision made in 1988 by the Belsize Square Liberal Synagogue to wave good-bye to the Union of Liberal and Progressive Synagogues. This would be of merely bureaucratic interest were it not for the special character of this congregation. It was founded in the 1930s by German and central European refugees, and was taken under the wing of the Liberals at that time. The founders of the new congregation came mostly from German *Liberal* communities (which were closer in style to Reform than Liberal) who made the understandable error of supposing that British Liberalism was a local variant of their own. However, the association proved convenient both for Belsize Square, which could take advantage of the burial and other amenities offered by the older organization, and for the Liberals, who benefited from the contributions paid by the sizeable new congregation. However, after that accommodation had been reached, the folk at Belsize Square went their own sweet way. They follow the Progressive practice of mixed seating, but use their own prayer-book. To confuse the matter further, their present rabbi, Rodney Mariner, is a member of the Conservative movement, a kind of staging post between Reform and Orthodox that has many more adherents in North America than in Europe.

The European refugees never felt at home among the Anglo-Jewish grandees and the *Ostjuden* and their descendants in the United Synagogue, nor among the radical but arid blandnesses of the English Liberals. So they created a home away from home. In the 1950s when the congregation achieved its highest membership (1,900, now shrunk to

1,300), you were more likely to hear German spoken than English. Belsize Square also provided a communal focus for the many refugees who had settled in the surrounding areas of Hampstead and Swiss Cottage. The congregation was not only European but middle-class and sophisticated; its cultural tone was very marked, and it was not free of a snobbery that looked down on the genial philistinism of much of Anglo-Jewry. Sixty-five per cent of the members today are over sixty-five years old. Many of their children, however, found the essentially European atmosphere of Belsize Square unappealing. If the founders could never wholly shed their attachment to the way of life, secular as well as religious, with which they had grown up, their children could and did. Some have returned to the fold, especially once they had children of their own. A stalwart of the congregation, whose parents were founders, told me: 'I wasn't attracted to Belsize Square initially. I found the atmosphere there heavy-laden, and there were always too many old ladies in fur collars. I even had serious doubts about whether to have my sons barmitzvah. Eventually I did join the synagogue, more, I suppose, to preserve continuity within my family than out of religious zeal. Funnily enough, I've come to admire the kind of Judaism represented here. At Orthodox synagogues I find that only the act of worship sustains the institution. Here we've got music and ceremony and family participation.'

The arrival of Rabbi Mariner six years ago forced the ageing congregation to realize it could not maintain its identity forever. If it were to be no more than a charming anachronism, it was doomed to extinction. So the community made quite successful efforts to attract new members who had no roots in the refugee community. Some of the new recruits live as far away as Watford. According to the rabbi, 'We attract many people who simply enjoy going to synagogue. It's a somewhat bourgeois Christian notion, but they just enjoy the experience of being there, of listening to the music. Their Hebrew tends to be quite good in terms of reading, less good in terms of understanding. The fact that they can still have that sort of service and sit with their family, and the music is good, and they're spared the rabble of the marketplace they associate with the United Synagogue – these are some of the factors that draw them here. When I came to England I found people full of questions. By having prayers in English there was an attempt to understand what it was they were praying. The truth of the matter is that in the end the English became a substitute for the prayer, and by just reading it in unison, it became almost as meaningless as Buddhist prayer. The only way language means something in prayer is if you read it silently in your own time. Reading English together in a community setting is as meaningless as reading Hebrew together in a community setting. To a certain extent the Hebrew is superior because you have a link with other generations and other communities, and at the same time it has a music of its own, a cadence. So I moved from a setting where people understood what they were praying into a congregation that didn't understand but nevertheless felt religious as a result of an experience.'

The old guard, who proved extremely tenacious, have gradually delegated to younger members, thus increasing the chances of survival. The changes have inevitably altered the character of the congregation. One young woman, the daughter of refugees, has mixed feelings: 'There's been an active campaign to bring in new people. But I worry about it. The congregation was built up by the German refugees and that gave it its character. Now our congregation is going all out to attract other people, and although it sounds a terrible thing to say, we're wondering whether we really want to be members of a congregation that's attracting that type of new member. We still feel we're part of an exclusive club. We still consider ourselves Continental. I've chosen Belsize Square not just because I was taken there as a child, nor is it a choice by default. I'm attracted to that German *Liberal* way of practice, and I like the services.' Yet the current rabbi is not only not European, but Australian. In all probability, his remoteness from the origins of the community may have proved a strength – 'We're all outsiders here,' he remarked – and he has had some success in reshaping the congregation into the Conservative mould he favours. Rabbi Mariner is a tall bearded man with a commanding presence, which must stand him in good stead when dealing with some of the dragons at Belsize Square.

'I would class myself as a right-wing Reform rabbi, but I painted myself into a corner by being a Conservative rabbi in a country that really didn't have a Conservative movement. My Conservatism has very much to do with form, in some ways even more than content. It's an attempt to preserve a particular style of Judaism that I felt was in some ways the epitome of civilized response to living in two worlds at the same time. Belsize Square gave me room to manoeuvre because it was frozen in time. There's a tremendous emphasis on music. In some ways it's almost in danger of becoming a museum piece by preserving the nineteenth-century romantic tradition. A Canadian colleague came to our Friday evening service and when I asked him how he liked it, he said: "It's very nice, but you can't listen to *Aida* every week." Well, we do. We have *Aida* every week.'

In terms of the liturgy, the service at Belsize Square is not unlike mainstream Orthodox, and almost all the prayers are recited or sung in Hebrew. The congregation employs a *chazan* with a splendid and express-ive voice, though there are those in the congregation who regard him as too 'florid'. The choir sounds larger than the congregation; it is packed with billowy sopranos and hefty basses. At times the service almost grinds to a halt as the choir lingers lovingly over a succession of cadences. Many references omitted in Progressive prayer-books, such as those to the return to Zion, have been restored by Mariner, sometimes after long grappling with the synagogue's own liturgical committee. He has also insisted that *kashrut* be maintained at all synagogue functions. 'I want the kind of synagogue where any Jew can participate and not feel barred. I'm making two statements: you can do what you like at home, that's your choice, but our type of Judaism is about choices, and that means the choice to do it as well as not to do it.'

– 11 –

Mavericks and others

Sephardi

Although British Sephardim and Ashkenazim have intermarried for nearly three centuries and the Progressive synagogues have long absorbed Jews from both streams, the Sephardi community still maintains its own institutions and identity. The religious leader of the community is known as the Haham, but that position has not been filled for a decade, ever since the then Haham, Rabbi Solomon Gaon, left for the United States. Over the last ten years the leadership of British Sephardim has been divided between Dayan Pinchas Toledano, the head of the Sephardi Beth Din, and Rabbi Dr Abraham Levy, who presides over the two principal Sephardi congregations at Bevis Marks and in Maida Vale, and enjoys the title of Spiritual Head of the Spanish and Portuguese Jews' Congregation. A Board of Elders administers the community, and there are subsidiary organizations that supervise such matters as *kashrut* licensing and burial rites.

The main difference between the Sephardim and Ashkenazim is liturgical. While the services are very similar in terms of their structure, the features that give them their character are very different: the prayer-book, the pronunciation, the melodies, and a certain stately feel to the flow of prayer. With so many Sephardi communities flourishing independently in parts of the world as diverse as Turkey, Portugal, Aden, and India, it is not surprising that even within the basic Sephardi *minhag* or rite there are strong local flavourings. Their religious leaders tend to adopt a less rigorous approach to halachic interpretation, and British Sephardim are spared the religious fanaticism that has crept into many ultra-Orthodox Ashkenazi communities. Medieval Spain was at times virtually adminis-

142

tered by its Jews, who were largely responsible for the golden age of Spain in terms of its culture, its learning, and its worldly sophistication. That influence did not spring from a tradition of inward-looking religious self-absorption and casuistry. The Sephardim never saw any contradiction between their religious code and participation in the secular world. After the expulsions of the Jews from Spain in 1492 and Portugal in 1497, the hundreds of thousands of Jews who fled fanned out into a new diaspora, settling as far afield as North Africa and Greece and the Middle East. Inevitably, as the centuries passed, they took on the colouring and trappings of their host cultures. I well recall attending the barmitzvah of a schoolfriend of mine who came from a Sephardi family. At the festivities the following evening, his relatives from Morocco and Algeria, who had flown over for the occasion, put on a display of singing and dancing that, one could have been mistaken for thinking, had far more in common with a Bedouin knees-up than with any specifically Jewish merrymaking.

No one knows how many Sephardi Jews live in Britain since only a small proportion of families is formally enrolled at the Congregation's synagogues. In many Oriental synagogues there was no such thing as membership; the expenses of the synagogue and its upkeep were met by the wealthiest members of the community. Consequently, many Oriental Jews still feel it is unnecessary to join a synagogue and pay their dues. The current estimate assesses the population at about 40,000, the vast majority of whom live in London or Manchester. While Anglo-Jewry as a whole is slowly shrinking, it's possible that the Sephardi community is actually growing, since many Jewish immigrants over the past twenty years or so have come from Sephardi enclaves. New arrivals from Iraq and Iran, from Morocco and Aden, are all Sephardim. A number of small congregations cater specifically to these groups; in Stamford Hill, for example, tucked among the Chasidic *shtieblach*, is a Persian synagogue in which services are conducted by *chazanim* according to three different Sephardi traditions: Persian, Israeli, and Moroccan. A synagogue catering to Turkish and Greek Jews has opened its doors in Holland Park, and this is one of the few places in London where one can still hear Ladino, the medieval vernacular language of Spanish Jewry, spoken. The Spanish and Portuguese Jews' Congregation formally consists only of the congregations at Bevis Marks and in Maida Vale and Wembley, but most of the splinter synagogues are affiliated to the Congregation so as to take advantage of such facilities as cemeteries.

The Ashkenazim have a mental picture of Sephardim as a collection of

City gents, rich grandees, worldly and aloof. In fact, the Sephardim have been just as socially diverse as their east and central European brethren. The marriage register kept at Bevis Marks through the nineteenth century lists the occupations of the bridegrooms. At one end of the social scale are the hawkers, the tailors, the fruit traders, the butchers, and at the other the cigar merchants, the diamond traders, and the stockbrokers. It was certainly true that many of the most distinguished Victorian Jews were of Sephardi descent – Benjamin Disraeli, Sir Moses Montefiore, the Mocattas – but so too were numerous working-class Jews. Although many Victorian grandee families have assimilated and are scarcely identifiable as Jewish any longer, there is still, as a visit to Bevis Marks over the High Holydays will make clear, a handful of well-to-do merchants and brokers at the core of the Sephardi community.

Nor are the recent immigrants impoverished. Many saw the danger signs in their native countries, notably Iran and Iraq, well in time and were able to emigrate with most, and in some cases all, of their wealth and possessions. Those without riches and useful connections, and there were hundreds of thousands in that less fortunate position, tended to make their way not to Britain or North America but to Israel, where they could be certain of a warm welcome and an absence of obstructive immigration officers. Just like most other rich newcomers to Britain, the prosperous Oriental Jews who came here have made themselves at home in the most fashionable corners of London, in Mayfair and Kensington, and those with a yearning for suburban life tend to live in Mill Hill. It has not always been easy to persuade many of these immigrants to become part of the Congregation. A disused synagogue in Maida Vale, complete with an Oriental *chazan* from Israel, is now being used by the Iraqi community on High Holydays. The Iraqis, with prominent exceptions such as Dr Davide Sala, do not play much of a part in communal affairs. An Elder lamented to me that 'the Iraqis are not terribly public-spirited, on the whole. Some give large sums of money, but from the point of view of going to synagogue I think they're terribly disappointing.'

The Sephardi community in Britain is both more cohesive and more fragmented than its Ashkenazi counterpart. More cohesive, because there was never such a thing as a Reform movement within the community and most Sephardi Jews accept the same standards of observance, whether or not they adhere to them. More fragmented, because the community is comprised of so many national groups. Rabbi Levy doubts that there is any other synagogue in the country with as diverse a congregation as his at

Maida Vale: 'Among our membership of 1,110, we have Jews from at least eighteen different countries: Iraq, Iran, Egypt, Syria, Morocco, Algeria, Gibraltar, India, you name it. It's not easy, for example, to give a sermon to someone whose family has been here for 300 years and to someone sitting next to him whose family arrived just a year ago.' He himself was born in Gibraltar, though he was educated in England at Carmel College and Jews' College. He is glad, however, to be spared the factionalism that mars the Ashkenazi synagogues: 'I don't like the word Orthodox. Orthodox only came into being as a concept when Reform started. The beauty of the Sephardi way was that with a little bit more tolerance and flexibility we managed to keep Jewry as one entity, and that's something we are very proud of.'

Dr Levy's London congregations retain a distinctively Sephardi ambience. In some of the grander United Synagogue congregations, the wardens and other lay dignitaries wear top hats during services. At Bevis Marks and Maida Vale, many ordinary members of the congregation do so too. The formality – some call it starchiness – of the services is reflected in other ways. Those called up for readings of the Torah are, as they return to their seats, congratulated on this *mitzvah* by their friends in the congregation. In Ashkenazi synagogues this takes the form of a simple shaking of hands. In these Sephardi synagogues the men exchange deep bows, directing them first at the wardens, then at other senior members of the congregation, and finally at friends who catch their eye. Choirs – male, of course, since Sephardim separate the sexes – are not hidden away in galleries, but ranged in ranks behind the desks on the *bima*. These Sephardi choirs manage to make a great deal of noise in relation to their relatively small numbers. No choirs will be found in the smaller congregations of mostly Oriental Jews in North London; they dispense with the ancient melodies and their services are conducted in a kind of drone.

It is always a joy to visit Bevis Marks, for it is not only the oldest synagogue in the country but easily the most beautiful. Huge brass chandeliers hang over the chamber, giving it the air of a ballroom. The ladies' gallery is concealed by a heavily latticed screen; all the fittings, the pews and panelling and screens, are stately and elegant. It is a most lovely setting for the elusive mixture of decorum and informality that constitutes a Jewish service. The publisher and novelist Anthony Blond, who attends Bevis Marks, remarks: 'When they march round with the scroll I always go forward to touch it, and I always cry. I'm moved by Jewish ritual, although it appears to many Gentiles to be uncannily easy and chatty and disrespectful. But I find it much more godly than the most ecstatic service in a cathedral.'

The Federation of Synagogues
When, just over a century ago, Samuel Montagu reorganized the chaotic jumble of East End *shtieblach* into the Federation of Synagogues, he was hoping to bring a dose of orderliness to the traditional forms of worship brought over by the immigrants without forcing them into the Anglo-Jewish mould of the United Synagogue. Through force of personality and abundant cash, he succeeded. When, after the Second World War, many East End families moved into the suburbs, it could have been the end of the road for the Federation. However, the synagogues eventually transplanted themselves along with their congregations, and today the most vibrant Federation synagogues are to be found in suburbs such as Ilford, Edgware, Finchley, and Golders Green. Despite the passionate loyalty of many Federation families, its numbers are not growing, and its membership stands at no more than 8,000. Many Federation members, on moving to the suburbs, joined the United synagogues already long established there, and in some cases the Federation was slow to set up new suburban congregations and continued to act as though the Jewish East End was still a community with a future.

Most Federation congregations are not only nominally Orthodox, but genuinely so, and the level of observance among their membership is probably higher than in comparable United Synagogue congregations. The disputes that divide Reform from Liberal, and Reform from United, and United from the Chasidim, do not trouble the Federation in its relations with the United Synagogue, and there seems no reason why the two organizations should not merge. The Federation is an anachronism, an accident of historical circumstances that decades ago ceased to have any significance. There is no reason, of course, why the Federation should lose its identity and the character of its congregations if it doesn't want to. What does seem absurd is the conscious attempt this relatively small and shrinking band of synagogues continues to make to set itself apart from the United Synagogue, with which it has so much in common.

In 1966 the Federation established its own Beth Din, and its own London Kashrus Board, a development that the Federation's official historian, Dr Geoffrey Alderman, has described as an 'unqualified success', though to me it seems yet another lamentable example of the fragmentation of Anglo-Jewry. At the same time the Federation established its own body to supervise religious education, yet another instance of needless duplication. The overwhelmingly elderly gentlemen who have run the Federation for decades still refuse to allow their female members any say in the management of synagogues. Even the Chief Rabbi – admittedly the Federation do not grant him any religious authority over their members – sees no reason why female members of the United Synagogue should not enjoy full voting rights, and he is no feminist. But his view is too liberal for the Federation, and they are the only synagogal grouping affiliated to the Board of Deputies whose representatives are not only exclusively male, but elected by an exclusively male body.

Supporters of the Federation argue that diversity and choice are no bad thing. Yet fractiousness is surely to be deplored. The Federation's institutions regularly come into conflict with their counterparts within the more powerful United Synagogue. Even within its own institutions, such as its *kashrut* board, quarrelling seems to be a way of life. In May 1988 a *dayan* of the Federation Beth Din was dismissed after he criticized the standards of *kashrut* at some catering firms and restaurants under Federation supervision. A committee of Federation rabbis then attempted to investigate this matter, but were denied standing by their own Beth Din. In the meantime, some of those institutions licensed by the Federation's *kashrut* board applied instead for licences from the London Beth Din, thus adding an inter-synagogal dimension to the row. The two Bloom's restaurants covered their bets by obtaining licences from both. The two *kashrut* boards do not always recognize the validity of each other's licensing procedures, and United synagogues are supposed to employ only caterers licensed by the London Beth Din. The Federation threatened to retaliate by refusing to allow caterers authorized by the London Beth Din to provide food and services at Federation synagogues. Abraham Levy put the whole silly business into perspective by simply stating on behalf of the Sephardi group: 'We will allow any caterer in any of our establishments who is under a recognized supervising authority.'

Attempts have been made over the years to merge the United Synagogue and the Federation, since their leaders acknowledge that on the important matters of belief and practice there is little distinction between them. No Federation member would baulk at worshipping in a United synagogue, and vice versa. Rabbi Alan Plancey feels strongly that the two organizations should join forces: 'There's no need for duplication whatsoever. Because it's the same service, the same burial, the same *kashrus*. It's because everyone wants to be president.' Indeed, each time the leaders of the two bodies make cooing noises at each other, another daft row erupts to sour the mood. In the end it is a question of control. As in the case of the Liberal and Reform merger talks, bureaucracies do not voluntarily relinquish control. Organizations do not vote themselves out of existence unless there is a compelling reason for them to do so. Neither do individuals, and the Federation has been run for decades by the formidable Morris Lederman, who is unwilling to give the impression of being pushed around by anyone, whether inside or outside his organiz-ation. The compelling reason that will surely force the Federation to come to some kind of accommodation with the United Synagogue is likely to be the continuing evaporation of its ageing membership.

New London Synagogue

If the disputes between the Federation and the United Synagogue can only induce a feeling of impatience, another blazing row of the 1960s exerted a greater intellectual fascination. Orthodox rabbis supposedly believe that the Torah was literally dictated to Moses on Mount Sinai, lock, stock, and barrel, and that later accretions of Jewish law are divinely inspired. Whether many rabbis outside the ultra-Orthodox community actually believe this fundamentalist line it is hard to say, for it would not be politic for them to chip away at this central pillar of Orthodoxy. It's certain that many of the new recruits to the United Synagogue rabbinate, *yeshiva*-trained rabbis such as Shlomo Levin, do hold fundamentalist views, but I doubt very much that rabbis of an older generation, now dismissed as 'middle-of-the-road', would have subscribed to it.

Most of them, if they did indeed entertain revisionist views, kept them to themselves. With one notable exception. Louis Jacobs is the very model of a rabbi. Seated in his study, flanked by enormous bookcases crammed with row upon row of tall Hebrew folios, he exudes quiet authority. Now in his late sixties, Rabbi Jacobs has a bleary-eyed look, as though he routinely sits up half the night poring over Talmudic commentaries. The appearance of weariness is undercut by his distinctly Mancunian twang. His story, as he tells it, is straightforward enough. 'I was the minister of the New West End Synagogue in Petersburg Place. I left there in 1959 to go to Jews' College as moral tutor, but it was understood that when the then principal retired, as he was about to do, I would become the principal – otherwise I wouldn't have left the New West End. It didn't work out because the Chief Rabbi, Israel Brodie, vetoed my appointment as principal. Then I was invited back to the New West End, and the Chief

Rabbi vetoed that as well. The people of the New West End Synagogue came almost *en masse* and we founded the New London Synagogue. I favoured a non-fundamentalist approach to the Jewish tradition. I believed that one could be an observant Jew but at the same time be open to questions of biblical criticism.'

Even before Rabbi Jacobs took up the post as moral tutor at Jews' College, he had attracted attention as the author of some mildly controversial books on Jewish theology. One might have been forgiven for supposing that this was a positive qualification for an academic post, but the Anglo-Jewish Establishment thought otherwise and were clearly horrified by his suggestion that the Torah should not always be read literally. Some delicate constitutional issues were touched upon when his reappointment to the New West End was vetoed, since a clear majority of its members favoured the return of their former rabbi. Who was to have the final say: the synagogue and its board of management, or the Chief Rabbi and his associates in high places within the United Synagogue, notably Sir Isaac Wolfson? From this impasse no clear resolution, no compromise, could be devised, and when the United Synagogue sought to sack the entire board of management of the New West End, the secession of the synagogue became inevitable. The position of the United Synagogue appears to have been that if you couldn't personally subscribe to the view that the Torah was dictated by God to Moses on Mount Sinai (which Rabbi Jacobs cannot accept, for very sound reasons), then you should keep your mouth shut. Rabbi Jacobs preferred to be intellectually honest, and paid the price.

The maverick congregation, based in St John's Wood at the New London Synagogue, has thrived for over twenty years. It has acquired a membership of about 1,000 souls, and there are additional associated communities in Finchley (with 300 families as members), Edgware, Ilford, and South London. Visitors to the New London cannot mistake the service for a Progressive form of worship. Women are still seated up in the gallery at New London (though at some satellite congregations women and men sit together), Rabbi Jacobs still chants the Torah in a distinctly unmelodious drone, and there are few differences between his form of service and that to be found in the United Synagogue which the Chief Rabbi attends a few hundred yards away. 'Most of our founder members', explains Louis Jacobs, 'came from the New West End, which was one of the United synagogues, although it was a bit unconventional, and we simply adopted its pattern of services. Now we are one of the few congregations in which the old Anglo-Jewish traditional pattern of service is preserved, so some people may come to the New London for that reason. We have a mixed choir, we don't repeat the *Musaf* [the additional service for the Sabbath], and there's decorum. I think we have an intellectual congregation, and there are still a few who are really sold on the idea of a non-fundamentalist approach to Jewish tradition. Last Shabbat, for example, I said that the modern way of looking at Noah's Ark is as a myth, but that doesn't mean it's not of value. And some members of the congregation said that it's good to be independent because you could say such a thing, whereas in other synagogues you couldn't. I was a bit disillusioned at this, because I'd have thought that after twenty-four years it wouldn't be terribly daring to say what I did, but that is the situation.'

At the time that the row erupted, the shift of power within the United Synagogue from the old guard to the immigrants' descendants had recently taken place. Although Rabbi Jacobs himself is no grandee, many in his fashionable Bayswater congregation were from older families, and deeply resented being pushed around by the new boys from the United Synagogue. If Louis Jacobs, unquestionably one of the most distinguished Talmudic scholars in Britain, wasn't good enough for the United Synagogue, then the United Synagogue evidently wasn't good enough for them. 'The difference between the New London and the United', according to Sir Monty Finniston, one of Louis Jacobs' ardent supporters, 'doesn't appear in the Bible, and it doesn't appear in the way the service is conducted. It appears in what Louis Jacobs thinks. He doesn't believe that the Bible was written once and for all on Mount Sinai, but he believes in the faith, he believes in one God. He believes all kinds of things, which of course as a scientist I have to tell you I'm rather hesitant about. It all comes down to the rabbi. They like him. Who thinks like him? I do, but I'm not a rabbi.'

In fact there are others who think like the rabbi. Louis Jacobs is a member of the Conservative movement, which is strongest in North America, and thus he has much in common, theologically, with other Conservatives in Britain such as Rodney Mariner of Belsize Square. Both men hold similar views on religious observance. Says Louis Jacobs: 'I've always taken the line that in the synagogue itself we are strictly observant. We wouldn't have a non-kosher *Kiddush* and we would keep the Sabbath strictly in synagogue. What people do in their private lives is a matter for them but I've always stressed the idea of a ladder reaching to heaven. I look upon Judaism as a quest. I'll encourage greater observance, of course, provided it rings a bell. I wouldn't be in favour of mechanical observance, just to be "respectable". I would stress the value elements of it, not the dogmatic elements.' Colin Shindler, editor of the *Jewish Quarterly*, believes that the appeal of Jacobs is his emphasis on the compassionate nature of Judaism and its relevance to modern life: 'Louis Jacobs is privately respected by many who shun him publicly. Many ordinary Jews feel that he has been treated shabbily by less worthy figures. And many Jews from traditional backgrounds find it difficult to relate to the contemporary leadership which purports to represent mainstream Orthodoxy, but are also uncomfortable with Reform or Liberal. Louis Jacobs provides the focus for a convergence of tradition and enlightenment.'

The furore over Rabbi Jacobs marked the end of the cosy accommodations of mainstream Orthodoxy within Anglo-Jewry. From the time of his resignation until the present day, the United Synagogue has moved steadily to the religious right, even if that means it often leaves its levy-paying membership shuffling behind in an embarrassed mumble of lip service rather than observance. Louis Jacobs is a thinking man's rabbi; much like any Orthodox rabbi, he conducts weekly *shiurim* on the Talmud during the winter months. His scholarly reputation and his courage and honesty have earned him the respect of rabbis with very different views. It probably doesn't help his cause, but Rabbi David Goldberg of the Liberal Synagogue told me: 'Louis Jacobs is my ideal. He's my exemplar of what a Jew can achieve as a citizen of a diaspora country. In other words, he is totally immersed in his Jewish sources, voluminously knowledgeable about that, yet equally at home in the general culture.'

Yakar
If Rabbi Louis Jacobs was an irritant to the United Synagogue twenty-five years ago, his role of gadfly and maverick has been taken in the late 1980s by Rabbi Michael Rosen of Yakar. The two men are very different, and I am sure there are many issues on which they disagree. What they have in common is a personal following from many people who feel disenchanted with the Establishment. Rosen is the director of Yakar, an institution that provides Jewish cultural and educational facilities. Although Rosen describes himself as Orthodox, events and discussions at Yakar are open to all, to non-believers as much as to practising Jews. There is also a synagogue on the premises, a small hall that becomes crowded on the Sabbath and could easily be mistaken for a Stamford Hill *shtiebl*. United

synagogues tend to be quiet and ill attended until about 9.45 or 10 on the Sabbath. Most congregants understandably prefer to limit their attendance at worship to two hours rather than the full three hours or more. I assumed Yakar would be much the same, and strolled in at 10.

The hall had been divided in two by a tall lacy curtain, and I could dimly make out the blurred silhouettes of the women behind the curtain. As in an ultra-Orthodox synagogue, the space was filled with oblong tables scattered with prayer-books. I found a seat, though many in the congregation were standing and davening with great intensity, their shoulders and even their heads swathed in their *tallit*. The ark was up on the stage, but the service was being led by Rosen from a reading desk placed in a corner. The hubbub was tremendous, the counterpoint of mumbling, declaiming, and chanting that denotes Jews at prayer. Then, just a few minutes after I'd arrived, it all stopped and the men began to remove their *tallit* and make their way towards the exit.

It is the custom at Yakar to start the service punctually at 9 and break for *Kiddush* and a *shiur* for an hour or so. The idea is to bring the congregation together in a sociable atmosphere during the service rather than after it, and also to expound and discuss the portion for the day. 'The point of the *shiurim*,' Rosen explained to me, 'is to inform us about what we're doing in *shul*. After the *shiurim* we go back to prayer.' Because of the numbers, there were two *shiurim* held simultaneously, and I attended the rabbi's. Rosen began it in characteristic fashion: 'I'm not terribly interested in this morning's *sidrah*, which gives the instructions for building the tabernacle. That doesn't inspire me much. All I have to say on the subject is a general observation that religious ritual is justified because it involves us physically in prayer, and the danger of such ritual is that it involves us only and merely in a physical way.'

So he talked instead about the uprising of the Palestinians on the West Bank. Rosen was concerned to discuss the problem from a moral standpoint, since we were in a synagogue and not at a political meeting. He referred to a letter from a young soldier which expressed the following dilemma: if ordered to beat an Arab suspect, should he disobey the order (which he would not have approved of), or execute the order on the grounds that the beating he would give would be less ferocious than that dished out by his fellow soldiers? When the discussion broadened into a more general discussion of Israeli policy and someone expressed the view that the government had no alternative, Rosen, with some impatience, intervened: 'We must beware when politicians make statements saying there is no alternative. It's the job of politicians to find alternatives. That's the whole art of politics, to find solutions to difficult problems. To say there is no alternative is a way of absolving oneself from having to think.' Returning to the question of using force against one's enemies, Rosen expounded the halachic view: religious law does give Jews the right to strike first if they feel they are in danger of death, but only if there is no alternative way of dealing with the threat. At this point others interrupted to say that this was precisely the situation in Israel, but Rosen disagreed.

This *shiur* at Yakar is not typical of the form. By discussing topics that were deeply controversial, dissension was inevitable. Moreover, Rabbi Rosen has the irritating habit of inviting comments and then immediately interrupting anyone who takes him up on the offer. Considerable heat was generated, not only by those who disagreed with Rosen's views, but from those whose arguments were truncated by the rabbi's short attention span. After a lively half hour, we all trooped downstairs again to the synagogue, divided ourselves according to gender, and resumed the service, with Rosen taking a back seat while other congregants led the service and read from the Torah. Like Shlomo Levin, he moved around the congregation, sitting in different places, exchanging a few words with everyone. To-wards the end, he leapt on to the stage to deliver a brief sermon, in which no allusion was made to Israel or politics.

Rosen is an unusual figure, an Orthodox rabbi with radical views. His father was Rabbi Kopul Rosen, the head of Carmel College, the only Jewish public school; Kopul Rosen was widely thought to be in line for the chief rabbinate, but died in 1962 before the expectation could be tested. His two sons, Michael and Jeremy, are both rabbis. Michael Rosen is a slight figure with a greying beard and thick-lensed glasses. Resolutely independent, he never hesitates to open his mouth, in or out of turn, and say what he thinks. Tact does not feature highly on his list of virtues. With independent views rarely expressed by those in high places in Anglo-Jewry, his forthrightness commands respect. He is highly critical of the ultra-Orthodox reactionaries, but has equally slight patience for the formalities of mainstream Orthodoxy. 'In a community which is over-structured, it's imperative to be as independent as possible. I'm Orthodox. I went to *yeshiva*. For Orthodoxy, Halachah is binding. That's a reason-ably objective criterion of Orthodoxy. Halachah is binding for me. But I believe the Orthodoxy that Anglo-Jewry receives is spiritually stultifying. One sees very little spirituality in this country. One sees the form without the real pulsating inner life, the holistic harmony.

'If you wanted a Jewish world where you felt there was an inner life, you would probably be in a group that you felt was not in the twentieth century. They might be admirable from a spiritual angle, but they would have opted out from the mainstream of cultural life . Of course, you can be out of twentieth-century cultural life and still not be into spirituality either! Myself, I'm after something spiritually intense, in the best sense of the word, within the twentieth century. I find it a perversion that somehow Orthodoxy should be identified with being a zombie, with someone who doesn't ask questions and has to keep his head down and do what he does because it's tradition. That might be the main Orthodox world, but it's definitely not mine. Faith is not an excuse for not thinking. Faith might be sensitivity beyond intellect but you can't use that to evade the issue.

'I'm not worried about disturbing the life of the middle-of-the-road Jew. It's just that I think it can be done in a far better way. My concern is that the image of Torah is not being projected correctly – because the message conveyed is one of halachic strictness and a sort of narrowness and antagonism. Orthodoxy's assertiveness has not really manifested itself in terms of spirituality, but in terms of learning and halachic behaviour. Meanwhile beauty, warmth, inner life, harmony – all that goes by the board.'

Battle lines: a polarized community

H AVE you heard the one about the shipwrecked man on a desert island? A devout Jew, he managed to construct a small synagogue from branches and driftwood. A year later he was rescued, and just as he was leaving the island his rescuers asked him about another small structure a mile down the beach. 'Oh that,' he replied scornfully, 'that's the *other* synagogue. That's the one I wouldn't be seen dead in.'

Jews have always been contentious. For those learned in the Torah, disputation and argument are a way of life. In recent years, however, the debate has become not only more vociferous but distinctly hostile. The buzz word among Anglo-Jewry today is 'polarization'. You'll hear it from the Orthodox and you'll hear it from the Progressives. You can read it every Friday in the *Jewish Chronicle* alongside choice examples of the phenomenon itself, notably in the correspondence columns. British Jews are no longer content to muddle along; now they feel they have to fight their corner – only their opponents are not the *goyim*, but other Jews. In a community that is slowly shrinking, there is a desire on the part of each synagogal group to increase its market share. In my youth which synagogue you attended was largely a matter of personal preference. That my father joined the United Synagogue and his brother the Belsize Square Liberal Synagogue had less to do with religious conviction, always in short supply in my family, than with the personalities of individual rabbis. Liberal, Reform, United, we all attended barmitzvahs and weddings at each other's synagogues and sipped the same sickly Israeli wines over *Kiddush* in the synagogue halls.

This easy-going attitude may still prevail in many sections of the

155

community. By no means all British Jews are constantly at each other's throats. But a good many are. A note of fanaticism and intolerance has crept into the debates between the different branches of Judaism, with attempts being made to deny the legitimacy of those groups the arguer doesn't support. The debate no longer has to do with style or preference or even belief, but with control and power. Although periodic attempts are made to find common ground, they have met with no success, and if anything the divisions are exacerbated with each year that passes. There are those who ascribe the polarization to the rise of extremism in most of the world's religions. Fanaticism and intolerance are not unique to modern Judaism. Islam is factionalized, and issues such as the ordination of women may yet cause a schism within that most placid of religious institutions, the Church of England. There may be some validity to such global explanations, but the principal cause of the animosity between Jews of different persuasions is none other than our old friend, Jewish status. Fifty years ago it wasn't much of an issue. You were Jewish if your mother was Jewish, and if you wished to convert to Judaism, for whatever reason, no major obstacles were put in the way of a sincere application. But with the establishment of the State of Israel, Jewish status became a central issue within the new state and rippled out into the diaspora. Israel was a secular state, but its identity was largely defined by religion. The new state felt obliged to allow the religious rather than the civil authorities to deal with, for example, the institution of marriage. If matters relating to status were kept in the hands of the secular authorities, then there was a danger that a situation would develop in which two parallel communities, one sanctioned by the secular branch and the other by the religious branch, could come into being and remain separated. By handing this matter over to the religious authorities, such a split could be avoided. The price paid for this move was an increase in ill feeling between Orthodox and Reform rabbis, who did not always agree on Jewish status. The Orthodox rabbinate, for the first time in modern history, exercised political power, and not only through representation in the Knesset; for the conferring of full rights as an Israel citizen was conditional on rabbinical validation of Jewish status. When the Falashas, the Ethiopian Jews, were airlifted to Israel in the mid-1980s, the rabbinate initially questioned whether they were in fact authentically Jewish. The Ethiopians believed themselves to be Jewish, they observed many Jewish rites and practices, but the rabbis weren't so sure. Their doubts affected not only the Falashas' religious status but their political status too.

156

This recent taste of power by Israel's Orthodox rabbinate has also affected British Jewry, as Rabbi Jonathan Magonet explains: 'Thirty years ago Anglo-Jewry was a backwater. People would argue and fight and there were fanatics at both ends of the spectrum, but it didn't really matter. Orthodoxy had no power-base and wasn't significant. With the rise of the power of Orthodoxy within Israel, the Orthodox elsewhere gained in self-confidence. The issue of who is a Jew and who determines who is a Jew is seen in terms of Reform versus Orthodox. What we're seeing is the Orthodox establishment of Israel versus the secular state of Israel, versus Progressive Judaism, and also, ultimately, versus any other Orthodox community that has the *chutzpah* to suggest that they can determine Jewish status. There's a move towards centralizing all power within the Israeli rabbinate. So the stakes have suddenly shot up. Jewish status is the only area where Halachah has sanctions. Every other bit of Halachah – defining how you tie your shoelaces to how you build your *mikveh* – can be determined by an internal group. If you don't want to follow those rules, no one can make you. The whole private arena doesn't matter any more. But the one area where rabbis have power still is status: who is married, who is not, who is Jewish, who is not. And that is the issue over which everything is being fought.'

This has made the Orthodox more aggressive in their relations with Progressive Judaism, while Reform and Liberal Jews themselves become more provocative in defence of what they see as their legitimacy. Moreover, the values of Orthodoxy are increasingly presented as the norm. With the remarkable growth in Jewish education in Britain, more and more children find themselves exposed to Orthodox views and values at their schools. Only one Jewish school in Britain is under Progressive supervision; all the others are monitored by Orthodox rabbis of varying degrees of severity. Not all the parents who send their children to Jewish schools are devout – far from it. Many parents choose Jewish schools because they offer better secular education than other schools in their area. Nevertheless, the upshot of sending your children to Jewish schools is that you may find yourself at the receiving end of a good deal of pressure to bring your own standards of observance roughly into line with those advocated by the school.

The religious control of the Orthodox synagogues, including the United, is firmly in traditionalist hands. The London Beth Din and the Chief Rabbi himself have no truck with the easy-going, mildly observant nominal Orthodoxy of fifty years ago. The line between Orthodox and

157

ultra-Orthodox has grown thinner year by year, and it is hard to avoid the impression that the United Synagogue is scrambling to keep up as the ultra-Orthodox slog their way up the steep slopes of the True Way. Middle-of-the-road Orthodox may be fighting a losing battle if only because Jews' College is no longer producing rabbis in their own likeness, or not in sufficient quantities. Many United Synagogue rabbis are trained at *yeshivot* and bring a much more combative style of Judaism to their pulpits and congregations. Memories of the Holocaust are a perpetual reminder to the Orthodox that they came close to extinction, and this has made them more strident in pressing their views. As Geoffrey Paul, the editor of the *Jewish Chronicle*, puts it, the Orthodox are no longer disposed to recognize Progressive Judaism as another way into Jewish life, but instead dismiss it as a way that leads out of Judaism altogether. As the Reform movement gathers strength, it is increasingly perceived as the enemy by defenders of the true faith. Some Jews, weary of the bickering, have turned to independent congregations such as Yakar or the New London Synagogue. With even the Reform and Liberal synagogues unable to agree on a merger, the hopes for reconciliation between Progressive and Orthodox Jews seem, to put it at its most optimistic, negligible.

The Chief Rabbi doesn't regard reconciliation as an achievable goal. He distinguishes between the fragmentation within Orthodoxy and the rift between Orthodoxy and Progressive Judaism. Orthodox groups, whatever their flavour, whether Chasidic or Federation or Adath, 'are all bound by the same law and acknowledge the same discipline. These distinctions are merely formal, organizational, or institutional – and sometimes personal – but not in terms of outlook. We pray in each other's houses of worship, eat in each other's homes, marry each other, and so on. I don't see anything unhealthy in the fact that we have our distinct Chasidic communities. It's enriched Jewish life. Anglo-Jewry is to my mind excessively preoccupied with the unity theme. But when you come to the non-Orthodox part of the community, that's a different matter. Here we differ both on fundamental beliefs and fundamental practices. There will never be a reconciliation. What I did on assuming office was to say that in areas where they have chosen to opt out or dissent, we cannot work together. Joint services we cannot have. On education we cannot join together, because what they teach is not what I teach. But on matters where these differences do not impinge – Jewish defence, Jewish-Christian relations, support for Israel – there we can work together.

I'm concerned to preserve the oneness of the Jewish people, not its unity.'

If you wish to put the best face on the situation, you may speak of religious pluralism. If you are more hard-headed, you will talk of fragmentation or polarization. The divisions do not only affect the religious preoccupations of Anglo-Jewry, they also impinge on its secular institutions. Welfare agencies, such as Norwood Child Care in London (patron HM The Queen), aid impoverished families in areas such as Stamford Hill, but have found that the ultra-Orthodox Establishment, despite a good sprinkling of multi-millionaires in its midst, is less than eager to contribute to such agencies, which serve the entire Jewish community without regard to religious affiliation. Nevertheless, it is true, as the Chief Rabbi said, that many other groups such as those campaigning for Soviet Jewry are unaffected by religious differences. On the other hand, Zionist groups, those hotbeds of pointless wrangling, are very much affected by the power struggle between Orthodox and Progressive. Jonathan Magonet explains: 'Four years ago the Reform and Liberal lobby tried to create a power-base within the Zionist set-up. They failed in those elections, but next time they won a desk. Why is that important? It's because desks are allotted according to the number of votes you get within the Zionist institutions. Who controls a particular desk – and we won education – gets Zionist money with which to control education and fund institutions. Before 1987, an Orthodox man was in control, and he wouldn't hand out any money to Reform institutions. Now our man is behind that desk, and this time it's the Orthodox who are anxious about who's going to get the money.'

There are many within the Anglo-Jewish Establishment who view this polarization with bewildered dismay. William Frankel, who edited the *Jewish Chronicle* from 1958 to 1977, recalls 'Chief Rabbi Hertz attending Reform and Liberal synagogues, on occasions not wearing a *yarmulke*. That would be inconceivable today. Hertz saw the United Synagogue in terms of Progressive Conservatism, but his own ideas changed after his daughter married a right-wing [in the religious sense] rabbi. And the community as a whole was influenced by the immigration after the war of comparatively large numbers of Chasidim and other ultra-right-wingers. At first they went off to Stamford Hill and did their own thing and didn't impinge much on the community. But in the course of time some of them became more successful and more assertive, and the Lubavitch Foundation started up. Everything came to a head during the Louis

Jacobs controversy, because that forced people to take up positions. Although it was a personal issue, it dramatized and gave a focus to what had been happening. I myself was very much on Jacobs' side.

'In the end the authority of the right-wing Establishment was maintained. But in the sense of trends, of who gains people's minds, I think the result was that there were quite a lot of people who saw the direction in which mainstream Orthodoxy was going. The results still aren't completely visible, as so many people are locked into the United Synagogue system because of burial rights, and it will take some time before that factor disappears. Not that I believe the individuals have become more Orthodox. But the institutions have. I see the situation not so much as a polarization than as a concentration of Judaism among the extreme Orthodox. Jews who join Reform and Liberal – many of them are very sincere about it – may have theological views but they don't have the zeal of the extremists. There isn't the same drive for perpetuation in Progressive circles. It's more gentlemanly, more toned down.'

I'm not sure how accurate that analysis is. Although rabbis are always anxious to assert how splendidly their own congregations toe the line, I don't doubt that the level of Jewish observance among many individuals within mainstream Orthodoxy has increased. Others have resisted the tug to the right and either hold their peace or have slipped away to join other congregations, just as William Frankel is now a member of the New London Synagogue. Despite calls for reconciliation, that doesn't seem to be on the cards, and the vituperative tone of much of the wrangling can be positively shocking. 'The nastiness of the argument here', suggests Rabbi Magonet, 'has to do with ignorance. The villains are all externalized and there's no self-criticism and no understanding. We dance on the graves of Auschwitz. We use the dead to score points.'

The current editor of the *Jewish Chronicle*, Geoffrey Paul, in an important lecture given to an audience of forty at the St John's Wood United synagogue, expressed his dismay at what is happening, and urged Jews from all sections of the community to respect each other's beliefs. Now that a scrutiny of family documents can lead the Beth Din to rule that a passionately anticipated marriage will not be acceptable in their eyes, many young people have to leave the community in order to marry and remain together. 'Can we', asks Mr Paul, reminding us that Anglo-Jewry is shrinking year by year, 'afford to cast off part of our strength so lightly?' Recalling that throughout the many centuries of Jewish history, learned rabbis have managed to solve seemingly intractable problems 'by following the spirit of Judaism rather than the letter' – even bastards have been absolved of their bastardy under certain circumstances, despite the legal strictures against them – surely, he argued, it should be possible for modern rabbis to apply halachic law in order to preserve the oneness of the Jewish people. He recalled that in his grandfather's day, membership of the Jewish community was extended to all those born into Jewish families, unless they either married out or adopted another religion. But as long as you stayed within the fold, whether you were a regular synagogue worshipper or not, you were, in such essential matters as burial rites, accorded the same dignity as the most celebrated rabbi. The hostility and rivalry between different sections of religious Anglo-Jewry is, to Geoffrey Paul, more troubling 'than the establishment of a new Conservative congregation or the growth of Reform, because this prac-tice of Judaism on the point of a pin is imposing an intolerable pressure on that middle-of-the-road Jewry which has always been the hallmark and strength of this community.' He deplores the way in which some Orthodox are setting themselves up as God's policemen. 'I cannot', he declared, 'accept a Judaism so exclusive that it withdraws itself even from fellow Jews, makes no contribution to the community's central welfare and representative authorities, and is concerned only with its own well-being.'

Observing Anglo-Jewry from his Liberal standpoint, David Goldberg takes a broad view: 'It's part of a general trend. This is a time of extremism, political, religious, anti-liberal. There's talk of a return to Victorian values, and we're seeing the deification of the Chief Rabbi as a custodian of positive morals. To be decisive is fashionable. This has rippled in to the Jewish community, and the Orthodox in Israel are affected by the same kind of messianic lunacy as the Ayatollah. The right wing is much more assertive and vociferous now. It feels it has a mission and a duty. It is much more dismissive of the values of acculturation, liberalism, liberal democracy, which throughout the nineteenth century were the touchstones of Jewish emancipation. In this century we've seen the rise of totalitarianism, we've seen what's happened to acculturation and assimilation, and there's a tendency to reject all of that. People are quite scathing now about Gentile culture and say our way, Orthodoxy, has always been the tried and true way, and we don't pander to false idols. Meanwhile we on the left of centre have become more diffident and tentative.'

A Manchester rabbi from the more gentlemanly school of Anglo-

161

Jewish ministers is harshly critical of *yeshiva*-trained rabbis. 'When I was being trained for the rabbinate over forty years ago, I was being trained to make the halachic burden easier rather than more insupportable. But now the right has penetrated centres of power, such as the *shechita* boards and the Beth Din. Organizations such as Lubavitch are amply funded with American money. Middle-of-the-road Jews either get out of synagogal life altogether or move to the left, while the right makes up the loss by having babies. These days even the title of "rabbi" has been degraded. Twenty years ago rabbis were trained at Jews' College, but the Chief Rabbi killed that off – he wanted to wipe out the "reverends". The title "rabbi" used to be given after long experience and great learning, and it entitled you to interpret religious law. It was inconceivable that you could be a rabbi without a university degree. Today a rabbinical diploma is easy to get, especially in Israel. The new *yeshivot* churn them out. There are even three or four *yeshivot* here in Manchester. It's a disaster.'

Raymond Goldman of the RSGB has no time for the fundamentalist argument. 'I can't make the intellectual presupposition that Moses sat on top of Sinai with his little typewriter and God dictated every word and therefore nothing can be changed. It is now a proven fact that the Five Books of Moses were not written at one time. If I believed that every word was God-given, then I'd have to be an Orthodox Jew with all the consequences attendant upon that. But since I cannot believe that, I believe that the Five Books of Moses were written by men of enormous religious insight and that God reveals himself through the minds of men. And since the minds of men are finite, their insight, however great, is limited by the time in which they live. You cannot ask me to believe the world is flat because the Talmud assumes that. I know it isn't. I'm in favour of maintaining Halachah in as far as it enhances the world in which we live. But to maintain that a divorcee may not marry a Cohen because possibly and very very notionally he may be of the line of priests of the Temple – that doesn't enhance Judaism or help Jews to live good Jewish lives.'

Julia Neuberger sees fundamentalism as the root of the problem. 'It's terribly easy to become really Orthodox because you don't have to ask any questions. You don't have to take any decisions of conscience because it's all perfectly obvious and you're told what to do. People who are now becoming fundamentalists have parents who probably went off to become hippies in the '60s or were tempted to do so. We're getting this polarization because people on the Orthodox wing who aren't born-again Jews are rather frightened by the fundamentalists and want to show that they are just as good as these born-again enthusiasts, so they keep tightening up their own practice. And at the same time all of us, who are absolutely horrified at this born-again stuff, we want to prove that it's a load of old rubbish and so become more and more trenchantly Liberal.'

Progressive Jews resent many of their Orthodox brethren not because of the religious views they happen to hold, but because the Orthodox consider those beliefs entitle them to have the last word on religious issues. Progressive Jews, and even mainstream Orthodox Jews, see the new Orthodox Establishment as obscurantist and ossified, reverting to old ways that should have been left in the ghetto and *shtetl*. They see Orthodoxy as a mummification of the past that shirks our common responsibility to deal with the need even of Jews to live and function in the modern world. They remind the Orthodox that Torah is not the sole component of authentic Jewish life, that being a Jew in the modern world is more than the scrupulous observance of outdated laws and rituals.

Yet there is an element of disingenuousness in all this, for if Progressive rabbis such as David Goldberg and Sidney Brichto give 'presumptive authority' to Halachah, then they cannot dodge out of the way whenever they see a halachic ruling that is not to their liking winging in their direction. When Rabbi Brichto proposes, as a way of solving the problems of the *get*, that the Orthodox Beth Din 'could even consider guaranteeing that every Jewish wedding allows for a technical basis for annulment'[1], it is clear that this kind of sleight-of-hand won't cut much ice with the Chief Rabbi and his court. When Brichto magnanimously declares he is 'prepared to entrust the Halachah to the Orthodox', he is offering nothing, for the Reform rabbinate has never claimed to be interested in being the guardians of Halachah. And when, by way of backing his offer, he goes on: 'I am prepared to accept the value of the myth that all the innovations of the rabbis of old could be attributed to Moses' conversations with God at Sinai', his very use of words such as 'myth' and 'conversations' suggests a lack of sincerity. The Orthodox couldn't care less whether Rabbi Brichto accepts 'the value of the myth', since what is in dispute in the first place is the status, literal or mythical, of the account of God's revelation to the Jews. But I shall let the defenders of Orthodoxy state their case in their own way.

Shimon Cohen, the executive director of the Chief Rabbi's office, discerns a shift throughout Anglo-Jewry towards greater Orthodoxy. He also maintains that Progressive Jews, increasingly left out in the cold, are

163

becoming more vitriolic in their attacks on Orthodoxy. Thus the aggression is coming from the left, not the right. Orthodox leaders have tended to ignore such attacks, though there was an occasion on which the Chief Rabbi had to rebuke an Orthodox rabbi who used 'out-of-order language to describe some members of the Reform community'. In Cohen's view, the gap between Orthodox and Progressive is widening not only in terms of religious observance but in terms of attitudes towards moral issues. This is undoubtedly true. The Chief Rabbi himself has observed: 'It grieves me deeply that of late, in very recent times, the focus of the attack on our traditional values is no longer limited to the ritual, nor even to the inter-personal status and relations, but also challenging the moral commitments that we thought would unite us.'[2] The Orthodox feel that Progressive rabbis who can't bring themselves to anathematize homosexuality or abortion on demand are abandoning traditional Jewish values, while the Progressives will respond that the Chief Rabbi has taken it upon himself to make increasingly reactionary statements on social and moral issues. Both are correct.

The current Orthodox line on Progressive Judaism was limpidly set forth by Rabbi Berel Berkovits. In a lengthy article, he declares that he loves all Jews equally, whatever their synagogal affiliation. Judaism, however, 'is for all time indivisible. In these beliefs I am at one with the great thinkers and leaders of Judaism throughout the ages.' It can never hurt to make sure the sages are on your team. Judaism is, he agrees, not monolithic, though how this is compatible with the indivisibility of Judaism is not clear. But, 'if everything is equally valid, or "equally authentic", as an expression of Judaism, then *nothing* is valid or authentic . . . It would simply boil down to a matter of taste, of what one feels more at home with, or to random chance. But is that religion?' The historical continuity which is a hallmark of Judaism cannot be claimed by Reform Jews, whose intellectual heritage only dates back to the iconoclasts of the early nineteenth century. Just as seriously, 'Reform and Liberal thinking accepts *mitzvot* at most as an optional lifestyle and has replaced Halachah with a broader emphasis on the more universal ideas of Judaism.'

Here's the rub. To an Orthodox rabbi such as Berkovits, this approach to Judaism is a denial of the very foundation of the faith. 'Judaism consists of 613 *mitzvot* which together form a unified system of coherence and structure. Torah is, by definition, a single harmonious entity; remove or omit any of its individual components (let alone most of them) and you have totally destroyed it . . . Torah is not just a religion, but a highly developed and precise system of law.' In the eyes of this former law lecturer, if you knowingly put yourself outside the law in one respect, you bring the entire structure into disrepute. 'A Judaism', he continues sternly, 'which cannot maintain its integrity without resorting to compromise and concession, is no Judaism.' Reform and Liberal teachings are 'essentially rootless, with a constantly fluctuating set of beliefs, and no central or cohesive authority ... The only "rule" which seems to be uniformly applied through Reform and Liberal thinking is that there are no rules.'[3] Of course he has a point. The Orthodox have logic, if not common sense, on their side.

Progressive Jews do have a reply to the accusation that they resemble diners picking out only the tastiest dishes from a menu. At least, they respond, we are intellectually honest, whereas everybody knows that the majority of nominally Orthodox Jews observe no more *mitzvot*, and possibly fewer, than many Progressive Jews. To this accusation of, essentially, hypocrisy, there is a classic counter-response, succinctly put, as so often, in the correspondence columns of the *Jewish Chronicle*: 'It certainly is not automatic that all Orthodox synagogue members are religious, but it is automatic that to belong to Reform or Liberal movements, both of which reject Judaism's basic premise of the Torah being binding on all Jews, one cannot be practising Judaism. The difference being that even weakly observant Orthodox members try to bend themselves to the Law, whereas Reform and Liberal Jews bend the Law to themselves.'[4] (I seem to detect a whiff of self-righteousness here, since it is common knowledge that many United Synagogue members care not a jot for 'the Law' but care a great deal about securing a burial plot at the Jewish cemetery of their choice. But we digress.)

How, then, does Berkovits propose that we deal with these tiresome Jews who claim to be religious while discarding the more inconvenient tenets of the religion? It's simple: you cast them out. 'There can be no agreement (no point of contact, even) between a Judaism which believes that God actually communicated the Torah to man at a revelation which actually took place, and a Judaism which maintains that men (albeit great men, or inspired men) wrote the Torah, or some of it, and that it is up to us to decide which bits of it are Divine and which are not.' We have come a long way from his initial expressions of 'love' even for Progressive Jews. 'I would be better able to respect or to give some credence to a non-Orthodox ideology if it did not so obviously aspire to the title of a Judaism which contradicts its very essence.'[5] In other words, Reform and Liberal

165

Judaism would be perfectly acceptable if their adherents would stop pretending to be Jews.

Although Rabbi Berkovits's fire is directed towards Progressive Judaism, there is also considerable ill feeling between mainstream Orthodoxy and the ultra-Orthodox. Cyril Harris, for many years the minister at St John's Wood United Synagogue and now Chief Rabbi of South Africa, accuses those ultra-Orthodox Jews who reject the State of Israel as 'colluding in a secular blasphemy that God did not help us to regain the Jewish homeland'. As many Jews are drawn to ever greater Orthodoxy, he warns, 'what we have gained in *frumkeit* [piety] we have lost in *menschlichkeit* [humanity]. There is great emphasis on ritual and ceremony and Halacha – all of which are important – but it has been at the expense of trying to understand basic human problems and living a Torah life in the context of the twentieth century.'[6] Rabbi Jonathan Sacks claimed in a recent lecture that the strictly Orthodox demonstrate 'a preference for the strictest halachic ruling, intolerance towards other positions, even of rival Orthodox groups, and oppositional stance to society, including Jewish and Israeli society as a whole.' Such élitist sectarianism, he continued, has no basis in rabbinic tradition, which always sought to find ways for Jews to live in the modern world without losing sight of their religious practice and ethical values.[7] And the forthright Rabbi Alan Plancey told me: 'The extreme right are as dangerous as the extreme left. The right shouldn't be throwing stones. The *Jewish Tribune* [published by Agudas] is always throwing stones at the United Synagogue. Always kicking us. It's wrong. They're ghettoized. They should leave us alone.'

The differences between mainstream Orthodox and ultra-Orthodox tend to be of style more than substance; there is far less common ground between Orthodox and Reform. Not all United Synagogue rabbis choose their words as carefully as Rabbi Berkovits, and for many it remains a deeply emotional issue. 'I've got to be frank here,' began one rabbi, which is always a good sign. 'What are Reform offering? I've even had one of their own high executive officers say to me he's a bit fed up with a religion which has to decide at an AGM whether they're going to ride on Shabbos or not. You've got to have something that has stability. The Reform are moving to the right because they're frightened, and they're trying to move with the times as well.' When the rabbi confirmed that the Orthodox 'don't recognize [Reform] converts at all, not at all, not for all the money in China', it was clear he was becoming very excited indeed. 'You go to the airport with them and they're eating meat sausages! They say it's not pork, it's only meat. What sort of religion is this, where even the dietary laws are thrown to the wind? As far as religious observances are concerned, I think they should be honest enough to admit it's not Judaism. When it comes to welfare or Soviet Jewry, we'll work together. I'll work for charitable causes with Jew or non-Jew. But what I do resent is when they try to tell me that my religion is too stringent, and therefore they have the right to represent the community on the media. They are very dishonest. They should say when they go on the media that they represent Reform, which is a minority group. My members, some of whom keep absolutely nothing, resent the fact that one of the Reform rabbis goes on television saying that she eats bacon or spends Christmas with nuns. My members like to see Orthodox Judaism being represented. If they don't keep it, that's their worry, their conscience. But they want their rabbis at least to be traditional. And if the Reform want to disagree with the Chief Rabbi, there's a respectful way of doing it. I would never even sit in the same room as Neuberger or Blue. If they walked in, I'd walk out. That's my feeling.'

I turned to cooler heads to try to find out why positions have hardened to such an extent. Rabbi Rodney Mariner tries to put the situation into some kind of historical context: 'The simplest answer is the failure of prophecy on the part of different areas of Judaism, prophecy that said that other areas of Judaism would disappear. The moderns really can't understand why the benighted medievalists haven't disappeared in the modern world, and the benighted medievalists can't really understand that, even though they keep on saying that Progressive Jews will never have Progressive grandchildren, nevertheless there are Progressive grandchildren. Both sides are expressing anger at the failure of their own perceptions of the dimensions of Judaism. Among the ultras, I think their response to the Holocaust has been this incredible leap backwards into a world in which the Holocaust hadn't happened yet. At the other end, the Progressives are saying that because of the Holocaust we've got to look at our relationship with the non-Jewish world in a entirely different fashion. On the one hand we've got to hold it at arm's length, but on the other we have to do more business with it. The lack of a middle ground is a mark of provincial Jewry. When Jewry becomes provincialized, it is always characterized by polar-ization. There's nothing in the middle. I didn't go back to Australia, because Melbourne was Manchester with better weather. There is a right and a left, and a similar newspaper full of vitriol, and people not willing to sit on platforms with their fellow Jews. What kept me in London was this tremendous variety of grey that stood between the extremes of left and right. The only other places where you could do that are New York and Israel.'

Others believe the degree of polarization has been exaggerated. Helene Bromnick maintains that 'it's an institutional animosity rather than on any personal level', and cites the many Jewish organizations supported and served by Jews of all factions. Some ultra-Orthodox figures, such as Rabbi David, take a similar view: 'I'm not sure the temperature has risen so much. But communication is so much better nowadays. People want to be in print, in the news. Newspapers stir up this sort of thing. They get publicity from it, they sell the papers.' Stanley Kalms prefers to stress the unity of the Anglo-Jewish community: 'Our community is sensationally cohesive and in agreement despite the efforts of the media to wind us up and say we're having arguments. This community hasn't had a split since the Louis Jacobs affair. We talk to the Reform, we talk to the Liberals, even though they have these crazy women rabbis who are adding nothing to the community. The only people we are frightened of are the fundamentalists. They don't talk to anybody.' Yet lack of schism is, surely, not the same as cohesion.

For Rabbi Michael Rosen, the stridency of the debate reflects the society around us. 'Part of the Thatcherite inheritance is that you don't work by consensus, but enforce your own particular position. Triumphalism, you might call it. And therefore would it be so surprising that Ango-Jewry is influenced by it? Orthodoxy is much more assertive than it used to be. Forty years after the Holocaust it's flexing its muscles. Anglo-Jewry as a whole has definitely moved to a much more halachic position. There's a real competitiveness, because Reform is consciously there to challenge. It's not an innocent party in this cycle. Neither party is blameless, and I find it very debilitating. This is about the only issue where I have not shown my true colours, because one has to choose one's battles and this is an issue I have chosen not to fight. And I wonder what sort of personality it is that needs to insult somebody in order to bolster itself. Nevertheless, I'm not as outgoing to the Reform world as I ought to be.'

Advocates from both sides of the debates have remarked on the shrinking of the middle ground. A traditional Anglo-Jewish rabbi such as Isaac Levy no longer feels wholly in touch with the United Synagogue he has served for over half a century. Some other rabbis are not prepared to concede the terms of the debate established by Orthodox and Reform. Dr Abraham Levy, a Sephardi rabbi for twenty-five years, says: 'I'm trying desperately hard to stand in the middle. It's not fashionable any more to be in the middle, but my philosophy is very simple. I say to my congregants that I will take anybody at any stage of the road, with one proviso: that you don't feel that you have to remain where you are, that you want to progress. I accept everybody. There are plenty of people who once came by car who are now ultra-Orthodox rabbis in Israel.' Another mainstream Orthodox rabbi, Jonathan Sacks, also seeks to keep his door wide open. Orthodoxy should 'include each Jew and make each Jew included' and should not 'give up on the marginal or irreligious Jew'.[8] The Chief Rabbi, with his distinction between the oneness of Jewry, which he accepts and works for, and unity, which is unattainable, appears to be prepared to live with the status quo.

Louis Jacobs actively seeks to defend the middle ground. Because Orthodoxy has grown more militant in its defence of Torah-true values, 'the middle ground, Anglo-Jewish muddling through, is no longer popular. I've always tried to present my view not as an attitude of muddling through, where you don't have the guts to go to the right or the left – that's not what I understand by the middle ground. I understand by it an openness to such things as critical and historical scholarship, and at the same time a loyalty to Jewish tradition, and I think that's possible. I think it can be shown that the strength of Judaism lies in its adaptability and creativity. Although overtly you have the notion that Judaism is unchanging and simply handed down from generation to generation, the facts are otherwise. I would say this is a myth, but that doesn't mean it's of no value. It seems to me to be quite ridiculous to say that there's no middle ground, because after all how many people ask when following a particular Jewish ritual, Was it given by God to Moses at Sinai? Surely they're saying, Is this the Jewish way, what I call the Jewish vocabulary of worship? The way Orthodoxy is defined today means that they have a monopoly on the True Way. They're saying that truth can have no truck with error; you can be nice to people who are in error, but you must never admit that they may have some truth – that's just not on, because from the dogmatic point of view if you do that, you're selling the pass. My own view is that there is room for all different shades in the community.'

The Lubavitch-trained rabbi Shlomo Levin, believes, like Michael Rosen, that this particular debate is not one that has to be joined, that sides do not have to be so vociferously taken, whatever the strength of one's personal convictions. 'The problem about tolerance is that it's always perceived, unfortunately, as a one-way street. You have to be tolerant of me – it doesn't always work the other way round. You cannot legislate for everyone. There are different kinds of communities, different kinds of needs. It's a question of live and let live. I personally think the Jew has to live in the world and there's a role to be played in the world. What I shall preach is the need for Jews to be wise in the world, and the kinds of people who come to my synagogue will be those who want to be involved in the world. The conclusion I've come to is that you do your thing in the very best way you can, with the deepest commitment and the greatest integrity, and if others want to jump on to your bandwagon because they've seen a lifestyle and an approach which is attractive and makes sense, they are very welcome to. But I can't see that it helps at all to go out and throw stones, physically or verbally, at people. When I first became religious, I thought I would change the world. Now I'm having enough difficulty trying to change myself.'

– 13 –

Being Jewish

To describe, as I have tried to do, the various synagogal groupings of Anglo-Jewry is to tell only part of the story. The fact is that there are as many different versions of Judaism as there are Jews. Two friends of mine who prop up their synagogue by giving a great deal of time to various committees, admit, when pushed, that their belief in God is a trifle shaky. To me this seems odd, as though some local stalwarts in the Conservative Party were actually socialists, but I dare say the same is true of churches, where many parishes must be dependent on the goodwill of local folk whose adherence to the articles of faith is hazy. Rabbi Alan Plancey of Borehamwood admits that some members of his synagogue choir are there primarily because they like to sing: 'There are all sorts of different ways to come to God: there's the gastronomic Jew, the Zionist Jew, the Jew in his heart. What's keeping them Jewish is this religion, this history, which they're passing on. As long as they're passing it on, I'm pleased.'

The Jewish concept of the deity, because it is central and indivisible, also seems diffuse, as though God were a given, and what counts is the implications of His convenant. Rabbi Abraham Levy refers to the story in rabbinic literature 'in which God symbolically speaks to the Jewish people and says: "Would that you would forget Me and keep My laws." In other words, keep the laws I have given you, live decently, and then belief in me will be automatic. Once I had a discussion with a young boy and he said to me: "I think I believe in God, but suppose the whole thing is a big hoax? What happens then?" I said: "Suppose it is a big hoax. You would have lived a decent life, helping other people, being kind to others, observing authority, teaching children proper values."' When I suggested to the

171

rabbi that this sounded very close to humanism, he replied: 'Historically, Judaism never understood the concept of Jews minus God. This only became an issue in the twentieth century. And that came about to a large extent with the introduction of political Zionism, surely.'

God, except vaguely defined as some kind of life-force, only just scrapes in to Arnold Goodman's theology: 'You only have to look at a leaf or an animal, a badger or a fruit tree, to realize that something incredible organized this. I have always held the belief that there must be some power that has organized it. I've not adopted a more superstitious approach, but I do believe somehow that there is some supreme force that has directed events, and it's as simple and as difficult as that. And I believe that on the whole the Jewish protestation of faith is a more tolerant, more civilized and more integral one than others.' Here Lord Goodman, like Rabbi Levy, veers towards an ethical justification. Rabbi Rodney Mariner agrees that many Jews like to keep their religious allegiance loose rather than precise: 'The majority of people involved in any religious system have some sort of religious connection. They'll talk to you at a party and say, "I'm Jewish but I'm not religious," or "I'm Jewish but I don't keep kosher" – reminding me of Woody Allen's famous line, "I'm Jewish with an explanation". We're living in a time of loss of Jewish capital. Years ago there was always somebody around who really knew, whom you could call upon to conduct a Seder or even tell you a bit about Judaism. We're losing that, we have been losing it by the yard. When I was in Australia, rabbis in the Progressive community never talked about God. They talked about the Vietnam War, they talked about social issues – it was a classic American style of Progressive Judaism.'

Another Reform rabbi, Barbara Borts, also concedes that God can easily be downplayed by religious Jews, certainly those on the Progressive wing. 'Judaism, because its bias has been towards leaving people free theologically but structuring their lives ritually, has not done a lot about teaching and thinking and speaking about God. We've assumed God. That assumption has not been grounded in a lot, which is quite opposite to the Christian church. That's left Jews with an uncertain basis to this thing they're just supposed to assume. They don't talk about it, and it's taken blows because of the Holocaust. I think Jews are embarrassed and reluctant to talk about spiritual thoughts, particularly in the Orthodox world where it's never been talked about. There's a lot of confusion and embarrassment about belief: it's not sophisticated.' She believes the lack of dogma within Judaism can be turned to advantage: 'The point of spiritual belief is to help people find and name their own experiences. To write down a catechism is a kind of dogma that Judaism has blessedly ignored. We've been very dogmatic about practices – you must put this shoe on and then that one – but we've not said, "You must believe such and such." Developing a spiritual awareness and a religious instinct in people is a different issue. We could have an advantage without a fixed dogma, if we take the initiative to talk about God.'

Progressive Jews are probably content to settle for Rabbi Julia Neuberger's formulation: 'The theological content of Judaism is simply the belief in one God – somewhat ill defined. If you want to describe what Jewish theology is you have to say there is a belief in a God differently defined by different people at different times, that It is a single being, and one to which we give thanks. That is very clear and universally established, and the rest is up to individuals. It doesn't matter in the same way as law and practice.' Rabbi Louis Jacobs's resolution of this matter is not much more definitive: 'The usual attitude is to say – and I would agree with this – that it's hard to believe in God but it's harder still not to. That's the sort of theological question we ought to be discussing. There's also the question of the hereafter. I don't know much about the geography of heaven, but I believe there is such a thing, and I think Judaism is impoverished if it's interpreted purely in this-worldly terms.' Of course the Orthodox have a problem too, for the central dogma is fundamentalist, and it is hard to understand how well-educated men and women can actually profess to believe what they are required to believe.

This is a point I put to Rabbi Berkovits of the London Beth Din, who, with his usual cogency and fluency, offered the following reply: 'If you ask me: do we believe that the Five Books of Moses were divinely given and are therefore immutable, though open to interpretation, the answer is: yes, of course. That has always been Jewish belief. We are aware of archaeological criticism, but archaeological discoveries tend to confirm the truth of the Torah rather than the opposite. An Orthodox Jew would say we do not believe a convincing case has been made out for us to alter our faith in the divine origin of the Torah. If you call that fundamentalist, so be it. I don't like the term, because it conjures up the image of a narrow-minded unintelligent person who clings to certain dogmas and doesn't want to open his mind. I've been a university lecturer, I have colleagues with classics degrees from Oxford and Cambridge. We're not as narrow and stupid as people imagine. On the other hand, we have certain beliefs that may seem unfashionable now.'

Rabbi Berkovits permits a qualification or two. 'Certain authorities, including Maimonides, do say that there are certain things in the Bible which are symbolic or allegorical. If you say that Abraham, Isaac and Jacob didn't exist, I think you'd be going a bit far. But if you ask whether there was a serpent in the Garden of Eden and did it speak, I don't think you'd be written off as a heretic if you said that was allegorical. Maimonides was fairly liberal on this, but Nachmanides was strongly opposed, so there's room for disagreement. Now, was the earth actually created in seven days or are the days referred to periods of time? There are different opinions about this. You're not written out of Judaism if you say that the seven days of Creation are seven eras. On the other hand, an Orthodox Jew would probably argue that much of the theory of evolution is exactly that, a theory, and hasn't been proved. An Orthodox Jew wouldn't dismiss science, but we would say, let's re-examine certain presuppositions and data and see whether they are as valid as you might imagine.'

Outside the Orthodox community such preoccupations would rarely be on the agenda. Even within it, soul-searching is not encouraged. The novelist Gerda Charles has written: 'I *am* Jewish. I relax within this accepted condition. I accept the moral laws given on Sinai. I accept the teachings (so marvellous in their delicacy and understanding of the human heart) of our great sages. I accept the lessons of history, I accept the mystical belief in the Jew's special purpose . . . In other words, I *believe*. I believe not with blind faith but because I see that, however outraged or distorted in the practice, orthodox Judaism *works*. If it didn't we wouldn't be here to deny it.'[1] Stanley Kalms, also an observant Jew, seems to have attended too many evangelical meetings: 'The whole philosophy of Judaism is about repentance. The rabbi's job is to keep saying, "Look, repent and all is forgiven." We're a very forgiving people. On the other side, it's about striving, it's about trying to improve oneself. If you can, you can reach that level of greater commitment to an Almighty, if you believe that. If not, you don't have to believe in God, but you can still believe in traditional Judaism.' Yes, but what does it mean to talk of a traditional Judaism from which God is missing?

Even heretical – in the eyes of the Orthodox – Reform Jews admit the centrality of God to their belief. Helene Bromnick, once United, now Reform, says: 'I do look upon Judaism very much as a religion. One hopes that Reform Judaism would always put more stress on the ethical side, and above all on the need of man to have a God.' For Sir Monty Finniston, ethical teachings are paramount: 'The rules of Judaic law are as applicable today as when they were first given. That's my test. The Jewish religion's got a series of principles which allows the majority of people to live together in reasonable harmony. It has minorities which don't, but these are small minorities. Judaism offers the best prospect. But of course you've got to practise Judaism, which is another matter entirely.'

Yet there are also many Jews who lack even those vague yet firm beliefs, but still consider themselves very much Jewish. Ian Mikardo simply declared: 'I think of myself as an ethnic Jew and the whole of my cultural basis is Jewish. I'm still much more at home telling a funny story in Yiddish than in English. I feel much more at home in the company of Jews. That's not universal. There are some *goyim* I get on with famously, and some Jews I hate the sight of.' For Wolf Mankowitz too, being Jewish is more a matter of culture than belief: 'Some people maintain that one is not Jewish unless one is a Jew in the strict and Orthodox religious sense. But the Jews are bound to each other not only because of their religion and religious past. They are also bound together because of their immediate secular history, their common heroes, their common enemies, their common contemporary predicament, their common myths and needs, their common concern for the State of Israel, by the common positive as well as negative aspects of "otherness", and even because of their present liking for certain foods, trivial as that may seem.'[2] Chaim Bermant cheerfully admits to the contradictions within his brand of Judaism: 'One does not . . . have to be a believer to enjoy religion, or to be pained by the lack of it, and I conform to observances which I cannot in logic defend – because they defend observances which I cherish. I take pleasure in the ceremonies and ritual of Judaism as impalpable antiques.'[3]

For Eva Figes, coming from a German background, Jewish culture means something quite different from Yiddish songs and gefilte fish: 'My Jewishness is a question of having been part of what happened in Europe and in Germany in particular. That will never go away, and that's always very strong. There are so many different ways of being Jewish. Middle-class German Jews were very assimilated anyway, and I'm one of those. For me the pride of being Jewish is not to do with religion, it's to do with Enlightenment, the intellectual heritage. For me Kafka is a Jewish author, not the Bible. Alienation and enlightenment and not being part of the herd and intellectual questioning.' An American friend of mine whose sense of Jewishness would overlap a good deal with Eva Figes' finds that the difficulties arise when passing on the heritage to his children, who are halachically non-Jewish: 'I very much want my children to be aware of

175

their cultural background. The trouble is that when I read them Bible stories and I come to an account of divine intervention, I find the talk about God bogus, and I baulk.'

The transmission of culture doesn't always succeed. Jonathan Miller once wrote: 'My father would create these Friday-night suppers with candles and an instant decor of Judaism. I had no interest in this whatsoever. I was told constantly by my father that I owed it to my people to identify with them. I didn't know how, and didn't want to. I could feel Jewish only for anti-Semites, not for Jews. As a child I resented being Jewish: it seemed designed just to prevent me having fun.'[4] As a middle-aged man, he has become even more impatient. Noting that a number of previously non-religious Jews, including some of his friends, have been creeping back towards their religion, he dismisses this return as 'a tedious regression': 'When I go to New York I sometimes get annoyed at the way some of my friends there have gone all Jewish on me. I fully grant that the universe is mysterious, but that isn't incompatible with saying it's un-supervised. If I were to get religion, I'd be attracted to Greek religion, with its many minor deities, rather than to the fantasy of monotheism. I'm all for admitting the mystery of the universe, but that doesn't mean you have to personify it.'

In contrast, Sir Claus Moser, the Warden of Wadham College, Oxford, is one of those who, as he grows older, is being drawn back to Judaism: 'To call myself a practising Jew in the sense of religious participation and synagogue-going would be rather pretentious. But being Jewish is the most important thing in my life. From the word go, being Jewish was a source of total happiness to me. I'm terribly proud of it. It dominates my life and I'm very active in the Jewish community. On actual religious belief and which bits of Judaism I feel strongly about, that, as with many people my sort of age, is a confusing business, because for much of my life I've been somewhat agnostic. As I get older, I've become less agnostic. When I do go to synagogue, as I've done all my life if not very frequently, I feel a tremendous sense of identity. I feel more at ease with Jews, on the whole. That's a natural reaction deriving from the fact that you both know you have one defining characteristic in common. I have an almost obsessional feeling about the Holocaust. I have very strong pro feelings regarding Israel. I just identify more with Jews than with non-Jews. Many Jews struggle over this if they don't naturally feel religious, but do feel this tremendous sense of pride, which is partly historical. As Elie Wiesel says, one can't be a passive Jew, and so five or six years ago I decided to spend a significant part of my life actually trying to do something. In my case it's taken the shape of active involvement in an embarrassingly large number of Jewish causes. As I retire and resign from other things, I will spend more and more of my time on Jewish activities, both here and related to Israel.

'Some people will say, What does it mean to be a passionate Jew but an agnostic? I can be proud of being all kinds of things, of being British, of being German. I'm terribly conscious of being Jewish, always have been. I grew up almost militantly atheistic, but a lot of things happen to one as one gets older. First of all one realizes that some of the people one admires are deeply religious. So it can't all be rubbish. One grows less intolerant. Secondly, lots of awful things happen: at the extreme end the Holocaust – I lost some members of my family, though not my immediate family – and at the personal end one comes close to personal tragedies. Also, as you get older, you feel a greater need to understand, to become more open to what religion as such has to offer. So over the last few years, with Hugo Gryn's guidance, I've been reading a great deal, I talk to people, and I could end up being a very observant Jew. It's quite possible. I've already changed a great deal. I now regularly go to High Holyday services. I go occasionally in between when I can. I'm wide open.'

So, in a very different way, is the publisher Anthony Blond: 'I'm a late-born Jew. I was never barmitzvah, though I had an inclination to be. I went to Eton and was very nearly confirmed. I saw the rabbinate as being unctuous lackeys, which is why I believe in alternative funding. That's why I like the Church of England. The clergy can be rude to parishioners, which the rabbinate couldn't. Twenty or thirty years ago rabbis were fairly low-level people. About fifteen, twenty years ago I learnt Hebrew. I say my prayers. I lay *tefillin*. I very much believe in ritual. I go to church and synagogue. I love services. Not that I regard my presence in a Christian church as anything to do with worship at all. It's like going to a concert. I'm a member of the Common Prayer Book Society. But I never pretend to be anything other than a Jew. The clergy don't care – turn up, that's all they want. They're so tolerant. It's the buildings that attract me too. I think I go to church much more than most Christians.'

Back to Judaism? 'The more I learnt about Judaism, the more marvelling and delighted and grateful I am. It's such an intelligent, practical, humane, courteous religion. I even tried to keep kosher for a bit, but that didn't work out. It drove everybody mad. That project was knocked on the head by going to live in Sri Lanka. I found Judaism arcane but delightfully so. All the oddities and absurdities and mysteries I enjoy just as much as the sense and sensibility of Judaism. It's the most caring and tender religion. The Jewish system of justice is marvellous. You're not allowed to deliver a judgement on the same day but must sleep on it – all these things thrilled me. And I read and read and read. I quite often go to synagogue. On Yom Kippur I walked from my home in Wapping to Maida Vale. Quite a hike, but it's these dramatic moments I go in for. My rabbi doesn't regard me as a good Jew, but he's quite pleased to have me around. I've disappointed him a lot recently – he hasn't mentioned anything, but I can see it in his eyes – what's a nice Jewish boy doing as the *Vogue* restaurant critic?

'I pray every day that I shall behave better. I thank God He's not made me a *goy* or a heathen or a woman. He's set on me the obligations of a man and a Jew. Whenever I have in front of me the temptation to cheat or to lie or to steal, I'm helped enormously by saying I'm a Jew and I can't. That's what I like particularly about being Jewish: the concern for the feeble and the horror of the powerful. Such observances as I practise are not linked with thinking I'm an improved person. I always had a sense of being a Jew, even when I was about to be confirmed, and that guided me morally. So I haven't gained any morality. What I've gained is a feeling that I'm inheriting a rather splendid set of values, with glorious anecdotes and precise attitudes to all sorts of problems. The Jewish religion is demanding. To be a good Jew is quite a hard task. Ritual is the cement. Religions which try and detach themselves from the physical, from the dirt, from the earth, fail. Take Unitarianism: an excellent, charming religion, but there are hardly any Unitarian churches left. And it's quite interesting what's happened to Catholicism, with this attempt at rationalism. Religions need mysteries and absurdities. Without the flesh of a religion, it all evaporates.' And what does his non-Jewish wife make of this newfound fervour? 'My wife regards all this with amused tolerance, tinged with scorn.'

– 14 –

Know your place: the role of women

FEMINISM and Judaism do not mix. Although women are not concealed behind Islamic veils, Orthodox Judaism requires them to be content with a role very different from that played by men. For the fundamentalists, with their unshakeable belief in traditional Judaism, this is rarely a problem: rigorous laws of family purity are part of the ultra-Orthodox package. If you're married to a Chasid, you're not likely to object to using the *mikveh*. Progressive rabbis, such as David Goldberg and John Rayner, argue that the separation of men and women was probably not introduced until the thirteenth century, and then only in response to the Islamic norms that prevailed in the lands where many medieval Jews were living.[1] Seven hundred years may be a fairly small slice of the cake of Jewish history, but it's still large enough to constitute a tradition of its own. In more recent times, with the rise of women's rights, traditional Jewish constraints on the role of women have inevitably come under attack. Nor is it solely a matter of separation in synagogue. The education of Jewish girls also used to be very limited. There was no need to educate them in their religion if they were not allowed to participate in many of its rituals. It was the menfolk who had the leisure or made the time to attend synagogue three times a day and to study the Torah before or after work.

German Reform Judaism banished the distinction between the sexes in the synagogue. Liberal and Reform Jews to this day pride themselves on the fact that men and women sit together and that women participate in the service to the same degree as men. Women rabbis are no rarity in British Progressive synagogues. The first female rabbi was ordained in Germany just before the Second World War, which she did not survive. In the early 1970s the American Reform movement ordained a woman, and a few years later the first British female rabbi, Jackie Tabick, was ordained as a Reform minister. Since then nine have been ordained and many have become prominent in the ministry. Even among Reform Jews, the innovation was regarded with mixed feelings. Logically inevitable, the ordination of women still met with considerable resistance. Reform Jews who were initially hostile to the idea admit that they soon got used to it. What mattered was whether she was good at the job, and fortunately the early entrants into the ministry were of high calibre.

Rabbi Jonathan Magonet, the principal of Leo Baeck College where Britain's women rabbis were trained, admits that the early reaction was 'hysteria and vast anxiety on the one hand, and a grudging welcome on the other. There were those who were gung-ho for it because it represented a progressive view. For the first women it was hellish, with the stereotypes and prejudice to be dealt with. The experience gained by the first ones is not easy to transmit to the newer ones. But there is beginning to be a recognition that something new is happening and is here to stay. It has great implications in terms of the language of the prayer-book, greater sensitivity to sexist language, an awareness of the position of women within Judaism. The sort of women coming to the college now are not radical feminists. One or two of them still are. Others are rather conventional, middle-class people who've found they want to become rabbis. The stereotype has been broken. Once women are seen to be competent and useful and valuable, then attitudes change. They become "our rabbi". But there's still a long way to go.'

Julia Neuberger doesn't feel she had a particularly hard time of it after she was ordained. There was little hostility, and, in contrast to Rabbi Magonet's view, she feels that hostility is greater now: 'Now we're a threat. There are nine of us and a lot more training. People now say there should be more young male rabbis. The response of the women rabbis, quite rightly, has been, "Either we're equal or we're not. If we are, what does it matter what sex we are?" And they can't answer that.' Barbara Borts, very much a feminist rabbi, recalls a more subtle response: 'I'm accepted as a rabbi, but whether they always want a woman is another issue. The way I do things may make people uncomfortable, but that's not an issue of my legitimacy.'

In January 1988 Jewish feminists sought to demolish another taboo. Male Jews at prayer wear a *tallit* or prayer shawl. Women, traditionally, do not. Women rabbis wear a *tallit*, and female congregants have begun, in small numbers, to follow suit. This has upset not a few people. Led by Barbara Borts, feminists within the Progressive movement decided to argue for the right to do so and published a crusading pamphlet entitled 'Women and *Tallit*'. The traditional line is as follows: because of the different role that women play – as guardians of the home and rearers of children – they are exempt from those *mitzvot* such as prayer that are 'time-bound' and cannot be performed regularly by those with domestic responsibilities. Moreover, some sages, including Maimonides, have actually ruled that women may not wear the *tallit.* To which the feminists reply: Just because women are exempt from certain *mitzvot* doesn't mean that we are forbidden to observe them should we choose to do so. The prohibition is a matter of tradition, not of Jewish law. Rabbi Borts argued in her pamphlet: 'It is indefensible for Progressive Jews to be progressive on most issues and then become "traditional" when it concerns women.' Women who wear *tallit* do so because of 'a genuine desire to increase their level of observance. The wearing of *tallit* by women has in all cases been accompanied by an increase in commitment and attendance at synagogue services and study sessions.'

The pamphlet was launched at the Manor House in Finchley, and about 120 people were present. Barbara Borts, in presenting her argument, said its opponents were people who attend synagogue as a source of comfort rather than challenge, who think of the synagogue as one of the few places safe from feminist inroads. Her intention is to see rituals as Jewish rather than as male or female. By wearing the *tallit*, she herself became more aware of the power and meaning of those rituals. There was an elegant response from Thena Kendal, a radio producer who grew up in a Chasidic household. In such homes, she recalled, there is no obvious association between prayer and *tallit*, and she questioned whether wearing *tallit* automatically enhanced the act of prayer. It was quite common for unmarried Chasidic males not to wear a *tallit* at all. Rabbi Fred Morgan of the North-west Surrey Reform Synagogue supported the aims of the pamphlet, arguing that rituals are derived from tradition but their meaning comes from personal experience, which, he mused, may have lost its freshness for many observant males. He admitted that he was enraged when his wife first donned the shawl, but patience won the day. He encouraged women to try wearing *tallit*, but added that if they derived no additional meaning from the experience, they should desist.

The Orthodox, for whom this is unlikely ever to be an issue, take a more philosophical view. Judaism, states Rabbi Shlomo Levin, assumes that men and women may be equal, but they are different. Judaism 'says equality is one issue; sameness is another issue altogether. I don't think Judaism and the Torah want to say that men and women are the same. Men are one kind of creature, women another kind. The way they are is a matter of creation rather than a question of environment. So a woman is exempt from certain *mitzvot* which are time-bound. The logical assumption made by Orthodoxy is that a man is obliged to do lots of different kinds of *mitzvot* because he has a tendency to stray away from godliness. The man traditionally has been the rover, the conquering male. All these things are distractions which can take a person away from an innate sense of religiosity, and therefore he's obliged to do things that will draw him back to his religious roots. A woman is created with different kinds of feelings of compassion. She has a different kind of inner structure, emotional and spiritual, as a consequence of which she is innately very much closer to godliness. She doesn't need to struggle as much. Therefore she doesn't have to be obliged to do things which men have to do, because she doesn't need them in quite the same way. That doesn't presuppose that she's inferior. On the contrary, it almost suggests that she's probably in a certain sense superior. But I wouldn't want to say that she's either inferior or superior. I'd want to say that men and women are different.'

Another Orthodox response is to upstage the feminist argument. Rabbi Berkovits of the London Beth Din was lofty in his dismissal of Rabbi Borts's pamphlet: 'I must say I found her arguments rather trivial. The question of wearing or not wearing a *tallit* is a very minor issue. She doesn't talk, I note, about wearing *tefillin*. Why not? I suppose because not many of her constituents come to *shul* in the morning and wear *tefillin*. This may sound unfair, but I have to make this point. If you want to assume privileges, you've also got to assume responsibilities. It's no good saying we want our women to wear a *tallit* and at the same time say that our women, and for that matter our men, can ignore much more important principles of Judaism: you don't have to keep kosher, you don't have to keep Shabbat, you don't have to come to *shul* every day in the morning, and so on. Now Orthodox Judaism says if you have a woman who is prepared to carry out those obligations and then wants to assume additional obligations, fine. There are precedents. Michal, the daughter of Saul, wore *tefillin*. But you can't isolate one thing, like the *tallit*, and say I'm going to ignore lots and lots of other important Jewish practices. There is an element of provocativeness about it, or there may be.'

182

Rabbi Berkovits, whose argument is persuasive, has an unexpected ally, though for different reasons, in Julia Neuberger, who, mincing her words as usual, declared: 'Women and *tallit*? I couldn't give a damn. This is really a non-issue. I do feel that if Jewish feminists were a bit more serious about where the problems lie, we would get a little further. The problems lie in discrimination, in recruiting women into leadership positions in the Jewish community, particularly in bodies that cut across the community rather than those just within the Reform or Liberal movement. With *tallit*, what's the big deal? Either you do or you don't. It does nothing for me. I've worn a *tallit* for thirteen years. Some women in my congregation do, some don't. Some men do, some don't. If you concentrate on things like that, you lose seriousness. I think there may be some great value in doing some serious feminist interpretation of rabbinic and biblical material. There's serious work to be done examining the writing out of women in the texts. You have strong female characters in the Genesis stories, but by the time you look at the Midrash, the women are gradually being written out or trivialized.'

If the arguments within Progressive Judaism about the role of women and the direction of feminist critique remain confused, at least the arguments are taking place. The Orthodox have battened down the hatches. There the emphasis is less on practice within synagogue – few Orthodox women wish to abandon the separation of the sexes – than with Jewish family law. Double standards do appear to prevail, so that adultery by a married woman was regarded as a capital offence whereas the same offence committed by a married man with an unmarried woman carries much lighter penalties. A woman whose husband is presumed dead, but of whose death there is no absolute proof, is forbidden to remarry, a prohibition that does not apply to a man in a comparable position. The *chalitsa* ceremony is also regarded by many as humiliating to women. Many would argue that the stipulations for Jewish divorce, the *get*, also discriminate against women. Judaic law prohibits women from being witnesses or judges. All these inequalities, remedied by the reforms of Progressive Judaism, are still, as it were, on the statute books of the Orthodox.[2]

Rabbi Berkovits does concede that women in some Orthodox communities may suffer from injustices: 'In certain Orthodox groups attitudes are formed which may not necessarily be reflections of Jewish teaching. In the Chasidic world women are treated as second-class citizens, and I find

183

no justification for it in Jewish law. They are very concerned about sexual problems. A Chasid will not look at a woman or talk to her. There's no justification in Judaism for that. My Chasidic cousin, when she was eighteen, would not speak to me.

'It's not entirely true that women can't be witnesses. For certain purposes they can be. Nonetheless they are not equal to men. There are explanations. Whether they will satisfy the feminists I don't know. One of the explanations is this. If you are eligible as a witness, then you are compellable as a witness. Judaism does not want women to be compelled to give evidence in the public arena, because the role of women is seen as somewhat more delicate or refined. We want to preserve that concept. Many feminists would say that in itself is sexist. Perhaps it is. But a lot of alleged discrimination depends on your perspective. There can be certain benefits as well as disadvantages. It's a benefit not to be compelled to go to court and give evidence. The important point is the idea of equality, that people can be equal but different. If women wish to observe voluntarily certain duties because they want to participate more fully in spiritual life, well and good. They're allowed to. But if the motivation is that they are dissatisfied with their lot and feel they are being treated as second-class citizens and want to rebel against that, then it's incorrect.'

The rabbi seems to want to have his cake and eat it too. He admits that there are inequalities in traditional Judaism's treatment of women, but is dismissive of any attempts by women to rectify the situation. It's not clear to me whether women should be more wary of Rabbi Berkovits's reasoned propping up of the status quo, or the more crude obduracy of strictly Orthodox rabbis such as Rabbi David: 'Women join in the prayer, but in the actual conducting of the prayer they play no part. It's always been like that. It's not that we've changed anything. A woman's got a place, she's got a place in the home, even in the *shul.* She organizes things, but she doesn't conduct prayers. They have their guilds and their organized events. But I don't think women should feel left out at all. A lot of them go out to work. They do what's comfortable. We've got women doctors in our community, women who own businesses, teachers.'

Rabbi Vogel of Lubavitch, not surprisingly, adopts a more sweetly reasonable tone in describing the Chasidic evaluation of the place of women in response to what he perceives as a feminist 'onslaught': 'It's unquestionable that the rise of the feminist movement and the creation of a sense of frustration and deprivation has affected the Jewish community. But we would see this as a challenge in the sense of an opportunity, not a

threat. We would want to redevelop a sophisticated and profound understanding of real values, real purpose, among women, so that they can
respond to this onslaught. We need to recreate or restate these fundamental truths in language which can meet this pressure from the
outside, and challenge the whole feminist movement and suggest to them
in no uncertain terms that this movement is in fact a creation of a male
chauvinistic society which has forced them into an unnatural position to
create this feminist movement. The establishment of a home, bearing
children for as long as a woman is physically capable – notwithstanding the
enormous physical pressures, the material pressures, the financial problems, that accrue from it – that in itself is a statement of the value system
which one has in life, so that a holiday in Spain or another car can never be
as valuable as, as worthy as, another child. They can never be equated.
Notwithstanding what I've just said, there are many women who are very
talented, very capable, creative, and they are encouraged by Lubavitch not
to stay home but to use their talents in the wider society. So we have
women members of the community who are lecturers, designers, who
work in a number of trades, having arranged their domestic life in a certain
way, usually with outside domestic help, so that they can pursue a career
because they are so gifted. Plus the fact that all the women are encouraged, as their menfolk are, to be activists in the regenerative process of
Judaism.'

There is something distinctly patronizing about the reverence of the
strictly Orthodox for their women while at the same time they are doing
their best to keep them in their place. *Challenge*, a Lubavitch tome
explaining the movement's aims, smugly expounds: 'The Torah's restrictions are the Jewish woman's safeguard ... Where has the modern
world's concept of equality finally placed the woman? She has become the
most potent instrument of advertising, subjected to every vulgarism, her
womanliness crudely exploited to promote sales ... We find that today's
woman, at the peak of her sophistication, has been stripped of her dignity
as a human being. Observing where man's concept of morality has led
society, how reassuring are the standards of the Torah! It imposes
differing demands on men and women because it recognizes their quite
natural Divinely given differences.'[3] Lubavitch has founded its own
Women's Organization to bolster this ideology. The statement of aims of
Lubavitch's Week of the Jewish Woman in February 1988 proclaimed:
'The Jewish woman has been endowed with special capacities, actual and
potential, to fulfil an important role in the preservation of our Jewish

185

people in every generation.' A member of the movement, Toebe Potash, stated: 'As women, maybe our main role should be raising children instead of money, to make a positive contribution to the world.'[4]

The more mainstream United Synagogue rejects the notion of equality espoused by the Progressives, but does allow its women a greater degree of participation in synagogal affairs than do the ultra-Orthodox. The Chief Rabbi, in a memorandum to the honorary officers of the United Synagogue in December 1986, let it be known exactly how far he was prepared to let its women members go. 'If what the women want is full participation, they can and will have everything.' What more could one ask? But wait. The next sentence reads: 'If what they seek is equal rights in a spurious quest for "women's liberation", they will have nothing.' What, you may wonder, is the precise difference between 'full participation' and 'equal rights'? The Chief Rabbi explains: 'The contribution of our women to enriching and intensifying our communal life can be invaluable . . . But their role must be played as women, and not as worshippers of a popular fad.' That's one in the eye for the likes of you, Neuberger. And what is their role as women? Read on: 'If by opening up our institutional leadership ranks to women we would lose or weaken their primary commitment to securing stable marriages' – nothing to do with men, of course, stable marriages – 'building happy homes and raising intensely Jewish children, the sacrifice of further eroding the strength of Jewish family life would not be worth the gain in improving the management of communal affairs . . . Once the primacy of the Jewish home and education is safeguarded, by all means, we should mobilize for community service the enormous resources of our women.'[5] It is not clear who decides, and when, that the 'primacy of the Jewish home and education' have been securely safeguarded.

What this all means in practice is that although the separation of the sexes is maintained in synagogue, women may be elected to boards of management and to the Board of Deputies. However, not all positions on boards of management are open to women, who may not be elected as wardens, who are the equivalent of floor managers within the synagogue. Boards of management are composed of the three honorary officers (male), twelve male members, and six female members, and the synagogue's representative on the United Synagogue Council. It seems probable that most United Synagogue women will settle for this limited role. Women not willing to be confined to running the ladies' guild or a middling position in the synagogue hierarchy have probably long deserted the United for the Progressive movement. It is hard to gauge what dissatisfaction there is, if any, with the Chief Rabbi's breathtaking condescension. Barbara Borts, a Reform rabbi, probably overdramatizes the reaction: 'People are very intimidated, easily bullied by men and by the rabbis' pronouncements. But if the United doesn't start to make moves towards women, it is going to flounder as the women's movement takes more hold. There have been a few little signs of being willing to accommodate women, such as the *bat chayil* confirmation ceremony which they've invented. Women are shunted upstairs because men assume that women are only sexual objects who are only there to distract while the men are the ones who are serious and who pray – never mind that the men are actually sitting in the body of the *shul* talking about the stock market, and that it's their responsibility for not having educated women to be able to follow the service – it's not justifiable on any level.'

Many rabbis find complaints along feminist lines an irrelevancy. Alan Plancey's view is not atypical: 'Any decent *shul* listens to what the women have to say. What can't they do? They can't take the service, and they can't sit in the warden's box. Separate seating will remain. That's Halachah. Everything else the women can participate in. Because you sit next to your husband doesn't mean you're a better person. I think people are making problems that don't really exist.' Other rabbis deflect feminist criticism with more finesse, but the basic argument remains that such criticism is irrelevant. Take Jonathan Sacks, who has written: 'Non-Orthodox feminists have targeted their objectives on the synagogue – from mixed seating to women rabbis. But the synagogue is *not* the focus of Judaism or of Jewish self-respect, except for those whose Judaism outside the synagogue is limited and secondary.'[6] In November 1988, Rabbi Dr Jeffrey Cohen of Stanmore United floated the suggestion that women could hold their own 'women only' services, but the proposal was denounced by most of his Orthodox colleagues.

In some synagogues separate seating has been taken to absurd lengths. I have attended one or two synagogues where I have seen women in wheelchairs placed just inside the entrance to the men's section, because there was no way to get a wheelchair up to the ladies' gallery. But there have been occasions when handicapped women have been denied this simple humane gesture. Chaim Bermant records an instance when a woman in a wheelchair was refused permission to remain downstairs, and was placed instead in a neighbouring room, from which 'she would have received a full view of the congregation and officiants, presumably with the help of mirrors and a periscope'. Bermant helpfully offers another suggestion, 'to jack her up to the roof of a nearby building, from which she could have followed the proceedings with a telescope.'[7] Rabbi Michael Rosen's congregation has come up with a *modus vivendi* that seems at least sensitive and sensible. Yakar being an Orthodox congregation, the sexes are separated by a tall curtain during the service. During the half-time break for coffee and *shiurim*, however, the sexes mingle and participate equally in study sessions and discussions.

The Masorti synagogues, headed by Dr Louis Jacobs, also try to deal with this problem in a non-traditional way. The Conservative movement in North America, to which Masorti is allied, has voted to ordain women. It seems unlikely that the Masorti group in Britain will follow suit, although the five congregations of which it is composed have a fair degree of independence in determining their policy on such matters as mixed seating. Colin Shindler believes that 'there are many younger observant women who feel that within the Halachah there must be some purposeful role for them. For example, *minyanim* and services for and conducted by women. There has been a flourishing of groups where women meet on the first of the Jewish month to celebrate and discuss a particular theme. Many regard the fashion parade on Jewish holidays as substitutes for spirituality. Many Jewish women are severely under-educated and that's a real condemnation of those who purport to represent Orthodoxy. Some Orthodox women have openly complained at the inferior role that the United Synagogue has allotted to them and to being closeted away in the women's gallery far from the proceedings. Even so, the difficulty of women's participation in services is a real one. Even at a Masorti synagogue such as New North London where there is separate seating on the same level, where women read the prayer for the Monarch and the State of Israel and even give sermons, there is still unresolved discussion. Has the role of women come about through the attitudes of men to women or is it something fundamental, rooted within Judaism itself?'

It is difficult to foresee any great changes in the status of women within Anglo-Jewry. A Jewish feminist magazine, *Shifra*, proved very short-lived, and academic groups such as the Jewish Women's History Group which compiles oral histories from the accounts of older Jewish women, and the radical Jewish publishing group, the Beyond the Pale Collective, make virtually no impact on religious Anglo-Jewry.

To ascertain the current state of play, I attended a meeting at Cockfosters United synagogue in March 1988. The theme was Jewish feminism. The main speaker was Rabbi Alan Kimche of the Ner Yisroel congregation in Hendon. He is a forceful figure, with ten years' experience at Israeli *yeshivot*, a philosophy degree from University College, London, and a pioneer of lunch-time *shiurim* for workers in the City. Rabbi Kimche got the session off to a good start by quoting Rabbi Dr Norman Lamm, the president of Yeshiva University in New York, who had stated that much discussion of Judaism and feminism is 'more hysterical than historical'. Judaism, explained Kimche, has always sought to protect women's dignity and welfare. The Torah, while patriarchal and consigning women to a supporting role, is not unbending, otherwise it would have collapsed as a source of religious authority centuries ago. The halachic system must respond to feminism by looking for places where we can and where we cannot adapt to changing modern realities. The first specific question he dealt with was whether women should be taught Torah. Maimonides and other sages had argued against it, but today there was no disputing that women could receive the full spectrum of Jewish education. As for time-bound *mitzvot*, the rabbi echoed the standard Orthodox objection to women wearing *tallit* or *tefillin*: although there was no overriding halachic objection to their doing so, one should not undertake extra *mitzvot* until the obligatory ones had been fulfilled. To go beyond the call of duty is to invite close scrutiny of one's motives, and the suspicion would be aroused that one is wearing *tallit* for political or provocative reasons.

He then surveyed the more important ban on Jewish women occupying any positions in the priesthood, judiciary, or *minyan*. He agreed that this didn't seem fair, but added that certain aspects of Jewish life are more important than fairness. The offspring of marriages not validated in Jewish law, *mamzerim*, are regarded as bastards without any claim to Jewish status; in cases, say, where a woman has been left by her husband who refuses to grant her a *get*, should she remarry the union would be regarded as adulterous and her children as *mamzerim*. This is unfair, he conceded, but justifiable on the grounds that adultery is such a heinous violation that the laws discriminating against *mamzerim* provide a deterrent. Their unfairness is less important than the sanctity of marriage. Nowadays we are worked up about the problem of *mamzerim* because adultery is not taken so seriously. A justification for the ban on women holding prominent positions, continued Kimche, is that they might attract the attention of men, which could be destabilizing for society. Why the attraction of women for men in positions of power isn't regarded as equally destabilizing, the rabbi did not make clear, but then clerics are

189

never very good at acknowledging female sexuality, as the Bishop of London demonstrated in opposing the ordination of women on the grounds that male congregants might be aroused by women wielding the wafer and this would undermine the religious experience. When during the discussion that followed the rabbi's remarks, a male member of the audience made precisely this point, Kimche replied that the present situation was more controllable because men were more likely to make passes than women. It should be clear by now that the expert on feminism was also an expert on primitive thought. In his concluding remarks, Rabbi Kimche fell back on the very dusty consolation that just because men occupy positions of power in Judaism doesn't mean that women lack influence.

Gradually the cat emerged from the bag. The core of the matter is that Kimche and the countless Orthodox rabbis who think like him do believe that the centre of a Jewish woman's life must be the home. Yes, women may pursue a career, but only if the domestic unit is preserved. 'You can't reject the critical position of women as homemakers. That's a value that lies at the very heart of Jewish life.' He climbed deeper into the bunker. In his many years in Israel, he confided to us, he had encountered female graduates of religious seminaries who complained that they had become unmarriageable because men were intimidated by their learning. This observation seems to run counter to his earlier statement that Jewish women were entitled to the full spectrum of religious education. Implication: men like their women ignorant, and Judaism should help to keep it that way. Because men feel weak and inadequate, penalize the women. Someone in the audience remarked that perhaps they needed to educate the men too, so that they no longer feel intimidated by learned women. After ninety minutes the discussion was drawing to a close. On a wild impulse I raised my hand and rose to speak. I normally keep quiet on such occasions, but I was unable to restrain myself. 'Over the past two decades I've attended a number of meetings at which feminist issues were discussed. This is the very first in which no women were present on the platform, and the very first in which all but two minutes of the evening were taken up by men sounding off.' A little speech that was greeted with silence.

Women members of the United Synagogue, not to mention of the proudly sexist Federation and ultra-Orthodox congregations, who imagine that they will in the foreseeable future be taken seriously and given positions of power and responsibility within the Jewish community are

190

deluding themselves. It is men who dominate the United Synagogue, the Board of Deputies, the Zionist Federation, the Anglo-Jewish Association. The secretaries are women, as are the worthy dames of the Ladies' Guilds and WIZO and their fund-raising bridge evenings, and so are the admirable tough women who run the campaigns on behalf of Soviet Jewry. These volunteers are rightly praised by the community for the work they do, but they are and will remain remote from the power bases of Anglo-Jewry.

✤ THE ESTABLISHMENT ✤

The Chief Rabbi

THE Chief Rabbi is not a diffident man. He basks in his role of religious leader. Pronouncements and pamphlets pour from his office at Woburn House, he delights in pastoral visits, he gives lectures and sermons and sits on panels. He is nothing if not visible. He is greatly revered, if not greatly loved, for he speaks his mind and does not court popularity.

When I read that he was coming to speak to members of the Cockfosters United synagogue, I made my way to that distant corner of London. As I was buying my ticket at the entrance to the synagogue hall, I was asked whether I would mind wearing a *kippah*. Although I am a non-believer, I readily follow Jewish liturgical and conventional requirements when attending a house of prayer; but a lecture hall is not a synagogue, and I saw no reason to cover my head, as I informed my hosts on this occasion. They repeated their request, with some urgency and emphasis, and I muttered something about coercion. This was not a battle I wished to fight to the death, so when they pressed a *kippah* into my hand and begged '. . . out of respect for the Chief Rabbi', I gave a testy reply, donned the skullcap, and entered the hall. (When, some months later, I went to interview the Chief Rabbi, his secretary asked me whether I would like a *kippah*. 'Only if the Chief Rabbi insists,' I replied, and she backed off. The Chief Rabbi himself betrayed no sign of interest in the back of my head.)

There were about 200 North Londoners seated in the hall. A quick survey established that there was one other male not wearing a *kippah*, so I removed mine. Nobody noticed. The middle-aged man seated next to me showed the customary hospitality Jews demonstrate to strangers, *kippah*-ed or not. The Cockfosters and Southgate congregation was, he confessed, 'not very *frum*, not very intellectual', but they had clearly turned out *en masse* to hear their spiritual leader. 'We don't normally get a crowd like this,' said my neighbour, 'certainly not in *shul*. It's the same here as everywhere else. Most members join for the burial rights. Where are you from?'

The speakers were assembling on the platform: Rabbi Yisroel Fine; Dr Robert Winston, the eminent surgeon specializing in problems of infertility; and the Chief Rabbi himself. Lord Jakobovits certainly looks the part. His trim white beard has taken on a truly rabbinic truculence. His placid smile suggests a sympathy with his flock, but also a consciousness of his role as their shepherd. He did his best to look modest, if not undeserving, as Rabbi Fine heaped praise upon the head of the recently ennobled cleric.

The subject under discussion was infertility and the means of dealing with it: embryo implantation and insemination, and *in vitro* fertilization. It is a topic of considerable interest, since it opens up the possibilities of dealing in the future with genetic defects, including disorders such as Tay Sachs disease which are of special concern to the Jewish community. Dr Winston spoke lucidly about the current state of research. Then the Chief Rabbi, an expert in medical ethics, rose to his feet. He is swooningly in love with the sound of his own voice. Convolutions, parentheses, qualifying clauses, and a barrage of synonymous epithets purr from his mouth. Sentences that appear to have come to an end have merely encountered a breath mark. A cogent three-liner appearing to end with 'common interests' has merely paused while the Chief Rabbi takes another breath and appends 'and common concerns'. There are no 'aims' unless there are also 'objectives'; a 'certain mentality' pulls in its wake 'certain attitudes' and vice versa.

Despite the tendency towards waffle, the Chief Rabbi gives good value, for views as reactionary as his still have a novelty value even in Thatcherite Britain. However, his stance on the vexed issues raised by the work of Dr Winston and his colleagues was not unsophisticated. Donor insemination troubled him since it represented an intrusion into marriage, and he was rightly wary of the possible consequences of genetic manipulations carried out without sufficient controls. On the other hand, he confirmed that, unlike Catholic dogma, Jewish teachings do not grant full human status to an embryo until birth has taken place. Thus genetic manipulation and even abortion are permissible, though only if there is the gravest medical justification for such procedures. What troubled the Chief Rabbi most, however, was the use of an anonymous donor of the ovum. If an implanted embryo has been fertilized by the husband and a birth results, the child is registered as the offspring of the woman who bore the child. Thus, argued the Chief Rabbi, the birth certificate, which cites the bearer of the child and not the provider of the ovum as the 'mother', is 'a legalized fraud'. It was not merely the legal implications that bothered the Chief Rabbi, but the possibility of incest. If a donor provided a number of fertilized ova to different women, then all the children born from those embryos would be half-brothers and half-sisters. If birth certificates are false, then questions of identity become uncertain. And although he did not voice this fear on this occasion, the Chief Rabbi is also concerned that, since Jewish identity is conferred by the mother, the child grown from an ovum provided by a non-Jewish donor would not be halachically Jewish, even though the woman bearing the child was Jewish.

Another doctor, speaking from the floor, raised the question of surrogate motherhood. Was there a halachic position on surrogacy? No, admitted the Chief Rabbi, it was halachically moot, though prudence should discourage outsiders from becoming involved in the generation of life. It was genuinely instructive to listen to the Chief Rabbi dealing with such issues. Here was an echo of ancient Jewish tradition, the taking of problems, ethical or otherwise, to sages who then apply their great learning to finding a solution. The Chief Rabbi was not attempting to make irrevocable decisions but was trying instead to discuss, albeit tentatively, some very delicate and contentious matters, and he did so eloquently and thoughtfully. The boom of the word 'moot' fell on the hall like a cannon shot. It is not a word one hears very often from this highly opinionated rabbi.

In the early nineteenth century the rabbi of the Great Synagogue in London was traditionally regarded as the senior rabbi of the British congregations. With the foundation of the United Synagogue, the position of Chief Rabbi evolved. He is elected rather than appointed, and those congregations and bodies that contribute to the funding of the Chief Rabbi's office have their say. The office has never been considered in parochial terms. Chief Rabbi Hertz, who was elected in 1913, came from South Africa, and Lord Jakobovits, an emigrant from Germany in 1936, was Chief Rabbi of Ireland and a minister of the fashionable Fifth Avenue Synagogue in Manhattan before his election to the Chief Rabbinate in

1966. Since it is not always clear whether the Chief Rabbi is speaking in a personal capacity or in his role as head of most of the congregations of Britain and the Commonwealth, I asked him to define his roles, of which there are three.

Formally, he explained, 'I am the religious authority of some 200 or so congregations, mainly in this country but some in the Commonwealth, which recognize my office as their supreme authority, historically, traditionally, and constitutionally. They have elected me and I am accountable to them and I speak for them, and I can make rulings for them.' Secondly, Lord Jakobovits sees himself as the religious spokesman of the Jewish community at large. 'On issues like Soviet Jewry, Jewish-Christian relations, Israel, anti-Semitism, anything that needs a religious expression, religious spokesmanship, I would generally be expected and authorized to speak on behalf of the entire community, and I myself would be careful to ensure that what I say does reflect the consensus of opinion.'

His third role is the most problematic and controversial. When wearing this third hat, the Chief Rabbi 'speaks not on behalf of the community but on behalf of Judaism. So that when I make a statement, let us say on abortion or AIDS or moral issues in society, I don't attempt to reflect the thinking of my members any more than the archbishop or cardinal speaks on behalf of his members. Even if I were to speak on Sabbath observance I don't speak for the majority of my community. Nevertheless they would recognize that I am the authentic interpreter of Judaism and speak with an authentic voice on Jewish teachings.' And this is where he gets himself into trouble, for in this admittedly interpretative role, he lays himself open to challenge. When the Archbishop of Canterbury's Commission on Urban Priority Areas published its report *Faith in the City*, there was widespread consternation. Its attack on what was depicted as governmental neglect of the inner cities and the consequent exacerbation of the already severe problems of those areas was seen, by government supporters, as overt criticism of Conservative policies, and everyone knows that it's bad form for churchmen to comment on political issues, although it's perfectly all right for politicians to rubbish clerics they do not favour. The Chief Rabbi was invited to offer a Jewish perspective on the report, and, in a paper entitled, with typical Jakobovitsian grandeur, *From Doom to Hope*, he did so. To get matters off to an uncontroversial start, he described the Commission's report with breathtaking condescension as 'a fairly even balance of Christian teachings, moral sensitivity and, at times, a measure of patent political bias'.

The Chief Rabbi derived his own view from the recollection that immigrant Jews had also lived in deprived inner-city areas. He admitted that the experience of Jews in Whitechapel in the 1890s and that of blacks and Asians in Brick Lane ninety years later were not identical, but also noted that Jews often had to endure additional disabilities, such as an inability to speak English and the hostility of Fascist gangs in the 1930s. He quotes the farewell sermon he gave to his New York congregation in 1966: 'How did *we* break out of our ghettos and enter the mainstream of society and its privileges? How did *we* secure our emancipation and civil rights? Certainly not by riots and demonstrations, by violence and protest-marches . . . Above all, we worked on ourselves, not on others. We gave a better education to our children than anybody else had. We hallowed our home life. We channelled the ambition of our youngsters to academic excellence, not flashy cars.' Moreover 'let them throw out from their pulpits leaders who profess to be men of God but who openly defy law and order.' So much, one assumes, for Martin Luther King.

Rabbi Jakobovits was not the only cleric who gave the American civil rights movement scanty support. But he must be one of the few to be entirely unrepentant and to quote himself with unequivocal self-approval. When he applies his wisdom to the situation in contemporary Britain, he has much advice to offer. He observes that 'Jews at the time were content to be patient and to wait and struggle for several generations to attain their social objectives, whereas we now live in an impatient age demanding instant solutions'. He then wags his finger at those impatient new immigrants: 'It may still be salutary to remind those presently enduring much hardship and despair that others have faced similar trials before them, and that self-reliant efforts and perseverance eventually pay off.' This must be music to the ears of a single mother living in a decaying council block in Tower Hamlets.

The practical solution offered by the Chief Rabbi in *From Doom to Hope* is the same as that offered to his suffering household by the retired Professor Serebryakov in *Uncle Vanya*: 'You must work, my friends, work!' 'No work', thunders the Chief Rabbi from the comforts of his study in St John's Wood, 'is too menial to compromise human dignity and self-respect . . . The key to true contentment, in the Jewish view, can only be found in economic self-reliance and self-sufficiency . . . Cheap labour is more dignified than a free dole, and industriousness generates greater wealth than increased wages for decreasing hours of work.' Social injustices can be rectified not by giving alms but by helping 'the poor man to rehabilitate himself . . . so as to make him independent of help by others'. Having somehow secured employment thanks to the philanthropy of the rich, the lucky chap must refrain from such measures as 'the immorality of inflicting massive suffering on millions of innocent victims by the periodic shut-downs of essential public services and utilities'. It is not only the government, in Jakobovits's view, that has a measure of responsibility for urban decay: 'the selfishness of workers' must share the blame. And the solution? 'No Jewish contribution could be more valuable than to help turn despair into hope, resignation into confidence that – given determination, patience, perseverance, and faith in the infinite capacity of man to prevail over adversity – the new ghettos will be transformed as were the old and the growing wealth of the nation will increasingly be shared by all through shifting the emphasis from rights to duties and from having a good time to making the times good.' This peroration is a classic example of Jakobovitsian rhetoric, plump with hot air, thin on practicality.

The publication of *From Doom to Hope* did not go unnoticed. Although the Chief Rabbi did not intend it to be read as an overtly partisan document, it was hardly cause for astonishment when about one hundred Conservative MPs put down an early day motion offering him their congratulations. The Labour MP Leo Abse declared that the bishops had turned Jew and the Chief Rabbi had turned Christian, 'because his emphases were all on self-help, and because he rewrote Jewish history in this country.' Others such as the Orthodox socialist Zionist Arieh Handler criticized the Chief Rabbi not so much for his views, as for his failure to speak out much earlier. The bishops had at least given a lead, in Handler's view, whereas the Chief Rabbi had merely responded to their initiative. Alan Greenbat, the director of the Association for Jewish Youth who was appointed the Chief Rabbi's adviser on the inner cities *after* the report was published, thought that Jakobovits's views had not been fully taken on board: 'What he is actually saying to the world is that self-help is important. I don't think it's right to read into that the corollary that you're on your own, mate, and no one is going to give you a helping hand, because the Chief Rabbi feels strongly and passionately that we do have an obligation to help and to be of service to other people.'

Others were less charitable. The historian Dr Geoffrey Alderman declared that Jakobovits's response 'amounted to the most blatant act of political partiality on the part of a holder of the office since Hermann Adler came out in support of the war against the Boers.' His exhortations 'reflected a lamentable ignorance of the very different experiences of Jewish and black immigrants to these shores.' Alderman did, however, accept that the Chief Rabbi's views 'undoubtedly reflected a feeling widespread among Anglo-Jewry'.[1] The Reform Synagogues of Great Britain pointed out in its journal *Manna* that the Chief Rabbi was writing as though full employment were likely to be achieved in the near future. The *Manna* editorial concluded: 'To exhort those trapped by society in appalling social conditions merely to work harder and marry wisely is as out of touch with reality as was Marie Antoinette.' This accusation is frequently heard from the Chief Rabbi's critics. The head of a charitable organization was more scathing than most: 'All the Chief Rabbi is doing is displaying his ignorance. The Progressives are much more in touch with reality but are not consulted. Indeed, nobody seems to be consulted by this Chief Rabbi. There are thousands of Jews with skills and experience and breadth, and they are all ignored.'

When I put this point, rather more politely, to Lord Jakobovits, his response was somewhat vague: 'On social matters I do not necessarily have a single group that are expert in every sphere and whose opinion I can invariably take as reflecting the opinions within the community. But I have numerous connections, friends, some experts in these respective fields. On all these matters I haven't gone through a consultative process, but I've tested my opinions against people whose judgement I respect. It's not a formal process. On the inner cities I was aware that I did not speak on behalf of the majority of Jews – that wasn't my task – I made it perfectly clear that it was a document on Jewish thought.' Since the Chief Rabbi admits that his views are in no way representative, one can't help wondering what the value of such pronouncements are. Although he grants himself the status of being 'the authentic interpreter of Judaism', there is no such thing as a uniform interpretation of social issues; they are simply not susceptible to that kind of lesson-drawing.

'I am unabashedly Orthodox,' he told me. 'I'm expected to be Orthodox. Nobody would ever expect me to be a spokesman of opinions I do not share and that are outside the purview of the congregations for which I am responsible. I hold that Jewish attitudes must govern contemporary attitudes on current issues, whether they relate to Israel or social or moral issues here. I have not yet had a challenge that anything I said in my document on the inner cities was not authentically Jewish.'

In 1986 the Chief Rabbi turned his attention to the problem of AIDS. He did not, it must be said, follow the lead of certain Christian fundamentalist preachers and declare that AIDS was a form of divine retribution for the committing of unnatural acts. 'We are certainly never entitled', he wrote in *The Times*, 'to declare a particular form of suffering as a punishment for a particular manifestation of wrongdoing.' He denied the existence of any 'simplistic relationship between evil and misfortune'. And what exactly is AIDS? Not a virus, as I'd always understood, but 'the price we pay for the "benefits" of the permissive society which, helped by the pill, liberal legislation and more "enlightened" attitudes, has demolished the last defences of sexual restraint and self-discipline, leading to a collapse of nature's self-defence against degeneracy.'

But how to combat the spread of this terrible disease? Not, declares the Chief Rabbi, by making condoms more widely available 'even if they temporarily reduce the transmission of AIDS'. Jewish law, he explains, cites the saving of life as the overriding value except in the case of forbidden liaisons, murder, and idolatry. 'The rule', declares the Chief Rabbi in more magnanimous spirit, 'might be invoked to treat more leniently the distribution of clean needles for drug abusers.' So what is the solution? 'The cultivation of new attitudes calculated to restore reverence for the generation of life and the enjoyment of sexual pleasures exclusively within marriage. Nothing short of a moral revolution will in time contain the scourge.' The phrase 'in time' reveals the extraordinary impracticality of the Chief Rabbi's nostrum. Thousands may, indeed will, die while the rest of us must endure uplifting sermons. In a memorandum on AIDS to the House of Commons Social Services Committee, the Chief Rabbi attacked those aspects of the government campaign to warn people of the dangers of the disease that stressed 'safe sex'. 'The campaign encourages promiscuity by advertising it. It tells people not what is right, but how to do wrong and get away with it.'

Not that it matters particularly what religious leaders say on moral issues. There is no evidence that Jews, at least outside the ultra-Orthodox community, adhere to conventional sexual morality any more or less keenly than any other segment of the British people. Lord Jakobovits would, however, like to see British sexual practices regulated by the law of the land. When rumours first reached me that the Chief Rabbi was seriously proposing the re-criminalization of sexual 'offences', I took this to be a slander spread by Reform Jews. So when I spoke to Lord Jakobovits, I asked him to dispose of these rumours if he wished.

'I would prefer', he began gravely, 'the offence of homosexual acts to be kept on the statute books, even if we do not have prosecutions under the act. Adultery, for instance, I would like to be regarded as a crime, still actionable – at least in theory, if only to express the public abhorrence, the public rejection, of these acts as being objectionable.' I hadn't been aware of a great public hue and cry against adultery, but no doubt the Chief Rabbi has access to different sources. 'Law', declared this newly appointed member of the upper chamber of Parliament, 'is there not merely to exact punishment. Law is there to set public standards of what is right and wrong. We have no other gauge by which to indicate society's standards as to what is moral and what is immoral.' What is peculiar about the Chief Rabbi's wish to see sexual practices of which Judaism disapproves outlawed under British law is his insistence that he doesn't care particularly whether or not the law is enforced. His declaration that legislation is the only way to set moral standards seems clearly flawed, not to say false. I cited the example of making wounding remarks that upset other people. We would all find this morally deplorable, but we don't need legislation to proscribe the act of hurting other people's feelings. But the Chief Rabbi is nothing if not consistent.

'I think it *should* be on the statute books. It should be included under the laws of libel, and slander. In Judaism it certainly is included. I'm not sure how this could be introduced here, but if I'm asked as a Jew how do I relate to this, I feel there ought to be certain offences that create a public sense of horror merely by being *stated* as being offences. For the same reason I would be in favour of restoring the death penalty, not to carry it out, because in Jewish law we abolished it 2,000 years ago, but because certain crimes ought to be looked upon as so heinous as to forfeit the right to live – at least in theory, even if we in practice don't carry it out.'

When I suggested that this was a mere indulgence in gesture – pressing for the passage of laws that were not intended to be enforced – the Chief Rabbi countered that he was hoping thereby to create certain attitudes in society, to reinforce the sanctity of life and of marriage. 'Society has no right to withdraw its collective judgement, and the only way to express a collective judgement is not by way of a gesture but by way of defining as only the law can define what is acceptable conduct and what is not. I'm not suggesting we should impose these standards. I strongly object to religious coercion, as I keep saying in Israel. I want to influence people by education and persuasion. I'd like the majority of our citizens to be so raised that they will vote such laws into force. I want the majority to

203

express itself. I believe the majority would support this, just as the majority supports the death penalty.'

'It's all very well for you to agitate for such moral legislation and then say you don't intend that the penalties should be carried out, but once a law is on the statute book, its enforcement is not dependent on your whim.'

'To the extent to which I could have an influence,' replied the Chief Rabbi, missing my point, 'I would hedge the imposition of the death penalty around with so many conditions – for instance, circumstantial evidence is unacceptable in Jewish law – and single out deliberate attacks on innocent third parties, such as hostage-taking and terrorism. Such people are outlaws and therefore may not have to go through the normal judicial procedure. Society itself is under siege, so society must protect itself. The law must reflect this new concern and the new circumstances that have arisen.' Such pronouncements, even though made in the course of a conversation, seem far removed from the interpretation of Judaism that he regards as his rabbinical responsibility. The careful distinctions and shading of grey areas that characterized his remarks on infertility at Cockfosters are a far cry from such shoot-from-the-hip suggestions as denying legal process to terrorists. The Chief Rabbi, whether casting his eye on urban decay or civil rights or serious crime, seems oblivious of causation but keen as mustard on grandiose remedies.

It is not his stress on individual responsibility, nor his reminders of the crucial importance of stable family life, nor his draconian puritanism that have endeared him to the Conservative rulers of Britain. Nor is there much evidence of overt partisanship in favour of Mrs Thatcher and her ministers. Instead, I suggest, it is his willingness to absolve governments of major responsibility for social conditions that must fall as the sweetest music on the ears of those who govern us. The Chief Rabbi's admiration for 'Victorian values' (though he has not, to my knowledge, used the fatuous phrase himself) and eagerness to play down social conditions that may have been brought about, at least in part, by specific government policies, have allowed him to supplant all but the most servile Anglican bishops as Mrs Thatcher's favourite cleric. Not surprising, then, that his elevation to the peerage was seen, even within the Jewish community, as a mixed blessing.

Might it not be preferable, I suggested to Lord Jakobovits, for the leaders of the principal religious bodies to be awarded *ex officio* peerages, as is already the case with Anglican bishops? Then there could be no suggestion of political patronage of religious leaders. The Chief Rabbi is unhappy about that idea, on the grounds that it might create more difficulties than it solves and raise the possibility of disestablishing the Church of England, which is not an issue with which he, as a Jewish leader, would wish to become involved. His peerage 'was a purely personal honour. It was given in that spirit and was accepted in that spirit and understood in that spirit. Therefore I do not see in this the raising of the office to the peerage. Personally, I by no means greeted this without reservations and pangs of conscience. Nevertheless, I think on balance many of my initial fears proved unjustified and I do not see any conflict of interest here. The appointment is not a political appointment and I sit on the cross-benches, and I am absolutely independent. There would be a conflict of interest if I chose to make it so, if I became a crusader for a particular political doctrine, but by conviction I see certain virtues in all the party platforms, and I will never identify with any one of them. I just am not by persuasion of any one political party.'

On the announcement of the Chief Rabbi's elevation in January 1988, the voice of the Jewish Establishment was loud in praise of the honour, as though all British Jews somehow shared in it. A few people, including some leading Progressive rabbis, were appalled, though they tended to keep their views to themselves. Julia Neuberger ('that woman'), on the other hand, was quite happy to express her views: 'I don't think there's any doubt that Jakobovits is a total Thatcherite. Some of my colleagues seem terribly upset that he's been given a peerage, but on the whole I think it's quite a good thing. On some issues he's been very good. He's been particularly good on campaigning for refugees, and spoke on this subject in his maiden speech. But his links with government are not particularly helpful, because I think it makes people perceive the whole Jewish community as being Tory, which it isn't. But it is plainly wrong that the Chief Rabbi is regarded as the spokesman for the community, and he very much presents himself in that manner.'

The peerage is in some respects a red herring. After all, few can remember which prime minister it was that dispatched the Methodist leader Donald Soper to the House of Lords, and Methodism seems to have survived Lord Soper's honest partisanship. The issue for Anglo-Jewry remains the reactionary stands the Chief Rabbi takes on social issues, since they seem to be at variance with the more liberal views held by a substantial proportion of the Jewish community. Leo Abse cites the Chief Rabbi's article in *The Times* on homosexuality 'in which he claims it's a sin, an evil, you may perhaps have some compassion for them but nothing must be done to allow them to exist as a community with community rights – because that in his view would undermine the family. I also deplore his attitude to, and the comments he made about, the blacks and trade unionists in his reply to the Church's Inner Cities report. I also believe that every effort should be made to assist the infertile. So I was appalled that the Chief Rabbi was giving support to Enoch Powell's bill that was in fact aimed at preventing scientists and doctors pursuing research which would enable them both to improve the techniques of *in vitro* fertilization and also perhaps to conquer inherited diseases. He recoils from the Warnock Report's suggestion that people who have had a child by such methods should be able to register the child as if it were their own, because his concerns are that a child that was not halachically Jewish might be treated as though it were. That's a racialist attitude. His approach to the family, which he's always talking about, and my approach are totally different, and they both stem from a commitment to the family. My attitude is rooted in the alternative Jewish tradition which has always existed, whether in the excommunicated Spinoza or a non-believer like Freud. I believe that I belong to the alternative tradition, and that makes me as much a traditionalist as he is. Mine is the approach of a Jewish humanist.' Of course that is, in the eyes of the Orthodox, tantamount to a contradiction in terms.

Nor do the Chief Rabbi's views win him many friends on the Progressive wing. Rabbi Barbara Borts was characteristically blunt: 'He may be regarded as a spokesman for Anglo-Jewry by the *goyim*, but not by us. The idea of a Chief Rabbi is a Christian concept anyway. The only chiefs there used to be were the heads of famous established academies. It's a nonsense. The Federation don't accept him, and he's not completely free because he's got his Beth Din to answer to. But the Christians, especially in England, like a focal point.' David Goldberg was more judicious. 'We accord an unspoken primacy to the Chief Rabbi.' Such a British formulation! 'Where he does speak on behalf of all of the community, we're perfectly happy to accept the fiction that he is Chief Rabbi, as indeed do the Federation to the right of him. But he's causing a lot of concern at the moment in Progressive circles because he appears to have moved to the right, of choice. His recent pronouncement on AIDS and his response to the Church of England report on the Inner Cities have been disappointing. He's a product of European culture, but he's not steeped in it the way that, for example, Louis Jacobs is. Fortunately my authority doesn't come from whether the Chief Rabbi and his cohorts recognize me or not. It comes from my 2,500 members, and I'm quite happy with that.'

Jonathan Magonet acknowledges the Chief Rabbi's status; it simply comes with the office. 'But there is considerable resentment towards him, and the more right-wing he gets, the less credibility he has internally in the Jewish world. But he does do a good representative job to the outside world. However, the right-wing Orthodox don't accept him, and the Reform and Liberal don't accept him, but no one calls the bluff entirely, though we're getting close to it now. The country likes to have representative figures, but what we gain from it I don't really know. The left-wingers feel very resentful, and quite rightly. What happens is that Julia Neuberger or anybody who argues against him is automatically marginalized. The Progressives who have become media figures don't speak as representatives, but tend to speak to issues. They are there by virtue of their talent. The Chief Rabbi is there by virtue of his office. Look at it the other way round. Why are there so few public spokesmen for the Orthodox point of view? The Progressives appear because they have something to say: Lionel Blue in terms of popular spirituality, Hugo Gryn in terms of statesman-like dealing with the formal Jewish issues like the Holocaust, and Julia as a gadfly.' (Or, as Barbara Borts put it: 'The Christians have got Lionel Blue as their spiritual Jew, Hugo Gryn as their Holocaust Jew, Julia Neuberger as their feminist Jew, and the Chief Rabbi's their Tory Party Jew.')

The supporters of the Chief Rabbi seem unable to warm to their task of dishing out the praise. Sidney Bloch, a businessman who has done much to reorganize the structure of Jewish charities, offered a somewhat tepid assessment: 'Obviously, because he's Orthodox, he's not prepared to bend the rules to accommodate those who are less Orthodox. But he's not intolerant. We can't have half a dozen Chief Rabbis. We are obliged to have one who conforms. He's not like the chairman of a committee, he's not speaking for the whole community on moral issues but for himself as Chief Rabbi.' Leon Brittan's anodyne tribute carried, perhaps unwittingly, a sting in the tail: 'The Chief Rabbi speaks with the authentic voice of Orthodox Jewry and the reason why he has reached greater prominence than some of his predecessors is that he does so in a way that appears to strike a chord within the country as a whole – among some people.'

'Some people' does not include Anthony Blond, whose eyes glazed when I mentioned the topic to him: 'The Chief Rabbi is just another cleric. I don't owe any allegiance to him.' Or Lord Goodman: 'The Chief Rabbi has just been ennobled. I was delighted and wrote him a polite note. But by my standards some of his views are reactionary and likely to fragment the community more than any liberalization.' Or former MP Ian Mikardo: 'The Chief Rabbi is an awful reactionary. He's well to the right of Thatcher. His reaction to the Church's report on the Inner Cities was absolutely disgraceful. I don't know what sources of Jewish teaching and tradition provide him with material for disputing that what the inner cities of Great Britain need is an influx of resources.'

Ivan Lawrence QC, a Conservative MP and a Progressive Jew, worked hard at a more balanced assessment. Reminding me that Progressive Judaism has been growing proportionately in recent years, he observed that 'it's less acceptable than it was to have the Chief Rabbi as a religious spokesman. But to me personally it's acceptable enough until such time as the Progressive groups produce a leader of like calibre. There are a number of leaders, splendid men, whom I admire immensely, in the Reform and Liberal communities, but none of them seeks to represent, nor is thought of by non-Jews as representing, the religious Jewish community. So I'm perfectly happy for the Chief Rabbi to broadly represent my Jewishness, in a religious sense, whilst it's understood that I don't agree with everything he says, and it's understood by the non-Jewish community that he doesn't represent all Jewry. He's a fine man and an outstanding leader. This has absolutely nothing to do with the fact that he has incurred the wrath of the political left in the Jewish community by his article on the inner cities. He has a difficult position. The Chief Rabbi is the safeguarder of the traditional religion. He has to deal with strong feeling from some Orthodox Jews who believe that the non-Orthodox are little more than a bunch of *goyim*. I can only say that my own relationships wit˙ the Chief Rabbi, which are tangential, have always been delightful, and he knows I don't agree with his Orthodoxy. He is as reasonable as it is possible for someone in that position to be. He is often misjudged by the Progressive community as being too reactionary, when I don't think he really is. He isn't a bigot and he does appreciate there are other points of view. I have great respect for him.'

Even some of the Chief Rabbi's most vociferous critics agree that he has taken an admirable position on the problems within the State of Israel. The Jewish Establishment in Britain has closed ranks on this subject in its anxiety to persuade the world that diaspora Jews are solidly in support of Israel, come what may. This unthinking attitude has not been shared by the Chief Rabbi, who in 1982, during Israeli military actions within Lebanon, was one of those who posed some difficult and timely questions about the morality of Israeli policy. 'Life is worth more than land,' he has often said. He has also expressed his disapproval of attempts at coercion by the religious parties within Israel and distanced himself from those who rule out accommodation with Israel's enemies. That the former Chief Rabbi of Israel, Shlomo Goren, has anathematized Jakobovits as a 'dangerous man' testifies to his stout independence of mind, which he again displayed after the Israeli general election of November 1988. That independence may have its limits. Some observers worry about the close links between the Chief Rabbi and the handful of rich men who bankroll the great institutions of Anglo-Jewry. He is obliged to work with them closely and cannot afford to alienate them, just as on religious issues he cannot afford to alienate his Beth Din. In a bold address to the St John's Wood United synagogue, the editor of the *Jewish Chronicle*, Geoffrey Paul, remarked of the Chief Rabbi: 'He can and does privately influence the interplay of the various forces active in Anglo-Jewry, on the whole positively. But he is also, to a major extent, their prisoner.'

It is some kind of tribute to Immanuel Jakobovits that virtually no one in the Jewish community is indifferent to him. He has stirred up debate, probably to a greater extent than even he would wish, and given his office an institutional power and prestige it had not previously attained. He has also been a major force behind the remarkable expansion of Jewish education in recent decades. He proclaims his views not exactly, it seems to me, out of courage, even though he must sense that the majority of British Jews don't really believe adultery should be made a crime, but out of a kind of obtuseness. The orotundity of expression gives a rhetorical gloss to what is often a paucity of thought. As *From Doom to Hope* showed, his analysis is often shallow, his solutions simplistic. While giving the impression of subtlety and fine distinctions, his rhetoric conceals thought-processes that are often narrow and inflexible and doggedly imperceptive.

Moreover, his attempts to put his ideas into practice can be woefully heavy-handed. Quite recently, the Lubavitch Foundation suggested to the Chief Rabbi that it would a good wheeze to discourage Jewish doctors from performing abortions or indeed from recommending abortions for 'social' reasons. A letter was drawn up and circulated with the approval of the Chief Rabbi, recommending that doctors opposed to abortions for 'social' reasons should not only refuse to perform them but should also refuse to refer patients to doctors of more liberal views. A Jewish general practitioner who received one of these letters felt deeply affronted that the Chief Rabbi should have the impertinence to tell him how to run his practice. In addition, the letter was circulated in a most bizarre way. Since there is no way of knowing which doctors are Jewish, Lubavitch combed the medical directory in search of Jewish-sounding names. Consequently a number of non-Jewish doctors called, say, Stern or Lewis were astonished to receive the advice of the Chief Rabbi, while Jewish physicians called Smith were left to fend for themselves.[2]

In a few years the Chief Rabbi will probably retire. It is difficult to speculate on who his successor is likely to be. One senior layman said to me: 'The fact that Jakobovits has such an overpowering position in this country is very bad for the development of the rest of the rabbinate. It's like a tall tree with too many leaves. Whatever is underneath doesn't get a chance to grow.' Much of the smart money is on Jonathan Sacks. He is exceptionally able and articulate, and sees eye to eye with the present Chief Rabbi on many issues, including some of the social ones that have caused such controversy. While firmly in the Orthodox camp, he is no zealot and, as has already been noted, is anxious not to freeze out of the community those Jews who are lax or indifferent to religious observance. There are others who fear that the more fanatical wing of Orthodox Anglo-Jewry will lobby for one of their representatives, which would lead to even greater polarization within the community. We shall have to wait and see.

– 16 –

The Board of Deputies

WHILE the Chief Rabbi and his court worry over religious and moral issues, it is the Board of Deputies of British Jews that constitutes the lay leadership of Anglo-Jewry. Delegates are elected to the Board from synagogues and other organizations; Progressive Jews are represented alongside more Orthodox congregations, even though they remain very much in the minority. The Board was founded in 1760 by Jews from the Portuguese community. 'Deputies' is an anglicization of *deputados*. Like all the other institutions of Anglo-Jewry, the Board remained firmly in the control of the old families, the Jewish aristocracy, until the early years of this century. It never occurred to some of the Board's senior figures that they were in any way accountable, and during World War I, at about the time of the Balfour Declaration, leaders of the Board and of the Anglo-Jewish Association took it upon themselves to write to *The Times* to register the distaste of the Anglo-Jewish community for nascent Zionism. Since the Anglo-Jewish community hadn't actually been consulted on this very important question, a huge row developed. As a consequence the Board was forced to change its character, and the representatives, and the interests, of sections of the community that had previously been either under-represented or not represented at all, such as the immigrants and the provincial communities, began to make an impact.

Not that the Board became overnight a responsive and democratic body. The instinct of its leaders has always been to pour oil over potentially troubled waters. Its desire is not to rock the boat; it has always been considered bad form for the Jewish community and its organizations to call attention to themselves. During the rise of Nazism in Germany, there were some British Jews who sought to express their disapproval by boycotting German goods, but the Board would have nothing to do with such proposals. The conventional wisdom dictated that for Jews to call attention to their plight might serve as a pretext for anti-Semitic attacks. Despite the absence of any evidence to support this view, it is an attitude that is still widely held. Geoffrey Alderman has pointed out that in the 1930s 'the Board publicly sought to counteract anti-Semitism at home by calling upon British Jews to adopt a deliberately low profile ... A handbook, in English and German, issued jointly by the Board of Deputies and the German Jewish Aid Committee in January 1939, warned refugees not to make themselves conspicuous, not to talk "in a loud voice", and not to take part in any political activities.'[1] The Board founded its defence committee in 1936 to guard and fight against anti-Semitism in British life, but was wary of supporting the activists who fought the Fascists in the East End, since many of those activists were also Communists. The Board prefers to work behind the scenes. Its leaders have regular contacts with politicians and other persons of influence, with a view to ensuring that Jewish interests are served or at any rate not harmed. The President of the Board, Dr Lionel Kopelowitz, told me: 'I'm a great believer in doing all sorts of things in private, because you achieve much more influence.' This makes the real achievements of the Board difficult to gauge, though observers familiar with its diplomatic activities assure me that in the 1960s and 1970s, for example, the Board was quite successful at defusing the activities of the National Front.

When one refers to 'the Board' one must be careful to distinguish the leaders of the Board from the deputies themselves. The Board is a parliamentary body whose deputies are elected for three-year terms. The deputies, who meet monthly, elect the executive officers who carry out the committee work and official representations that constitute the daily grind of the Board. It resembles the distinction between government and Parliament: what happens at Cabinet level is crucial, but what happens on the floor of the House is usually of trifling importance. The deputies represent about 250 congregations and organizations, many of which are entitled to elect more than one deputy. In addition the Board staffs a Statistical and Demographic Unit, which has produced many fascinating and detailed surveys of Jewish communities in Britain. The Board takes an active part in the Council of Christians and Jews, and supplies lecturers to schools and other interested groups. The deputies also elect the members of ten committees that deal with such matters as

Israel, education and youth, Jewish defence, *shechita*, public relations, and parliamentary relations. These committees draw up reports, which are then submitted to the monthly plenary sessions to which all deputies are invited. Recommendations and resolutions are discussed and voted upon.

Even though many of the deputies, especially those representing provincial communities, make but infrequent appearances at the plenary sessions, that didn't prevent some of them from objecting strongly when in 1988 the number of deputies was reduced to about 460 from 660 in order to produce a more manageable parliamentary body. Dr Kopelowitz explains the reasons for the decision: 'The principle I adopted was that the Board must be big enough to be representative of all sections of the community, but small enough to be effective.' Under the old system, there was one deputy per 500 Jews; under the new, there will be one deputy per 700 Jews, which still seems remarkably generous. There used to be no maximum number of deputies per congregation, however large; in future the maximum number of deputies per congregation will be five.

The Board is not concerned with religious matters, though there is clearly an overlap between the religious and lay dimensions of certain issues. Where religious matters are inextricably involved in the Board's deliberations, its constitution requires the officers to seek and accept the views of the religious authorities, including the leaders of the Reform and Liberal Synagogues. The ultra-Orthodox communities play no part in the Board. In the early 1970s, when it was agreed that the Board should consult Progressive as well as Orthodox religious authorities, the ultra-Orthodox Adath Yisroel group walked out, since they couldn't bring themselves to accept Progressive rabbis as religious authorities – at least not on Judaism.

I asked the secretary general of the Board, Hayim Pinner, to explain how on an issue such as *shechita* it was possible to differentiate between the religious and lay aspects. 'We are clear about our role,' he told me. 'Our role is the defence of *shechita*. A Jew should have the right to slaughter animals according to our beliefs, rites and rituals. The government has always recognized that and continues to recognize that. Now the arguments as to whether the animal should be upside down, inside out, these are religious matters and not our business. If the rabbis say it's okay, we're not going to argue.' The Board is essentially a political organization, and concerns itself with such issues as anti-Semitism, parliamentary matters, race relations, education, and Sunday trading. 'Sunday trading is an example of a very complex issue, because there are exemptions to

Sunday trading laws for religious Jews. The Home Office entrusts us with enforcing those laws. We interview every applicant for an exemption. There can be a lot of money in this for the person concerned, and he has to satisfy us that he has a conscientious objection on religious grounds to trading on the Sabbath. If we're satisfied, we can issue him with a licence to trade on Sunday. An important new problem for us is security. We advise synagogues and schools on security matters. That means co-operation with the police, because we ourselves don't have policing powers.'

The most common criticism made of the Board is that it is little more than a talking-shop. Many of those who find it wearisome to listen to rambling speeches from fellow deputies nevertheless defend this aspect of the Board's activities. Ivan Lawrence, who is a Member of Parliament as well as a deputy, believes 'that in a free society a body which raises issues, discusses them, gets everybody's point of view, which allows for the venting of criticism, working feelings about certain issues out of the system, such a body is absolutely vital. If the Board did no more than provide an outlet for discussion, debate, and argument, it would be a success, because that function is very important. Of course the Board does much more than that. It acts as a link between the various synagogues and Jewish organizations and the wider Jewish community. There are the Board committees, and the views which they represent to government, either directly by Board representations or indirectly through people like me. We can feed back into our parliamentary committees the feelings of the Jews in their constituencies. And this can work in reverse. Sometimes people like Michael Fidler stand up at the Board and put a Conservative Party point of view. I think that's extremely valuable. Any institution with such a substantial membership which articulates existing policies and constantly reviews future policies on such vital areas as *shechita*, Soviet Jewry, or Jewish education, has to be very important.'

One Sunday morning, as the deputies were gathering for their monthly session, I made my way upstairs to the small half-empty gallery. I looked down on the throng of deputies below, milling as though at a cocktail party, while at the far end of the hall the honorary officers were gathering on the platform. This main auditorium at Woburn House looks as shabby and makeshift as a school assembly hall, and the figures on the platform could easily pass for a band of housemasters. Hayim Pinner, short, plump, and dapper, with neatly waved hair, exudes the benign self-confidence of the efficient mandarin. He, after all, doesn't have to conduct the plenary sessions; his work is done before and after these often unruly meetings. At the centre of this band of officers sat Dr Lionel Kopelowitz, who has the unenviable task of chairing these meetings. Dr Kopelowitz is an old hand at this line of work, as he seems to have adorned every committee of the British Medical Association over the past thirty years.

At 10.15 sharp the meeting began and the deputies seated themselves parliamentary fashion, in rows facing each other across a gangway, even though at the Board there is of course no such thing as government and opposition. Although women are conspicuous by their absence among the honorary officers, there is a fair sprinkling of women among the deputies, a body otherwise dominated by elderly gentlemen. Dr Kopelowitz rose to his feet to give his presidential address. Although a kindly man, Kopelowitz has an impossible public manner. He glowers at his audience, wagging fingers and jowls in what is supposed to be an air of decisiveness but which comes across as plain bad temper. When he wishes to emphasize, he berates; when he seeks to implore, he hectors.

A lengthy debate on Israel was followed by a constitutional debate prompted by the decision to reduce the number of deputies. There is nothing any debating body enjoys so much as a constitutional wrangle, for it allows masters of the form to play all the tricks in the parliamentary book – points of order, amendments, improperly drawn-up amendments, motions back, motions forward, closure, insufficient majorities. Some of the younger deputies have mastered this art, and run circles round the older, less nimble deputies, who never seem to understand what is supposed to be going on and are continually rising to their feet to give passionate addresses on the wrong amendment. The agility of the younger deputies is admirable, but sheer force of numbers means that all this deftness goes for nothing; when the vote is taken, the old gentlemen usually have a clear majority, and life goes on just as it did before the debate began.

A deputy called Levin got the debate off to an excellent start by suggesting that synagogues that did not hold daily services shouldn't be entitled to representation on the Board since they were halachically out of order. This delicious dig at the Progressive synagogues was widely enjoyed by the other deputies, but as a serious proposal it was a non-starter since the Board is simply not interested in halachic eligibility. Various amendments were then put by one of the young firebrands ('young' at the Board means under forty-five), Jerry Lewis, who sought

215

to increase the representation of women and young people. In so doing he touched upon the sensitive matter that the Federation of Synagogues, for instance, denies its womenfolk a vote (though widows inherit the vote of their departed spouse). The Board, roared Lewis, must insist that the women of the community should enjoy full rights and that includes voting rights. A little old man rose to his feet – yes, Morris Lederman himself, born in Poland in 1908 and, it seems, President of the Federation ever since. Like a lovable character out of Yiddish theatre, he shuffled up to the microphone and began, in heavily accented English: 'I'm not against ladies to be represented on the Board . . .' The deputies must have heard it all before, since they cried with one voice: *'But!'* And Mr Lederman obliged: 'But . . .' and he argued that synagogues were autonomous and it was not for the Board to tell them how to elect their deputies.

After a few more speeches, a vote was taken, only to be followed by wrangling about whether correct procedures had been followed. Deputies shouted at each other across the floor, points of order were made rebuking the Chair, while another deputy tried to incite Mr Lewis's supporters to walk out. By now it was almost 12.30; absolutely nothing had been achieved, and it was time to break for lunch. I went home.

Only to return a month later. The Board, after much procrastination, had drawn up a statement on the situation in Israel and the Occupied Territories. It was a vacuous and inoffensive document, a few paragraphs of judicious waffle. A number of deputies rose to their feet to argue that the statement was too weak. Michael Fidler, a former Conservative MP and President of the Board from 1967 to 1973, stressed the need for unity and then delivered a scathing attack on Arthur Hertzberg, a distinguished American rabbi and academic who had dared to reveal that diaspora Jewry was split in its attitude towards Israeli policies. Another deputy savaged an article by the historian Geoffrey Alderman, whom he accused of 'irresponsible mischief' and of being virtually an anti-Semite. These *ad hominem* attacks are one of the more enjoyable features of the plenary sessions, and such attacks are invariably addressed at people who are not present.

This sideshow came to an abrupt end when the arrival of Yehuda Avner, the Israeli ambassador, was announced. All the delegates rose to their feet as he processed up the central aisle. Avner discussed the unrest without once discussing its causes and argued that the restoration of public order had to be the first priority of any government. When he sat down there was a standing ovation, although some deputies stubbornly remained seated. Dr Kopelowitz's voice rose to its most excited high pitch as he acclaimed 'your thrilling address' as 'a *tour de force*'. Now that Israel was out of the way, the deputies could turn their attention to more important matters such as constitutional changes, this time in protest against the steep rise in affiliation fees for synagogues; this, it was plausibly argued, would hit small congregations very hard indeed. Dr Kopelowitz took a vote on a constitutional amendment, which was clearly passed, but then announced to the astonished deputies that it hadn't been passed at all because a three-quarters majority was required. Although he happened to be right, he had neglected to inform the electors of this requirement before the vote was taken. Deputies demanded a fresh vote, but Kopelowitz was having none of it. Uproar, and even the president of the United Synagogue rose to his feet to protest. But the President of the Board wasn't going to be bullied by anyone. The vote stood. I went home.

Who does the Board of Deputies represent? Eighty per cent of the deputies are elected by synagogues, the remainder being selected by organizations such as the Association of Jewish Ex-Servicemen, the Federation of Women Zionists, the Union of Jewish Students, and so on. That half of Anglo-Jewry which is not affiliated to a synagogue or organization is in effect denied representation. This is a valid criticism, although it is difficult to see how it could be otherwise. Dr Kopelowitz points out that 'as long as there is no census of the Jewish community, how do you carve out an electoral roll of the community? Synagogue membership continues to be the most effective criterion for demonstrating Jewish identification. We've also always recognized that there must also be an institutional and organizational representation. But everybody on the Board must represent somebody. You don't speak for yourself. You're accountable. Whilst deputies are not delegates and can't be mandated, nevertheless there are times when their accountability can be tested. Take *shechita*. If you represent an Orthodox synagogue and you regard *shechita* as antiquated and cruel, then I think you would be called to account by your constituency because you wouldn't be representing their views.' He also made the point that unaffiliated Jews are denied representation not only because it is very difficult to identify them, but because they have no organizational status and coherence. Nevertheless, the unavoidably unrepresentative nature of the Board weakens its claim to speak as the united voice of Anglo-Jewry.

217

A more serious criticism of the Board is that Jews of eminence not just in the Jewish community but in British life play virtually no part in it. When I asked Sir Isaiah Berlin about the Board, he murmured blandly that 'it did no harm', but it was clear that he had very little interest in the formal bodies that make up the Jewish Establishment. Ivan Lawrence admitted that the Board is unrepresentative and that 'some of the leading people in the country whom you would think would be on the Board are not, either because they're not interested or don't find it constructive or effective enough. But that doesn't mean that the Board is no good. It means that the Board could be improved by devising some way in which more important people of leadership quality could be encouraged to go on it.' Fair enough, only no such reforms are being proposed. Arieh Handler, a deputy who grew up in Germany, compared the Jewish organizations there before the war with those in Britain. 'We had *Einheitsgemeinde*, unity committees. It was like a small Board in every town. The elected officers were usually the top people in the community – not the rabbi or someone who had a lot of money, but top academics, medical men, lawyers, businessmen. So the level of discussion was very, very high. Here in Britain, though it's improving a little bit, the academics, the top professional people, are usually not members, though you do get the occasional MP.

'The people who are elected are not necessarily the best men for the job. Often a certain type of intellectual doesn't even want to be elected. Anglo-Jewry is very well organized, but anything connected with scholarship, with culture, with art, here we are very weak. Prominent Jews are not integrated into the community. Sometimes somebody in a congregation wants a bit of honour, so they send him to the Board. This also applies sometimes to the honorary officers. Anglo-Jewry is very formalist. We don't want the discussion of serious matters to be in the centre of our discussions. We are a Judaism of dinners; we go from one to another. That's the centre of all our Jewish activity. It's better now, but it was this way for many years. That is one reason why Anglo-Jewry plays a very unimportant part in the councils of world Jewry. We hold many positions, but in reality our voice is not heard. We have wonderful people in the community who could contribute, but they say they don't want anything to do with the Board.' The feeling sometimes seems to be mutual, as in Stanley Kalms's assertion to me, in a tone of such confidence that he made it seem incontrovertible: 'You don't expect the intellectuals to share the same platforms with the lay activists.'

Arieh Handler would rather that the plenary sessions were addressed by community leaders on such matters as Jewish education or youth movements, so that deputies would be properly informed before sounding off on such subjects; this would give better guidance to the Board's committees as they pursue such issues. But the crucial issues – education, polarization, whatever – are scarcely ever raised, let alone discussed, at the Board. 'The Board should focus the attention of the community on certain problems, force the community to think about these things. Instead, when you look at the Board agenda or minutes over the last ten years, you'll find the same discussions on the same problems: a little bit of anti-Semitism, a little bit of Israel, *shechita*. What we don't do is focus on certain issues and go more deeply into them. Even if we come to the conclusion that we're split on certain issues, that doesn't matter. But we're too formal. It's the same in the United Synagogue. Presidents and vice-presidents are often elected on the basis that it's your turn, which means that the person who holds high office isn't necessarily the best.' His views were echoed by Professor Ludwik Finkelstein, a Hendon deputy, who told a plenary session that 'it is disgraceful that this Board wastes endless time on totally irrelevant issues largely concerned with the self-esteem of members.'[2]

Jonathan Magonet, the head of Leo Baeck College, while believing that 'if we didn't have the Board, I don't suppose it would make much difference', does nevertheless find some value in its existence. The Reform synagogues were, he told me, somewhat reluctant to participate in the Board, even though they had fought for their right to representation. 'We were forced to enter that sphere, which I wasn't happy about at the time, but on the other hand it matured us a bit. You can't just be a spiritual movement. You've got to have your feet on the ground. The more the Board becomes polarized and politicized, the more you're forced to be there and be represented. There's a whole group of people for whom synagogue life is not very meaningful, but for whom that sort of argy-bargy is their Jewish bread and butter. The Board does provide an outlet for harmless fun, and it gives a frame of reference to outside bodies. The difficulty is that all such establishments tend to be seen as more important than they are. They get the press coverage, whereas other things which are perhaps far more important get ignored because they don't have that status. It's totally different from America, where this problem about being a minority within an established society doesn't exist. Here we imitate the Establishment by creating our own Establishment hierarchy. It's a

219

necessary British institution, but in America Jews are a minority among minorities, which gives them far greater self-confidence. The Reform and Liberal groups here are looked down upon not so much because of our theology but because we are not part of the Establishment.'

Stanley Kalms, very much an Establishment figure though an attractively rough-edged one, defends the Board as a forum. 'The United Synagogue and the Board are fairly good forums for the activists to express themselves. Do they actually do anything? Yes. Not a lot. It's a bit like electricity, only 30 per cent efficient. For every ton of fuel you burn, you get 30 per cent heat out of it. The Board is probably 90 per cent heat and 10 per cent effective.' But so cumbersome a body as the Board has to do more than provide a platform for Morris Lederman and Michael Fidler and Jerry Lewis to sound off once a month. They can make as many speeches as they like, but in the meantime Jewish charities continue to run up huge deficits, religious Jewry continues to fragment, and every other ailment that afflicts the community goes unchecked – by the deputies. Clearly the Board at its executive level has some influence, but probably less than it likes to imagine. William Frankel has his doubts: 'The government and the media will listen to them sometimes as an expression of Jewish opinion, but whether the Board influences governments or influences anything, is extremely doubtful. It has some statutory functions. With those limited things it does a useful service. And it's one of the very few institutions we have where Jews from all sections of the community do meet. I suppose that's useful.' Like Sir Isaiah Berlin, he remarked: 'I don't think it does very much harm. It's a bit of Anglo-Jewish history, but it's obviously overblown. It's a ridiculous size. One of the few sensible things Alfred Sherman ever said was when he remarked the Board was composed of fourth-raters who couldn't find a platform anywhere else.'

Ivan Lawrence points out that much of the most important work accomplished by the Board is achieved behind closed doors. He recalled the period when Greville Janner, the Labour MP, was president: 'He used to have – and Lionel Kopelowitz has followed on, but obviously can't do it quite as effectively as Greville because he's not in politics – a series of lunches with the leaders of the Anglican community, with the Catholic cardinal, with leaders of the main political parties. Leaders from all walks of life were brought in to hear what the Board was, what the Board did, how important the Board considered itself to be, and to forge links between the Jewish community and the rest of British society.' Greville

Janner himself is in no doubt as to the influence wielded by the Board. 'However it may be regarded in the Jewish community, it is regarded outside it as the voice of the British Jewish community, and as such it is believed to be very powerful.' He cites an occasion some years ago when a plane carrying Iranian Jews en route to the United States had been denied permission to land in Britain in order to obtain American visas. Janner secured an appointment that day with the Home Secretary, William Whitelaw. Whitelaw asked how long the Iranians would wish to stay in Britain. Three weeks, replied Janner. And if they stay longer? 'Well, you won't let the next lot land, will you?' replied Janner, thus persuading Whitelaw to grant permission. Janner attributes his success, and other effective interventions, not to personal influence but to the weight of the Board.

If the Board does have influence, it often seems to be in spite of the organization rather than because of it. The director of a Jewish charity was blunt: 'The problem lies with the quality of the people. Grassroots representatives like meetings for their own sake. The elected forum produces mediocrity – sad but true. The most impressive people in the community want nothing to do with the Board, which they regard as a waste of time, playing games.' And Ian Mikardo was even blunter: 'I call them the Board of Dead Bodies. They live with memories of the time when they were the voice of British Jewry. They're no longer the voice of British Jewry. The Board is overwhelmingly synagogue-based and therefore people who are not synagogue members aren't represented. The Board is now a lobby, a PR organization, and one that's not taken very seriously. It's pretty low level.' In Geoffrey Paul's view, even some Board committees are essentially powerless, since they are obliged to worry about matters over which they can have no control.

Time and again the Board's critics are able to focus on its unrepresentative nature, even though it is difficult to see what the Board can do about it. Tony Lerman, an assistant director of the Institute of Jewish Affairs, observes: 'The Board arrogates to itself the prerogative of calling for community discipline. When a subject like community radio comes up, the Board feels that they are the ones that should be organizing and controlling it. My own experience suggests that they act more to stifle creativity and the flowering of different views and ideologies and ideas. There is still some fear in the Jewish community about speaking out and about contradicting those who are saying they are our representatives. There have been various ideas proposed for reforming or replacing the

Board, but they've all died the death. Frankly, I think they are very much out of touch.'

At the root of the matter is the notion that the Board exists to express some kind of consensus among Anglo-Jewry. Unfortunately Jews don't find it easy to arrive at a consensus; to use the Chief Rabbi's distinction, there may be oneness but no unity. Colin Shindler, the editor of the *Jewish Quarterly* and a deputy himself, is very much aware of this lack of consensus. The divisions that do exist within the Jewish community are masked by the unrepresentative make-up of the Board. 'They are not so much the Board of Deputies of British Jews, more the Board of Deputies of British Jewish Organizations. Yet there are tens of thousands of Jews who do not belong to Jewish organizations or involve themselves in synagogue life. That doesn't mean they are assimilated. It indicates that they do not wish to join a formal structure. The Board's solution to this difficult problem is to ignore them. I represent my own synagogue at the Board, but I hope that I also voice the opinions and concerns of large numbers of the affiliated and non-affiliated who espouse broadly liberal views but who are aghast at some of the things that are done in their name as British Jews by their so-called representative body. The fact that June Jacobs' – a number of the Executive Committee hounded by deputies because she co-signed a letter to the *Independent* critical of Israeli policies in the Occupied Territories – 'and others like myself who hold liberal views are so few in number is an indication of the unrepresentative nature of the Board. The wide expanse of liberal opinion simply isn't represented there, especially by intellectuals. Writers and intellectuals don't go near the Board. These people cannot be accommodated within the formal structure. I'm an oddity in that I've got a foot in both camps.'

Michael Rosen, as a rabbi, is ineligible for election to the Board – its constitution maintains its own equivalent of a separation of Church and State – but that doesn't prevent him from voicing severe criticisms of the Board. A panellist during a meeting to discuss the problems of Jewish youth, Rabbi Rosen turned to his co-panellist Dr Kopelowitz and quite simply laid into him in his quiet-spoken way. 'The Board is an organization of consensus, concerned with presenting a Jewish face to the Gentile world. This is a recipe for the lowest common denominator, not for the airing of creative differences. The Board thinks of itself as a parliamentary body, but this is a nonsense. In a parliament you have a government and an opposition. The Board is simply a deputation to the *goyim*.' At this point he was interrupted by the great conciliator, Rabbi Yisroel Fine of Cockfosters United synagogue, who was chairing this particular meeting. Kopelowitz took the criticism in his stride, and observed that the problem was a lack of feedback from the grassroots, who don't make enough noise and don't make their views felt. This is rather odd, since with one deputy per 500 Jews of whatever affiliation or non-affiliation, it shouldn't be hard for people at grassroots level to make their voices heard through their deputies. My own view is that they could make as much noise as they liked, but it wouldn't make the slightest difference unless their views coincided with the consensus. On my visits to provincial communities, I heard their leaders express time and again their deep concern and even strong criticism of Israeli policies in the Occupied Territories – but to listen to the honorary officers of the Board of Deputies speaking about Israel, one could suppose that the Board was a paid-up affiliate of Likud.

I put this dilemma to Dr Kopelowitz. 'How do you express a community consensus that doesn't exist?' 'One endeavours to get a consensus if one can,' he replied, 'but if it's impossible you've got to take a majority view, haven't you?' Wouldn't that view be more accurately reflected if the majority of deputies weren't occupying their seats as a kind of reward for long service by their synagogues or organizations rather than on account of their personal merits? 'There are people I'd like to see on the Board,' admitted Dr Kopelowitz, 'but however distinguished they might be in other spheres, that does not qualify you automatically to represent any part of the Jewish community. The Board's great strength is that it has always been an elected body, not an appointed body. I'm elected, but I can be deposed as well. If I don't articulate the views of the Board overall, then I'm accountable to those who elected me. If there are people of distinction who want to have a voice in the policies of the community overall, and not just sit on the outside and make comments, they can only do it by going through the well tried and tested system.'

'But they're not doing this. They join the Institute of Jewish Affairs or other more focused organizations.'

'Intellectuals are all very well,' said the doctor, 'they're all very nice people, but they must also recognize that the IJA and these bodies are talking-shops and don't have much muscle. They're convivial get-togethers.'

'How much muscle and influence does the Board have?'

'It's very hard to measure, isn't it?' was Dr Kopelowitz's frank reply. 'If you measure it in terms of the monthly meetings, it's like measuring the House of Commons by what goes on in the debating chamber.'

223

'But in the Commons there's a government with the power to legislate, which is not the case with the Board.'

'But the Board has ultimately to speak out and represent the Jewish point of view. You have to listen to that democratic voice. The very fact that members of the government and leaders of all parties are always anxious to receive us and be received by us is an indication of the esteem in which the Board is held. After all, when Mrs Thatcher entertains the prime minister of Israel there are very few members of the Jewish community invited, but the President of the Board is invited and so is his wife. They don't pick anybody else. I often think that the Board is held in more respect outside the community than within it.'

No doubt. But perhaps Dr Kopelowitz mistakes access for influence. Does a victory over *shechita* legislation or a reiteration of complaints that the British media are biased against Israel amount to influence? And if so, does that justify the cumbrous and far from representative machinery of the Board of Deputies? Is there no more efficacious way of bringing together the leading voices of Anglo-Jewry, from all sections of the community? The strength of the Board is its democratic structure: the opinionated loudmouth from even the most parochial synagogue can sound off to his fellow deputies. The weakness of the Board is, likewise, its democratic structure: most men and women of any distinction have better things to do with their time than spend a dozen Sundays watching Dr Kopelowitz mismanage a meeting. In the end the Board will be judged by its effectiveness. Does it perform? The lamentable conclusion would appear to be that while it is better to have an elephantine yet non-representative Board rather than no Board at all, there simply must be better ways both of giving a platform to Jewish lay men and women, and of giving their views weight in the political and legislative arena.

The Board may have succeeded in persuading governments and the other non-Jewish institutions with which the Jewish community must deal that it is the principal and most representative source of power within Anglo-Jewry. Yet this is far from the truth. The true lay leaders of the community are the few very rich men who, by their benefactions and their genuine devotion to the community's welfare, control the major institutions: the Joint Israel Appeal, the welfare agencies, the educational bodies. They control them not because they interfere with the daily workings of those institutions, but because they finance them, and without the millionaires' support many of the institutions would be in even more severe financial difficulties than they are at present. Dr Kopelowitz is accountable, but trivially so. It doesn't terribly matter what he thinks or what he says. The opinions of men like Stanley Kalms or Cyril Stein or Sir Sigmund Sternberg are far more important in terms of the functioning and survival of Anglo-Jewry; but these men, because they are philanthropists, are not accountable. They are the latter-day equivalents of the grand old men who ruled the community in the nineteenth century. If you want to know who wields power within the Jewish community, you need not devote too much attention to the Board of Deputies.

– 17 –

Passing the baton: education

ENTHUSIASTS for Jewish education like to compare the excellence of the many recently established Jewish primary schools with the defects of the '*cheder* system' that preceded them. They are right to do so. I am one of many authentic authorities on the subject of the *cheder* system, as I endured it in person for many years. Classes took place not only on Sunday mornings, but after school two evenings a week. They were little more than cramming sessions, for we could not be called up to read from the Torah in synagogue until we had passed the barmitzvah test, which was certainly the most arduous examination I have ever had to take. Candidates were required to memorize page after page of prayer, not to mention blessings so numerous as to cast a general benediction over all of creation for a hundred years. There's a blessing for smelling fragrant woods or barks (terribly handy, that one), a blessing for witnessing lofty mountains, a blessing on seeing giants or dwarfs. Nor was it sufficient to have memorized the lengthy *Amidah* prayer; you had to know what every word of it meant. Some weeks before my barmitzvah I was put through my paces by some dour greybeard. I do believe I failed. It was back to the books and long evenings of committing to memory the blessing for consuming liquor other than wine (most useful to a twelve-year-old), and second time around I passed. (This dispiriting routine, requiring the regurgitation of Jewish 'knowledge', has, I am glad to say, been replaced by a written examination, scarcely more than a quiz, that tests knowledge of Hebrew, the Jewish calendar and liturgy, and some Jewish rituals. It is not very demanding. The quiz is followed by an oral test conducted by the boy's rabbi; this consists of the memorization of the principal blessings and a familiarity with the significance of the portions assigned to the boy

226

when he is called up to read the Law for the first time.) By now I was thoroughly disillusioned with the whole thing, and not only because of my difficulties in passing the test.

It was Rashi who nailed the lid shut. Rashi is the sobriquet of Rabbi Shelomo Itzhaki, a French sage of the eleventh century who wrote one of the most celebrated, and lengthy, Talmudic commentaries. The study of Rashi is not beginner's stuff, and the texts we studied were printed without vowels. Hebrew script consists of letters that mostly represent consonants or silences; vowels are conveyed by a series of dots over, beneath, or alongside the consonants. Even though most us could construe the script and even, given sufficient clues, translate some of it, I doubt whether any of us had the faintest idea what it was all about. It was rather like being taken through a chapter of *Principia Mathematica* shortly before sitting O Level Maths. To relieve the tedium, I would throw in questions such as: 'If God created the universe, who created God?' Rather a good question, and still something of a tease in theological circles, but the response from my teachers would invariably be along the lines of, 'Shut up and translate the next verse of Rashi.'

And so a few months after my barmitzvah, I grew tired of being rebuffed every time I showed any intellectual curiosity. When asked why I had grown so indifferent to the faith of my ancestors, I would reply: 'I've spent five years or so studying Hebrew and my religion every week, often three times a week, and at the end of that time I haven't the faintest idea what Judaism is all about. I know how to bless a *lulav*, but nobody has ever explained why I *should* bless a *lulav*.' I have told this story to a number of rabbis, who have all nodded sadly and said, yes, we've heard this kind of thing so often. Rabbi Dr Isaac Levy, now retired, agrees that 'the old-fashioned method of instruction was appalling. It always emphasized the dos and the don'ts, never the whys, never the historical background or development of Judaism. As Louis Jacobs once said: "Theology is a dirty word." Throughout all my years of study at Jews' College, we were never given any instruction on theology or philosophy. We had to make it up on our own, as I did, from our own reading and research, but it wasn't part of my instruction. This is a great loss.'

Stanley Kalms, now the chairman of Jews' College, admits: 'My Hebrew teachers were without exception the antithesis of everything one would today associate with education. I left *cheder* the way the Israelites left Egypt: in a hurry. In fact what I took with me by way of Jewish knowledge was a bit like the *matzah* the Israelites took with them: thin, flat, and indigestible.'[1] The Reform Rabbi Dow Marmur provides evidence that the situation was no better in Progressive communities: 'The Synagogue Sunday School as it now exists, whether or not augmented by Hebrew classes during the week, is a failure. It brings together, with the help of parental coercion, tired and confused youngsters for brief episodes of Jewish study and fragments of Jewish living. It creates in the minds of the children a suspicion of and a disdain for Judaism ... Only such learning as is conducive to a creditable performance in synagogue is being sought.'[2]

That's history. Twenty years ago the proportion of Jewish school-age children attending Jewish schools was about 5 per cent. Now that figure stands at 35 per cent, and in some provincial cities the percentage is far higher. By 1983 some 14,000 children attended Jewish nursery, primary, and secondary schools. The *cheder* system totters along, and about thirty-six United synagogues in Greater London retain 'religion classes' for some 6,000 children, but they no longer constitute the principal means of acquiring knowledge of Hebrew and Judaism. In 1967 the proportion of Jewish children enrolled in *cheder* classes was almost 70 per cent; twenty years later it was less than half. This revolution in Jewish education affects primary schools only. Nor does it take into account the numerous *chedorim* and *yeshivot* among the ultra-Orthodox communities of north London and Manchester. Secondary schools, such as the large London comprehensive called the Jews' Free School (JFS), Hasmonean High School, and the public school of Carmel College (chairman of the governors: Cyril Stein), have been prominent for some time. Carmel has 325 pupils, of whom the parents of two-thirds pay annual fees of £7,500, said to be the highest of any public school in Britain. Carmel has been in existence for forty years, but what is new is the plethora of Jewish primary schools throughout Britain. There are two principal bodies that organize and fund these schools: the Jewish Educational Development Trust (JEDT), and the Zionist Federation Education Trust (ZFET). There is no significant ideological difference between the two bodies.

The JEDT was founded in 1971 and its very active president is the Chief Rabbi, who takes a keen interest in such matters as curriculum development and who visits the schools under his aegis as frequently as possible. The Trust does not run the schools. It is primarily a funding organization, which accounts for the presence of some very rich businessmen – such as Stanley Kalms, Trevor Chinn, and Gerald Ronson – among its senior executives. It has funded resource centres and new buildings and curriculum development programmes. Nor does the Trust restrict its funding to schools affiliated to the United Synagogue. It has provided assistance to the ultra-Orthodox Yesodey Hatorah schools and the Akiva school, which is part of the Manor House centre. 'Of course,' says Simon Caplan, the director of the Trust, 'the schools do have to be ideologically acceptable to the Chief Rabbi. So we won't build a Reform school but we might provide teaching materials or a computer room within a Reform school.' It provided some of the funds required to establish the Independent Jewish Day School in Hendon which, together with one or two other London primary schools, represents what the Trust hopes will be a model for Jewish education in the future. Not only is Hebrew taught, as in all Jewish day schools, but classes in Jewish studies are taught in Hebrew. In educational terms, these new schools are sophisticated, with special provisions for slow learners and many extra-mural activities. Jewish schools are intended to be every bit as good as, if not better than, their secular counterparts.

The United Synagogue also sees education as a high priority. Out of the 1988 budget of £7.5 million, £1.9 million was spent on Jewish education (23 per cent more than in 1987), notably the Jews' Free School (which also receives financial support from the Zionist Federation) and two primary schools in Kenton and Ilford. Through its Board of Religious Education the United Synagogue funds Hebrew studies at these schools and, of course, continues to support what is left of the *cheder* system, which still absorbs some 6,000 children. With the expansion of Jewish primary education and the immobility of the secondary sector, the educational organizations are under considerable pressure to establish a third Jewish secondary school within Greater London, with the JEDT favouring a location in Bushey.

Unlike Yesodey Hatorah, some Jewish schools are eligible for voluntary-aided status and thus integrated into the State system. The North West London School in Willesden is a case in point. Although the primary education is State-funded, the parents make voluntary contributions to finance the Hebrew education, which of course is not covered by the local authority. Security is another feature of the school that has to be paid for by the parents, many of whom participate in a rota system to keep an eye on the children. Founded in 1945, the school, which has strong Zionist

229

leanings, is mainstream Orthodox – 'just to the right of United,' says the headmaster, David Collins.

The school day begins shortly after nine, when the headmaster conducts morning assembly and prayers. Some of the boys davened and took the prayers more seriously than the less attentive younger children, who regarded prayers as a pretext for a singsong. The first class of the day that I attended was in Hebrew studies, and George Albert, a kindly Irishman with the softest of Dublin accents, was leading the children through the story of Moses in Egypt. The children clearly yearned to be allowed to answer whatever question Mr Albert posed. They stretched their arms high into the air, raised their bodies some inches above their seats, and moaned, 'Please, sir, please.' Some of these eight-year-olds even had their hands up before Mr Albert had asked his question. He didn't simply require the children to translate the Hebrew text, but elicited from the children the significance of what they were reading.

About one-third of the curriculum is devoted to religious and Hebrew studies. Moreover, language studies and art work all tend to have religious themes. Mr Collins conceded that because of the need to provide both religious and secular education, certain other aspects of school life, such as art work and physical education, tended to suffer, though he stressed that there was no shortage of extracurricular activities. Unlike the pallid children at Chasidic *chedorim*, the pupils at North West struck me as fresh and lively. Mr Collins seemed delighted with them. In the bad old days, when Hebrew classes were held on Sundays and after school, the kids were tired and their studies lacked continuity. 'At this school', added Mr Albert, 'Jewish education is integrated into the curriculum. The kids feel no resentment, as they do when they have to give up a Sunday morning or two evenings a week. One of the problems at *cheder* schools is that teachers' pay is lousy. Nobody who's any good will teach there, and in some places the only people they can get to teach are other children. The trouble is that parents just can't accept that if you want quality education, then you have to pay for it.' His point was well illustrated when in 1988 the United Synagogue attempted to increase annual *cheder* fees from £50 to £75. The proposal was voted down.

Although North West is Orthodox, not all the children come from Orthodox homes. Thirty years ago all the children would have been *frum* and would have lived locally. Now the religious mix is greater and the 265 children come from all over north-west London, some from as far away as Harrow and Edgware. Applications far exceed the number of places available, and David Collins has to make hard choices when interviewing not only the children but their parents. Teachers at numerous schools around the country confirm that many parents are by no means Orthodox, suggesting that a desire for sound religious education is not the sole reason for enrolling children at Jewish day schools. 'This school has blossomed', says Collins, 'because the standards of secular education are so high. For many parents the religious education we offer is a bonus. Some send their children here because we have higher standards than the other primary schools in the area, because they want their children to be aware of their Jewish heritage, and because they want them to be imbued with high moral and ethical standards at school. The parents tend to be professional people: lawyers, psychologists, doctors, publishers. Our standards have to be high because the parents insist upon it being that way.'

The imbalance between the provision of Jewish primary and secondary education means that not all the children could continue their studies at a Jewish secondary school even if they wanted to. Some children do go on to JFS and Hasmonean, but many others enter schools such as City of London and Haberdashers'. Parents who may be keen to give their children a solid grounding in Jewish studies and Hebrew may baulk at entrusting them for the next seven years to the rabbis who direct the studies at Hasmonean. And many parents, rightly or wrongly, are convinced that JFS and Hasmonean, however thorough their provision of Jewish education, aren't quite up to the mark on the secular side of the slate – or not in comparison with the other schools mentioned. Attempts are being made to improve standards at JFS, notably by the introduction of sophisticated computing facilities largely financed by the Ronson Foundation – illustrating yet again how dependent the community remains on the munificence of a handful of benefactors. If there is any ulterior motive behind Gerald Ronson's generosity, it is probably no more than a wish to ensure that JFS remains firmly rooted in the modern world and does not follow in the footsteps of the Chasidic schools or, in the eyes of many, Hasmonean.

JFS, with 1,400 students, is essentially a large urban comprehensive school. The vast majority of the pupils have to travel, some of them considerable distances, to attend the school. Simon Caplan estimates that about two-thirds of the children come from homes where they are not instilled with any great sense of Jewish commitment or identity. Hasmonean offers a far more traditional Jewish education, rooted in the

231

study of set texts, to about 600 boys and 300 girls – educated separately, of course. Of the 600 boys, about 400 would come from United Synagogue families, and the remainder from more strictly Orthodox Adath homes. Both JFS and Hasmonean are good schools in the eyes of dispassionate observers, but neither is outstanding. In 1987 the A Level pass rate at Hasmonean for subjects such as mathematics and Hebrew was a gratifying 100 per cent, but for English a worrying 40 per cent and for biology 56 per cent. Comparable O Level grades for the same year suggest this is not an isolated occurrence.

Early in 1988 a performance of *Macbeth* to be given at the boys' school by a local theatrical troupe was cancelled at the last moment because, it was reported, the troupe consisted of men and women, as is customary; this, however, did not meet with the approval of the rabbis who teach at Hasmonean and the boys studying *Macbeth* were left with Shakespeare on the page instead of on the stage.[3] (The school claims the cancellation took place because the performance clashed with another activity.) And, if Chaim Bermant is to be believed, and the school says emphatically he should not be, the rabbinical authorities – the Sacred Society for the Prohibition of Just About Everything, in his felicitous phrase – who watch over the girls' school have followed in the steps of nuns at convent schools by banning patent leather shoes on the grounds that the shoes might reflect the girls' knickers, or worse.[4]

Simon Caplan points out: 'One can see what's lacking there by looking at schools like Haberdashers' or City of London, which not only have enormous numbers of Jewish pupils but quite large numbers who come from committed homes. Many parents don't think that Jewish secondary schools have enough to offer them. It may also have something to do with private education compared with State education, or the nature of Jewish education, and, perhaps even more importantly, the communal ethos of the school. I can't disguise that there are issues within Jewish education that worry a lot of parents. The classic modern committed Orthodox Jewish parents today are strongly pro-Israel and very committed to Hebrew; and Hasmonean, for example, is tentative in its position *vis-à-vis* Israel. It's certainly not a strong element on the curriculum. JFS is strongly pro-Israel, but it has a much lower level of commitment and achievement in Jewish studies. So for the modern Orthodox community, which is growing, there's a big gap in the provision of schools.'

One would imagine that the tremendous growth in Jewish education, whatever the gaps, would result in a more observant Jewish community, with the new generation showing far greater commitment to a Jewish way of life than their parents' generation. Yet there is a considerable evidence to suggest this simply isn't so. Research studies, such as the Redbridge Survey undertaken by the Demographic Unit of the Board of Deputies, have failed to demonstrate that Jewish secondary education has any noticeable impact on the inculcation of Jewish values. Such findings are extremely upsetting to the Jewish educational establishment, as Simon Caplan is the first to admit: 'It's very worrying. A pupil who'd left his primary school and not gone to a Jewish secondary school was more likely, the studies showed, to be a synagogue attender than a person who'd gone all the way through the Jewish educational system. Is it the fault of the schools or the system? Do we create new schools and try to get it right, or do we channel our expenditure into the area where most of the children are: part-time centres and youth movements, for example? Or do we channel those funds into more adult education?' Perhaps in response to such findings, the United Synagogue in particular is trying to provide community centres and special teenage centres, such as the one at Brent Cross in north-west London, where young people can gather in a more informal yet intensely Jewish setting. Additional ideas, such as proposals for a new Orthodox youth movement, videos for home education, and a *yeshiva* for adult education, are all being considered.

Rabbi Abraham Levy, spiritual leader of the Sephardim, recently opened a primary school in Maida Vale. As in many such schools, not all the teachers are Jewish, for almost every school experiences difficulty in finding first-rate Jewish teachers. The private school is open to all Jewish children, whatever their background. Rabbi Levy also places great emphasis on the quality of the school's secular education, although his primary reason for founding the school was dissatisfaction with the *cheder* system. 'I'd like to give them, at least until the age of thirteen, Jewish education – say a couple of lessons a day – and give them a secular education that will lack nothing in comparison to what people are getting at any other school. If at thirteen they go to a non-Jewish school, at least I've given them ten years of Jewish education. If you don't expose your child to a sophisticated understanding of Judaism, the chances are he's going to have a juvenile picture of it all his life. Nothing upsets me more than seeing a brilliant university student, with a maturity which enables him to do any job in England, yet with a picture of Judaism identical to that of a young child.'

Rabbi Levy stressed that in imparting Judaism to his students he puts

233

great emphasis on theological aspects. 'I try very hard in my school to make the children exceedingly aware of God as almost their second father. If we can achieve that, then I think we have a chance of making them appreciate what Judaism is.' Rabbi Vogel of Lubavitch also assures me that modern Jewish pedagogy no longer discourages the inquiring mind and the awkward question: 'If there's one thing we can say emphatically, it's that we encourage questioning and understanding of the very fundamentals of our faith. Other Chasidic groups may not be so eager for those questions to be asked and would frown upon the time that is spent in pursuit of Jewish theology and philosophy, but our fundamental tenet is that one has to know God. Maimonides emphasizes the importance of the knowledge of God as opposed to belief in God, and our philosophy was built up on this. Once a question is posed, it has to be dealt with. One has to understand the process of continuous creation – it touches on metaphysics, the cabbalistic system – essentially it is a mature knowledge of what religion is about. If you had gone to a Lubavitch *cheder* as a child you would have been welcomed as the model child who was asking the questions, and they would have been dealt with.' Maybe, but I'm not sure the answers would have been satisfactory.

Since almost all Jewish education is in the hands of the Orthodox authorities, the Progressive community has a problem. Reform parents have long complained that children from their community who attend JFS are treated as second-class citizens. The Chief Rabbi has declared that only children who are halachically Jewish may attend Jewish schools. Calderwood School in Glasgow has a few Muslim pupils, which doesn't bother the religious authorities, but the child of, say, a Jewish father and non-Jewish mother would be denied admission to many Jewish schools. From about 1985 onwards the schools began to demand from parents documentation to establish beyond any doubt that prospective pupils were halachically up to scratch. The grandson of Rabbi Louis Jacobs was admitted to JFS without any difficulties being raised, but when the boy's younger sister applied a few years later, her Jewish status was questioned and documentation called for. Now if the boy is a bona fide, fully paid-up Jew, then so, as a simple matter of logic, is his sister. The parents became so exasperated by the obstacles put in their way that they sent the girl to a different school. Evidently, the Orthodox authorities are now prepared to go to extraordinary lengths in order to deny Progressive Jews any scrap of legitimacy. Even if the children in question come from nominally

Orthodox families, a single blot on their copybook – a divorce of a German grandmother, say, that was not obtained through recognized authorities – may be sufficient to deprive them of their right to attend Jewish schools. The Chief Rabbi's justification for this is that 'parents have a right to expect that [Jewish] schools will not even indirectly promote marital liaisons with children deemed as non-Jewish by any section of the community'.[5]

The full, and richly absurd, consequences of the Chief Rabbi's dogmatism can be seen from the saga of the King David primary school in Birmingham. The school has admitted Jewish children of all shapes and sizes, from all sections of the community; indeed, half the pupils at King David are non-Jews. Along came a rabbi, Leonard Tann, whose brief it was to supervise religious education at the school. 'You cannot give Jewish religious instruction to non-Jewish children,' he declared, referring not, as you may have supposed, to the Christian children but to the children regarded as Jewish by their parents but not by Rabbi Tann. Uproar ensued, to the bafflement of some Orthodox leaders. Rabbi Singer obtusely declared: 'I can't understand the issue. If you belong to an Orthodox congregation, you must accept the Chief Rabbinate's decision.'[6] Must? He argues that it would be harmful to allow halachically suspect Jews to be educated as though they were strictly kosher, though what harm such a religious education could do it is hard to see. Negotiations continue.

Reform children obtain Jewish education either through the religion school attached to their synagogue or from synagogue youth clubs. Such clubs, however, attract a mere 1,500 teenagers. There is a reasonable provision of adult education, especially for Reform Jews in north London, since the Manor House offers a full range of courses and seminars. Akiva, the only Reform school in London, is also based on Manor House as part of the Centre for Jewish Education. When this Centre was founded, the Orthodox authorities in the form of the powerful trustees of the JEDT were unhappy about the wide embrace of the title. Simon Caplan was asked to write a polite letter to Manor House requesting a change of name. Rabbi Tony Bayfield, who runs Manor House, replied that they would gladly oblige if JEDT could come up with some suggestions? Would they consider, he wondered, the Centre for Schismatic Jewish Education? The correspondence came to an end.

The Reform community probably exerts less pressure on its leaders to set up schools because it is not as ideologically committed to the whole notion of separate Jewish education. Even among Louis Jacobs's sophisticated congregation at New London, very few parents send their children to Jewish day schools. Not that Progressive Jews are prevented from sending their children – provided they are halachically pure – to Orthodox schools. Some Progressive parents do think it desirable to send their children to schools where they will acquire a knowledge of Hebrew and Judaism. Other Jews, whose personal religious commitment may be low-keyed, may still wish to discourage their children from excessive assimilation or, the ultimate horror, out-marriage, and may hope that attendance at a Jewish school will root their children more firmly within the community. Others, such as Colin Shindler, send their children to Jewish schools as an act of cultural self-determination: 'I send my children to a Jewish school for reasons of ethnicity rather than for overriding reasons of belief or religion. I want them to learn modern Hebrew and Jewish history as well as how to daven. Originally, I sent my children to the local school because I wanted them to recognize and understand the world outside of a purely Jewish lifestyle. It soon became apparent that Barnet's multicultural policy as it affected Jews was little more than tokenism. In part it was due to Barnet's educational backwardness, but also to the indifference of Jewish parents themselves. I had to choose between the narrowness of a Jewish school and the narrowness of a non-Jewish one. I chose the Jewish school.'

It is difficult to assess the strength within the community of objections to separate education. Not everyone actively involved with Jewish education finds separate education problematic. David Collins said that when he first began to teach in Jewish schools, he had reservations about the notion. But after many years in the profession, he could find no evidence that children who went on from his school to non-Jewish secondary schools had the slightest difficulty in fitting in to a secular environment; nor had he heard of the graduates of Jewish secondary schools encountering such difficulties when they went up to university. 'The only thing that's keeping Judaism alive today is the religion. Since the Second World War, Judaism has been in decline. If that decline is being reversed, it's going to be because of day schools.'

Simon Caplan suspects that some parents cite a dislike of separate education as an excuse for not sending their children to Jewish schools – as though it were some kind of duty. 'There's certainly a suspicion in society about separate education. You've got to ask yourself what actually creates a harmonious multicultural society. Is it the physical placing of young children in the classroom so that they are confronted with a display of all faiths and all cultures, or is it by creating a kind of education which gives each individual a strong internal base of identity, combined with a commitment to be part of society? The Jewish approach has been a struggle to find a fusion of the two. Separatism left to its own devices can produce intolerance. But if it's separatism combined with a certain ethic about the community, then it can have an opposite effect. There are religious Jews who feel that their own identity would be threatened by any kind of encounter with secular society, but that attitude isn't expressive of mainstream Orthodoxy. We take the view that Jewish tradition encourages the Jew to reside within his society and be law-abiding and try to achieve success within it without losing his identity. Carmel College was founded to sit astride the two cultures, to be a public school that was Jewish and to provide leadership for the Anglo-Jewish community. The whole ethos of the school was precisely this, to be part of society, and to succeed within it, and yet to do it as a Jew. To me the strength of one's identity and the depth of one's cultural background are actually an intrinsic part of one's being and one's mechanism for dealing with the world. That's what I hope the best Jewish schools are trying to achieve.'

Caplan went on to admit that he wasn't certain whether the schools were achieving this goal. Those who defend separate education point to the long existence in Britain of Catholic schools. 'We've had church schools, and we've had Catholic schools,' says Rabbi Dr Isaac Levy, 'and the Catholics have never said that because they go to Catholic schools they can't integrate into the wider community. When Carmel College was founded, people said it was a bad thing because it was going to stop the process of integration, and isolate the Jewish pupils. In actual fact it didn't, and the kids feel they are part and parcel of the wider community. I don't think that the Jewish school necessarily is a contribution towards segregation or ghettoization. It gives the kids a certain measure of stability, which they need.' Some parents consider this element of stability exceedingly important, since it is far better to feel secure within your own culture than rootless and uncertain within the wider culture.

That graduates of Jewish education feel fully able to participate in society at large I do not doubt. But that separate education is of itself desirable I am not at all sure. One of the pleasures of my secondary education was that I could count among my best friends an Indian, a devout Anglo-Catholic, a nominal Christian who would later achieve notoriety as a member of the Angry Brigade, a Quaker with a flair for

237

cooking, as well as many Jewish friends. Such a mix is broadening and a source of stimulation and delight. I can fully appreciate that many Jews wish to live in a predominantly Jewish environment. Yet, while acknowledging the right of parents to educate their children according to their beliefs and principles, I retain a distrust of separate education, whether for Jews or Catholics or Muslims. Tony Lerman of the Institute of Jewish Affairs expresses similar doubts: 'There's a side of me that believes that ethnic groups should be able to assert their identity if they wish to and that includes educating their children in the way they want to. That side of me says that day schools are fine. But there's another part of me that has a vision of various religious groups taking their children and giving them very very narrow education, the kind of education that makes children think of themselves as not necessarily part of the mainstream of British life – and there I do have doubts. I find this impinging on my consciousness more now that there are demands for Muslim schools. But there's probably a strong desire on the part of people who have come to live in this country to make a success of their lives here, in which case it would go against their own interests to educate their children in such a way as to separate them from society.'

Mike Anderson, the director of Manchester Jewish Social Services, is, however, convinced that Jews educated in separate schools do find it difficult to integrate into wider society. 'Bernard Crick once distinguished between tolerating things and approving of them. I disapprove strongly of separate schooling, yet it's people's wish and I think we should tolerate it. But it worries me because I see what's happening in Northern Ireland. At the King David School in Liverpool, only 60 per cent of the pupils are Jewish. For once in their lives they are in the majority, but they can never get into thinking that their viewpoint is the only viewpoint. They have to come to terms with racism and cultural relativism, because the Christian pupils remind them of it. I'm worried about whether separate schools can sort out those issues. In separate schools the kids can simply ignore some of the painful issues.' The Liverpool experiment certainly seems successful. While the Jewish pupils spend a quarter of their school week engaged in Jewish studies, the non-Jewish students take courses in more general social and religious studies. The non-Jewish children participate in the Jewish festivals celebrated at the school, and such participation encourages the Jewish pupils to examine their religious observance, which they must explain to their non-Jewish schoolmates. Such joint education, maintains Clive Lawton, the headmaster, 'encourages intelligent integration and discourages assimilation'. The latter is achieved by making it easier for Jews to identify as such in the constant company of non-Jews.

Clearly the Chasidim who finance and run the *chedorim* and *yeshivot* of north London have no wish to see their children integrating into wider society. Theirs is a deliberate and very successful attempt to erect the strongest possible defences against the encroachment of the host society. That, of course, is far from the intention of mainstream Jewish educationalists. Whereas Chasidim will almost never seek admission to universities, higher education is the natural goal of the most able students in Jewish secondary schools, although some parents at Hasmonean Girls' School have complained that girls are dissuaded from studying scientific subjects and from seeking university places.[7] The qualms expressed by Mike Anderson are probably not widely shared, certainly not within the Orthodox community. But many others do criticize Jewish education in Britain on the grounds that standards simply aren't high enough.

Despite the expansion of Jewish education, it is less widespread here than in many other parts of the world. Greville Janner points out that 'compared to Australia, Canada and South Africa, we have an abysmal record. The average Jewish family doesn't send its child to Jewish schools in this country. In other countries it does.' Michael Rosen, always keen on hyperbole, describes religious education in Britain as 'catastrophic': 'The day school system has certainly grown since 1967. Its blossoming relates to the weakness of the state system and the arousing of Jewish consciousness after the Six Day War. But it mainly affects the primary schools. If you look at the secondary schools in Britain, for the mainstream community there are really only two schools, and both are so easy to criticize – and not because one wants to be critical. JFS is a school for Jews rather than a Jewish school. JFS and Hasmonean – that's not much of a choice. There are only two really excellent Jewish schools in London: one is Haberdashers' and the other is City of London. I believe passionately in Jewish education. What we're discussing is the ability of a minority group to maintain its culture in a majority civilization. It's not specifically a Jewish problem. It seems to me much easier to be a Christian, where there's such an emphasis on faith rather than acts. It's much more difficult for the assimilated Jew to identify with his culture when he feels this barrier of not knowing what to do, when to stand up, when to sit down. Take any secular subject and imagine you stop at the age of eleven. How much can you learn? That's why we need first-rate Jewish education. But you can't paper over the cracks. Haberdashers' has a calibre you won't

239

find at the Jewish day schools. We should be building a first-rate Jewish day school. At least Jewish education is on the agenda of the Chief Rabbi and others. But over the past fifteen years all the creative ideas on education have come from outside the formal structure, from individuals. If you're lucky, the Establishment follows. The Establishment is afraid to experiment with a multiplicity of approaches. It's afraid to fail.'

Michael Rosen is himself, as the founder of Yakar, one of those who has experimented with educational ventures outside the formal structures. Yakar has three functions: it provides a variety of courses and lectures for adults; it is a cultural centre and library; and it is a synagogue. Despite Rabbi Rosen's Orthodox commitment, no religious pressure is exerted on those who attend Yakar. He is trying to provide a place where those who wish to know more about Judaism can do so without feeling they have to join a synagogue or participate in the community in any formal way. The cultural events are as wide-ranging as possible, so as to bring to the attention of the Jewish community not only aspects of their own culture (Chasidic music, for example) they may know little about, but issues relating to broader ethical and social matters that ought to be of concern to Jews. Archbishop Desmond Tutu has spoken at Yakar – could one seriously imagine the Board of Deputies playing host to such a man, or to another of Yakar's guests, Trevor Huddleston? – and black politicians such as Diane Abbott and Paul Boateng have participated in Yakar seminars. You may enrol for courses on Jewish meditation, or Zionist ideologies, or the Ten Commandments, or for Rebbetzin Schlesinger's *shiurim* (women only).

'Yakar is trying to break the preconceptions people have of religious Jewry,' Michael Rosen explained. 'It tries to marry roles. It attracts the widest spectrum of any organization of its kind, precisely because it is more than a secular cultural centre. So you'll have an exciting fusion of people who are into being religiously Jewish and people who are totally oblivious of it and who are coming along because of the cultural occasion. We also attract people who are ready to admit that their knowledge of Judaism is negligible. When you get people of forty and fifty who say that they can't read the Hebrew alphabet, that means they've already over- come a certain hurdle of embarrassment by admitting it. They wouldn't feel able to go to their local synagogue and tell the same thing to the rabbi. Here they can come to neutral territory.' He doesn't know to what one should ascribe this revival of interest, especially among middle-aged people who previously regarded themselves as thoroughly assimilated. He speculates that it could be an attachment to Israel, or contacts with their children or with nieces and nephews who communicate their own excitement about Judaism.

Rabbi Rosen keeps Yakar as informal as he can. There is no formal membership, though modest fees are charged for certain courses and events. The informality is a direct reaction against what he perceives as the excessive aloofness and tendency towards pomposity of the rabbinate. 'The dangers of familiarity are far less than the dangers of distance. I don't believe in a stuffy lecture presentation. I believe very much in participation. If there's no argument, then one has failed. We encourage questions and challenges – we don't pretend to have all the answers.' My own experience at Yakar meetings has borne out this claim. The strenuous arguments that characterize Rosen's *shiurim* also mark the lectures and debates in the evening.

Equally important are the more structured programmes and courses offered by the Spiro Institute for the Study of Jewish History and Culture, which was founded in 1978. Robin Spiro was a property developer who was keen to transmit his passion for Jewish history, which he shared with his wife Nitza (then a lector in Modern Hebrew at Oxford University), to sixth-formers, whether Jewish or non-Jewish. From modest beginnings as a one-man band, the Institute has expanded in a most remarkable way. Its seven full-time staff members and thirty-five part-timers offer not only evening courses and cultural events, but correspondence courses and weekend seminars and foreign tours to places of Jewish interest. There are courses on, among other topics, Israeli politics, Jewish art and music, Hebrew, and the history of Jewish food. The Institute has 1,200 students on its books, both in London and the provinces. Each July it mounts a Jewish film festival at a Hampstead cinema. One of the Spiro Institute's great triumphs was the establishment of an AO Level examination in modern Jewish history which is by no means restricted to students in Jewish secondary schools. Those studying for such exams in non-Jewish schools are mostly taught by teachers and lecturers supplied by the Institute.

As at Yakar, all this has been achieved outside the Jewish educational Establishment. Judging by the success of both organizations, the Establishment has wildly underestimated the desire for further knowledge on the part of unaffiliated Jews, Jews uncomfortable with the clubby atmosphere at many adult education meetings arranged by synagogues. Of course both Yakar and Spiro would never have got off the ground, nor be able to maintain their activities, without substantial injections of capital from private sources. With no strings attached to the Establishment, they are free from the narrowness of mind that afflicts so much thinking among Anglo-Jewish leaders, religious and lay, and they have provided a means by which unaffiliated and disenchanted Jews can re-establish contact with their community. Rabbi Jonathan Magonet points out that the emergence of Yakar, the Spiro Institute, and the Manor House 'have proved far more important than their mere scale suggests, because there's nothing else going on'.

The universities also provide a measure of further education for those members of the community with more scholarly interests. Apart from the extensive writing and lecturing undertaken by prominent Jewish historians – such as Professor Aubrey Newman, Dr V. D. Lipman, Dr Geoffrey Alderman, and Dr David Cesarani – university departments such as the Oxford Centre for Postgraduate Hebrew Studies also offer classes and seminars on subjects such as modern Jewish history and modern Hebrew. The Oxford Centre has been a notable pioneer of Yiddish studies, a programme that has proved of interest not only to Jews. Cambridge offers courses in Hebrew and rabbinics but not in Jewish studies as such. Jewish studies programmes at other universities – notably University College, London, Warwick, Newcastle, Glasgow, and Manchester – have been harmed by the general cutback in funding for tertiary education. In an effort to keep some of these departments alive, Sir Monty Finniston chairs an appeal to raise over £1 million: 'I'm not sure it's going to do much good, but it might keep something alive that would otherwise die.' Manchester University bucked the trend by announcing in October 1988 the founding of a new chair in Jewish studies, funded by a local family trust.

Whatever the deficiencies of Jewish education in Britain, the situation has improved vastly since my early encounters with it. In terms of quantity the expansion has been extraordinary, and if the quality does, as Rabbi Rosen maintains, still leave much to be desired, there is at least an awareness of the importance of education within the Jewish community and a genuine desire to improve its standards. Factionalism, as in so many other aspects of Anglo-Jewish life, may yet have a ruinous impact on those efforts, but there does seem to be a sufficient number of people within the community determined to prevent that from happening.

– 18 –

The charity network

TWO men were shipwrecked on a desert island. One was deeply
apprehensive, while the other, nonchalant, sunbathed. 'How can
you be so calm?' said the anxious man to the calm man, who
replied: 'Two years ago I gave £200,000 to Jewish charities. Last year I
gave £500,000. Don't worry – they'll find me.'

Which reflects two truths: that Jewish charities are very proficient at
fund-raising, and that Jews are very generous. Charity, among Jews, is
culturally inbred: one of the greatest *mitzvot* is to give aid to the poor.
Helping the needy, in Jewish law, is not the conferring of a favour, but the
fulfilment of an obligation. Nor is charitable aid supposed to glorify the
donor, and rabbinical tradition regards anonymous giving as the most
admirable form of charity. To identify oneself as a benefactor, argued the
rabbis, is to expose the recipient to the possibility of humiliation. In
practice, however, the preservation of anonymity places too great a strain
on the vanity of most people, however generous. Chaim Bermant has
described synagogues in the East End of London 'where almost every
inch of wall space was taken up with the names of benefactors written in
letters of gold (as they had to donate a mere 20 shillings for the honour,
immortality was cheaply bought)'.[1] In most synagogues, prayer-books and
pews and stained glass are donated by the wealthy or the grateful, who are
duly identified. Jewish old people's homes and day centres and libraries
are often named after philanthropists.

If many generous Jews find anonymity too great a strain, that does not
detract from their open-handedness. The community is, in relation to its
size, magnificently serviced. Apart from the large welfare agencies such as
the Jewish Welfare Board, the Ravenswood Foundation, the Jewish Blind

Society, and Norwood Child Care, innumerable provincial communities have their own agencies, their day centres and old people's homes and burial societies, groups that distribute *matzoh* and other Passover foods to the elderly and housebound, and volunteers who visit the old and the lonely. Melvyn Carlowe, the present director of the Jewish Welfare Board, points out: 'Each new community mimics the structure that exists in the host community. In many ways the welfare structure of Anglo-Jewry mirrors the welfare structure that existed during the mid-Victorian period.' It is the reflection in the charitable sphere of the same mimetic principle that prompted the establishment of a Chief Rabbinate, a hierarchical institution closer to Christian forms of organization than traditional Jewish ones.

The first comprehensive agency to be established was the Jewish Board of Guardians, founded in 1859 and now known as the Jewish Welfare Board. Before then other charitable bodies had been in operation; some, indeed, such as the Jewish Bread, Meat and Coal Society and the Norwood Jewish Orphanage, dated from the eighteenth century. The Board of Guardians, however, was the first attempt to integrate social services. Very much an arm of established Anglo-Jewry, the Board was positively hostile to the needs of immigrants later in the century. Indeed, the Board was keen to see the repatriation of the more indigent immigrants. Yet for all its conservatism, the Board was in its welfare policies a remarkably forward-looking institution. 'Our whole history', remarks Melvyn Carlowe, 'is a mixture of establishment rigidity and Jewish creativity. We were the first organization in the world to recognize that poor hygiene and poor living conditions actually had a direct effect on health. Our medical committee in the 1860s introduced the first public health service, and the first midwifery service to people in their own homes.' The Board is now responsible for eleven residential homes, hostels for the mentally ill, and teams of social workers.

With the institution of the welfare state after the Second World War, the Jewish community looked at ways of providing specific services that would augment those offered by the State and the local authority. Individual agencies cherished their autonomy and traditions, but over the years it became obvious that they should co-ordinate their activities to the greatest possible extent. In 1972 an umbrella organization, the Central Council for Jewish Social Service, was formed – incorporating the Welfare Board, Norwood, the Blind Society, and the Jewish Home and Hospital at Tottenham – in an attempt to co-ordinate the delivery of services. 'It was a great idea,' says Carlowe, 'but it never worked. There was no money behind it. Everybody thought it was a fantastic idea, but people resist any degree of centralization or nationalization. The concept of having a huge conglomerate was seen as impersonal, and people feared it would create a massive bureaucracy. Groups that came into being to meet the needs of the blind or the mentally handicapped or those with multiple sclerosis feared that they would be lost, and you have to acknowledge that the beauty of having lots of smaller organizations is that they can simply focus on the needs of a particular group rather than having to worry about overall needs and priorities.'

Yet the need to which the Central Council was intended to respond has not diminished. Even though the community is shrinking, demands for the provision of social services are greater than ever. Carlowe observes: 'We're going to have fewer working members of our community who are going to have to provide support for an increasing number of handicapped and elderly. The government has made it crystal clear that it sees the holes in the safety net it is willing to provide getting very much bigger.' At every AGM of every Jewish charity, the directors warn that, as the Conservative government cuts back on the provision of benefits to the needy, the burdens are falling ever more heavily on the private agencies. The financial strains, inevitably, are considerable. Meanwhile, the network of small, individual, localized charities and agencies becomes increasingly outdated. By the late 1980s the Jewish community still sustained just under one hundred welfare organizations, with, inevitably, considerable duplication of bureaucracies, if not of services. Mergers have begun: in the mid-1980s the Ravenswood Foundation merged with the Jewish Society for the Mentally Handicapped, and Norwood Child Care took over the Jewish Society for Deaf Children. In 1990 two of the largest agencies, the Welfare Board and the Blind Society, will formally merge. Stark economic reality has had to prevail, not simply because of duplications, but because institutions established, in some cases, almost two centuries ago, were often located in areas that have long ceased to be centres of Jewish population.

A serious attempt is now being made to reorganize the whole structure of Jewish charities. The businessman Gerald Ronson has been a prime mover in the attempt to achieve greater co-operation and co-ordination, but it has not been easy, for individual bureaucracies are loath to surrender any of their authority. Nevertheless the directors of the various charities do acknowledge that such co-ordination is essential. As Carlowe points out: 'In social work you can't divide people into segments. You can't send a social worker round to a family and say that's a mental handicap problem, that's a family therapy problem, and put four different agencies to work. We have to look at the family as a whole.' While agency directors are unhappy about the changes in government benefits policy, some, such as Melvyn Carlowe, welcome the impetus those changes have given the community to reorganize the charitable network. 'Economic circumstances are going to force us into doing all the things that people were talking about 150 years ago and never got round to. Parochialism is being phased out, though painfully.' Moreover, the Jewish community that helps to fund these agencies is a shrinking pie from which they are all trying to cut a slice. While individuals may have their favourite charities, many other Jewish families are bewildered and impatient when, as may happen over the course of a year, they are approached by no fewer than sixty-five organizations, all appealing for funds. Ronson has been trying to set up a unified appeal, which will then distribute the funds on the recommendations of an allocations committee.

The latest experiment in co-ordination is the foundation in 1987 of the Federation of Jewish Family Services, a consortium of four agencies – the Jewish Welfare Board, Norwood, the Jewish Blind Society, and Ravenswood (which serves the mentally handicapped) – which now share a building in Golders Green. 'The sum of the whole', hopes Melvyn Carlowe, 'will be far greater than the sum of the individual component parts.' The Federation is now responsible for 80 per cent of social services. Carlowe is untroubled by the fact that the remaining 20 per cent is dealt with by almost eighty agencies in the London area alone. Some of them are self-help organizations or already work in close co-operation with the Jewish Welfare Board. The Federation will fund some projects jointly, such as the provision of day centres, and will soon initiate joint fund-raising. Manpower will be shared, as are computing facilities. The extraordinary thing is that it has taken so many decades for such an obviously sensible idea to be put into practice.

Not all the funds need to be raised from within the Jewish community. Some 60 per cent of operating costs are reimbursed by the DHSS or local authorities in return for services provided in place of statutory services. Money is raised in three principal ways: through fund-raising efforts, legacies, and investment. All the principal agencies are heavily dependent on the largesse of a handful of individuals. According to Melvyn Carlowe, the Welfare Board relies on fewer than twenty-five major contributors for about 80 per cent of its fund-raising income, and the same is true of most other agencies. The donations of charitable foundations such as the Wolfson, Rayne and Ronson Foundations can maintain the financial health of individual agencies and occasionally underwrite in full some urgently needed project. During its first fifteen years, the Wolfson Foundation handed out some £15 million, though only a small proportion went to Jewish causes[2], while by the late 1980s the Ronson Foundation was giving away almost £3 million each year, mostly to educational and welfare projects, though, again, not exclusively to the Jewish community, and not exclusively in Britain. Alan Sugar, head of Amstrad, is offering about £2 million to Jewish charities through his recently established foundation. The primary purpose of establishing such foundations may be to lighten the burden of taxation, but this doesn't lessen the gratitude of those agencies on the receiving end, and it certainly doesn't diminish the influence and power of those individual donors. Geoffrey Paul, the editor of the *Jewish Chronicle*, observes that the community has a disproportionate regard for its wealthiest members, while Jews distinguished in other ways – whether through piety, scholarship, science, or artistic achievement – are scarcely noticed, let alone esteemed. Meanwhile, not even the best efforts of the philanthropists can save the major agencies from growing deficits. The agencies must compete for funds with the powerful Joint Israel Appeal, which has long been able to persuade diaspora Jews that if they aren't prepared to go on *aliyah*, they should at least make generous contributions to Israeli projects. About 60 per cent of all funds raised within the Jewish community pass through the Joint Israel Appeal, amounting to £13.5 million in 1987, leaving the welfare agencies and other domestic charities with the remnant.

A survey conducted by Dr E. Krausz in Edgware in the late 1960s showed that while only about 13 per cent of Jews were regular in their attendance at synagogue, at least 35 per cent supported Jewish charities. For many people whose religious commitment is weak, such support is, together with backing for Zionist organizations such as WIZO, their major form of identification with the Jewish community. Dr Krausz's findings, however, are no longer valid, according to some directors of charities. Mr Yochanan Pre-el of the Jewish Blind Society maintains that only 20 per cent of British Jews give to domestic and Israeli charities.[3]

Nor could the agencies survive without the contributions of volunteers. Norwood alone makes use of more than 200. Among many other activities, they staff the day centres, distribute meals on wheels, and organize a ceaseless stream of fund-raising events. The help of volunteers is obviously welcome, but doesn't fully compensate for a shortage of professional staff. Mike Anderson, the director of Manchester Jewish Social Services, observes: 'There are plenty of Jewish social workers but not many Jewish social work managers. Many old people's homes and other Jewish institutions have to be run by non-Jews. Jewish professionals don't want to work for Jewish agencies, partly because some Jewish agencies have a reputation for not being professional in their employment practices. It's difficult both being a helper in the community and living within it. And the smaller the community, the more difficult it is. The more exposed you are to the public, the more arm-tugging is likely to go on.' Moreover, many volunteers are happy to perform the handful of rewarding tasks required by welfare agencies, but far less willing to pour the coffee, however necessary such relatively menial tasks may be.

Charitable bodies have retained greater freedom from religious interference than have Jewish schools. 'The rule of thumb, as far as the Welfare Board is concerned,' says Melvyn Carlowe, 'is that if anybody actually has any kind of Jewish background, we'll try to help them. We don't inquire whether somebody is halachically acceptable to the Beth Din. But all our services have to be run on strictly Jewish lines. If somebody was to come into one of our homes or receive our services, we would have to ask ourselves whether they would actually be able to live with that service – because if they were brought up in a totally non-religious way they would find it very difficult not being able to do certain things on the Sabbath. Of course we don't force people to go to synagogue.' Other agency directors, such as Mike Anderson, do find that religious militancy is encroaching on the provision of social services. With so many guardians of *kashrut* stomping the land, the pressure is increasing on those who run, say, old people's homes, to supply unimpeachably kosher food. 'But you can buy kosher food and the very religious won't eat it because it's not kosher enough. There are homes here where the less religious don't feel comfortable any longer. Some rabbis do try to tell people what they can and cannot do. So in Manchester a lot of people prefer to go into private nursing homes that are not religious even though they are half filled by Jews. They're happy to be with Jewish people but they don't want the religion thrust down their throat. The homes within the Jewish community are subject to management committees, and it's hard for agencies such as ours to interfere. But as an agency, we are there for all Jews on a self-identification basis. Anybody who comes to our door and says, "I am a Jew", or doesn't say it even but just comes to our door, gets help.'

In London the Welfare Board is doing its best to maintain and increase links with the ultra-Orthodox community. That community will have nothing to do with the institutions run by the Board, on the grounds that standards of religious observance are unacceptably slack. However, both the Board and Norwood are establishing small nests of social workers on the fringes of the ultra-Orthodox community. There is some understandable resentment that the bulk of the community has to underwrite social services for Jews unwilling to make any contribution towards them. 'The wealthy Orthodox', says Sidney Bloch, a former chairman of Norwood and present chairman of the Central Council for Jewish Social Service, 'don't always cough up. They'll pay for the *yeshivas*, for education, they'll pay for a new synagogue.' They appear to see social problems in terms of individual cases, which can be remedied by single acts of generosity. And of course they have established some institutions of their own, such as the Agudas Housing Association and Vad Voezer, which is founding residential homes for handicapped children.

The social problems afflicting the Jewish community are not very different from those troubling the wider society around it. Ageing is certainly a major problem, prompted by out-marriage and the subsequent 'loss' of the resulting children and by the simple fact that people live longer than they used to. Within some families there are often two generations of retired people, and this preponderance of elderly people places a great burden both on the younger members of that family and on the community as a whole. The other major problem is family breakdown, resulting in the human wreckage of deserted wives and struggling single-parent families.

Melvyn Carlowe detects an alarming complacency within some sections of the community. 'The myth that we try to perpetuate both within and outside the community is that we are the religion of the family, that we look after our old and our sick, that we're not abusers of ourselves or others. That's complete and utter rubbish. The divorce rate in the Anglo-Jewish community has gone up dramatically in the last twenty years, because the social and religious pressures that used to prevail are less punitive. Many women no longer see themselves just as being the wife and dutiful mother. They want to pursue their own interests and careers, and are not prepared to put up with a marriage for the sake of the family.

There's a tremendous increase in single-parent families. Norwood and the Association for Jewish Youth commissioned a recently issued report that will probably perpetuate the myth that there's no problem with drugs in the community. The people they tried to interview proved unco-operative: the schools, the youth movements, everybody else, said it's not a problem. And yet when we spoke to non-Jewish doctors and specialists in this field, they all say that there's an increasing number of kids from Jewish backgrounds attending the clinics. We have a younger group of people who are much more affluent than their parents or grandparents were. Jewish yuppies are certainly experimenting with drugs. We're probably less prone to playing around with heroin but more prone to being involved with pot and cocaine. And alcoholism is an increasing problem. Many Jews with drugs or alcohol problems are totally alienated from the community. They don't want support from the community, but many of them certainly come from traditional Jewish backgrounds.' That schools did not co-operate with the survey of drug use among Jewish teenagers is hardly surprising. As Alan Greenbat, director of the Association for Jewish Youth, put it: 'Imagine the Jewish reaction if they discovered at this school or that school that there was even a suspicion of drug-taking!' As for alcoholism, if the Jewish community enjoys a relatively low incidence of the disease, it is less fortunate when it comes to the great Jewish vice of gambling, which can be as socially disruptive if not as physically ruinous as hitting the bottle.

The other great problem is poverty. 'We're dealing', says Carlowe, 'with an increasing demand from people who are poverty-stricken. They are people on low incomes, mostly people entirely dependent on their old-age pensions. Longevity makes it worse. Many of these people are left behind in inner-city areas such as Hackney and Stepney. We're also finding a high incidence of mental illness. And the fact that there are many single-parent families means that we have more and more young people trying to cope on social security. But it's too uncomfortable for us as a community to acknowledge that we're anything other than middle class.' Just as Jews are unwilling to admit that there are alarming pockets of poverty within the community, so too they would wish to disguise the incidence of child abuse, an offence so antithetical to Jewish values. Yet in 1987 Norwood dealt with 120 cases of child abuse, though not every allegation could be proved. In the great majority of cases the children suffered physical rather than sexual abuse. Yet four years ago Norwood didn't deal with a single case of child abuse. Whether the rise in incidence is one in actuality as well as in reporting is difficult to say, but the trend certainly alarms Jewish social workers.[4]

I thought I must be in the waiting room at Waterloo Station at the start of a summer bank holiday. But no, it was only the reception area of the Michael Sobell Day Centre. While at the front of the building on Golders Green Road administrators keep the Welfare Board and three other agencies running, here at the back charity is put into practice. The Sobell Centre is the largest Jewish day centre in Europe, and it looked it. I had arrived just as minibuses full of elderly and handicapped people were unloading, and the doors and halls and coffee lounge were jammed. Every visitor, and there are on average 250 each day, registers on arrival, so that the centre can keep track of the 1,500 people it caters for. The registration desk can monitor any members who are ill or in hospital and ensures that all members receive birthday cards. A sign by the registration desk reads: PLEASE LABEL YOUR WALKING STICK. Wise counsel, for if you mislaid it, or anything else, in this mayhem, your chances of recovering it would be slender. Volunteer 'hostesses' as well as full-time staff were shepherding the new arrivals from door to desk, from desk to coffee bar, and from coffee bar to any available seat. An old and very lame whiskery man was shuffling his feet but his movement was imperceptible. A hostess slid up and offered to take his arm and guide him to his chair. 'With you, anywhere,' he replied in a strong Polish accent, gallant to the last. There was a brief outburst of peevishness from a blind man, bewildered by the noise and confusion around him, and who could blame him? Yet everybody else seemed unfazed by the racket. No doubt widespread deafness increases tolerance for noise in old age, but the din all around me was equally likely to have induced deafness. At least you know you are still alive.

At the registration desk the arrivals hand over £2.10, which entitles them to coffee and biscuits, a three-course lunch, tea and biscuits in the afternoon, and any of twenty-seven different activities organized each day, ranging from opera appreciation to quizzes and cookery classes. The centre is run by twenty-four paid staff and a pool of almost 350 volunteers. For the visitors the highlight of the day is lunch. The dining-room filled up while the cooks were still warming the soup; people seek each other out week after week to resume their conversations. Talking, indeed, is the main activity at the centre. Television sets are stowed away except for rare occasions such as royal weddings that excite general interest.

Very few of the regulars come from institutions. Indeed, many make their own way here and don't need the centre's minibuses. They come from all over north London, from as far away as Barnet and Southgate. Despite the clusters of Jewish residential institutions throughout north London, only about 5 per cent of people over seventy-five require or have opted for residential care. The great majority of those who come to the Sobell live alone in their own homes, and for them the centre provides a whole range of services, quite apart from the pleasures of sociability. There are five shops within the centre, including a grocery, a dress shop with new clothes at discounted prices, and a gadget shop full of items such as devices enabling the arthritic to hold playing cards, large-print telephone cards, and simple inventions enabling the infirm to put on their tights without bending double. For £1.40 you can have your hair cut and enjoy the warm high aromas of lacquer and spray and the noisy, cushioning blast of the hair-dryer.

Each morning a discussion group gathers, and the session on which I eavesdropped was thrashing out the rights and wrongs of Israeli policy in the Occupied Territories. The more articulate regulars can also contribute to *Emet*, the house magazine largely written by those who attend the centre. Grave issues are addressed – notably morality and politics – but the contributions tend to be diffuse and imbued with sentimentality. Less garrulous members can sit in comfort in the library, or head for one of the quiet rooms with a book or a chessboard. Upstairs there are crafts rooms equipped for dressmaking or basketwork or pottery, and finished items are sold off. A supervisor wandered up to an old gentleman who was staring with a puzzled look at the work table in front of him.

'What are you going to make today?'

'Good question.' And he nodded soberly, and continued to stare at the table.

Other activities have a more overtly therapeutic purpose. At the keep-fit class a few women in wheelchairs were participating in some of the exercises. At the 'training flat' widowers were learning basic skills they had not previously needed to acquire, such as cooking an egg. Men and women recovering from strokes were learning how to get in and out of baths without assistance. There's rehabilitation for the mentally ill or those recovering from mental breakdowns; simple tasks such as stuffing envelopes or stringing beads are undertaken with earnest application. Quite a few of those in the rehabilitation room were young men.

About 35 per cent of those who attend the centre are refugees, mostly from Germany, central Europe, or Poland. A few of them experienced the horrors of the concentration camps, but the great majority made their escape in time. Although most refugees rebuilt their lives after they came to Britain, and many of them prospered, there is an increasing problem within the community of 'survivor syndrome'. The syndrome is usually spurred by some watershed in the pattern of one's life, such as the death of a spouse or retirement. Long-buried memories begin to surface once again, and many refugees, aware of their own good fortune, feel growing guilt at the thought that they survived while dozens of their relatives and friends perished. I was told of one classic instance of the syndrome, when an old lady was taken, for the first time in her life, to hospital, where she grew confused and insisted that she was back in a death camp and that the nurses were her guards. The Sobell Centre and other organizations have established groups to assist the growing number of those beginning to encounter problems of this kind.

Melvyn Carlowe is understandably proud of the day centre, not only because it provides a necessary service but because it is innovative and responsive. In 1987 the Sobell even whisked fifty-two members, including some handicapped people, to the Mediterranean for a holiday. Carlowe is full of praise for his hundreds of volunteers, though he chides some rabbis for neglecting the social aspects of their work. 'Most rabbis accept that they have a responsibility for overseeing the welfare needs of their flock as well as their spiritual needs. All the synagogal organizations acknowledge that the synagogue has to do very much more to deal with the needs of their members. Some congregations are doing the job very well. Others just see their role as dialling a telephone number and referring the problems that arise to the appropriate agency.'

One difficulty that crops up when the provision of welfare is partly in the hands of a religious group is that certain problems cannot be admitted to exist. With the Chief Rabbi thundering from pulpit and leader page about the hideous sins of adultery and homosexuality, it is far from easy for, say, Jewish homosexuals to obtain support from within the community. The religious services held each week by the Jewish Gay and Lesbian Group have to be conducted at Friends' House, the Quaker headquarters in London. The Jewish National AIDS Co-ordinating Council has wisely decided to keep its distance from the religious establishment, even though there are no doubt individual rabbis – especially from the Progressive wing – who are sympathetic. Even the Chief Rabbi has declared that AIDS victims must be treated with compassion and not scorn, yet it has not been possible for the community as such to create support mechanisms for AIDS sufferers or for those troubled by their 'abnormal' sexuality.

Administrators of Jewish charities must also ask themselves whether it would be sensible to make radical changes in their structure. Morton Creeger, the director of the Ronson Foundation, points out that the provision of old people's homes is a perfectly reasonable aim for the community, since there is no way that stretched local authorities can provide facilities that cater exclusively to the stringent requirements of a small religious minority. On the other hand, what purpose is served by institutions that care only for Jewish handicapped children, many of whom are so handicapped that they have no notion of what it means to be Jewish? In such cases, the provision of Jewish care clearly satisfies the wishes of the parents rather than the needs of the children. There is nothing wrong with that, but perhaps it should be recognized as an indulgence of sorts that may soon have to take a lower position on any list of priorities.

That so small a community has developed, in the main, such impressive charitable institutions is a reflection of the fact that it had little choice if it wished to ensure that members with specific needs would be cared for appropriately. Yet despite the affluence of the community, there have to be serious doubts about whether such largesse can continue. The treasurers of the major agencies point out that the generosity of Nigel Lawson's lavish tax cuts in 1988 mean that many Jewish families are vastly better off than they have ever been, and should thus be able to increase their support for Jewish charities without it affecting their standard of living. At the same time the treasurers report that there is little evidence that much of that extra loot is coming their way. Manchester Jewish Social Service, for instance, is operating with an alarmingly high, and worsening, deficit. With the private acquisition of wealth legitimized by the prime minister and others as a positive goal in itself, the moral imperative to apply some of that wealth to relieving the misfortunes of others is no longer convincingly maintained, despite the lip service paid by the philosophers of *laissez faire* capitalism to the values of charity and volunteerism. There are, it is safe to predict, going to be tough times ahead for Jewish charities.

✤ THREE COMMUNITIES ✤

– 19 –

Fading away: the East End

THE poverty of which Jewish social workers speak must be a perplexing notion to the inhabitants of London suburbs such as Bushey or Edgware or Finchley. Those dreary seamless expanses of comfortable enclosed houses, each neatly set within its garden, may conceal many a heartache, but not, I think, poverty. Jewish poverty has become invisible. It is the consequence of being left behind, both physically and emotionally. The East End of London which fifty or seventy years ago was teeming with 100,000 Jews is now parcelled out among Pakistani and Bangladeshi immigrants, the English working class in their council housing, a handful of yuppies who have colonized some of the more architecturally distinguished streets of Bow and Spitalfields, and a small community of mostly elderly Jews. The Jewish exodus from the East End began after the Second World War when returning evacuees and servicemen and women chose not to resettle in the streets where they had grown up, but moved to the suburbs of Gants Hill and Ilford and Edgware. When Helene Bromnick worked at an East End primary school in the early 1950s, 'one-third of the children in that school moved out annually. Of those the vast majority were Jewish.' Some 15,000 Jewish families now live in Ilford and the neighbouring suburbs of Wanstead, Chigwell, and Redbridge. When Dr E. Krausz surveyed Edgware Jewry in the 1960s, well over half those he interviewed had been born in the East End.

Those who still live in the East End are overwhelmingly elderly. The only Jewish day centre left in the area, the Stepney Settlement, set up shop in 1938 just as the flight to the suburbs gathered momentum. In 1956 it constructed a nursery school, but five years later handed the facility over to the Inner London Education Authority, since there were so few Jewish children left in the East End. A few synagogues, a remnant of the eighty that used to flourish in the area, still open their doors on Saturday mornings. On paper their membership figures look healthy enough, but that merely reflects the fact that for sentimental or financial reasons, or both, many suburban families have maintained their membership of East End synagogues. In this way they can still claim some kind of allegiance to their original community and, what's more, the burial fees are lower than in the suburbs.

The Jews still living in the East End inhabit Mile End, Bow, Spital-fields, and, in far smaller numbers, Bethnal Green, Poplar and Lime-house. Nobody knows how many there are. Trudy Schama, the director of the Stepney Settlement, estimates about 3,000, but other people who know the area well think there may be twice that number. A walk down Mile End Road or Whitechapel Road will take you past small workshops, mainly gown and mantle distributors, operating under Jewish names. While their owners may indeed be Jewish, you can be sure they no longer live in the East End: Blackman's shoe shop on Brick Lane, for example, is owned by a Jewish couple but they live in Highgate. Very few of the Jewish businessmen or artists or publishers who have moved into Wapping warehouses and luxury Docklands developments joined the indigenous Jewish community. In recent years the Jewish Welfare Board and the Jewish Blind Society even ceased operations in the area, much to Mrs Schama's annoyance, but now they supply some volunteers to help out at the Settlement. The rabbinate is also conspicuous by its absence, although one Lubavitch rabbi from Finchley makes regular appearances. In its structure the Stepney Settlement does not differ greatly from larger venues such as the Sobell Day Centre. Of course the numbers are far smaller: there's a total membership of just under 800, of whom about eighty visit the centre on each of the four days on which it is open. The local authority contributes a grant and the lunches are subsidized, but the rest of the money required to run the centre has to be raised privately. Two hundred kosher meals on wheels are distributed each day, and Passover parcels are delivered to home-bound Jews. Like most welfare agencies, the Settlement doesn't ask too many questions of the applicants for its services. Mrs Schama tells of an elderly Pole who received meals on wheels for many years. On his ninetieth birthday she paid him a visit, and couldn't help noticing that there was no indication in his flat of Jewish observance: no *menorah*, no *mezuzah*, no prayer-book on the shelf. A few gentle questions confirmed that the old gentleman wasn't Jewish at all, but he was so distressed at the thought that Settlement workers would cease their visits that Mrs Schama assured him that he would continue to receive their services, and he did so until his death.

When I visited the Settlement, one of the regulars, Jack Miller, showed me round the art class, pointing with pride to his own paintings on the walls. An autodidact, he also talked books to me. We had both just finished reading Martin Amis's *The Moronic Inferno* – he was less impressed by Mr Amis's sizzling prose than I am – and we also exchanged views on the work of D. J. Enright. When Jack Miller mentioned that he had taught himself French, I had a hunch that we would soon be discussing Proust, and indeed we were, until Mrs Schama whisked me off to visit the dining-room. A gang of old ladies had taken over the adjoining lounge, their merry old-fashioned print dresses scarcely distinguishable from the chair coverings. A visiting social worker said to me: 'It does the old dears good to come here once a week, not just because they get a hot meal, but because they're competitive. If they're coming to the centre, then they know they've got to put on a dress and comb their hair.'

I didn't have to be in that dining-room for more than ten seconds to identify the principal problems of the Jewish East End: old age and its ugly sister, senility. Although old women outnumber old men, the men provide the greater problem, since they tend to be less well equipped to cope with their circumstances. Fortunately the Settlement and its volunteers are not the only agencies at work in this area. Organizations such as Age Concern and the local authority provide facilities and services that far exceed anything that was available twenty or thirty years ago. Nevertheless the future is grim for the Jewish community, even more so for those Jews whose identification with the community is so attenuated that they have no contact with the Settlement and the Settlement has no contact with them.

Of course not every East End Jew is old and impoverished. A handful still live much as they have for half a century. Manny Penner and his wife occupy a pleasant council flat in Stepney. A dignified man, he has long been active in politics and trade-union affairs, and in 1983 became mayor of Tower Hamlets. I first met Manny at his local synagogue in Rectory Square, a side street flanking a large housing estate just south of Whitechapel Road. The synagogue, built in 1877, is a grim grey-brick building that gives no indication of the splendour of its interior. I wandered in one Saturday morning expecting to find a service in full swing, but though the doors were open and the lights were emitting a dim yellow glow, the synagogue was deserted. The dark wood of the *bima* and the pews and galleries gleamed richly against a gaudy backdrop of brick and tile, and the atmosphere was as Victorian and ecclesiastical as any Butterfield chapel. The only discordant features were the exceptionally tawdry light fittings that resembled milky tumblers suspended upside down. There was a wealth of useless ornament, such as carvings of foliage chiselled by hands that were familiar with the cut and edge of Grinling Gibbons, and the delights of bright colour and self-conscious grandeur.

Yet I could hear voices chanting, and so I made my way towards their source, a small upstairs room. I pushed open the door and saw in front of me four women, one wearing a *sheitl*, seated behind a long table and thus separated from the dozen or so men, all elderly. A young rabbi, Yitzhak Macmull, was at the desk, chanting from the Torah. I was waved over and prayer-books were pressed upon me. I took an empty seat in the front row; there were only two rows in the room, which I later learnt was the former children's synagogue. No sooner had I sat down than the warden came up and asked me to help bind the scrolls after the reading. I said I'd rather not. But he had no intention of taking no for an answer. It was not that he wished to press this *mitzvah* upon me for the good of my soul, but because the tiny congregation was desperately short of hands. They wanted my body, not my soul. I gave in. 'Good, good,' said the warden, 'and it's a *mitzvah*, you know.' As in all Orthodox synagogues, the noise level was high. In so tiny a room even a whisper carried from wall to wall. The man seated behind me insisted on talking at the top of his voice during the most solemn parts of the service, but he was so obviously not in his right mind that his verbal meanderings were tolerated. Towards the end of the service, the bearded reader asked us which version of the concluding hymn we'd like to sing. A brief discussion was held and we plumped for a version I recognized and so I could show good will by joining in.

I hadn't realized it, but this was the last service ever held in the old building at Rectory Square. The site had been sold, for it was absurd to maintain so large and elaborate a building for a Sabbath congregation of fewer than twenty people. The fate of the building is still unclear. There had been talk of replacing it with sheltered housing, and then of converting it into a mosque, but there were objections to both schemes. There is no permanent rabbi at this synagogue, and Rabbi Macmull is a graduate of Gateshead Yeshiva and a teacher at the Avigdor School. Despite his piety and devotion to the dwindling congregation, the young rabbi, in his Homburg and beard, seemed even more out of place among this pack of raw working-class elderly East End Jews than I did. There had been a full-time minister here, but he had died, and after his death a part-time rabbi had been taken on. He and the congregation did not see eye to eye, and so he departed and his place was taken by the young rabbi, who now led the congregation in prayer but performed no other ministerial functions.

After the service I found myself in conversation with a congregant, who turned out to be Manny Penner. He told me that despite the pitifully small Sabbath morning attendance, the actual membership of East London is close to 700, of whom three-fifths are women, mostly widows. There hasn't been a barmitzvah at Rectory Square for four years. As the active congregations of various East End synagogues continue to shrink, synagogues have been forced to amalgamate; Penner recalls five in five years. 'But there's no one left to amalgamate with. At burial society meetings, I'm often the youngest person in the room.' It's much the same story at the Fieldgate Street Synagogue, which has a membership of over 1,000, the majority of whom live far from the East End and never attend services.

Manny Penner and his wife have six children, scattered on both sides of the Atlantic. Despite the dispersal of their children, none of whom lives in the East End, the Penners still maintain a traditional Jewish home, and are joined by some of their children and grandchildren each Friday night. Penner attaches enormous importance to education and dissuaded their children from leaving school at too early an age. 'It's the old saying: When you educate a man, you educate one person. Educate a girl, and you educate a family.'

Penner feels that the synagogal and welfare authorities seem oblivious of the real hardship in the East End. 'A funeral and stone can easily cost £1,600. I know an old lady who can't afford a stone for her husband's grave, and she feels ashamed. She thinks she's dishonoured his memory. The Jewish organizations have deserted the community. Some of the people here have made contributions to Jewish welfare services all their working lives, and now that they need those services they're not getting them. In fact many old Jews around here have to apply to the Christian missions instead.' As the Jews moved away, other immigrant groups moved in to take their place. Where Jewish sweatshops once thrived, Pakistani and Bangladeshi manufacturers have taken up the slack. There is little tension between the Jewish and Muslim communities. Alan Greenbat, director of the Association for Jewish Youth, which is based in Stepney, recalls how Muslim extremists painted vicious slogans on the door, but this was an isolated incident. Manny Penner agrees: 'Many of us have done our best to welcome the Muslim community. After all, they are immigrants, just as we were. It's important they should feel that they're citizens too. When the local Hindu society has its AGM, they ask me along as a mark of respect.' A lifelong socialist, Penner abhors racism: 'I still feel an outsider. The moment someone realizes you're Jewish – and with a name like Manny, you can't hide – they think of you as a foreigner. People think of Jews not as a religion but as a race. When I'm riled I find myself using Yiddish expressions. When I arrange for leave for the Jewish holidays, even though I always offer a quid pro quo and cover for other people over the Christian holidays, I'm conscious of being a Jew. When you go into the community, what one Jew does, every Jew does. People judge us by our behaviour, and so if I come across a Jew who's behaving badly or denigrating other people, I'll pull him up. If I hear someone referring to a "schwarzer", I boil. The role of the Jew is to be a soldier of God. Racism is not part of our way of life.'

Bella Aronovitch feels much the same way. A remarkable woman of eighty, she now lives in Kilburn, but spent most of her life in the East End. Bella was born to Russian parents in Bow but grew up in Shoreditch. Her father was a loser, but a highly literate one; he would regularly invite round like-minded friends, and Bella would listen in on their discussions of poetry and art. The only problem was that they didn't have enough to eat. She recalls her childhood and her adolescence as a struggle to find the next meal. Her mother did her best to disguise their poverty, but malnourishment took its toll and Bella suffered from very poor health as a young woman. Before and after her prolonged stays in hospital, eloquently described in her book *Give It Time*, she was employed in the fur trade and, like Manny Penner, was active in trade-union organization. She describes working conditions in those days as absolutely appalling, since no professional qualifications were needed in order to set up shop, and the trade was entirely unregulated. 'It took us thirty years of negotiations before we earned the right to a week's paid holiday.' Although Bella, like her father, is in no way religious, she feels very conscious of her Jewishness. 'I don't really feel assimilated at all. My sister and I didn't mix with non-Jewish children except at school, and at home we spoke Yiddish. I remember one day our teacher showed the class a globe, and pointed to the pink bits and said, "This is all ours." I didn't really understand what he meant. I just grew up thinking that the English are supremely confident and socially at ease, and I'm not.'

Bella Aronovitch and Manny Penner must, I imagine, have felt somewhat baffled when in the summer of 1987 the East End was filled with exhibitions celebrating Jewish life in the area. There were performances of Yiddish theatre, readings from the works of Jewish East End writers from Israel Zangwill to Steven Berkoff, concerts and displays, guided walks, talks and film shows. The events I attended were evocative and full of fascinating material. Yet in a sense this splendid Jewish East End Celebration marked the extinction of the area as a living community. You memorialize what is dead. You evoke scenes that can never be duplicated in the modern world. You sing songs that have to be exhumed from the archives. The Jewish East End has become as remote as the *shtetl*. Three singers and actors who kept the Yiddish theatre tradition alive – Anna Tzelnicher, Harry Ariel, and Bernard Mendelovitch – performed only as a travelling troupe, moving from venue to venue, from charity event to charity event, and in 1988 the partnership, and Yiddish theatre in London, came to an end.

The Celebration was an undoubted success, and a well deserved one too. People who had grown up in the East End, even though they have lived most of their adult lives in Gants Hill or Finchley, came back in droves, for it was an opportunity for them to show their children and grandchildren the way things used to be. The revival of interest had no religious content. It was an exercise in cultural nostalgia. But the Celebration was a particular success with younger Jews, not only with nostalgic grandparents. By reacquainting themselves with the Jewish culture that once flourished in the East End, they became aware of their own loss. The suburbs may be humming with bridge parties and Ladies' Guilds and other social events that bind the Jewish community, but the music and the food and the languages of the East End will soon be gone for ever. Rabbi Dr Isaac Levy points out that the Holocaust has heightened that sense of loss. 'The eastern European communities were a source of Judaism that's lost for all time, and people feel they have to recapture it somehow, or at least ensure it isn't forgotten.' Others see dangers in this kind of revivalism. 'Part of me', says Helene Bromnick, 'does hate a Judaism that is too much composed of fried fish and Yiddish song. That to me is not what Judaism is about and I think the vogue for the Jewish East End can be facile. I don't want to equate Judaism with life in Russia.' To Jews of German and central European descent, the revival of Yiddish – not only in musical performances but at Oxford University – is a form of regression. Their ancestors fought their way out of the ghetto and into the modern world. The last thing they wish to see would be, as Mrs Bromnick put it, an equation of Jewish life with a particular slice of Jewish culture.

Some rabbis do see a connection between this cultural revivalism and the reawakening of interest in Judaism among many younger Jews. 'Sentiment is there,' says Barbara Borts, 'but it's a powerful emotion, an irrational one, one that comes upon you in waves, and one that motivates you to do something. Some of that can be considered in the same way as a religious manifestation. Something is compelling Jews in times when it makes no sense to continue to survive as Jewish people. Why should a Jew who's had very little contact with the religion suddenly want to proclaim their Judaism? You can't sing Yiddish songs without being aware of the religious traditions as well – the two things can't always be separated. There are political songs and love songs in Yiddish culture, but a lot of songs have to do with Shabbat and the festivals. And I find it quite ironic that the quintessential English university has the only department of Yiddish in the country. Terrific!'

Nevertheless the religious element should not be exaggerated. The majority of Jewish East Enders were never especially devout. Many of those that remain still observe *kashrut* and make an effort to attend synagogue at least on major festivals, but this kind of observance is far removed from the piety of Stamford Hill Jews. Monty Richardson, a former chairman of the Tower Hamlets Society, has observed: 'The assumption is that the East End . . . was very Orthodox. This is complete nonsense. The vast majority of the people had no connection with the synagogue. They were Jewish because they lived in a Jewish *milieu*. A greater proportion belongs to a synagogue today than in a previous generation. My own experience is that many people only became members of the community when they moved to a suburb . . . In the East End, although there was quite a rich synagogal life in terms of worship, there was no room – no space. Hebrew classes and Talmud Torahs were not part of the synagogue establishment, nor was social work. Don't exaggerate the past.'[1]

– 20 –

Manchester

IN the spring of 1988 the Jewish community of Manchester decided it was 200 years old – though pedlars had been plying their trade in the city since the 1740s – and celebrated accordingly. The Board of Deputies, which holds one plenary session each year in a provincial centre, naturally chose Manchester for the 1988 meeting, and I hitched a ride on the deputies' bus from London early one Sunday morning. At eleven we arrived at Manchester Town Hall. We sat among the neo-Gothic splendours of the main hall, with its elephant-hide stone and wan murals, while a row of dignitaries seated up on the dais regaled us with platitudes. I arrived half-way through the speech of Dayan Gavriel Krausz, a Swiss-born rabbi wearing a long black coat. 'Without fear of contradiction,' he informed us, 'I can say that Manchester is one of the finest Jewish communities in the world.' There was, he tried to convince us, harmony between religious and lay leaders, in which case Manchester must be unique indeed. At the same time there was an abundance of institutions of Torah learning and Torah-true schools.

The speakers were introduced by Henry Guterman, the president of the Jewish Representative Council (JRC), the local equivalent of the Board of Deputies. He presented a somewhat bizarre appearance, since he was wearing a bright blue *kippah*, a red bow tie, and an extraordinary gold chain that looked like a giant version of something that had fallen out of a Christmas cracker. Guterman read out telegrams of congratulation from Buckingham Palace, President Herzog of Israel, Mrs Thatcher – the Dalai Lama was about the only person who hadn't wired the JRC. He began his own speech by overwhelming us with his sense of humility at actually giving an address on such a historic occasion. This seemed rather peculiar since it was he who had organized the whole thing. Observing that the Manchester Jewish population was larger than that of all the other communities north of Watford combined, he went on to praise the liberal multicultural tradition of the city. This must have pleased the quaintly titled Chair of the Council, Eileen Kelly, who noted in a somewhat lacklustre drone the contributions the Jewish community had made to Manchester.

The Duke of Devonshire proved even humbler than Henry Guterman – 'Thank you for allowing me to be privileged to take part in your celebrations' – and he used the word 'undeserving' again and again, though there was no evidence that the audience shared his view. Indeed, it was quite a coup to have secured his presence. He spoke with evident sincerity of the warmth he had felt towards the Jewish community all his life. His speech over, he sat down next to Dayan Krausz, a most delightful juxtaposition. Dr Lionel Kopelowitz spoke next, reminding us that this was 'a great and historic occasion', in a tone that suggested we were somehow to blame for this state of affairs.

The speeches were not yet over, and now Lord Young rose to his feet. I had heard David Young address Jewish audiences before and had noted his gift for ignoring the subject under discussion and giving us instead a little pep talk about the glories of private enterprise. He was on typical form. The immigrant Jews of Manchester, he informed their descendants, 'recognized the world owed them nothing and realized that if they did not look after themselves, no one else would.' After about an hour and a half of speeches, the formalities came to an end. Like any good reporter, I'd already found out where the food was, and made a beeline for the adjoining hall, where I refreshed myself with a glass of kosher wine, and then conducted a thorough inquiry into the kosher buffet. I was soon followed by the rest of the audience and the dignitaries. I was keen to make contact with some of them, and adopted the tactic of approaching anybody who was immobilized by balancing a glass and a plate while trying to eat and asking them if they were Sir Sidney Hamburger. One of those I approached was wearing a chain of office not unlike the vast necklace weighing down Henry Guterman. Could that be Hamburger? No, it was somebody from Liverpool and he didn't know a soul either. I never found out why he was wearing a chain round his neck.

After lunch everybody went home, except for the Board of Deputies, who began their meeting at 2.30. There was no visitors' gallery, so, at the suggestion of a vice-president of the Board, I sat among the deputies themselves. The temptation to rise to my feet and attack the inadequacy of the *kashrut* supervision at the preceding banquet was intense, but I restrained myself. The meeting consisted of complaints about media bias in the reporting of events in Israel, and complaints about increased affiliation fees. I shall spare the reader further details. After the deputies went home, the celebrations continued – for months. Through the spring and summer of 1988, there were exhibitions and lectures and musical events, and a garden party hosted by the Duke of Devonshire at Chatsworth.

The first settlers in Manchester were of German and Dutch origin, and mostly engaged in the textile trade. In 1799 a young man by the name of Nathan Mayer Rothschild spent some time in the city. Many of these immigrant merchants and traders prospered as the industrial revolution gathered momentum. Ships arriving from eastern European and north German ports brought fresh immigrants from Poland and Russia later in the century. Just as in other cities, the nascent Jewish community soon established its own institutions, religious and charitable. A Hebrew Philanthropic Society was founded in 1826, and a school for the Jewish poor opened its doors in 1842. This was the only city other than London where the Reform movement secured a foothold, drawing strength from the German Jews who had settled in the city, though absurd infighting inhibited the growth and development of Reform either in Manchester or anywhere else in the north of England. But the great majority of the newer immigrants were faithful to the more Orthodox traditions of eastern Europe. In 1867 a Jewish Board of Guardians was established, though this was a less munificent measure than it at first appears, since aid was extended only to the 'deserving' poor; the now thoroughly settled Jewish Mancunians had no wish to encourage riff-raff to remain in their midst. True to the liberal traditions of the city, the Board did offer loans to those who wished to establish their own businesses.

Manchester has always had a distinctive Sephardi presence, many of them originally traders from the Middle East, and there are three Sephardi congregations. By 1875 the Jewish population was 10,000, and by 1914 had risen to 35,000. The more recent arrivals followed the same pattern as their counterparts in the East End of London, establishing workshops and factories that produced clothing, boots and shoes, tobacco products, and furniture. Sweatshops and small workshops employing up to twenty workers sprang up in Cheetham and other parts of the city with substantial Jewish populations, notably in north Manchester. The more prosperous middle-class Jews, many of whom had entered the professions, moved to south Manchester, especially Didsbury and Withington. Palatine Road in Didsbury has long been known as Palestine Road. As in suburban London, there was considerable assimilation, and a desire for propriety that led to an impersonation of British institutions and British ways. As Bill Williams (to whose studies of the Manchester community I am heavily indebted) has pointed out, 'in the Jews School, the speaking of Yiddish became a punishable offence'.

Zionism thrived in Manchester, and no Jewish Mancunian will let you forget that Chaim Weizmann was not only the greatest of the early Zionists but a teacher of chemistry at Victoria University in Manchester. The passionate Zionism of the Marks and Sieff families is directly attributable to the close friendship between Weizmann and the founders of those two dynasties. Fascism too infected the streets of Manchester, where Mosleyite Blackshirts and Jewish Communists battled it out in the 1930s. During that decade some 2,000 refugees from Nazi Europe also came to Manchester. By this time the dispersal of Manchester Jewry into suburban areas was thoroughly under way, with the community divided between north and south. South Manchester attracted the wealthier and more successful Jews, though it is misleading to generalize. Many south Manchester Jews who had originally settled in Didsbury and Withington have now moved even further to the south to the more verdant suburbs of Sale, Cheadle, and Gatley. Jewish day schools have been established in the suburbs to cater to the numerous young families who have been moving out there. Their religious allegiance tends to be middle-of-the-road Orthodox, since Progressive Judaism has never managed to make great inroads into the city.

The kinds of Jewish organization that flourish in Greater London – the welfare agencies, the Zionist groups, the fund-raising circles, the social and cultural clubs – all have their equivalents in Manchester. Lubavitch is active, handing out Chanukah candles and visiting the sick in hospital. The same kind of ultra-Orthodox revival one finds in Stamford Hill and Golders Green can be observed in Broughton Park, a square mile of suburban streets containing seventeen synagogues. Indeed, the richness of Manchester's Jewish life is the main reason why the community is said to be expanding. As Jewish communities in, say, Sheffield or Leeds go into a decline that may prove terminal, observant Jews, anxious to be close to facilities such as active synagogues and kosher butchers, have little choice other than to move to London or Manchester. Some Londoners too, especially those with young children, were driven out of the capital by high property prices, since they discovered that their inadequate little house in Hendon could be exchanged for more spacious and luxurious accommodation in the north.

To walk out of central Manchester up Cheetham Hill Road is a saddening yet evocative experience. The broad street was once lined with synagogues, for in the last century this used to be the heart of Jewish Manchester. No longer. The New Synagogue, founded in 1889, is now a factory that produces lampshade frames. The United Synagogue, established in a former Methodist chapel in 1904, is now a cash and carry. Just to the north, another former thoroughfare associated with the Jewish community, Bury New Road, is now known as the 'Asian Petticoat Lane'. In London it was the policy of the United Synagogue to erect its synagogues along side streets, probably in an attempt to be self-effacing. This is not the case in Manchester, where synagogues were regarded as important public buildings in the same league as churches, libraries, and the neo-classic headquarters of insurance companies. The Sephardi Synagogue, built in 1874, was also on Cheetham Hill Road, and it has been most charmingly converted into Manchester's Jewish Museum. The synagogue itself, which was built by Edward Solomons in what the curators call a Hispano-Moresque style, has been impeccably restored and the former ladies' gallery is now an exhibition centre. (Unfortunately the Jewish Museum itself may yet end up as another cash and carry, since the withdrawal of a grant from the hard-pressed city council has put its future in jeopardy.) The bulk of the Sephardi community is now based in south Manchester. No clear division is maintained between Sephardim and Ashkenazim; Dr Maurice Gaguine, the retired rabbi of the principal Sephardi congregation, told me that forty years ago he opened the doors of his synagogue to Ashkenazim, and the two communities have been intermarrying for generations. As in the London Sephardi synagogues, the *minhag* is distinctive, with its own pronunciation and liturgy and a greater formality during the services.

Nobody is quite certain how many Jews live in Greater Manchester, but most community leaders estimate a population of about 30,000. Henry Guterman notes that the influx of Orthodox Jews into Broughton Park is offset by the departure of many suburban Jews for London and other cities. If the community is growing, it can't be by much. As president of the JRC, Guterman is understandably anxious to stress the unity of the community rather than dissension within it, but he admits that Manchester Jewry is far more polarized than it was twenty years ago. The important ultra-Orthodox Machzikei Hadass congregations can't be bothered even to affiliate to the JRC, though they don't object when the JRC campaigns on their behalf. Some Orthodox rabbis in north Manchester apparently view the southerners with suspicion and have been accused of blacking south Manchester rabbis by refusing to invite them to give lectures to north Manchester communities. Guterman is doing his best to pull the different strands of the community together by setting up committees composed of the heads of welfare agencies and the school principals, and another committee that brings together the heads of the JRC, the Beth Din, and the Manchester Shechita Board. Since most Mancunians are sceptical about the efficacy of the JRC itself, there has to be considerable doubt as to whether Guterman's well-meaning attempt at co-ordination will add up to more than the superimposition of fresh layers of bureaucracy.

Guterman certainly has an uphill struggle, as criticism of the JRC is severe. It is derided as a talking-shop. One rabbi asserts that most people in the community don't want anything to do with it, as they don't want to waste their time or be pilloried in public. Consequently it has very little influence on the community. As that veteran observer Sir Sidney Hamburger remarked, the JRC provides a platform for some people, but that doesn't mean they are active in the community. The JRC used to be more influential, in the days when it was led by men such as Abraham Moss, a Lord Mayor of Manchester and, briefly, President of the Board of Deputies. Another lay leader pointed out: 'The JRC doesn't have any clout. Henry Guterman is a progressive man, and his heart's in the right place, but he is ineffectual and too fond of his chain of office. By its very nature, the JRC is forced to be nice to everybody, so it really ends up speaking for nobody. At the level of platitude, it's operating quite effectively. At the level of really making an impact, it's got bugger-all effect.' Nor do Mancunians have any more respect for the Board of Deputies. 'If the Board didn't exist,' says Sir Sidney, 'it would make very little difference to the life of the Manchester community. Our synagogues are all independent. We make a very minimal contribution to the Chief Rabbinate fund and to the Board. Whereas Londoners expect Mancunians to go down to London at the drop of a hat for a meeting at five o'clock, you can't persuade a Londoner to come up to Manchester. You don't get the feeling that it's a two-way traffic.' This, of course, is a common complaint from all provincial communities.

Mike Anderson, who as director of Manchester Jewish Social Services must reach all sections of the community, deals with at least ten different groupings, many of which are antagonistic to the others. Even the Sephardim are divided, with the Iranians hankering after their native country while the Iraqis are eager to integrate and settle down. Yet Sir Sidney Hamburger insists that 'one of the main differences between us and the London community is that we seem to be a more homogeneous unit. I know there's a division between north and south Manchester, but if you ignore that division, the rest of it constitutes one community. London is quite different, a series of peripheral communities that have no common point of contact. Geographically we are more compact.'

Sir Sidney was born here in 1914, and has held just about every conceivable office in the Jewish community. Having handed over the daily running of his electrical fittings business to his sons, he now devotes all his time to charitable work. He has been honoured not only by the Jewish community but by the local Catholic hierarchy too. Active in Labour Party politics, he spent over twenty years on the Salford city council, including a year as mayor. 'The Conservative Party held nothing out to attract us, not so much because of economic differences, but because they were known to be anti-Semitic. A Jew could not become a Member of Parliament in a Conservative constituency. You couldn't make any headway. Today the situation is that the Jewish community probably feels itself more threatened by the extremism of the left than of the right. Because of the improved economic situation we probably have more in common with the liberal philosophy of Conservatism than with the very extreme economic philosophy of the Labour Party.' Nevertheless the JRC and other communal organizations report no difficulties in working closely with the Labour-controlled city council.

Sir Sidney is not alone in worrying about trends within the community that are causing the same polarization that afflicts London. 'We dispense charity to people irrespective of their religious attitudes. But the religious community is very much more powerful than their numbers would justify. My complaint about them is twofold. One, their attitude to Israel I regard as quite indefensible. Their response to that is we worry about religious Israel, and you can worry about secular Israel. The other complaint is that they are very introspective. We don't get enough co-operation from them. There are a large number of men who are young professionals and have

271

everything to offer, but instead of giving the wider Jewish community the benefit of their knowledge, their experience, they build a new ghetto around themselves. I think this is self-defeating and an attitude we can ill afford. And they have their own charities. Polarization is going to increase. It's in the nature of things that as you drive a wedge into anything, the wider become the extremities of the thing that's being divided. However extreme you think you are on some subject, somebody has to go one better than you. Some teachers in the Orthodox schools wanted to segregate children at the ages of five or seven; others said you've got to segregate them at three. And now the Beth Din has decided we're not allowed to have Brussels sprouts served at public functions.'

Yes, indeed, Sir Sidney had touched upon the great sprouts controversy. Until 1988 even the most scrupulous observers of *kashrut* had been able to enjoy the occasional sprout or salad with a perfectly clear conscience. Then the Manchester Beth Din ruled in its full majesty that sprouts and asparagus were off – on the grounds that the folds and leaves could conceivably conceal tiny organisms that were not in themselves kosher. There is a proviso: as long as you check the asparagus thoroughly, peeking into every crevice and fold, and as long as you fail to find a creepie-crawlie, you may consume the asparagus. To this, however, there is a drawback, for by the time the inspection is completed the asparagus will resemble shredded cabbage. Individual families may decide that Dayan Westheim and his colleagues are round the twist and refuse to give up their sprouts, but the ruling does affect caterers and restaurants who would have their *kashrut* licence annulled should they contravene the Beth Din's judgement.

The Manchester Beth Din has also made the separation of the sexes in synagogues more rigid than before, and partitions screening the women's section have been heightened. The growing inflexibility of the religious authorities infuriates some of the lay leaders. One snorted: 'They say they're trying to raise standards, but it just makes everything ridiculous. It trivializes the religion. The greater the prohibitions, the greater the chances of getting round them. And for the Orthodox it's a question of power. They now think they have the authority to frighten the shit out of people. I resent walking into a school playground and being told to cover my head. The community shouldn't be run for the benefit of a few zealots.' Such zeal also has an impact on Manchester's Jewish schools. King David School is a comprehensive with some 1,100 children enrolled in its infant, primary, and high schools. Two-thirds of the teachers are non-Jewish and the headmaster of the high school, Stephen Williamson, is especially proud of the fact that 20 per cent of the students go on to university. Well aware that most of the pupils are not from religious backgrounds, the Jewish studies programme covers a surprisingly wide spectrum. The Jewish Grammar School, on the other hand, is run by the strictly Orthodox. There are also a number of primary schools in the suburbs and dormitory towns, such as Bury. And within the Orthodox enclave of Broughton Park there are no fewer than fourteen *chedorim* and *yeshivot*. Mike Anderson worries about 'the rivalry between schools to see who can be the most religious. The children are ending up far more religious than their parents, which in turn is forcing the parents to become more observant.' Which, no doubt, is pleasing to the religious authorities, if worrying to those who find the drift to ever-greater Orthodoxy a mixed blessing.

It would be difficult to expect Mike Anderson to be very sympathetic towards the ultra-Orthodox community, since Manchester Jewish Social Services receives no support from them. 'On the whole their money goes back into their own communities. They certainly don't give us any money. Their care of the elderly is probably excellent, but the child care does worry us. The mother's health is often weak and the children are often unruly. The older children spend a lot of time with the younger ones, perhaps sacrificing part of their own childhood. But then they have the compensation of being part of a large, warm family. Where it works it can work extremely well. Where it doesn't work you get very serious child-care problems. But we're not into those communities enough to be able to get to grips with them. As a voluntary agency we can only be involved by invitation. We have in the past attempted to do some bridge-building but we haven't had great success.'

The agency is funded mostly by investment income, topped up by a grant from the local authority and by individual contributions. Many Mancunians are sensitive to the view that Jews are excessively pre-occupied with their own welfare, and this attitude is something that Sir Sidney Hamburger has argued against: 'Our welfare services are all very well supported. And the Jewish community doesn't separate itself when it comes to contributing to non-Jewish charities. I've strongly resisted attempts to have a Jewish appeal for a scanner or a particular hospital. I feel we are part of a wider community and to segregate ourselves for fund-raising is counter-productive. We are part and parcel of this city.' Manchester Jewry supports not only JSS (which among other activities employs five social workers and provides sheltered accommodation for the elderly and rehabilitation for mentally ill patients), but a Jewish Blind Society, and the highly regarded Brookvale home for the mentally handicapped – a total of twenty-three charities, plus various Friendly Societies. Arthur Sunderland, a former editor of one of the city's two Jewish newspapers, the *Gazette*, looks back to the good old days when there was less money around but greater good will. 'Today people feel that if they give a few pounds, they've justified their existence.'

As in London, there is still a remnant of Manchester Jewry that is impoverished, that has not made the leap to Cheadle. Jewish Social Services disburses about £30,000 each year in direct relief to the poor, and each spring about 200 people make their way to the JSS offices to collect their Passover packages. Government cutbacks are going to increase the burdens on the poor, and thus on JSS. According to Mike Anderson, 'We have a steady stream of people coming through these offices who are as scruffy as any people social services offices deal with. But we also get better off people, who may have problems with their children or with mental illness in the family. We have a fair number of very poor people – mostly elderly – but we also have our share of mad and bad. A small share of bad, a higher share of mad – young, middle-aged and old – from all sections of the community. We've got half a dozen prisoners in Strangeways, but we seem to be a low-crime community. Or if we're stealing we're not getting caught. The community is also storing up problems for itself by having very weak provisions for youth. There is no one central youth centre. Maccabi has folded. The Lads' and Girls' Brigade and Habonim are quite strong. But the provision is patchy. There's no real pulling together.'

Manchester Jewry has long taken pride in its Zionist tradition. The Zionist Central Council acts as an umbrella organization under which political groups such as Mizrachi, fund-raising groups such as WIZO (the principal women's Zionist organization), and youth groups such as Habonim, can all work in harmony. The Council provides information and arranges meetings and dispatches speakers on political and cultural aspects of Zionism. Its director, Steven Fruhman, prefers to keep the Council aloof from the infighting that afflicts other Zionist groups: 'There's no point fighting out the minutiae of Israeli politics in Manchester.' He tries to avoid interfering in the activities of the forty-two groups that huddle under the Council's umbrella: 'I remember once learning that Mapam had slipped Ken Livingstone into one of their meetings. I knew nothing about it until it was over, which was probably a good thing, as it saved me from having to make a difficult decision.' He regrets that many of the ultra-Orthodox Jews in the city tend to be anti-Zionist. When the Israeli ambassador came to address a meeting early in 1988, he attracted a crowd of 600, but certain prominent figures, such as Dayan Krausz, were conspicuous by their absence.

If Manchester Jews are particularly fervent in their Zionism, they differ little from Jews in other communities in terms of their politics or culture. Although most Manchester Jews have risen contentedly into the middle classes, and working-class Jews still living in the city tend to be elderly, their politics used to be fairly left-wing, if only because fifty years ago the ranks of Conservative associations were closed to the likes of Jews. But the old left, once represented by Sir Sidney Hamburger and many others, is fading out, and few Manchester Jews are attracted to the radical left. Nobody has surveyed the political leanings of Manchester Jewry, but community leaders suspect that Jews remain strongly attached to the welfare state and other aspects of communal care, and so it would be rash to assume that, for example, the Jewish yuppies of south Manchester are necessarily Tories. Yet the MP for Bury, David Sumberg, can probably count on a good deal of support from the many fellow Jews within his constituency. In the cultural field, many Jews not only patronize theatres and concert halls and museums but also give active support to those institutions. The community also funds an annual tribute concert to honour one of its more formidable rabbis, Felix Carlebach. But the involvement of Anglo-Jewry in artistic life has always been exaggerated, and the patrons of the arts in Manchester form a noticeable but relatively small proportion of the community. The Orthodox in particular seem to feel their money is better spent on a new *mikveh* than on assisting the Hallé Orchestra. Within the Jewish community itself there are a few literary societies, but it is hardly a thriving intellectual milieu.

One can only hope that the community's two newspapers are not representative of the intellectual tone of Manchester Jewry. Critics of the *Jewish Chronicle* should take heart. That newspaper is much maligned, usually for trivial sectarian reasons. One glance at the *Manchester Gazette* or the *Telegraph* should reassure the *Chronicle*'s critics that its faults are slight and its merits considerable. The two Manchester papers are parochial, badly written, banal. The best that can be said for the *Gazette*, the senior of the two, is that it does make a serious attempt to reach not only the Jews of Manchester but other more isolated communities.

The print run of 16,000 comprises three editions, one for Greater Manchester, another for Leeds (including news of Bradford, Harrogate, Sheffield and Hull), and one for Merseyside and Chester. Up to twelve pages are printed separately for each edition. The sixtieth anniversary edition of the *Gazette* displayed headlines such as 'the super new-look *Gazette* is tops for pictures', confirming that the paper is mostly a vehicle for snapshots of barmitzvahs and weddings and school prize-givings, birth announcements, and recipes. The *Gazette* and *Telegraph* function as community noticeboards, but steer well clear of serious reporting or reflection.

The cosy inward-looking insularity of large segments of Manchester Jewry is deplored by many community leaders. Mike Anderson told me: 'I would like to see Manchester Jewry give of itself in a more formal way to the wider community. On issues like race we should be standing up and talking loud. It doesn't do Jews any good to be silent on these issues. I'd like to see us extend all our services, open our schools, spreading what we have that we think is good to the outside world. You've got to hand it to the Sir Sidneys of this world, because they were very willing to do this. There's a ghetto mentality in Manchester and it rather alarms me. It may be easier for a Christian family to settle alongside very religious families in Broughton Park than it would be for a Reform family – because the Reform remind the very religious of a different way of doing things that they claim isn't even Jewish, and that's very threatening to them.'

Henry Guterman was saddened when the community expressed no wish to be represented on a subcommittee on race that was being set up by the city council. A compromise was eventually reached by which Guterman himself attends meetings as an observer but plays no part in its deliberations – an honourable but not very useful solution. In October 1988 he upbraided the community for its failure to take a stand on issues such as racism, immigration laws, and urban deprivation. Sir Sidney Hamburger applauds Guterman's attempts to foster good relations with other ethnic groups in Manchester, though he stresses it has to be a two-way operation: 'We try very hard through the Council of Christians and Jews. The trouble is that many of the immigrant groups here are Asian or from the Middle East. There's an unfortunate and unpleasant anti-Semitism among many of the new ethnic immigrant groups, though we haven't had any open manifestation of anti-Semitism on any large scale in Manchester. I always like to feel that we can give the newer immigrants the benefit of our advice, our experience. I tell some of the Asian groups, look, you've got to integrate, but that doesn't mean rejecting your own cultural background. You must retain that while accepting that you're part of the wider community.'

Anti-Semitism in Manchester does seem to be a thing of the past. Fifty years ago, and no doubt more recently too, there were, for instance, golf clubs that excluded Jews. The Jews, consequently, founded their own and that was that. Anti-Semitism is far more of a problem for some of the students at Manchester University and UMIST, who have to fend off anti-Zionist resolutions from well-funded Arab students. The Jewish students have had a fair measure of success at defeating attempts to ostracize them, but it is they, rather than the comfortable suburbanites of Greater Manchester, who are in the front line so far as anti-Semitism is concerned. At UMIST, the fifty Jewish students are outnumbered by a thousand Arab students, many of whom press, so far without success, for the expulsion of 'the Zionist entity' from the student union.

Such conflict, of course, takes place in the somewhat rarefied environment of student union chambers. Seen in a wider perspective, Manchester Jewry does seem to be in harmony with the wider community around it. Manchester, after all, is an hospitable environment for Jews; its manufacturing and trading traditions have long been congenial. Non-conformist religion and the entrepreneurial spirit put few snobbish obstacles in the way of immigrant Jews, who were invited to make their way in the city just as other immigrant groups were. And no doubt the Jews' own commercial skills proved indispensable to Mancunian industrialists. Manchester was and remains a more open society than London, and its institutions, being younger, are less stultified. It is not surprising that even today Jews from other parts of the country continue to settle there. The city also continues to attract Jewish refugees from the Middle East. Although different in many respects from London – despite the physical division between north and south, there is considerable cohesiveness within Manchester Jewry – the community experiences the same problems that beset Anglo-Jewry in general. Whether the cohesiveness of Manchester Jewry is sufficiently strong to survive the flight to the suburbs is less clear. Most Manchester Jewish institutions – Mamlock House, home of the Zionist Central Council, the Levi House day centre, the relatively new Tannenbaum Jewish Centre – are all located in north Manchester, close to the Orthodox powerhouse of Broughton Park. More and more Jews, however, are living far to the south in Cheadle and Sale and other suburbs. The very lack of homogeneity that Sir Sidney Hamburger discerns as afflicting London Jewry may soon be replicated in Manchester too.

– 21 –

Glasgow

I F Manchester Jewry in many ways mirrors the complexities of London Jewry, the Glasgow community goes about its business with typical Scottish disregard for anything happening south of the Cheviots. Its very independence gives it a confidence one doesn't sense in, say, disputatious Manchester. The problems facing the Glasgow community – assimilation, shrinking numbers – are typical of Anglo-Jewry as a whole, but the Glaswegians seem relatively free of the bitter infighting of many English communities.

Although some Jews arrived in Scotland as early as the seventeenth century, the Glasgow community did not establish itself until the 1820s. The original immigrants were Lithuanians, though by the end of the century Polish and Russian immigrants swamped the indigenous Jewish community in Scotland just as they did in London. By the turn of the century there were about 7,000 Jews in Glasgow. The more settled families lived close to the city centre while the new arrivals moved into the less salubrious Gorbals. Gradually welfare agencies and cultural institutes were established to serve the growing community. Just as those who'd settled in the East End of London moved to the suburbs when the opportunity arose, and just as the Cheetham Hill residents dispersed in Manchester, so too in Glasgow the Gorbals dwellers, as they prospered from the 1930s onwards, moved south into more fashionable districts. Sir Monty Finniston recalls: 'I was born next to the Gorbals. The people were all working class – no, that's wrong really, they were all poverty-stricken. There were no rich people as we know them today. People who became rich moved out of that area.' They moved to Queen's Park, Pollokshields, and Newlands, planting synagogues as they went, and inhabiting the solid,

279

detached, stone villas with large bay windows so typical of those districts. The migration into the South Side continued, into Merrylee and Whitecraigs and Giffnock, which today still has the largest Jewish population of any part of Glasgow. After the Second World War, many Jewish families moved yet further south, to the bland modern suburb of Newton Mearns, though this only became possible after the death of an estate agent who refused to sell houses to Jews.[1] Giffnock and Newton Mearns support not only spacious synagogues but ample communal and educational facilities. Today, Muslim immigrants are following a similar pattern, and a large mosque adorns the redeveloped Gorbals.

Relatively few refugees from Nazism came to Glasgow. Many who did so arrived as children – there used to be a hostel for refugee children next to the Garnethill Synagogue – and left for Israel after the war. According to one of those children, now the writer Chaim Bermant: 'Anyone brought up in Berlin or Vienna . . . was unlikely to be overawed by Glasgow Jewish society. Indeed, they were hardly in it before they took the measure of it, and were out of it. They were widely read, cultivated people and where they remained part of the community they enriched it immensely, but in the main they kept to themselves.'[2] The indigenous Jewish community used to complain that they were patronized by the new arrivals because of the differences in cultural outlook, and that is entirely plausible. According to the local newspaper owner Dr Ezra Golombok, a few elderly refugees still maintain a *Kulturkreis* but nobody else seemed to know anything about it.

The Jewish community of Glasgow is not immune from the traditional rivalry with Edinburgh. Edinburgh has never had a large Jewish settlement. Glasgow, as the more industrial city, offered better opportunities for employment than its more refined neighbour. The two communities intermarried and, for much the same reasons, couples tended to settle in Glasgow, thus depleting the Edinburgh community further. There are roughly 1,000 Jews in Edinburgh, compared with about 9,000 in Glasgow. Edinburgh, as the seat of Scottish government and law, doesn't disguise that it feels vastly superior to its unruly neighbour, and the attitude has rubbed off on Edinburgh Jews. Their desire to be the leaders of Scottish Jewry has, however, been defeated by sheer lack of numbers.

If Glasgow lacks the social pretensions of Edinburgh, there is no shortage of well-established Jewish families and until quite recently they were extremely influential. Many local boys have made good in other ways. Emanuel Shinwell, though born in London, began his political career by being elected to a Scottish constituency in 1922; however, he took virtually no part in local Jewish life. The Regius Professor of Medicine at Glasgow University is Sir Abraham Goldberg. Lord Kissin, though born in Danzig, grew up in Glasgow, as did Sir Monty Finniston and Ralph Glasser and Jeremy Isaacs. Among the moneyed class, whisky magnates such as Sir Maurice Bloch and Samuel R. (for Rosenbloom) Campbell flourished in the 1930s. The Walton family made a fortune from property and then gave away a substantial amount of it to endow a university chair and fund medical research. The Goldberg family, which founded a department store, is among the current grandees, and the Jesner family is also heavily involved in local fund-raising. Despite the presence of such philanthropists, wealth, according to Dr Walter Sneader, a pharmacist at Glasgow University and president of the Jewish Representative Council, no longer confers status automatically. You won't become chairman of your synagogue just because you are the richest man in the congregation: flaunting your wealth is simply not a Scottish thing to do. Philanthropic donations are usually made through the Jewish Community Trust, an unelected body. Should a project attract the fancy of a member of the Trust, there is a fair chance that he will be able to persuade his co-members to support it too. The trust is currently mulling over whether or not the community really needs a new community centre; if it decides it does, the trust will then put its mind to raising the £900,000 required to finance it.

As in Manchester, the vast majority of Glaswegian Jews are nominally Orthodox. There was no Reform synagogue until 1931, and Liberals are non-existent. Even today there are fewer than 200 Reform households in a community with a total synagogue membership of well over 3,000. After the community became more settled, it began to follow the pattern of mainstream Anglo-Jewry in its imitation of the host religion. The oldest extant synagogue in Glasgow is the Garnethill Hebrew Congregation close to the city centre. Dating from about 1880, it is an extremely handsome building, with its white and blue coffered ceiling, and smart gilt and oak furnishings. The entrance hall is divided by an exotic arch that would be entirely suitable for a Turkish bath. Garnethill catered to the 'original' settlers of the West End of Glasgow rather than the newer arrivals who had gone to live in the Gorbals. It was a worldly congregation and still is. It survives more through sentiment than practicality, for scarcely any Jews now live within easy walking distance of Garnethill.

Almost all the forty or fifty members who attend Sabbath services come by car. The rabbi, Adrian Jesner, is realistic enough to tolerate the situation, though it would be mischievous to suggest that, as a qualified motor mechanic and garage proprietor, Rabbi Jesner has a vested interest in the matter. His spacious and very lovely synagogue is, at least in architectural terms, the jewel of Glasgow Jewry, and a sufficient number of people in the community are keen to ensure that it survives. The fairly lax attitude towards religious observance persists, not only at Garnethill but at some of the suburban synagogues too, and while the strictly Orthodox do maintain a presence in Glasgow, they are less powerful and far less strident than their counterparts in Manchester or London.

The synagogues are all independent, yet broadly sympathetic to the United Synagogue. They contribute to the Chief Rabbinate fund and draw their ministers from the pool of rabbis maintained by the United Synagogue. On the other hand, according to Dr Sneader, 'there is less pomp and formality in Scotland, and no attempt to behave like English gentlemen'. With typical Glaswegian scorn he pointed to other differences between the Glasgow and London communities: 'London is the largest provincial community in Britain. People forget that Scotland is a different country, with its own educational and legal system. Young people tend to study in their native city, and most of them live at home. We're less synagogue-dominated than the English communities, and the main religion of the community is Zionism. The Board of Education and other groups will sometimes even fly in lecturers from Israel to address meetings, and the attendance is sufficiently high to make them financially feasible. But there's a constant drain on the community, to London, to Israel, to Australia.' It is an irony by no means exclusive to Glasgow that fervent Zionism persuades a fair number of the community to go on *aliyah*, thus depleting the native community further.

Despite the fact that Glaswegian Jews are identifiable, by their manner as well as their accents, as Glaswegians as much as Jews, the community does tend to be fairly inward-looking. It is difficult to generalize, but the profusion of charitable, musical, literary, and Zionist organizations – quite apart from synagogal activities – suggests that the community is, in terms of its cultural and social life, largely self-sustaining. Mixing with non-Jews is certainly not frowned upon but is undertaken, it seems, with a degree of caution and reserve. Even though the religious standards of Glaswegian Jewry are lax, there is a powerful sense of communal identity. The Jewish thirst for education is comfortably slaked by the Scottish academies, and the city is well stocked with Jewish doctors, lawyers, accountants, and academics. Dr Ezra Golombok, who edits the *Jewish Echo*, Scotland's only Jewish newspaper, is not alone in thinking that the origins of the community have helped to shape its character. Few pious Polish found their way to Glasgow. It was the Lithuanians, more progressive in their social and religious attitudes, who settled here. 'The Litvaks are hard-headed people, and the immigrants devoted themselves to earning a good living. They transmitted material benefits but not Jewish culture. It's only in more recent times that a generation has begun to return to its Jewish roots.' This view is echoed by one of the community's lay leaders, Mark Goldberg: 'The Lithuanians aren't like the Chasidim, who liked to latch on to ideas through thick and thin. Litvaks are more analytic, and that may account for the independence of our community.'

Glasgow's geographical isolation has allowed the community to retain that independence, but it's a mixed blessing. Many rabbis are unwilling to move from the comforts of south-east England to the rigours of Glasgow. If the sense that Glasgow is on the fringes of Jewish life has helped to keep away the religious extremists, it has also made life increasingly difficult for the 5 per cent of the community that are estimated to be fully observant and for the many more people who at least keep a kosher home. There are now only two kosher butchers serving Glasgow Jewry, and Edinburgh Jews in search of kosher food have no choice but to come and shop in the neighbouring city. Even Lubavitch have made little impact in the city, despite a presence here and a willingness to make contact with Jews on the fringes of the community who feel uncomfortable within mainstream Orthodoxy. There is rivalry between Lubavitch and the *kollel*, a kind of postgraduate *yeshiva* with about a dozen members pursuing advanced Torah studies. Moreover, anyone in the grip of a conversion experience drawing them towards strict Orthodoxy soon feels compelled to head for Broughton Park or Stamford Hill or Jerusalem. Dr Golombok expressed a sentiment that I imagine is widely held: 'Lubavitch rejects no one, however irreligious. That's admirable. But I still can't stand them.'

Glasgow's Jewish Representative Council is the oldest in Britain and looks after all the Jewish communities in Scotland. The Board of Deputies is seen as remote from Scotland and largely ignorant of Scottish Jewry. Local leaders are particularly irritated when, for example, the Board dispatches an Israeli embassy spokesman to Scotland without consulting the local community. Although the synagogues raise a levy to support the Board, many individual members refuse to pay it. Dr Jack

Miller, a veteran Glasgow deputy, points out that it costs him at least £100 to come down to London for a plenary session mostly devoted to rubber-stamping committee reports. Thus the Representative Council is a much more significant body, and some fifty organizations are affiliated to it. Its leaders place great emphasis on inter-faith work – another indication of Glasgow's rather old-fashioned Anglo-Jewish style. Constant contact with church leaders allows both sides to discuss matters of common interest, such as inner-city policies and religious education. A speakers' panel dispatches about twenty lecturers to Rotary Clubs and church guilds and any other non-Jewish group eager to learn about any aspect of Jewish life. A community relations committee has established close links with other ethnic groups. According to Jack Miller, Glaswegian Jews may not mix much socially with the rest of the community but they are anxious to be on good terms with them, notably with the 25,000 Asians. Recent events in Israel have proved a threat to those amicable community relations, as there was talk in the Muslim community of boycotting Jewish businesses. Fortunately, the Muslims proved far more fragmented than the Jews, and the boycott never materialized.

The well-supported structure of welfare agencies found in other cities with a large Jewish population is replicated in Glasgow. Not all Glasgow Jews live in comfortable houses in Giffnock and Newton Mearns. There are some 200 families that depend to some degree on the largesse of the Welfare Board, which also rents out seventy houses and flats to the needy. The local old age home and the home for the mentally handicapped are supported in part by the local authority, but other amenities, such as the Board's sheltered housing, receive no such subsidy. Apart from the hardships suffered by those few Jews on supplementary benefit, and the inevitable indignities endured by the old and the lonely, there are relatively few social problems in the community. Alcohol and drugs are thought not to be widely abused. Some 40 per cent of young Glaswegian Jews belong to youth movements, and their conduct is closely monitored by community elders, and any infringements of alcohol and drug laws are rapidly stamped on by the JRC. In general, Glasgow's Jews are light drinkers. 'People in the licensed trade', remarks Walter Sneader, 'don't relish being asked to cater Jewish functions.'

Since 1962 there has been a Jewish primary school in the city. According to the community's historian, Dr Kenneth Collins, there was considerable opposition to the founding of the school from the religious authorities, who feared a diminution of their control over religious education through the *cheder* system. Support from some of the grander families among Glaswegian Jewry, who were among the first to enrol their children at Calderwood, put the school on a firm footing. 'The plan', says Dr Golombok, 'was to give Calderwood snob appeal, and it worked.' The school is associated with the Zionist Federation, which supplies teaching materials and keeps an eye on the religious education, but great emphasis is placed on secular education. Glasgow has some excellent primary schools, and Calderwood must compete directly with them. It does so successfully. Now with 220 pupils, the school is full. Mrs Dianna Wolfson, the headmistress, remarks: 'They say the Jewish birthrate is falling in Glasgow, but if so, we don't notice it here.' As Calderwood is a State school, parents pay no fees but contribute £45 per term for the six hours each week of religious and Hebrew studies.

The school council seems unconcerned by the Chief Rabbi's strictures, for among the pupils in 1988 were not only four Muslim children but a number of halachically suspect Jews. Reform Jews are not excluded, for the antagonism between Reform and Orthodox found in London is largely absent in Glasgow. The community hasn't made an issue of Jewish status, and Reform Jews are welcome participants in community events and organizations. The Muslim parents, according to Mrs Wolfson, send their children to Calderwood because they recognize the value of religion in education – even if it isn't quite the right religion. Those children apparently speak Urdu at home, learn Arabic at the mosque and Hebrew at the school. In its religious orientation, the school is mainstream Orthodox, and the teachers, not all of whom are Jewish, are well aware that not all children come from observant households. Mrs Wolfson is satisfied if the pupils leave the school 'with a good feeling about being Jewish'. The local Board of Jewish Education, run by the youthful Glasgow-born Rabbi Maurice Pinder, supervises the religious education at Calderwood but can't impose any changes without the headmistress's approval.

On leaving Calderwood about two-thirds of the children go on to private schools, such as Hutcheson's Boys' and Girls' Grammar Schools, Glasgow Academy, and Kelvinside Academy. Further religious education is provided, for those who want it, at the *cheder* run by the Board, and at after-school classes organized by the *kollel* and by Lubavitch. The community leaders are well aware that the provision of Jewish education at secondary school level is inadequate, yet a higher proportion of Jewish children are receiving religious education now than was the case fifty years ago. A network of Jewish youth movements ensures that few children grow up without any access to Jewish culture and knowledge. However, Rabbi Michael Rosin, for many years Jewish chaplain at Glasgow University, acknowledges that most of the university's 150 or so Jewish students are not religious.

In their politics, Glasgow Jews have taken on Scottish colours. Jewish Tories are, of course, far from thin on the ground. The Conservative minister Malcolm Rifkind comes from Edinburgh, and JRC president Walter Sneader shares that political allegiance. At the same time, he insists, the Jewish community, whatever the individual sympathies of its leaders, knows full well that Glasgow is a Labour city, and has always cultivated good relations with left-wing councils and unions. With so many professional and self-employed people within the Jewish community, Sneader believes that there is a higher proportion of Tory voters among Glasgow Jewry than among the non-Jewish population, but it is difficult to be certain. (In the mid-1970s a survey established that 81 per cent of Jewish men living in Newton Mearns were self-employed, as compared with 28 per cent of non-Jewish men.)[3] Before general elections, Jewish voters are canvassed about issues close to their hearts, such as Israel, and Members of Parliament representing constituencies with large Jewish populations, such as Allan Stewart, no doubt take heed of those findings. Yet the surveys reveal little about Jewish voting preferences.

It's only in recent years that Glasgow has begun to rival and even overtake Edinburgh as a major cultural centre. The construction of the Burrell Centre in the city brought thousands of new visitors to Glasgow, even though the city has always housed magnificent art collections. Glasgow can also take justifiable pride in such institutions as the Scottish National Orchestra, the Scottish National Opera, and the Citizens Theatre; and Jews, notably Michael Goldberg, were heavily involved in their establishment. According to Dr Golombok, the number of Jewish subscribers to the musical seasons in particular is disproportionately high. He also believes that the present community leaders are less actively involved than some of their predecessors.

Despite the vibrancy of Glasgow's Jewish community, demographic trends are working against it. The birthrate, between fifty and sixty per annum, has remained static for twenty years. Although in recent years the city has been experiencing a cultural and financial revival, many ambitious young people are still leaving for the richer pastures of south-east England. Some nurture the hope that the arrival in the city of new service industries will slow down the rate of departure. 'The problem', remarks Rabbi Rosin mournfully, 'is not that all the young people are leaving Glasgow, as has been happening in Newcastle, but that many of the best people leave.'

If Glasgow is a long way from London, it's even further from Tel Aviv, yet Glasgow, like Manchester, is proud of its long support for Zionism over the decades. The community fosters ten WIZO groups and the usual range of Zionist youth groups, and makes substantial contributions to the Joint Israel Appeal. Nevertheless the community leaders have been openly critical of Israeli policy in the Occupied Territories. I was visiting Glasgow during the worst of the troubles on the West Bank and Gaza. With growing stupefaction I had been monitoring the response of the Board of Deputies as it toed the Israeli government line without qualification, and I expected to find the same rigidity among lay leaders in Glasgow. Not a bit of it. Walter Sneader, while denying that the community was split on the issue, confirmed that Glasgow Jewry was highly critical of current Israeli policy and deplored the lack of leadership displayed by the Board. June Jacobs of the Board's Israel committee had just come under heavy pressure to resign after expressing reservations about Israeli policy in a letter to the *Independent*. But Sneader snorted: 'You can't criticize June Jacobs for going against a party line that doesn't exist.' Henry and Judith Tankel, both prominent members of the community, used even stronger language to express their dismay. They were highly critical of Defence Minister Rabin's justification of the beatings that were being dealt to Palestinian protesters at that time. Furthermore the Glasgow community had made its feelings known to the Israeli authorities, though the Tankels were rightly sceptical about the effect of such protests. Yet it was foolish, they argued, for the Israelis to dismiss the criticisms of people of goodwill in the diaspora. Indeed, I didn't encounter a single member of the Jewish community in Glasgow who expressed unequivocal support for Israeli policy.

I was even more astonished to learn that the Glasgow Zionist Organization has for some years been in the control of the Peace Now group, led by, among others, Mark Goldberg. Goldberg, an articulate and unassuming man in his forties, comes from a family with a long Zionist pedigree. His grandfather planted orchards in Palestine, and as a young man Mark spent a year in Israel. By the late 1970s he was deeply disenchanted by the policies of Menachem Begin, and his reservations came to a head with the war in Lebanon in 1982. He was fully aware that war plans had long been in existence for an invasion of Lebanon, and thus also knew that the propaganda issued by the Israelis to justify the invasion was simply untrue. At that time community leaders in Glasgow tended to suppress all criticism of Israel, so Goldberg, together with twenty-eight other signatories, wrote a letter of protest to the *Jewish Echo*. The response, he recalls, was one of hurt and outrage. But six years later the situation was reversed and hardly anyone in Glasgow now openly supports Israeli policy. Goldberg is opposed to unity for unity's sake, which appears to be one of the Board's principal justifications for sycophancy: 'There's no sense being united in a wrong cause. Glasgow is less politicized than London, and that makes it easier for us to say what we think. There are no big prizes to be won here. The guy who is president of the Glasgow JRC has to work for the community seven days a week and earn a living too.'

If public opinion among Glaswegian Jews has swung against Israeli policy, some of the responsibility must be placed at the door of Dr Ezra Golombok. The banality of the Manchester Jewish papers had not prepared me for the *Jewish Echo*, a most extraordinary newspaper. It has its critics: there is a lack of local news and book reviews. On the other hand, the *Echo* offers the most complete range of information about Israeli politics and life that you can find it Britain, unless you subscribe to the *Jerusalem Post*. If Glasgow Jewry is highly critical of Israeli policies, it cannot be, as Dr Kopelowitz and others would have us believe, because they do not know the facts. Diligent readers of the *Echo* must know far more about what is happening in Israel than any other section of British Jewry.

The paper was founded in 1928 by Dr Golombok's father, who intended the *Echo* to be a mouthpiece for Zionism. He died prematurely; his son Ezra, who was working towards a career as a chemist, took over the paper in order to keep it going, and decades later he is still the editor. He acknowledges that the role of a local newspaper is to act as the voice of the community, but he also feels compelled to put local issues in the context of wider Jewish interests – hence the international flavour of the paper and the consecration of the entire front page, and many that follow, to news from Israel. His office even maintains a computer linkup with the offices of the *Jerusalem Post* and he tells with glee of occasions when he has scooped the *Jewish Chronicle*. One would expect the editor of such a paper to be a leading figure in the community, but Dr Golombok is known as something of a recluse. A refreshingly opinionated man, he clearly relishes his independence. He sees no point in disguising his impatience with the more trivial aspects of provincial Jewish life: 'The prize-giving at Calderwood shouldn't be the top story.' He is equally scornful about politicking within the community. Some years earlier, a delegation of Orthodox businessmen had called on him: they were unhappy about the *Echo*'s policy of publicizing the activities of the local Reform synagogue, and were prepared to guarantee a certain amount of advertising if Dr Golombok would cease to print information about Reform. He seems to have taken great pleasure in telling them to get lost.

Although Golombok is certainly critical of Israeli Prime Minister Shamir, he is by no means a supporter of Peace Now. He is loath to put himself in the position of telling Mr Shamir how to run his country. On the other hand, Golombok is happy to open the columns of his paper to a variety of voices, and feels that both Peace Now and the few supporters of the unspeakable Rabbi Kahane have had their say in the columns of the *Echo*. Dr Golombok's paper pays his readers the great and rare compliment of not underestimating their intelligence.

The *Jewish Echo* is merely one manifestation of the independence of Glasgow Jewry. Although not exactly Scottish Nationalists, Glasgow Jews express pride both in their Lithuanian ancestors and in their adopted Scots culture. Some Calvinism has rubbed off on them; they work hard and those who have prospered don't flash their wealth. They also participate without inhibition in the local culture; Jewish football fans are divided in their loyalties between Celtics and Rangers. Jack Miller does concede that there are limits to the Jews' Scottishness: 'There's been a rash of Jewish Burns' Nights, but as far as I know Jews don't wear kilts.' Dr Henry Tankel finds London suburban communities far more provincial than their counterparts in Glasgow: 'We take a broader view of the world, we're less blinkered. In London people seem completely baffled that I should be addressing the Church of Scotland's General Assembly, but in Glasgow it seems a perfectly natural thing to do.' Dr Golombok, however, sees the Jewish community as still unsure of itself and unwilling to integrate into the wider community. Their social life is incestuous, he argues, if only because of the shared understanding of Jews with a similar past. Few agree with this analysis. Jews in Glasgow, as in other parts of the country, do (as Tova Benski's remarkable study of the Newton Mearns Jewish community established in 1976) prefer the company of their co-religionists since so many shared values can be taken for granted, but I discerned no ghetto mentality in the city. Scottish Jews are Scottish as well as Jewish.

With most British Jews living in Greater London, it is inevitable that Londoners should dominate the community and its institutions. They would do well, however, to acknowledge that the provincial communities are not faded carbon copies, but have a distinct character of their own. The independence and efficiency of the Glasgow community is an object lesson to Anglo-Jewry. That their views and interests count for so little at, among other bodies, the Board of Deputies, is an indictment of those institutions rather than an expression of feebleness on the part of the provincial communities themselves.

– 22 –

The provinces

M ANCHESTER and Glasgow are provincial communities that are very much alive. That makes them atypical. As Anglo-Jewry shrinks, it is inevitable that the smallest communities should prove the most vulnerable, especially when they are located in parts of the country so stricken with economic difficulties that new arrivals are deterred from settling there. Brighton, one of the few strongholds of Reform Judaism outside London, is one of the exceptions, for the lively cultural and academic life has been attracting new residents. Another seaside town that used to draw thousands of vacationing British Jews, Bournemouth, is in a less fortunate position. In the 1930s there were thirty kosher hotels in the town; now there are two or three. In Sheffield, too, it's a very different story. One native of the city told me that out of a family consisting of himself, two brothers, and four cousins, only one had married a Jew. The 800 Jews of Sheffield are almost all professional people, doctors and lawyers and academics, many of whom maintain only the most tenuous links with the Jewish community. When in June 1988 the Liberals let it be known that they were thinking of opening a house of worship in the city, the Orthodox leaders reacted with fury on the grounds that such a move would split the community. That may be so, yet how ironic that a new synagogue is seen as a threat rather than as a sign of hope to a declining community.

Most of the provincial communities were founded in the eighteenth or early nineteenth century, either by itinerant pedlars who put down roots, or, in the case of the seaport towns, by merchants who specialized in ship chandlery and other forms of marine commerce. Many of these communities are now on their last legs. Plymouth, the site of the oldest

Ashkenazi synagogue in the country – it dates from 1762 – is home to no more than 150 Jews. The Jewish cemetery at Chatham contains gravestones from the end of the eighteenth century; now there are fewer than one hundred Jews in the town. By 1918 the Jewish population of Liverpool had reached 11,500, but seventy years later, only 4,400 remained. Compared to Bristol, Liverpool represents quite a success story, for Bristol, a once-flourishing community, has a mere 450 Jews.

The early settlements were given a boost at the turn of the century when immigrants were dispatched there from overcrowded London or Manchester or Leeds. They were given interest-free loans to induce them to try their luck in Reading or Blackburn, or anywhere that wasn't already stocked with impoverished Jews. In most cases, these human injections had no lasting effects, although sheer determination has kept some small communities in existence. A mere thirty families constitute the Jewish community of Darlington, but that didn't prevent them from opening a new synagogue in 1967. Yet by 1974 no more than ten children were studying their religion, and it would be miraculous if they all remained in the town, married other Jews, and brought up their families in Darlington. Derby is another melancholy example: its synagogue closed in 1986, and its thirty-five Jews must now make their way to Nottingham if they wish to maintain a Jewish way of life. Grimsby has a splendid neo-Romanesque synagogue but hasn't had a rabbi since 1965; the entire Jewish population could fit into the first three rows of the synagogue. In the autumn of 1988 the Cardiff community sold its nineteenth-century Cathedral Road synagogue, which was far too large for its needs. Belfast, with 280 Jews, can no longer maintain a rabbi, and its synagogue, which is only twenty-five years old, may have to close its doors before very long. A visit by members of the Board of Deputies executive must have provided scant comfort to the Jews of Belfast. Vice-president Eric Moonman is reported to have said: 'It is foolish, however, to judge a community by numbers alone. We have been impressed by your leadership and by the community: you are a devoted and committed group of people.'[1] Fine words, sadly, do not keep shrinking communities afloat.

Other communities survive because of special circumstances. Gateshead, home to the best known *yeshivot* and girls' seminaries in the country, is very much an ultra-Orthodox enclave. Leeds is one of the few Jewish communities still with a strong working-class component, and its Jews played a significant part in the history of British trade unionism. The community gives the impression of exuding vitality – its JRC is very active, trained speakers are dispatched to non-Jewish clubs in the area, regular open days are held at the synagogues so that non-Jews can learn about the Jewish community in their midst, and Zionist organizations proliferate – yet Leeds is often mentioned as being high on the list of endangered species. According to a recent demographic survey of Leeds Jewry, the population has declined over the past two decades from 17,500 to 10,500.[2] Dublin, which has a smaller Jewish population of about 2,000, presents a similar profile. The community, which dates from about 1660, is an active one, sustaining an old people's home and Jewish schools, yet assimilation and emigration are leading not only to a dwindling of numbers but, as a direct consequence, to a shrinking of the financial base required to sustain the community's institutions. One of Dublin's most famous sons, apart from the fictional Leopold Bloom, is Chaim Herzog, the President of Israel. There are three Jewish members of the Dail, the Irish parliament, and the present Lord Mayor of Dublin, Ben Briscoe, is Jewish, and his father held the same post. Even such illustrious graduates can't save a community in decline. The *Dublin Jewish News* recently ceased publication, and the outlook is gloomy.

The Stratford schools of Dublin have as many non-Jewish pupils as Jewish, and this compromise has been adopted by other shrinking communities. Liverpool supports a Jewish school, both at the primary and high school level. The King David School now admits 40 per cent non-Jews, which may or may not be a good thing, depending on your viewpoint, but which at any rate ensures the immediate survival of Jewish education in the city. The same situation obtains at the King David primary school in Birmingham. About 90 per cent of Jewish children in Liverpool attend the King David schools, which gives the Jewish community a cohesiveness few others can match.

It is hard to see how communities such as Derby or Hull or Swansea can be reprieved from fairly rapid extinction, and Liverpool and Cardiff and Dublin from long-term eradication. The fecundity of the strictly Orthodox, of which they are so proud, can't help provincial communities because of their insistence on the most exacting support system. Yet Geoffrey Paul, the editor of the *Jewish Chronicle*, is convinced far more could be done by Anglo-Jewish leaders to mitigate the losses. 'We have to ensure that when they close their schools, their *chedorim*, they do not also close the doors on their or their children's Jewish identity.' He notes as a 'disgrace' that Anglo-Jewry supports only one part-time minister whose brief it is to maintain contact with the smaller communities – and that rabbi wouldn't be in business if the *Jewish Chronicle* hadn't underwritten his activities for the past seven years. There is a shortage of practical ideas for keeping Jewish ways alive in such communities. Why not, he has suggested for starters, have a travelling kosher supermarket on the lines of a mobile library? Yet such measures, while desirable, would only prolong the agony, for Mr Paul confirms that 'our provincial communities are in a decline which is never likely to be reversed . . . We continue to bury more people than we give birth to in all but the most strictly Orthodox segments of Jewish society.'[3]

Yet there are instances of new communities that are thriving. Most of them are satellites of major London suburban congregations. The Reform movement seems content with the growth of membership in Cambridge, Milton Keynes, and Hatch End. Of course the average new member at Hatch End or Pinner is likely to be a Son of Edgware or a Daughter of Finchley. The Brighton and Hove area has a Jewish population of some 10,000 which supports a kindergarten, welfare agencies, an old people's home, even a *shechita* board. The two Orthodox synagogues staff a *cheder* attended by 120 children. The Progressive Synagogue has over 500 members, and at the other end of the spectrum the Lubavitch Rabbi Pesach Efune has arrived to ginger up its Jewish life. Brighton has no tradition of religious militancy and Rabbi Efune will have his work cut out for him; on the other hand the community clearly welcomes another dedicated rabbi who can assist with services and education in the town. One can never accuse Lubavitch of not trying. Yet despite Brighton's relative strength of numbers, community leaders are far from hopeful about the future. Most of the synagogues have experienced or are still experiencing difficulties in filling their pulpits. Hillel House, the social centre for Jewish university students, is moribund. The day school has closed. Despite a community of some 10,000 souls, there is clearly a shortage of involved congregants in the area.

For most, the issue of communal survival is perceived as a balancing act between demographic decline and religious revival. For others, it is the most profound issue facing Anglo-Jewry, for Jewish survival is in their eyes paramount, if only as a form of belated triumph over the massacres of the past.

✤ JEWS AS BRITONS ✤

– 23 –

Making a living

I F there is one stereotype that irritates Jews more than all others, it is
that of the grasping businessman. The stale joke – 'That'll be twelve
pounds, but as a special favour to you, my boy, I'll only charge you
fifteen' – and its many variants, delivered with a Fagin-like accent and
Heep-like hand-rubbing, are back-handed tributes to supposed Jewish
commercial acumen. That Jews do have a great deal of entrepreneurial
skill is undeniable. What is less well understood is that this came about
because Jews in the past had little choice in the matter.

When Jews were readmitted to Britain in the late seventeenth century,
they were not discriminated against because of their faith, but their civic
rights were limited. Until well into the nineteenth century many professions remained closed to them. Exactly the same was true of Jews in
many other parts of Europe: in Habsburg Vienna the preponderance of
eminent Jewish physicians and lawyers and journalists could not be
divorced from the fact that Jews were ineligible for more prestigious
professions. The situation, of course, had been far worse in the Middle
Ages, when Jews had had to suffer religious bigotry as well as civic
discrimination. Never knowing how long they could remain in any city or
country, Jews had to develop skills that were adaptable and portable.
Trade and moneylending and banking were ideally suitable – but bore
within them the ticking bomb of social ostracism. There is nobody people
are more likely to hate than those to whom they owe money. There was
also a certain ambiguity in the Jewish attitude towards money. Commanded by the Torah to deal honourably with each other, there were no
special constraints against Jews taking a slightly less noble line when it
came to business relations with Gentiles. This is not to say that Jews were

297

necessarily given to sharp practice. On the other hand personal enrichment through skilful exploitation of particular circumstances was certainly not frowned upon, so long as it didn't involve patently dishonest behaviour.

Those early immigrants from Holland and Germany came, many of them, already equipped with financial skills far more sophisticated than those routinely encountered in the London markets. It is said that Jews more or less invented the profession of stockbroking in Britain. By 1700 one-fifth of all London brokers were Jews. Their familiarity with European markets gave them a further advantage denied to their more parochial English counterparts. They were marvellous packagers, assembling deals that, in central Europe, bailed the Habsburgs out of grave financial difficulties, and, in England, sustained the government during such crises as the Jacobite Rebellion of 1745. The broker who organized the consortium that saved the government of the day from a probable run on the Bank of England was Samson Gideon, and so grateful was the government that Gideon acted as its financial adviser for many years. The Rothschild brothers performed similar services across Europe. Nathan, like Gideon before him, advised the British government in times of financial peril. The great advantage he had over other London brokers was the international network he and his brothers, in Naples and Frankfurt and Paris and Vienna, could offer each other. It was an unparalleled development, and the Rothschilds prospered hugely from their skill and discretion. Confidants to half the governments of Europe, their reputation would have been shattered in a moment had they not earned the great trust placed in them.

Of course not all British Jews were City men, but a substantial proportion of those who earned large fortunes and secured a measure of social respectability were financiers. Others were attracted to retailing or small manufacturing. The Lyons empire has its origins in the enterprise of the four Gluckstein brothers in the 1880s. Their catering business soon developed into the chain of tea-shops that by the 1930s had almost become a hallmark of British life, like John Bull or warm ale. Jews, as outsiders, were quick to spot any gaps in the market. In Leeds, especially, it was the immigrant Jews from Russia and Poland and their children who developed the clothing trade, supplying inexpensive but well-cut suits to the respectable working and middle classes. Technological developments were also monitored by the quick-witted immigrants, who rapidly moved into new industries such as radio and cinema and electrical goods. Few

Jews of humble origins could raise the capital to finance any large-scale manufacturing enterprise, but a family might well be able to pool its resources and set up a workshop or small factory specializing in an item for which there was, they sensed, a definable market.

If manufacturing had the disadvantage of being a hit-and-miss occupation, prone to slumps, fluctuating costs of raw materials, and plain bad luck, retailing was more flexible. Isaac Wolfson, the Glaswegian son of immigrants, epitomized the successful entrepreneur. He began commercial life as a small-time trader in household items, but it was after he joined Great Universal Stores that he found himself in a position to wheel and deal and amass his great fortune. 'By the late 'fifties, when a series of dramatic takeover bids brought Wolfson inexorably into the public eye, he had under his hand 2 per cent of the country's shoe shops, 5 per cent of Britain's furniture business, an important stake in both men's and ladies' tailoring, a whole string of clothing factories, plus an embyronic supermarket chain, a house-building company and a travel agency; not to mention important interests in Canada, South Africa, Holland, France and Israel.'[1]

The property business also proved a gold mine to many Jews of immigrant stock. Again, it was not only their nimbleness and flexibility that helped them succeed in this field, but the eye of the outsider which enabled them to spot opportunities that other more experienced, but more conventional, property brokers overlooked. If a prime site was undervalued, Jewish entrepreneurs were more likely than most both to realize it and to be willing and able to exploit the situation. They had the instincts of gamblers, but the professionalism and capacity for hard work of consummate businessmen. Jack Cotton was typical of this generation. Born in 1903 into a respected Birmingham family, he blazed his way through the property game, eventually acquiring a half share in what was said to be the largest office building in the world, the Pan Am building in Manhattan. The great legend of the 1950s and 1960s, the heyday of the Jewish property men, was Charles Clore, who would buy and sell anything, not only property, if he thought he could make a profit, as he usually did. During his lifetime he, like Wolfson, gave away millions to charitable causes, many of which were not Jewish. Stephen Aris estimates that between 1945 and 1965 more than one hundred people made a personal fortune of over £1 million each from property deals; about seventy of them were Jews. Men like Harry Hyams and Harold Samuel, at one time the single largest owner of property in the world, made immense fortunes.

They were not only owners of property but developers, willing to gamble on the likelihood that a new site or building complex would attract a sufficient number of tenants to cover their investment costs many times over.

Property still remains a powerfully attractive option to British Jews. Godfrey Bradman's Rosehaugh Group is valued at £600 million. Less conventional than most in his philanthropy, he has bankrolled the Freedom of Information campaign and Friends of the Earth. He also underwrote the legal costs of 1,500 people claiming damages against the manufacturers of Opren, a drug for arthritis sufferers, costs that could amount to £2 million. Naturally these worthy causes only mop up the small change from the huge profits he can expect to make from the Broadgate redevelopment in the City, a Docklands scheme, and the £6 billion King's Cross redevelopment, which should generate for Rosehaugh and its partner Stanhope Properties (run by another Jewish property developer, Stuart Lipton) profits of over £1 billion.

Yet Jews, like other businessmen, have diversified. Contemporary tycoons such as Cyril Stein of Ladbrokes, Gerald Ratner the jeweller, Alan Sugar of Amstrad, Robert Maxwell of Pergamon and the Mirror Group, Lord Bernstein of the Granada group, Arnold Weinstock of General Electric, Stanley Kalms of Dixons, Gerald Ronson of the Heron Corporation, Sir Ralph Halpern of Burton's, and Ephraim Margulies of S & W Berisford have, apart from their money, far less in common than the tycoons of earlier generations. Few have risen diligently through a corporate structure; indeed, most of them have created their own corporate structures beneath them. Most are not averse to a spot of self-promotion, nor do they hesitate to identify themselves loudly with Jewish causes. There are countless others whose names are unknown outside the narrow world of the City or their businesses: the travel agents, the drapers, the impresarios, the publishers.

If there is one branch of business from which Jews tend to be absent, it is manufacturing industry – what's left of it. Arnold Weinstock is a rare example of the Jewish captain of industry. Even though he married into Sir Michael Sobell's electrical goods company that was soon taken over by General Electric, Weinstock's rise to the top was rapid indeed. His subsequent career has been marked by takeover bids, ruthlessly executed, that have consolidated the company but have not won him the affection of the thousands of workers who lost their jobs as a consequence. Another Jewish industrialist who is more in the public eye than Lord Weinstock is

Sir Monty Finniston, who despite his gaunt appearance exudes great vigour for a man in his late seventies. He is, however, not only an industrialist, but a distinguished metallurgist with more honorary degrees to his name than a cat has whiskers. Indeed, his appointment to the chairmanship of the British Steel Corporation in 1973 seems almost like a footnote to his career. He has little doubt about why few Jews were attracted to heavy industry. 'When I was a young man, parents who wanted their children to do better than themselves pushed them into a few professions. You entered these professions not only as a means of improving yourself, but as a way of improving your family. In those days it was a real sign that the family had made its way. But manufacturing was not a profession. Manufacturing was a dirty job.' Manufacturing businesses, moreover, tended to be well established, with their roots in the last century. Mining and heavy goods and machinery production were not the kinds of enterprise into which outsiders could easily penetrate. Managerial rather than entrepreneurial skills were required.

Nor are British Jews well represented in banking. In Germany and Austria, Jewish bankers were much more common; banking was often a family business rather than a profession. In Britain the only Jewish banking dynasty that survives is Rothschilds. Many other banks founded by Jews, such as Hambros, have long ceased to have any Jewish identification and the founding families, where they still exist, are entirely assimilated. Nor are Jews well represented in banks outside the merchant banking sector. In 1950 Dr Ernest Krausz reported as follows: 'There are no Jews on the Board or among the directors of the Bank of England, and – in recent years – of the 150 directors of the Big Five commercial banks, only four were Jews.'[2] Sir Claus Moser offers the following explanation: 'Jews are prominent in merchant banks but not the clearing banks, because in a clearing bank one isn't an entrepreneur. Their hierarchical structure doesn't attract a Jew.' Yet the Jewish character even of a merchant bank such as Rothschilds has altered in recent years. It was not that long ago that a Jewish bank would conduct no business on the Sabbath, but today the most outwardly Jewish manifestation at Rothschilds, apart from the presence of family members among the partners, is the *mezuzah* over the door. Nor do Jews constitute anything like the majority among the partners: not one of the four managing directors is a Jew. One of the present partners is Sir Claus Moser, who is concluding a very varied career by taking up the profession the Nazis prevented him from entering in the 1930s. Had he remained in his native Berlin he would have joined the family bank, but he had to leave Germany for England as a boy. Sir Claus finds it difficult to define what it is about Rothschilds that is characteristically Jewish. The Rothschilds play little part in the deliberations of Anglo-Jewry, though Edmund de Rothschild is an active vice-president of the Anglo-Jewish Association, but they practise their internationalism by taking a deep interest in Israeli affairs. Supremely well connected, the family can operate as behind-the-scenes fixers on those occasions when their powerful assistance is required. And in times of crisis, such as the Six Day War, the Rothschilds emerge from the boardroom and from their elegant offices at New Court and make more public declarations of their support.

My meeting with Evelyn de Rothschild, while amiable enough if regarded as a conversation, was, in terms of investigative journalism, a non-starter. I am not easily intimidated, and intellectual and social bullies, notably vain politicians, bore me. Yet there was something genuinely intimidating about Sir Evelyn, and it was nothing other than the extraordinary and effortless self-confidence of the very rich, of men who all their lives have known no other condition than perpetual good fortune. He combined languor – the way he flopped into a chair – with a kind of energetic impatience. A tall imposing man in his late fifties, with a handsome face just on the edge of fleshiness, he was wearing a well-cut suit that seemed a fraction too large, as though he'd recently shed a few pounds. The languor was not offputting; it's preferable to the earnestness of most businessmen; but it did suggest that he would rather be playing polo than talking to me, which is perfectly understandable.

I had come prepared with a number of questions but never got a chance. It was Evelyn de Rothschild who was putting the questions to me, as though I were somehow in his employ and was expected to furnish him with information about the people I had met and the issues I was pondering. We spent a pleasant half-hour, but I learnt nothing about the mysteries of banking, let alone Jews in banking, and that no doubt was exactly as he intended it to be. Not that he was coy or inarticulate; he offered forthright opinions on a dozen or more topics, few of which had anything to do with why I was sitting in his office. The Rothschilds are loath to give interviews – Victor Rothschild visibly backed away when I was introduced to him – and I had the impression that ill-kempt writers are rarely seen at New Court, and that Evelyn de Rothschild was inspecting me with the bemused if disengaged curiosity that might be applied, say, on first encountering a benign alien from the planet Xzorq.

The most remarkable of the Jewish bankers operating in Britain in recent times is now dead: Siegmund Warburg. Although Sir Evelyn de Rothschild told me he still encountered people who were convinced he was French, despite the fact that his branch of the family has been thoroughly settled here for a century and a half, Warburg was unmistakably German. After the war he took up merchant banking almost as an afterthought, and adopted an originality of approach that was to shock and outrage the British Establishment. In the 1950s he masterminded various takeover bids, notably the takeover of British Aluminium in January 1959. Warburg always managed to find himself working for the consortium perceived as hostile to the City Establishment. The latent anti-Semitism of a section of the British upper classes was unleashed against this aloof intellectual German refugee, all the more so because he was so very successful at his profession. He was fully aware that he was viewed by the City as – in his own words – 'the Jew, the newcomer, the fellow who had not been brought up in British schools and who spoke English with a foreign accent'[3]. Warburg was not an observant Jew, but did retain glimmerings of religious feelings, a diluted legacy of the German Reform tradition in which he was brought up. He was, however, passionately interested in Zionism and became deeply involved in the creation of the State of Israel. Like the Rothschilds, he took no great interest in the Anglo-Jewish scene. No doubt its parochialism did not appeal to a man whose outlook was so effortlessly internationalist.

'Jews are very much drawn to moneymaking,' observes Sir Claus Moser, 'which is not a disgrace. Jews are natural traders. Negotiation comes naturally to us. The typical business-minded Jew is an entrepreneur. In finance and in property there is a speculative element, which is what appeals to the Jewish instinct. We are more natural risk-takers and loners than we are organization men. There's nothing wrong with that. And so we're very much drawn, and always have been throughout modern history, to property and to banking.' And to self-employment. A disproportionate number of Jews work for nobody other than themselves. It cannot be the lure of the traffic jam that persuades Jews to drive one quarter of London's taxis. When in 1948 the Trades Advisory Council surveyed over 70,000 firms in cities with large Jewish populations, they discovered that 14 per cent were Jewish-owned. Nothing sinister about that, but it does reflect the eagerness of Jews to be controlling rather than controlled.[4] Jews, it would seem, prefer to take the risks involved in running a small firm or shop rather than take orders from a superior. For the Orthodox Jew, self-employment can mean that he regulates his working hours to suit himself, which would include the freedom not to work on the Sabbath or on Jewish festivals. Unfortunately Mosaic law did not take into account standard working practices in the modern world. The Sabbath happens to be the busiest day for most retailers, and few shopkeepers willingly give up about a third of their turnover. As Stanley Kalms remarks: 'To think that a modern economy can be constructed, or a business run, on *purely* Jewish lines, seems to be an impossibility. So in business, I am less Jewish than I thought I was; and I don't know how it could be otherwise.'

If Kalms is realistic about the difficulties experienced by a small-time retailer who isn't prepared to risk bankruptcy in order to get to synagogue on Saturday morning, he also stresses the emphasis Jewish law gives to business ethics. Jewish law, he has said, 'covers both the transaction, and what lies behind it – the intent. It has historically covered such detailed ground as weights and measures, and acceptable profit margins. It was anti-monopolistic. Its strength was to recognize both the entrepreneurism and the greed-element in man, and to try and create a mechanism to encourage one and contain the other.'[5] Sir Monty Finniston, during a panel discussion on business ethics held at the Westminster Synagogue, gave some examples of how Jewish law lays down what is acceptable business practice: it is contrary to Jewish law to mislead people in business or to defraud; Jewish law requires the fair treatment of those whose labour is hired, and prohibits the withholding of payment. The shaking of heads from the rabbis' front bench, manned by Rabbis Friedlander and Rayner, both learned Progressive rabbis, suggested that Finniston might be making it up as he went along, especially when he declared that Jewish law would probably be opposed to strike action, though strikes were not a major headache in biblical times.

Lord Murray, the former head of the TUC with whom Finniston was sharing the platform, disputed this: 'After all, the Children of Israel withdrew their labour from Pharaoh.'

'Yes,' replied Sir Monty, 'but the Children of Israel were not contractually allied to Pharaoh.'

Such debates may seem somewhat arcane. After all, do we really expect businessmen to check the Talmud before signing a deal or ordering redundancies? Lubavitch hold *shiurim* for businessmen during lunch hours in the City or West End, but whether such studies merely assist the devout Jew to fulfil his obligation to study the Torah or whether they have any influence on his everyday conduct of business affairs it is hard to say. Certainly the publisher Anthony Blond, who not long ago found himself bankrupt, didn't experience any wonderfully ethical behaviour from his fellow Jews. 'I approached people I've known all my life, Jewish publishers. And who succoured me? Naim Attallah. I've come to the conclusion that none of my best friends are Jews. There's no Jewish mafia. The reverse, the reverse. There's never been and never could be a Jewish conspiracy. If there were, it would be almost entirely directed against other Jews.' Yet suspicions as to whether or not Jews conspire together in high-flying financial circles are voiced from time to time, especially when, as occasionally happens, a City scandal erupts and prominent Jewish businessmen are alleged to be involved. This is precisely the case with the Guinness scandal, which brought into the open issues that Jews have long recognized as potentially troublesome: whether Jewish bragging about high ethical standards is essentially hogwash, whether Jews are unscrupulous and willing to bend if not break the law in pursuit of wealth, and whether Jews will cover for each other in times of trouble. There seems no evidence that Jews are any more or any less prone to criminality than any other section of the population, but the alleged involvement of some very prominent Jews in the Guinness scandal is, to say the least, worrying.

The charges all relate to the £2.7 billion takeover by Guinness of the Distillers group. Millions of pounds were paid out to individuals who had supported the Guinness share price, and it was this aspect of the operation that violated the law. The former chairman of Guinness, Ernest Saunders, was charged with theft to the tune of £20 million, and Gerald Ronson of the Heron Corporation was charged with stealing more than £6 million from Guinness. Saunders vehemently denied the charges, as did Ronson, who claimed he did not know he was doing anything wrong when he agreed to participate in the share-support scheme on Guinness's behalf. Moreover, the accusation of 'theft' in this context is not the same as a charge that these gentlemen had their hands deep in the till. The stockbroker Anthony Parnes, who was responsible for putting the scheme together, was also accused of stealing over £13 million and of false accounting. (At the time of writing, the case has yet to come to court and none of these charges has been substantiated.) The operation was launched because Guinness was competing directly with the Argyll group in the bid to take over Distillers. If Guinness were to succeed, it was essential to maintain its share price. Ronson agreed to spend up to £25 million buying Guinness shares, on the condition that he was indemnified against any loss and would receive a fee for his services. That Ronson paid back his fees did not prevent charges being brought against him. Ephraim Margulies of S & W Berisford also agreed to participate, and would receive payments of around £3.5 million. Other men arrested in connection with the bid included Roger Seelig, Lord Spens, and Sir Jack Lyons.[6]

It has not escaped notice that many of the protagonists are Jews. Mr Ronson in particular is a pillar of the community and a major contributor to charitable causes. Despite a reputation for toughness in his business dealings, Ronson has prided himself on his integrity and is said to be devastated by the charges. A self-made man, he earned his first million by the age of twenty-three and was the first developer of self-service petrol stations in Britain. Heron is now said to be worth over £1 billion, and remains a private company, active in the entertainment and property business as well as garages – all under the tight personal control of Ronson. Parnes, Lyons, and Margulies are also Jewish, though Roger Seelig, despite a 'foreign' name that leads people to suspect the worst, is not. Saunders is half-Jewish but was not brought up as a Jew. Eyebrows were also raised when half of Gerald Ronson's £500,000 bail was put up by another Jew, Trevor Chinn, the chairman of Lex Service. British Jews were most unhappy about the scandal, aware that, whatever the innocence or guilt of the accused, the scandal itself was potentially very damaging to the Jewish community as a whole, even if it was pure coincidence that so many of Anthony Parnes' invaluable contacts were, like himself, Jewish.

The press, in reporting the scandal, was for the most part impeccably behaved. But there were newspapers that transgressed the bounds of decency in the eyes of the Jewish community: the *Mail on Sunday* made slighting references to the Kosher Nostra – guaranteed not to go down well with the professional defenders of the faith at the Board of Deputies – and the *Sunday Telegraph* also printed some rather peculiar articles in which the Jewish factor loomed large. Jonathan Lew of the United Synagogue argued: 'Why does Mr Ronson have to be described in the media as a Jewish businessman, not as a six-foot-three businessman? I think the world went out of its way to prove that Mr Saunders did have some Jewish ancestry back there somewhere along the line – poor fella.' A distinguished Jewish intellectual to whom I was giving lunch one day construed the scandal less as an unfortunate event in which prominent Jews appeared to be implicated, than as an Establishment conspiracy against successful Jews. 'One key figure in the whole scandal, David Mayhew, of the stockbrokers Cazenove, hasn't been touched. And it's no coincidence, since he's close to the Bank of England and the royal family. I'll bet you a lunch that Mayhew will never be arrested.' The next day I heard on the news that Mr Mayhew had just become the latest casualty of the Guinness scandal and had been arrested. The distinguished intellectual phoned later that morning to concede that he had lost the wager and owed me a lunch.

Jewish responses to the scandal, apart from paranoia, were mixed. Some expressed disgust at what seemed to be the extraordinary greed of the protagonists. A Jewish politician declared: 'A chap that gives back several million pounds that has been paid to him doesn't do it without a *de facto* admission that the acquisition of that money is at best highly improper.' A Jewish solicitor thought it possible that the greed that motivated the protagonists could derive from communal insecurity since the last war, but that was a charitable explanation. 'Businessmen equate money with security, but it's got out of hand. Some of Harold Wilson's Jewish cronies, like Lord Kagan and Sir Eric Miller, were in trouble with the law. These days the rich businessmen give away large sums to charity, but it's just a sop to their conscience. Of course non-Jews do exactly the same thing.'

Rabbi Jonathan Magonet admitted that such issues as the Guinness scandal were disquieting. 'There's a lot of discussion off stage among the rabbis. There's a certain necessary paranoia that Jewish leaders have. It confirms Jewish stereotypes. There is no way you can win in a community that is still emotionally perceiving itself as a minority, where anything that is writ large is potentially disastrous.' Others accuse the rabbis of a strange silence when it comes to talking about business ethics. Leo Abse suspects that the community is so dependent on its wealthiest members that any criticism of their conduct or values has to be muted. It's not a direct correlation, rather an issue that is best avoided. Abse also believes that the influence enjoyed by the very rich gives them a kind of arrogance, as though keeping kosher would more than make up for any ethical failures in their professional life. It is certainly true that many of the idols of Anglo-Jewry have pasts that are shaded if not shady. Jack Cotton's abuses of his position as an auctioneer caused him to be struck off the lists of that profession, and even his sympathetic biographer is compelled to remark: 'Cotton's action was entirely reprehensible.'[7] Sir Isaac Wolfson also sailed close to the wind. Stephen Aris remarks: 'It was often difficult for outsiders to discern exactly where Isaac Wolfson's private empire stopped and his public one began, and this later led to some controversy and confusion. In 1943 . . . it became clear that Wolfson and his family had made a profit of nearly £60,000 from selling privately acquired companies to Great Universal Stores.'[8]

Most people within the Jewish community tended to play down the Guinness scandal. Leon Brittan was convinced that, in statistical terms, Jewish wrongdoing in the City was not especially significant, though he added: 'There's no doubt at all that when people who are known to be identified with being a member of any minority group are reported as having done something wrong, that is bad news for the group of which they are a member.' Sidney Bloch, who moves in financial circles, commented on the lack of criminality among Jews – 'outside of commerce. How often do you come across a Jewish mugger? To draw conclusions because there's a handful of people that might be in a court case at any given time would be very misleading.' Anthony Blond made a similar point more succinctly. While believing that the Jewish factor in the Guinness allegations is mere coincidence, he also declares: 'Fraud is the great Jewish crime, I'm afraid.'

Unfortunately the finger of suspicion did not cease to wag. In 1988 the Department of Trade and Industry launched an investigation into Burton's, the retail clothing group restored to vibrant profitability by Sir Ralph Halpern. The investigation subsequently cleared Sir Ralph of all charges of wrongdoing. The combination of revelations about Sir Ralph's fascinating sex life and the shadow of the DTI investigation only added to the unease of the Jewish community, which was further compounded when in February 1988 an investigation was announced, to the astonishment of those outside as well as inside the community, into the business dealing of John Ritblat, chairman of the British Land Company.

Stanley Kalms, with whom I raised these worrying issues, especially the Guinness scandal, gave a spontaneous and heartfelt response: 'The people you are talking about are meticulous in the way they run their businesses. They are of the highest repute. They are the purest of businessmen. If you ask in the City about these people, you'll find they're regarded with the highest respect. It's an unfortunate situation. It's semi-technical, it's a case of convention being changed into hard rules retrospectively. It's not a major thing, if you look at it in context. These people have sensational reputations as industrialists, as philanthropists, and whatever the facts of this case are, I don't think it stands as a reflection on Jewish businessmen, who can err like anybody else. If they err, the law deals with it. I don't think it shows a fundamental weakness. Every day a non-Jew is charged with an offence, and what do you say to that? We are sensitive to the most extraordinary degree.'

Kalms himself worries articulately over such issues as halachic attitudes to wealth. It may seem odd that a man whose annual salary is £650,000 should be given to such ruminations, but it is indeed the case. Once, when involved in a takeover bid, he handed out 50 per cent more in redundancy payments than he was legally required to do.[9] In a talk to the Cambridge University Jewish Society, he said: 'In business, because I am Jewish, I have to be *seen* to behave in a certain way. But that is not because of how my Jewishness seems to *me*. It is because of how it might seem to *others*, who aren't Jewish. The image on the outside might seem more powerful than the values on the inside.'[10] The Chief Rabbi gently rebuked Mr Kalms for such excessive scrupulousness: 'What makes you feel that there is something Jewishly unethical in making profits and gaining wealth?'[11] To me his worrying aloud seems strangely at odds with his robust defence of Jewish business practices. Kalms is clearly anxious that no opportunity should be given to those who would exploit the fallibility of Jews by generalizing from the particular to the universal.

There's a further contradiction, for Kalms feels that rabbis, who after all are supposedly charged with upholding Jewish ethical values, often fail to understand the rich: 'Rabbis do understand how to glean money out of wealthy people. Some are geniuses at it, some are poor at it. But rabbis don't understand wealth as such and what wealth actually means. They've never quite understood a rich man other than as a milch cow. But a rich man is a poor man with money. They never quite understood the problem of wealth, and they're very unsympathetic to it. They really do not understand the thrust of life as represented by wealth. Wealth brings vast responsibilities, vast pressures, vast influences on a man who accumulates it. Rabbis don't always understand the pressures, and they see it in rather simplistic terms, as a source.' When I mentioned the Chief Rabbi's rebuke, Kalms responded: 'The Chief Rabbi is totally wrong. If you read many rabbis, time and again they are critical or cautious or suspicious of wealth. There's nowhere it says you shouldn't be wealthy, but it does say in an enormous number of writings that you should beware of the rich man and that to have what you've got is enough.' I don't think many would share Kalms's view. Indeed, some members of the community find the relationship between religious leaders and the powerful businessmen far too cosy. A Progressive rabbi, however, dismissed such theories of rabbinical conspiracies to protect the wealthy as 'absolute nonsense. It's entirely up to each individual rabbi to say whatever they want. The fact that they're a lily-livered bunch of twits is a separate matter altogether.'

It is easy to understand what Stanley Kalms means by the stresses experienced by successful businessmen: he has built up a huge retailing empire, employs 18,000 people, and will be held personally responsible for its fluctuating fortunes. But the stresses and responsibilities entailed in the management of, say, the Dixons empire is an entirely different matter from the impulses that prompted those accused in the Guinness scandal to behave as it is alleged that they did. Yet Kalms uses his assertion that rabbis don't understand wealth to suggest that they should refrain from passing judgement on Jews who, let us say, misbehave. 'If you're asking me', he told me, 'whether rabbis should be critical of an individual Jew who does something wrong, I don't think that's what the rabbi should really be doing.' Which does rather beg the question. Certainly rabbis appear to agree with Kalms, for the Guinness scandal, whatever anguish it provoked behind closed doors, remained resolutely undiscussed in public by the Jewish community.

Even the leaders of Anglo-Jewry, normally so circumspect, agree that the conduct of many strictly Orthodox Jews in their business affairs leaves much to be desired. The possession of an ethical code cannot of itself abolish wrongdoing, and nobody seriously believes it does. Yet it is widely acknowledged that, paradoxically, the ultra-Orthodox who claim to have derived the greatest and most life-sustaining nourishment from their study of Jewish law and lore also have the worst reputation for shady practice in their business dealings. Both the Berger family, which controls 400 companies, and the Freshwater family are reputed to be among the worst landlords in London, and in July 1988 the Bergers again attracted unwelcome attention when the Charity Commission revealed that some share dealings relating to Berger charities were being investigated.[12]

An Orthodox social work manager said that strictly Orthodox Jews tend to be legalistic, and thus will push the law to the limit of what is permissible. Chasidic Jews 'display a great deal of warmth, but in many ways it's a selfish warmth. They don't concern themselves with the rest of the world, so that the generalized view of the Jewish people as being a light unto nations would be interpreted by them as being so happy in your own environment that other nations would want to be like you. There's a school of thought among Orthodox Jews that says: What do I care what people say, because they're going to say this sort of thing about me anyway?' The Torah requires Jews to be especially scrupulous when it comes to treating fellow Jews; unfortunately, this injunction is often turned on its head and taken as a justification for treating non-Jews differently, and hence less honestly, than fellow Jews. And there may be a tendency among the ultra-Orthodox to look down on those not as blessed and enlightened as themselves. A prominent businessman was even more scornful of some strictly Orthodox attitudes to business. 'They're élitists. They only look after themselves. At the moment there are two Chasidic Jews serving a few years in prison on a VAT charge. What's interesting is that they are totally unrepentant. They can't see that what they did is wrong and they couldn't care less about it. Fiddling VAT is not a Torah-based sin. Their attitude is: I'm in a *goyish* prison, so I'll suffer. We Jews have been punished for 2,000 years, so two more won't make much difference. With that kind of attitude, you can't be too surprised when landlords with poor non-Jews living in their properties decide it's okay to screw them. It doesn't say you shouldn't anywhere, does it?'

Rabbi Berkovits of the London Beth Din acknowledges that some ultra-Orthodox Jews behave badly and inconsistently. 'But many people are inconsistent in their personal behaviour. The average Englishman is law-abiding in that he won't commit murder or steal. But he may not be so law-abiding when it comes to his tax return. The question is: what does Jewish law say about it? Jewish law says you must obey the law of the land. If a Chasidic Jew is not paying his taxes or is swindling somebody, then he is failing in a whole area of Judaism that is important. I don't think you'll find any leading rabbinic figure condoning it. If you ask me why more of this sort of thing goes on in the Chasidic community, I'm not sure. The answer may be that it's very close-knit. Jews were persecuted for a long time and had to use their wits to earn a living. In the ghetto, practices evolved because certain professions were excluded to them. They tended to go into business, where life is tough – and in Poland the average non-Jew was an anti-Semite, so you felt a little bit at liberty to cheat him. These are attempts at sociological explanations – but by no means are they justifications. My feeling is that the leaders of these communities should be seen more often and more publicly to be condemning these practices. Some of them do, to their credit.' In the summer of 1988, for instance, Manchester rabbis and *dayanim* issued a statement deploring the activities of property speculators and pointing out that Halachah forbids gazumping.

The self-imposed isolation of some of the ultra-Orthodox groups must be part of the explanation. If you pretend you are still living in eighteenth-century Poland and educate your children in Yiddish, your sense of connection with the host society and its customs and conventions – not to mention its laws – is bound to become tenuous. Steeped in the study of Jewish law, it may be tempting to regard British law as of lesser consequence. Stanley Kalms, like most other Jewish businessmen, has no sympathy with ruthless property owners, however deep their piety: 'The *frum* Jews of course have *their* morality, but it's an in-group morality, one that can become exploitative of outsiders . . . We could do with more Jewish values from the very people who most profess to live by Jewish values.'[13] Chaim Bermant has written scathingly of the strictly Orthodox businessman William Stern who secured a place in the record books by going bankrupt to the tune of £110 million and shortly afterwards gave a lavish wedding feast for his daughter. 'One cannot really tell people what to do with their money,' remarks Bermant, before putting the boot in: 'Mr Stern's case is different in that the money wasn't his own.'[14] Stern had been prudent enough to ensure that his million-pound house was in his wife's name, so he lived on much the same lavish scale after his devastating – to his creditors – bankruptcy as he had before it.[15]

Not surprisingly, those within the sub-society of the ultra-Orthodox are somewhat bemused by their disrepute. Ita Simons admits that some strictly Orthodox landlords such as the Bergers (the fortune of Sighismund Berger alone is over £200 million) have a lousy reputation, though she adds that she has never experienced any problems with them or with other Jewish landlords. 'A religious person doesn't condone any behaviour which gives us a bad name. There are some people who are too avaricious, but they don't always realize it. Religion, unfortunately, can do very little about somebody who's extremely greedy. I do know people living in some of the Bergers' flats and they have loads of arrears and think it's just a shame to pay the Bergers. Some of the landlords are probably not as considerate and compassionate to others as they are to their own community. But when somebody in our community is doing something clearly objectionable, the only thing we can do is go to a rabbi and say: "Look here, this guy is doing this and that, and it's not on." Sometimes it works.'

And sometimes it doesn't. Yet if a certain contempt for non-Jews is, regrettably, implicit in some of the teachings absorbed by the ultra-Orthodox, there is no reason to suppose that such an attitude informs the behaviour of the vast majority of Jews engaged in business. Moreover, that some very rich Jews are alleged to have been involved in the Guinness scandal has nothing to do with their Jewishness. If money-grubbing has become respectable in Thatcherite Britain, there is no reason why Jews should be exempt from the yearning to grow rich and become richer, even if it sometimes means bending the rules in the process.

Business, and related professions such as accountancy, are not, of course, the only ways in which able British Jews earn their living. They are also drawn to the standard middle-class professions. There is nothing mysterious about this. Jews have always placed high value on good education, especially education that leads to qualifications and a career; hence the plentiful seeding of Jews in medicine and dentistry and the law. In eastern Europe the doctor was regarded with a veneration approaching, and possibly exceeding, that felt for the rabbi, for the Talmud advises Jews not to live in a town that has no doctor. The veneration persists, especially in the United States. The aunt of my first wife, an American, had urged her niece to marry a cardiologist. When I came along, it was conceded that I had some positive qualities, but I always knew I hadn't quite come up to scratch. Fortunately my ex-wife's sister married a cardiologist, and family ambition was satisfied.

In Britain, although Jewish doctors are plentiful enough, there are relatively few Jewish surgeons. Jonathan Miller explains: 'Surgery has always been associated with a rather patrician side of the profession. It's been associated with a sort of stylish metropolitan grace – it's a craftsman's job, and I suppose that Jewish manual craftsmanship has always been rather slight. Because the emphasis among Jews has been on learning rather than handwork, they tend not to go into surgery. In the early days in general medicine it was felt that surgery was a profession for gentleman, and Jews weren't gentlemen. But now there are certain hospitals in London – University College, the Middlesex – where Jews are very well represented.'

Jews may inhabit the medical world in considerable numbers, but they used to overwhelm the psychiatric profession. Some twenty-five years ago, three-quarters of the staff at the Tavistock Clinic in Hampstead were Jews, although the proportion has since diminished. A senior psychoanalyst at the clinic was uncertain about why Jews were so attracted to the profession: 'It may be to do with Jews' need to understand their personal past as well as their historical past. Jewish families are very strong, and there is a need to sort oneself out in relation to one's parents, who are often seen as controlling and dominant. There's a need to free oneself from restrictive control.' But those sound like reasons to consult a psychiatrist, not to be one. She pondered further, admitting that she had never previously given the matter much thought: 'Jews are searchers after truth, and psychoanalysis is a search for truth as well as a method of treatment. Jews have an awareness of suffering and a desire to alleviate it, whether through traditional medical practice or psychiatry. To be in touch with pain and emotion is very Jewish. There is a need to make sense of it all, to understand what everything means in terms of feelings.'

Not only are many of the Tavistock psychiatrists Jewish, but so are many of their patients. Of course the explanation may simply be that the clinic is based in Hampstead, close to districts well populated by Jews. Among children, there are more male patients than female; among adolescents an equal number; among older patients, more women than men. The analyst suspected this had less to do with a gender-based pattern of mental illness than with the stage at which Jews feel it's all right to seek psychiatric help. Delinquency and aggression, which are common among boys, worry parents, whereas withdrawal, which is more common among girls, is perceived as less of a problem requiring treatment. Among the juvenile patients are many Orthodox and ultra-Orthodox Jews. Bad behaviour, even violence, is quite common, and she suspects that the severity of the school regime is partially responsible. 'The discipline, like the Torah which is instilled in them, is punitive. The acting out and delinquency that can result are simply unacceptable to their parents.' She herself found the 'internal super-ego figures' of Orthodoxy hateful, and the punitive element in the rearing of Orthodox children equally so. 'Ritual can be positive,' the analyst conceded, 'but punitive laws represent primitive thinking and can result in cruelty.' Certainly the many Jewish psychoanalysts I have encountered have been profoundly Jewish in their culture, intensity, and (sometimes) warmth, yet completely out of sympathy with the Jewish religion.

If a passion for the welfare of others motivates large numbers of Jews to enter the medical professions, a love of justice, despite the exhortations in that direction through Jewish prayer and lore, probably plays a relatively minor part in their attachment to the legal profession. Jews are naturally disputatious and argumentative. Those who have experienced a Jewish education that goes beyond learning by rote will feel entirely at home in a courtroom. Sir Alan Mocatta, a retired judge, also remarked with some candour that the legal profession was relatively easy to enter. Brains are an advantage in the legal profession as in any other, but less academic gifts such as a good memory and a nimble wit can be equally important. And certainly a passion for social justice does play a part in the commitment of some Jews to the legal profession. The partners of the firm of Seifert Sedley & Williams are almost all Jewish, and relish taking on controversial cases such as the Blair Peach killing, and defending controversial clients such as the National Union of Mineworkers.

Some of the snobbery that attaches to the surgical branch of medicine has its counterpart in some of the snootier barristers' chambers, but Jewish lawyers face no institutional obstacles in the path of their career. In 1875 Sir George Jessel was appointed Solicitor General and then Master of the Rolls; Rufus Isaacs, Marquess of Reading, was the first Jew to become Lord Chief Justice. Jewish solicitors remain at the head of the profession: men such as Arnold Goodman, Sir David Napley, and Lord Mishcon. Jewish judges – Dame Rose Heilbron, John Hazan, Lord Salmon, Israel Finestein – are a dime a dozen. The present Director of Public Prosecutions is a Jew, Allan Green. Louis Blom-Cooper, after decades of work as a crusading barrister, legal journalist and leader of official inquiries, recently made an interesting shift in his career when he accepted the chairmanship of the Press Council.

Given the dominating presence and outstanding contributions made by Jewish journalists in Europe, notably Austria, earlier this century, it is surprising that few British Jews have risen to the top in this profession. Carey Labovitch, the founder of *Blitz*, is a publisher rather than a journalist, and at present the only Jewish newspaper editor is Eve Pollard of the *Sunday Mirror*, though Sydney Jacobson (former editor of *The Daily Herald*) and Louis Heren were respected newspapermen in their day. Editing Sunday tabloids may carry some kudos within the profession, but hardly counts for much outside it. When the Tavistock analyst was speaking of the Jewish search for truth, I doubt that she had the likes of Wendy Henry in mind, for it was she who, while employed by the *Sun* 'newspaper', lifted an interview with a severely wounded Falklands veteran from another publication without acknowledgement. This may have offended those of us who naïvely believe that newspapers should at least strive to tell the truth – an increasingly old-fashioned notion – but it clearly went down well with Mr Rupert Murdoch, who rewarded her with the editorship of *The News of the World*, Britain's largest-selling Sunday 'newspaper'. In December 1988 her reign ended and she was sent back to the *Sun* as deputy editor. Perhaps Jews are more comfortable writing speculative and ruminative journalism than occupying essentially

315

managerial positions as newspaper editors. There are certainly a number of distinguished Jewish columnists and journalists who contribute to some of Britain's better newspapers. Among others, one thinks of Nora Beloff on the *Sunday Times*, Bernard Levin on *The Times*, Neil Ascherson on the *Observer*, Samuel Brittan on the *Financial Times*, and Melanie Phillips on the *Guardian*. Their contributions are rarely overtly Jewish, but they are often imbued with a concern for social and moral justice that one would like to think of as quintessentially Jewish. Another corner of the journalistic profession that has appealed to Jews is the occupation of agony aunt, currently represented by Claire Rayner and Marjorie Proops.

It has already been noted that the passion for self-employment is the most likely explanation for the hordes of Jewish taxi drivers in London. Nor is the equally independent profession of market trader defunct. The traders and stall-holders that used to line some East End streets have followed their customers to the suburbs. Of the stall-holders at Lea Valley market in Waltham Forest, close to the large Jewish settlements of Ilford and Redbridge, 70 per cent are Jews.[16] Many of the stall-holders at the new Jubilee Market at Covent Garden are also Jewish. London taxi drivers cannot match the bizarre and often bigoted repartee of their New York counterparts, but unlike the New Yorkers they do usually speak English and know how to get to Oxford Street. Alan Weinberg, the deputy mayor of Redbridge where hundreds of Jewish taxi drivers live, himself drives a cab. Many taxi shelters, where drivers stop for a meal and a cup of tea, are run by Jewish families and offer cuisine to match. One obviously Jewish taxi driver who once drove me across London regaled me with some entrancing showing off: 'Had Michael Crawford in the cab tonight. Picked him up from the theatre. Nice fellow, he is, but doesn't say much. They're not all like that, though. X [famous actress], she was one of the worst. Started to talk to her, and she leaned forward and slammed the connecting window shut. When I arrived at her place, she sort of apologized, said she'd had a hard day. You should try driving a taxi ten hours a day, I said to her. Then she asked me if I wanted her autograph. No, I said, I only collect them from stars . . . Did you know Y [famous American film star] is gay? How do I know? Well, I took him and Z [famous English actor] – he's a known homo, everyone knows that – to Heaven one night. Soon as they got out of the cab, I yelled down the radio, "Y is gay!" Five thousand other drivers all got the news at the same time.'

Just as there are professions that attract Jews, so there are callings that no Jew ever seems to have given a moment's thought to entering. Jewish coalminers, for instance, must be as rare in Yorkshire or South Wales as wild parrots. Few Jews would seek employment as unskilled or manual workers. Most Jews instinctively distrust the country, for entrepreneurial skills are largely wasted in the middle of a large field in Norfolk. Ernest Krausz, in a study compiled in the early 1960s, noted that Jewish participation in occupations such as the aircraft industry, shipbuilding, and the car industry was 'insignificant', which is not hard to believe.[17] There are few Jewish policemen, and it warranted a news item in the *Jewish Chronicle* when a part-time policeman won a long-service medal after eleven years. The paper also unearthed the sole Jewish dog-handler in the Metropolitan Police. There are no more than 250 Jews in the armed forces, mostly in the army. According to the senior chaplain to the armed forces, Malcolm Weisman, few Jewish members are strongly committed to their religion. Anthony Blond plausibly speculates that there are very few Jewish army officers because their mothers wouldn't let them join up. Major-General Sir James d'Avigdor-Goldsmid, who died in 1987, rose to a higher rank than any other Jew in the forces. As commandant of the Jewish Lads' and Girls' Brigade, which was founded almost a century ago by an earlier Goldsmid, he tried to instil some old-fashioned virtues into a younger generation.

On those rare occasions when the thoughts of British Jews turn to crime, it is more likely, as Sidney Bloch said, to be a commercial than a domestic or thuggish offence. Rabbi David insists that even though an Orthodox Jew occasionally comes up before the beak on a VAT charge, the crime rate among the strictly Orthodox is very low. Nevertheless, British prisons contain their fair share of Jewish murderers, burglars, and drug dealers, and there is a handful of Orthodox Jews behind bars too. Some senior judges have told Sir Alan Mocatta, himself a retired judge, that they rarely find themselves sentencing Jewish wrongdoers. 'I hope it's true,' says Sir Alan, 'but I'm not altogether convinced. Once when I was at Leicester I went round the jail there and saw the list of prisoners and remarked with some pleasure, "Ah, only one Jew." And the governor replied, "Yes, and he's one of the worst of the lot."' Today there are about 300 Jewish prisoners in Britain, neither more nor less than one would expect. Many if not most Jewish prisoners are non-religious. Curiously, non-Jewish prisoners often pay their Jewish co-inmates a fine compliment by declaring to the prison authorities that they are Jewish. Monty Richardson, who served as a chaplain at many British prisons, suspects that is because some Gentiles believe there's a kudos attached to being Jewish, that Jews are seen as cleverer and more skilled than your common or garden jailbird.

Juvenile crime is low, but in general Jews participate in the full range of criminal behaviour, though financial crimes dominate. Jewish gangsters such as the Krays are relics of the past, but fraud remains popular, if only because many Jews are employed in financial services or in occupations such as antique dealing, which offer splendid opportunities to the dishonest. Mr Richardson notes that many Jews convicted of financial crimes are curiously unrepentant, possibly because they feel they are in prison out of sheer bad luck or miscalculation while many of their colleagues, equally guilty, are still happily pursuing their crooked careers on the outside. British Jews, lagging behind the Americans as usual, simply can't match the dubious record of the New York community, where two Lubavitch rabbis ended up in prison after masterminding a $130-million fraud scheme. A successful middle-class community, British Jews have little need to step outside the law in order to live prosperous and contented lives. Arnold Goodman, for one, is unabashedly proud of the Jewish appetite for professional success in their chosen fields: 'The disproportionate number of Jews in public life is largely due to the fact that they are of superior quality. One is slow to say this, but it is unarguably so. On the whole, the Jews are cleverer, they are more conscientious, basically they are more honest. They are a splendid community, and it's a pleasure and a privilege to belong to them.'

– 24 –

Art and intellect

THE Jewish contribution over the past 150 years to the arts and to intellectual life is hard to exaggerate. Think, on the one hand of Karl Marx and Freud, and at another extreme, of Hollywood producers. Whether in high culture or low, the Jews, in relation to their numbers, have made a unique impact on the Western world. To this glorious state of affairs the Jews of Britain seem to have declared themselves the great exception. Many explain this cultural barrenness by reflecting that during the great waves of immigration during the last century no Jews with brains got off the boat in England. 'The Jews who came here were stupider,' asserts Anthony Blond, the publisher. 'They were sold tickets to New York and – my grandfather was one – they got off in Hull thinking it was New York. It sounds like a joke but it's absolutely true. They were not the brightest.' The novelist Clive Sinclair also takes what he calls a Darwinian view: weedy or indecisive immigrants stopped off in Britain, while the tougher and more determined specimens endured the discomforts of the voyage until the boat docked in New York. Jonathan Miller's maternal grandfather came from Vilna and disembarked at Cork.

The Jews who landed in America, moreover, found a very different society from that which the tamer souls discovered in England. Apart from the dwindling bands of native Americans, everybody in America, even the snobbish Cabots and the Lodges, were immigrants, and Jews were as welcome to join in the free-for-all of making your way in America as anybody else. True, they weren't welcomed at Harvard or most medical schools, but there were plenty of other avenues, plenty of other opportunities. Jews in Britain, on the other hand, had to struggle laboriously against a whole string of civic disabilities. The eastern European immigrants arrived here to find not only a strongly class-based host society but a Jewish Establishment modelled on institutionalized England. Establishment Jews in the last century were mostly merchants and financiers; excluded from so many other fields of endeavour, they had concentrated their energies on those occupations they were permitted to practise and had succeeded nicely. Thus the role models for the new arrivals tended to be worldly businessmen, and the immigrants followed in their footsteps.

Yet this can provide only a partial explanation of the relative feebleness of Anglo-Jewish culture. Almost a century has passed since the immigrants arrived, more than enough time for the difficulties and anxieties of those days to have been absorbed and forgotten. Even a novelist and translator of distinction, Elaine Feinstein, concedes that Anglo-Jewry, while well represented in law and science and politics, is scarcely in evidence at all in British literature. Feinstein believes that because the Jews had to model themselves on the societies in which they were implanted, in Britain they couldn't help but absorb the philistinism that runs like rich marbling through British life. Feinstein's ability to deal with Jewish themes in her fiction may well be related to her own sense of balance between being a Jew and an Englishwoman – neither epithet can take precedence. The English language must be one of the very few in the world to possess a phrase such as 'too clever by half'. The Jew relishes cleverness, especially his or her own, but in Britain where such manifestations are clearly bad form, it must have been tempting to play down any such leanings. The Jews of Vienna and Budapest, as Feinstein remarks, also penetrated the host culture and absorbed its values, which in the case of central Europe effortlessly took in political philosophy, medical research, and *Kultur* with a big K. To use your mind and to cultivate the arts was not considered an eccentric foible.

Eva Figes, the novelist, who came to England from Germany as a child just before the Second World War, finds that British philistinism persists. 'English people generally feel it's *infra dig* to talk intellectually. You must always pretend to know very little. Everything has to be sort of amateurish. It makes me impatient and I'm bored with it. The French aren't like that, and in Germany there is a literary life, and writers do get together to discuss politics and ideas and what they're going to do about it. Here they just go on about Thatcher and do nothing.' I recall a small conference of university lecturers in English which I attended in the late 1970s. An evening session was addressed by George Steiner, who is very much a

European intellectual in his preoccupations. He spoke for an hour, and was questioned for a further half-hour, at which point the academic chairing the meeting, glancing at his watch, thanked Steiner for his talk, and proposed that anyone wishing to continue the discussion should do so in the bar, which would be closing in twenty minutes. Whereupon Steiner rose to his feet and said with cool politeness that he had recently returned from somewhere in eastern Europe where he had given the same talk, and there the discussion had continued until three in the morning. He couldn't help regretting that even among university lecturers it was seen as more important to get to the bar before it closed than to continue to explore an intellectual dilemma. Of course only a few of those lecturers were Jewish, and Steiner was merely drawing attention to British anti-intellectualism even in academic circles. It is hardly surprising, then, that many British Jews should place a similarly slight value on the arts and the mind.

Of course, numbers have a great deal to do with it. 350,000 British Jews can scarcely compare with the 5,500,000 American Jews who are concentrated in, and thus dominate, the great cities, where intellectual and artistic life are likely to flourish. A novelist who writes about the Jews of England, unless her name is George Eliot, is likely to have a rather small audience. Bernice Rubens's *The Elected Member*, a fine novel that very much explores Jewish themes, is a critical success but not a best seller. In contrast, an American-Jewish novelist such as Philip Roth can write almost exclusively about his fellow Jews and their tortured relationships with themselves and others, since he knows that there is a sufficiently large audience out there to identify with his protagonists and ensure that the books are best-sellers. Hundreds of thousands of readers will have shared, to some degree, the experiences he writes about and the peculiarly Jewish feelings that accompany them; that is a luxury no Anglo-Jewish novelist or poet can enjoy. British Jews, moreover, share the reticence of the host society and do not welcome personal exposures such as those Roth delights in. Clive Sinclair observes that personal experiment is not encouraged in Britain, whereas Americans are always reinventing themselves. Dissatisfied with an old model, it's easy for them to trade it in for a new one, whether in the form of an identity, a fad, a political philosophy, even a religion. The British are too fastidious for that kind of continuous self-appraisal. In addition, America has a pluralist culture: the Jewish novel is just as good, in terms of its subject matter, as the Western or the Hollywood caper. American writers do not have to worry quite so much about the weight of a native tradition as capacious and awesome as that offered by English literature. Arnold Goodman put to me the notion that English writers can tap the native literary tradition while Jewish writers lack that kind of access. Yet if one considers the case of 'foreign' writers such as Joseph Conrad or Henry James, they were anything but hampered by their lack of immediate connection with British literary tradition. You don't have to be related to Jane Austen or Charles Dickens in order to write well.

Since Jewish themes do not offer a rich seam for exploratory British artists, Jews who do excel in the arts often have no interest in dealing with, or even alluding to, their own Jewishness. Many would argue that the finest British playwright is Harold Pinter, and yet his Jewishness seems incidental, with the one arguable exception of *The Birthday Party*. If Pinter tends to ignore his Jewishness, the Jews of Britain ignore him in return. A writer who produces a saga about an Anglo-Jewish family might be fêted by the Jewish community, but even that is questionable. Anthony Blond's *The Family*, which clearly drew upon his own family – the revered Markses of Manchester – was not as successful as one might have predicted. Hilary Norman, whose first novel *In Love and Friendship* sold at least 150,000 copies, has done well with a Jewish saga.

An Anglo-Jewish artist who is not actively involved in the Jewish community is likely to be ignored or even disdained by fellow Jews. They are simply not interested. Successful American writers are lionized; successful British writers, Jewish or not, are not even celebrities. Clive Sinclair observes that the Anglo-Jewish community will flock to hear Teddy Kollek, the mayor of Jerusalem, give a talk, but wouldn't turn up to hear an Israeli novelist or poet. Sinclair had an unhappy time of it in 1987 as literary editor of the *Jewish Chronicle*. The weekly paper is much maligned, but it does a difficult job well, reporting on Reform and Liberal Judaism to the irritation of its more Orthodox readers, and giving space to columnists – notably that scourge of the pompous, Chaim Bermant – whose ideas are bound to displease a substantial proportion of its readership. On the whole the *Chronicle*, with its fashion and property pages and titbits about Israeli life, accurately reflects the preoccupations of the community it serves, though the editor, Geoffrey Paul, gives the paper some intellectual content with long feature articles on contentious issues. His decision to appoint Clive Sinclair as literary editor was a perceptive one, for Sinclair is one of the few Anglo-Jewish writers who is obsessed with his Jewishness and the problems of identity it poses.

Inevitably, it was not long before Sinclair was under attack as being too intellectual, too disdainful of the general reader. Sinclair was well aware that the average *Jewish Chronicle* reader did not read Wittgenstein in the bath and was more concerned with having the kitchen redone than with contemporary Israeli poetry. Nor did Sinclair add to his popularity with the publication of his novel *Blood Libel*, with its rough language, scathing introspection, and sexual explicitness – especially in recounting the exploits of a certain Rabbi Nathan. Sinclair can be abrasive, but he is an honest and often very funny writer and it was certainly cause for regret when he was sacked.

Sinclair finds it symptomatic of Anglo-Jewry that dead intellectuals seem greatly preferred to living ones. His view is corroborated in a passionate speech Gerda Charles gives to one of her characters in her old-fashioned novel *The Crossing Point*: 'Do we care twopence about literature, for example, or about any Jewish, living artist – for the value of his work? All *we* want to know is – is he still one of us? In other words, is he on one of those dreary committees? . . . We've gone soft. Our "life", our "vitality", our "culture"; where is it? Drained out over the card table and the business deal and those never-ending committees. Who invented this colossal fiction about Jewish culture anyway?'

Eva Figes suggests that British Jews tend not to be creative because 'they're too comfortable. When I think of English Jewry I think of Golders Green, of suburbia, and accountants, people who are very comfortable and liberal and quietly feathering their own nest – but not interested in ideas.' Her view is echoed by Jonathan Miller who finds the Anglo-Jewish suburbs 'very mercantile and rather complacent'. I asked Figes, who lives in Hampstead, whether she was conscious of living among a Jewish intelligentsia – for if there is a Jewish intelligentsia anywhere in Britain, it would have to be in Hampstead. She laughed: 'I know some writers who are Jewish and some who are not, and it never enters my head to make any sort of distinction. The notion of the literary life is an illusion people have who are outside and who imagine writers lead this glamorous life of discussing ideas. When we do meet, the only thing we talk about is royalties and who's cheating whom.'

George Weidenfeld speculates that Anglo-Jewish writers may not have achieved much distinction because they simply lack themes. American-Jewish writers have observed or participated in powerful political convulsions such as the Vietnam War and the civil rights movements. Artists and intellectuals in Britain have fewer causes. He may be right. And those

323

causes which might stimulate artistic and intellectual explorations – such as the conflict in Northern Ireland – are not ones to which Jews have any special access. Clive Sinclair is one of the few writers who has explored his own identity as an English Jew, though he himself places the emphasis very much on the Jewish side: 'You can't identify with the English, for God's sake,' he told me. 'At least the Jews are interesting. But I'm not interested in Anglo-Jewry as such, but in world Jewry.' There is also a shortage of outlets for Jewish writers within the community. The *Jewish Quarterly* is the only publication with any intellectual or literary pretensions other than the religiously preoccupied *L'Eylah*, and, despite its excellence, it sells fewer than 2,000 copies. It was lamentable that an article in the *Jewish Chronicle* commenting, in reasonably favourable terms, on the quarterly's thirty-fifth anniversary, should have carried the headline 'Vehicle for dissenters', thus relegating the sole Anglo-Jewish literary and cultural magazine to the margins of the community. The prolific Chaim Bermant, who has written some fifteen novels about Jewish life, in addition to some excellent non-fiction studies of Jewish life and culture, had admitted that he survives on the basis of his sales in the United States, not Britain.[1]

But we should not allow the indifference of Anglo-Jewry to disguise the number of very good writers – poets as well as novelists – who are British Jews. Apart from those already mentioned, we should include David Benedictus, Frederic Raphael, Jon Silkin, Dannie Abse, Wolf Mankowitz, Bernard Kops, Gabriel Josipovici (also a very distinguished literary critic), Michelene Wandor, Ruth Fainlight, Arnold Wesker, Stephen Poliakoff, Anita Brookner, the South African Dan Jacobson, Howard Jacobson, Peter Shaffer, Ronald Harwood, and that dangerous, tender poet of disgust, Steven Berkoff. And, at a pinch, one might be tempted to sneak in that most distinctive novelist Muriel Spark, who had a Jewish father but a resolutely Catholic faith and personality. Of course not all these writers touch on Jewish themes, and those that do so are not always thanked for it. As an admiring rabbi remarked, 'Only writers like Howard Jacobson and Clive Sinclair are prepared to be determinedly and vulgarly Jewish and to say to hell with the consequences.' Sadly, Mankowitz, who once called himself 'a Jewish writer writing in the English language' and described his work as 'a synthesis of English and Jewish cultural elements'[2], is no longer prolific. Frederic Raphael is articulate in defining his stance: 'I am not basically a Jewish writer at all if by Jewish one means working within the Jewish community or finding any characters among the figures of traditional Jewish writing . . . I have no interest in saving the phenomenon of Jewishness, but I find it senseless to proclaim my divorce from a group in which my family quite recently took an active part . . . My Jewishness is the Jewishness of the disillusioned diaspora Jew, the Jewishness of loneliness.'[3] It is significant that the only academic study of recent Anglo-Jewish writing is entitled *Beyond Marginality*, for as the author Efraim Sicher rather despairingly notes, most of the writers are 'outside the organized Jewish community and distant from traditional Jewish life'.

Jews are more conspicuous in theatrical life, though they tend to be active backstage rather than on the boards. In ballet, Alicia Markova was famous as a ballerina, but Dame Marie Rambert enjoyed more lasting fame as the founder of the school and company that still bear her name. Although there have been Jewish actors – Constance Collier and Leslie Howard, and more recently Claire Bloom, Anthony Sher (if we can admit a South African to the ranks of Anglo-Jewry), Maureen Lipman, Miriam Karlin, Lee Montague, David Suchet, Georgia Brown, and Eleanor Bron, among others – Jews have been much more prominent as producers or agents. The paucity of Jewish actors can probably be ascribed to cautious gentility; aspiring immigrants were conventional in their ambitions, and preferred to see their offspring as dentists rather than as movie stars. What kind of a job can it be where you don't get paid half the year? It is not hard to explain why Jews tended to find their way into the managerial side of show business, just as Jews seem happier being art dealers rather than artists. In America, explains Jonathan Miller, 'orthodox routes to promotion through banking, business, and stockbroking and so forth were ruled out. Showbiz, trade unions, and crime were the ways which were available to immigrant communities – black, Irish, Italian, and Jewish.' With anti-Semitism rife in universities and banking institutions, 'showbiz, vaudeville, agency work, and production were the only routes in. It was a disreputable profession, and therefore there were possibilities.' In England the entrepreneurial side of the business suited those whose skills were thwarted in other, more conventional professions.

Yet they kept their distance from classical and innovative theatre. Few Jews were associated with the pioneering seasons at the Royal Court Theatre in the 1950s and 1960s; nor are they associated with avant-garde theatre today. Just as Jews thrived in American vaudeville – think of the Marx Brothers – so they made their mark in the British music hall and its successors. Max Miller, Bud Flanagan (whose improbable real name was Chaim Reuven Winthrop)[4], Frankie Vaughan, Alfred Marks, Bernard

Bresslaw, and Bernie Winters thrived in this tradition, as did impresarios such as Bernard Delfont, his brother Lew Grade, and Joseph Collins, the father of Joan and Jackie. Some Jews have been attracted to the more prestigious side of theatrical production, such as Michael Codron and the executive director of the National Theatre, David Aukin. A few impresarios straddle both sides of the business. Harvey Goldsmith is best known as a rock group promoter, but it was he who helped bring to Earl's Court the extravagant Vittorio Rossi production of *Aida* that packed in 100,000 people in June 1988. Goldsmith thus joined the ranks of such well-established Jewish impresarios as Victor Hochhauser. Jewish playwrights rarely draw on their heritage for their material, though Stephen Poliakoff and Arnold Wesker are obvious exceptions to this. Jack Rosenthal, whose play *The Barmitzvah Boy* was a triumph on television, was not slow to remind me that out of the many plays he has written, only two have had Jewish themes – so to dub him a 'Jewish playwright', while not false in terms of identification, would be misleading in terms of preoccupation.

Just as there are few Jewish actors but many Jewish theatrical managers, so too there is an abundance of Jewish publishers. Many of the most distinguished publishers – Walter Neurath (Thames & Hudson), Bela Horowitz (Phaidon), George Weidenfeld, André Deutsch, Paul Hamlyn, Ernest Hecht (Souvenir) – are or were refugees from Germany or central Europe, where Jews had been involved in publishing houses for decades. A few Anglo-Jewish families also have publishing interests: the Franklins, as well as having a stake in the former Jewish bank of Keyser Ullman, have for two generations directed the academic publishing house of Routledge & Kegan Paul. Anthony Blond says he was drawn to publishing because it was an occupation that combined idealism and commerce. In broadcasting too, Jews are well represented in senior managerial positions. Jeremy Isaacs was succeeded as head of Channel 4 by Michael Grade, and will add lustre to his already distinguished career once he has settled in as the new director of the Royal Opera House, Covent Garden. Paul Fox and Alan Yentob of the BBC and Michael Kustow, commissioning editor for arts for Channel 4, also enjoy a high reputation. It's not clear why so many Jews were attracted to television at roughly the same time. Television did enjoy a blossoming in the 1960s, with satirical series such as *That Was the Week That Was* setting a new tone and establishing new possibilities for a medium that had hitherto, for all its virtues, been seen as somewhat staid and conventional. Television also attracts Jewish writers, such as Jack Rosenthal, and Laurence Marks and Maurice Gran, the authors of, among other series, the splendidly subversive *The New Statesman.* A gift for more easy-going light entertainment informs the radio broadcasts of Denis Norden, David Jacobs and Alan Keith.

In the world of music, Jews again gravitate towards the managers' offices, rather than on to the stage or into the pit. There are of course many Jewish musicians, including the composer Robert Saxton and some very fine soloists such as Robert Cohen and Steven Isserlis, but, with the exception of Solomon and Myra Hess, Anglo-Jewry has not managed to produce virtuosi that one can mention in the same breath as Isaac Stern, Heifetz, Schnabel, Perahia, Barenboim, Ashkenazy, Rubinstein, Perlman, or Zuckerman, or conductors of the calibre of James Levine, Lorin Maazel, Michael Tilson-Thomas, let alone the likes of Klemperer or Bruno Walter. In America the cantorial tradition produced opera singers such as Richard Tucker and Robert Merrill, but there are no great Anglo-Jewish opera singers that I am aware of. Jonathan Miller points out that Judaism cannot match the English choral tradition, which generates from the ranks of cathedral and church choirs considerable numbers of professional singers. Nor is there a Jewish equivalent of the massed choirs that were once ubiquitous in Wales. If British Jews are indifferent performers of the arts, they are more avid consumers. It was often said that about half of any West End theatre or opera audience was likely to be Jewish, but that is not wholly accurate, for a high proportion of those Jews would be refugees. In Germany every city of any consequence has an opera house, often of international renown. Attending the theatre and opera came naturally to many middle-class Germans and central Europeans, and as refugees the habit persisted. But if one excludes the refugees, I would suspect that the proportion of Anglo-Jewry that regularly patronizes the performing arts is no higher and no lower than that of the rest of the population.

The absence of Jewish performers to be cheered from the boxes has not inhibited Jewish patronage. Glance at the names of board members of and major contributors to such institutions as the National Theatre and Covent Garden, and the large proportion of Jewish individuals and organizations will be apparent. Jonathan Miller is not entirely happy about this state of affairs, since he argues that Jews mostly support only the most prestigious institutions. 'That I think reflects not so much a commitment to the arts as a commitment to getting a place in the British Establishment. It's a short cut. You can buy your way into the centre of the Establishment. I think it's rather pathetic. I don't believe wealthy Jews are committed to opera. They have a canny eye for the fact that opera is smart and snobbish. It appeals to the Gentile snob and it appeals to the anxious upwardly mobile Jewish snob. If they really liked opera you'd find Jews giving money to the Kent Opera, and they don't. Or to the ENO. But being on the Board of Covent Garden gives you entrée. It's a very good way of laundering your money, to put a large section of it through the operatic washing machine.'

Sir Claus Moser, a former chairman of the Royal Opera House, doesn't agree – not surprisingly. 'Most people who sponsor the arts do want a little bit of publicity out of it, and most people are on the whole more inclined to sponsor the established and conservative and élitist rather than the experimental and innovative. But it's nothing to do with being Jewish or non-Jewish. It's easier to get sponsorship for events to which you can take your clients and entertain them grandly than to performances held in a bicycle shed. That's natural.' Sir Claus also concedes that many generous contributors are also social climbers. 'A lot of people are in it not for the finest of reasons. They're in it in order to curry favour or to gain fame. But that can be true of anybody, and it's ridiculous to pin that on the Jews as particularly characteristic. In fact, I think it's possibly less true of Jews because Jews are more genuinely interested in the arts than perhaps the average non-Jew – it's in the blood. Also Jews are natural givers.' Sir Claus is especially proud of the fact that while he was chairman of the Royal Opera House, Arnold Goodman was chairman of the English National Opera, and Max Rayne was chairman of the National Theatre – all unpaid jobs, of course. Lord Goodman dismisses the notion that Jews sponsor and patronize the arts in order to worm their way into British society. 'That's nonsense. It's a way *out* of British society. If you believe that British society is enamoured of the arts, that's pure rubbish.' Nor is social ambition a sufficient explanation for the amassing of one of the finest collections of avant-garde painting by the Saatchi brothers, a collection they have opened to the public.

Earlier in the century there was an abundance of Jewish painters and sculptors: Jacob Epstein, Isaac Rosenberg, Mark Gertler, David Bomberg. Today, too, many of the most distinguished names in British art are those of Jews, though their Jewishness is more an accident of birth than a religious commitment. When Lucian Freud attended the wedding at Bevis Marks of the painters R. B. Kitaj and Sandra Fisher, it was, he couldn't help mentioning, his first appearance in a synagogue. Kitaj himself, however, has discovered in middle age an increasing fascination with Judaism, although his family background was militantly secular. An

American, he has lived in London for some thirty years, and has written: 'I think I'll live and die here, under English skies.'[5] Like many secular Jews, his rediscovery of Judaism sprang from his study of the Holocaust; he became 'a mad expert in this whole lugubrious business'. He is not greatly interested in the religious content of Judaism, and its services and rituals, made more perplexing by his inability to read Hebrew, bore him. The only religious aspects of Judaism that intrigue him are those which he can intellectualize, as it were, and use in his painting. He is especially fascinated by the whole notion of exegesis, as exemplified in the Midrash, and Responsa. He dislikes formal interviews, and prefers to have questions submitted in writing to which he can give a considered written response, just like a rabbi dealing with an ethical conundrum.

There were Jewish elements even in his earliest work. Of the six paintings by him now hanging in the Tate Gallery, two, including 'The Murder of Rosa Luxemburg' (1962), have Jewish themes. Aware of his Judaism while still beginning his career, it was only after 1970 that he made a conscious effort to explore it. Other Jewish painters working in Britain, such as Lucian Freud, Frank Auerbach, and Leon Kossoff, and the sculptor Sir Anthony Caro, have not followed in his footsteps. In Kitaj's view, their religion is art and they are mildly amused by his preoccupation with Jewishness. In his paintings, the Jewish elements are ruminative rather than overt. Always a literary painter, if that is not a contradiction, he is a master of allusion and symbol. His obsession with the Holocaust, for instance, is adumbrated by the inclusion of a chimney-stack motif in some of his recent work. He does not agree with those who insist that the Holocaust cannot be handled satisfactorily in art, though his own allusions to that time of horror are delicate. He is dismissive of critics who try to tell painters where they may or may not tread, and insists that you can't tell artists what to do. Eva Figes takes a similar view: 'There's long been this discussion about whether the concentration camps have killed the possibility of art. That seems to me nonsense, though it does horrify me when people exploit it as an easy tear-jerker. Elaine Feinstein is right in that if you have no direct experience you should leave it alone. I tackled it fictionally only once. I had to get it out of my system. I found I did it in a mythic, indirect kind of way. On the whole, it's better to avoid the subject than tackle it, as it's sort of unforgivable to fail in that area.'

Anglo-Jewry has not only a mostly undistinguished record in the arts but, it is sad to reflect, has made an equally uninspiring showing in the academic world. Perhaps this is because Anglo-Jewry perceives education as a means to an end: to have a degree in medicine is splendid, but a degree in philosophy, while nice, is a less useful commodity. Geoffrey Paul has remarked that 'we live in a community where academic or professional achievement is regarded as secondary or even tertiary to financial success'.[6] 'Consequently the Anglo-Jewish Establishment has never made intellectuals welcome within its ranks. Again, we must distinguish between the more established British Jews and the refugees from Nazi Europe and their children, who come from a very different cultural tradition with a much higher regard for learning and intellectual achievement. Most of my Jewish contemporaries at Haberdashers', and there were a good number of them, didn't share my own yearning, never fulfilled, for academic glory. They were clever boys, some of them obviously cleverer than me, and although they sailed into the Oxbridge colleges of their choice, it was always clear that their university career was a means to a more practical end. My contemporaries did well enough at university and have since enjoyed respectable careers in broadcasting, banking, and various other professions. At Cambridge, I found few Anglo-Jewish dons. Many believed that the literary critic F. R. Leavis was Jewish (his fierce wife Queenie, also a fine critic, definitely was), but he always denied it.

I studied in two faculties, the English faculty and what was charmingly known as the Moral Sciences faculty, where I read philosophy. Among the philosophers, the only Jewish don I encountered was Casimir Lewy, my supervisor at Trinity and the possessor of a magnificently operatic Polish accent. In the English faculty, the only Jewish don of any stature was George Steiner, who in those days was being given the cold shoulder by the faculty and could only find a perch among the scientists of Churchill College. He was considered suspect by the faculty partly because of his assertive manner but chiefly because he not only possessed but relentlessly displayed a breadth of learning and culture that were quintessentially European. When Steiner lectured on Romanticism, he didn't only talk about Coleridge and Wordsworth, Keats and Shelley, but threw in Mme de Staël and Schlegel too. Although we students packed into the lecture hall for his performances, it was very much a fringe activity, for the philistinism and parochialism of the British extended then as now even into its most ancient universities. To Steiner, intellectual issues impinged on matters of life and death, and this to most English dons was taking scholarship far too seriously. My few ventures on to the high tables of

Oxbridge have been soporific occasions for the most part, and clearly the experience of presiding at high table for years at University College as its master provoked some exasperation in Arnold Goodman: 'Anyone who thinks that conversation at a university high table is of scintillating quality has another think coming. It's largely concerned with the prices of houses, the inadequacy of the train service from Oxford to London, the need for more adequate bicycle racks and parking space, and grumbles about the food – unless you happened to be sitting next to a very amusing man such as Herbert Hart, who is Jewish. Then the conversation became more interesting.'

In the two decades that have elapsed since I frittered away four blissful years at Cambridge, much has changed. Many Jewish heads of colleges, especially at Oxford, have been appointed, for a start. Yet here too Anglo-Jewry is thinly represented. Sir Claus Moser, Warden of Wadham College, is German-born; Sir Isaiah Berlin, first Master of Wolfson College, was born in Riga; Sir Zelman Cowan, Provost of Oriel, is an Australian; and the new Master of Balliol, Baruch Blumberg, is an American. Two other foreign-born Jews, Sir Hans Kornberg and Sir Hermann Bondi, are heads of Cambridge colleges. The plain truth is that virtually no academics of the highest distinction have been produced by the Anglo-Jewish community. Even V. D. Lipman, a far from radical historian, had to admit: 'In the field of Jewish culture and scholarship . . . the Anglo-Jewish native community was not outstanding. Its scholars, who were not numerous, came in the main from abroad.'[7] Here too the community simply mirrored the values of British society. As Arthur Koestler, another foreign-born intellectual, once wrote: 'I was intrigued by a civilization . . . which admired "character" instead of "brains", stoicism instead of temperament, nonchalance instead of diligence, the tongue-tied stammer instead of the art of eloquence.'[8]

The contrast with Europe or the United States is extraordinary. George Steiner tells of the time when a fellow of the Institute for Advanced Studies at Princeton, probably the foremost postgraduate research institute in the world, died and had to be replaced. At a meeting a number of names were put forward, and then someone asked, rather plaintively, whether it might be possible to come up with a single candidate who wasn't a Jew. Recognizing the justice of this, the scholars tried, but failed. 'I can see why the Russians are so reluctant to let the Jews leave the Soviet Union,' says Steiner. 'The Jews of Russia are a major resource, a pool of the country's best brains. Not so here. In Britain not

331

even the chess players are Jewish. Safety puts us to sleep. Think of the giants of British science – Darwin, Huxley, Rutherford, Thompson, Crick, Hodgkin, Hawking – not a single Jew.' George Weidenfeld told me how he and Isaiah Berlin, at loose ends for half an hour, did their best to name one twentieth-century British-born Jew of outstanding intellectual achievement. They came up with one name, but then agreed that their candidate wasn't really in that Olympian league at all. It cannot be simply ascribed to lack of numbers, for France, with an equally slight Jewish population until supplemented by recent waves of North African immigration, managed to produce the likes of Bergson, Proust, Lévi-Strauss, and, more controversially, Derrida.

Isaiah Berlin recalls that very few of his Jewish contemporaries sixty years ago went to university. When he was appointed a lecturer at Oxford, it was considered distinctly unusual for a Jew to hold such an appointment – not because of anti-Semitism, but because there weren't that many Jews around. Although I have tended to point a finger at the philistinism of the host society, even that explanation will not do entirely. For, as George Weidenfeld pointed out when I offered the observation, at the time that Isaiah Berlin was an atypical figure at Oxford, British intellectual life was dominated by such figures as Bernard Shaw, Virginia Woolf, and Bertrand Russell among others. No, a more plausible answer is that Anglo-Jewish energies and abilities, which are considerable, are directed towards achieving practical rather than academic results. In 1942, it was estimated that the Jewish enrolment at British universities was proportionately three times higher than that of the non-Jewish student population: 'Medicine, law or accountancy was their first choice, for here was an opportunity for good rewards and added prestige in the community.'[9]

It was the refugees and foreign-born Jews who contributed their brilliance, as thinkers and researchers, to British academic life, men such as the art historian Sir Ernst Gombrich, the Italian scholar Arnaldo Momigliano, the historian Sir Lewis Namier, the political theorist and Marxist historian Eric Hobsbawm, the South African-born zoologist Solly Zuckerman, the psychologist Sir Martin Roth, the astronomer Sir Hermann Bondi, the historian Geoffrey Elton, the political scientist Elie Kedourie, the Nobel Prize-winning chemist Sir Aaron Klug, the biochemist Sir Hans Kornberg, the statistician Sir Claus Moser. The four Jewish holders of the only British honour of any worth, the Order of Merit, are all foreign-born: Isaiah Berlin, Solly Zuckerman, Ernst

Gombrich, and Max Perutz (who, strictly speaking, is a Catholic, though of Jewish descent). It would be unfair to overlook entirely such native-born Jewish intellectuals as Victor Rothschild, the Islamic scholar Bernard Lewis, the economic journalist Samuel Brittan, the economist Lord Kahn, the Nobel Prize-winning physicist Brian Josephson, the astro-physicist Dennis Sciama, the biologist Miriam Rothschild, the literary editor John Gross, the historian Martin Gilbert, a younger generation of historians such as Raphael Samuel and Simon Schama, and a few free-floating intellectuals such as the splendidly articulate and versatile Jonathan Miller and another doctor, Oliver Sacks (although Schama, Gross and Sacks now live in the United States). Yet, given that Jews revere learning for its own sake and delight in intellectual daring and specula-tion, the British contribution to academic as well as to artistic life in Britain seems disproportionately modest.

– 25 –

Eyes right: Jews in politics

SINCE the principal opponents to allowing Jews and others their full
civic rights in the nineteenth century were Conservatives, the
political sympathies of Anglo-Jewry lay with the Liberals. Indeed,
the first six Jewish Members of Parliament were all Liberals. The first
Jewish MP to be elected was Lionel de Rothschild in 1847, but he had to
wait eleven years before he was permitted to take his seat. Having taken it,
he then remained silent for the entire period of his membership, which
does seem rather a wasted opportunity. The first Jewish Conservative MP
was Saul Isaac, who was elected in 1874. This marked the beginning of a
drift away from a Liberal Party which under Gladstone was perceived as
unfavourable to Jewish interests, which were thought to be better served
by Benjamin Disraeli. With the mass immigration of eastern European
Jews towards the end of the century, the pattern began to change. The
Jewish Establishment aligned itself with the ruling powers, and Anglo-
Jewish leaders seemed as concerned as the most reactionary Tories about
the unwelcome effects of this sudden influx of strangely garbed Polish and
Russian Jews. The concern, of course, was that the impoverished immigrants would prove a burden to the long-settled Anglo-Jewish community
and to the institutions and infra-structure of the districts they were
crowding into. In essence, it was a concern for image. Having devoted
the best part of two centuries to becoming English gentlemen, with
splendid carriages and country houses and baronetcies, they didn't want
to see that good work undone by a rabble of ill-kept impoverished Jews
who spoke little English and with whom they had no more in common,
other than religious rites and beliefs, than they did with Scottish
crofters. Jews in both political parties tried to slow down the pace

of immigration and to deter the newcomers from settling in this country.

In 1903 the Royal Commission on Alien Immigration delivered a report which formed the basis of the Aliens Act of 1905. This did not ban further immigration, but it greatly increased the restrictions. There was no serious objection to the bill's provisions from Anglo-Jewish organizations, neither from the Board of Deputies nor from the Chief Rabbi. As Dr Geoffrey Alderman writes in his excellent study of *The Jewish Community in British Politics* (to which this brief account is heavily indebted), 'The immigrants brought into Anglo-Jewish life three political elements which had been but barely discernible within the community before: socialism, trade unionism, and Zionism. Powerful pressures were brought to bear by the established Jewish community to eradicate these novel tendencies.'[1] Given their provenance, it was not surprising that the political sympathies of the immigrants were more radical than those of the Anglo-Jewish gentry who were giving them so frosty a welcome. Nevertheless formal socialist and anarchist groups attracted few members; the nascent Labour Party would soon be drawing support from the immigrant community, and more radical organizations attracted little measurable support.

The drift of the Jewish East Enders into the Labour Party continued in the early decades of the twentieth century, both because this working-class community identified with its ideals and because Labour supported Zionist aspirations. The allegiance was consolidated during the 1920s and 1930s, and in 1934 four Jewish Labour MPs were returned to Parliament. At the same time Jewish support for the Liberals, especially in such places as Manchester, remained strong. Lord Goodman recalls: 'In my day almost every Jew was a Liberal, largely because of the prominence of one or two Jewish Liberals, Lord Reading and Herbert Samuel.' Jewish support for the Communist Party has been considerably exaggerated. Many Jewish intellectuals were drawn, like thousands of others, to what were perceived as being the ideals of Communism, but for East Enders the appeal of the Communists lay not so much in their ideology as in their uncompromising resistance to Fascism, which with the rise of Mosley and his Blackshirts became a genuine threat. As Sharman Kadish has observed: 'As in Russia, those Jews who were active in the general socialist and anarchist movement were unrepresentative of the Jewish community as a whole . . . Marxist atheism and anti-nationalism ran directly counter to the aspirations of an overwhelmingly traditional community – and one moreover, increasingly affected by Zionism.'[2] Yet the Communists were

335

willing to face the Fascists on the streets, while the Board of Deputies, as usual, wanted to keep their heads down and to prevent any direct confrontation on the grounds that such clashes played into the hands of anti-Semites.

The willingness of many prominent Conservatives to appease Adolf Hitler did little to endear Conservatism to the Jewish community. The party forfeited even more support when it signalled its intention to dispense with the major provisions of the Balfour Declaration. A White Paper of May 1939 making this abundantly clear could not have been worse timed. Despite the loyalty of some Establishment Jews to the Conservative banner, the vast majority of Jewish MPs returned in the 1945 election stood for Labour, which, it must be understood, is not the same thing as saying that the overwhelming majority of Jews voted Labour. The votes were counted, of course, before the foreign secretary Ernest Bevin antagonized Jews by opposing large-scale immigration into Palestine; during the war years the Labour Party had given every indication that it supported Zionist aspirations, but by November 1945 the government was supporting the very White Paper it had claimed to be opposing. Nevertheless criticism of government policy on this matter from Jewish MPs was muted, for to come out strongly in support of the struggle for Zionism could be perceived in unfriendly quarters as backing for the Jewish underground organizations that were blowing up installations and troops.

Yet if the Labour government's policies were deeply and disturbingly wrong-headed in the eyes of many Jewish voters, there was no mass desertion of the party. At Westminster Jewish Conservative MPs remained conspicuous by their absence until 1955, when Sir Henry d'Avigdor-Goldsmid was elected, to be followed by Sir Keith Joseph; these two were the only Jewish Tories in the Commons until the 1970 election. From that time on the balance began to alter, and by the 1980s the Labour Party had long ceased to be the natural home of the Jewish voter – if it ever had been – and there was considerable evidence that, at least in suburban London, Jews were supporting the Conservative Party in ever greater numbers.

Growing up in the 1960s it was natural to assume that anybody with brains and a conscience supported Labour. Among my fellow sixth-formers it was virtually impossible to find ardent Conservatives, and the few that held Tory views were regarded as blimpish eccentrics. Jews of my age were attracted almost *en masse* to the more forward-looking Labour

Party, largely because of its enlightened views on social matters. The Labour governments of the 1960s and 1970s included a number of Jewish ministers, such as Harold Lever, John and Sam Silkin, Joel Barnett, and Gerald Kaufman, and some of the most powerful figures in the government, such as George Brown, Ted Short, and Richard Crossman, were ardent supporters of Israel, which couldn't have lessened the appeal of Labour to Jewish voters. The back-benches were stuffed with more colourful figures, too wilful to be obvious choices as ministers, yet powerful guardians of a tradition that combined, in their view, socialism with Jewish values.

Leo Abse, who sat in the Commons from 1958 to 1983, was born and raised in Cardiff and to this day retains a pronounced Welsh accent. His childhood was dominated by two grandparents. His maternal grandfather was a glazier by trade and a Talmudic scholar by inclination and, according to his grandson, 'the first man ever to have spoken Welsh with a Yiddish accent'. He prepared his grandson for his barmitzvah, and they studied rabbinical texts together after Sabbath services. 'Then I would leave him to go some 400 yards up the road in Cardiff to the other set of grandparents. The dominant figure there was my grandmother. She was born in Germany, brought up against the background of the Enlightenment. She observed no *kashrut*, very deliberately and defiantly. So in my early years I oscillated between a very religious household and a defiantly atheistic pugnacious grandmother, and this meant I've had the great advantage on the one hand of understanding the conventional Orthodox Jewish tradition, and on the other was brought up to be highly critical of it. And all this was being done against a background of Welshness, which of course also played a significant part. I was brought up in a minority within a minority, so later in my life it was quite inevitable that I should be particularly sensitive to the needs of minorities.' Leo Abse was indeed instrumental in changing the laws regarding homosexuality and illegitimacy.

'The great advantage of a Jew in politics is that he can participate but also be an observer, because he belongs and he doesn't belong. I could address all those issues to do with family relationships because I wasn't burdened by the Christian view, which would tend to accept existing laws, nor was I burdened by the ghetto Orthodoxy. When I entered the House, Nye Bevan took me through Westminster Hall for the first time and said to me, as he had no doubt said to many others, "Leo, cultivate irreverence." The irreverence meant that one could become the idiosyncratic member who could take a contrary view. It wasn't an accident that Sydney Silverman and I were largely responsible for bringing about the abolition of capital punishment. The confident sense of identity which comes from belonging to an older culture meant that you were not intimidated by the prevailing ambience. It also enabled you to have, even while you were acknowledging what was good, sufficient irreverence to be critical. In that sense the older Jewish tradition was very influential. I think this attitude was shared by the Labour members of my generation. They came from similar backgrounds.'

Leo Abse also drew some intellectual and moral sustenance from the history of East End radicalism. 'There was great antagonism towards the Chief Rabbis of the day, who were very ambivalent towards the immigrant Jews, particularly those with a background of the Bund, of commitment to a socialist view.' It's the same tradition that inspired Manny Penner, the former mayor of Tower Hamlets. 'When people ask me about my basic tenets, I tell them: "I'm a Jewish socialist. My faith makes me that way."' Ian Mikardo too, another long-serving Jewish Labour back-bencher, has inherited some of that tradition, though he spent his childhood and youth in Portsmouth, in a small Jewish area near the dockyards.

Mikardo's parents were immigrants at the turn of the century. He attended a Jewish seminary in Portsmouth, established by a local Jewish magnate. 'But I got into bad odour, first of all because I started questioning some of the things we were being taught. Secondly, because I discovered that the principal of the college was a phoney and an impostor and I wasn't afraid to say so. Thirdly, because I was simultaneously studying science, and this was a matter for excommunication. What was a Yiddisher boy doing with physics and chemistry? So I broke away totally and became a rationalist at sixteen. Since then I've had no connection with Jewish religious affairs whatever. It was also during that period that I became a lifelong Zionist. I made my first speech on a Zionist platform in January 1922 when I was thirteen years old. I spoke in Yiddish, which was my first language. I only learnt English when I went to school, despite having been born here. English is my second language, which is maybe why I still don't speak it so good. To this very day, when I play bridge, I bid in English and score in Yiddish.' From 1964 he represented Bow in the Commons, and his own memories of growing up in an immigrant family made him especially sensitive to the problems encountered by the then current wave of immigrants from Bangladesh. Less transfixed by moral and family issues than Leo Abse and taking a particular delight in the infighting within the Labour Party, Ian Mikardo is, like Abse, a product of his Jewish upbringing, benefiting from its disciplines and social concerns. Abse is a practising lawyer, while Mikardo credits his skills as a debater to his Talmudic studies: 'Nobody who has ever studied Talmud can fail to be a good debater.'

Both Leo Abse and Ian Mikardo are retired from Parliament. The Labour Party has long ceased to be the obvious home for Jewish political activists. In Mrs Thatcher's Cabinet, Jews occupy many senior positions, and this is no accident, for her partiality to a people that display the very entrepreneurial skills and initiatives that she values so highly is no secret. When Leo Abse first entered Parliament in the late 1950s, the only two Jewish Conservative MPs, Henry d'Avigdor-Goldsmid and Keith Joseph, both baronets, were both representatives of upper-middle-class Anglo-Jewry who had absorbed aristocratic values to a sufficient degree to moderate the frequent reluctance of Conservative Associations to send a Jew to Parliament. Mrs Thatcher, to her credit, has no truck with such snobbery and has never been politically dependent on Tory grandees. In Leo Abse's formulation: 'The Tory Party has become the party of the *petit bourgeoisie*, of popular capitalism. It's inevitable that this appealed to many Jews.' As Jonathan Miller puts it: 'The entrepreneurially successful Jew is in fact the model in many ways of Thatcherite achievement. The Conservative Party now underwrites the values of Jewish entrepreneurial initiative, thrift, and ingenuity.' Moreover Jews, like anybody else, tend to vote in accordance with their economic interests, and as the Jewish community has grown richer it has become easier to shove into the background any lingering collectivist ideals and reward the government for making all that worldly success possible.

The growth of Jewish involvement in the Conservative Party has been paralleled by a remarkable disillusionment with the Labour Party. Many old-school middle-of-the-road Jewish socialists no longer feel at ease in a party that until recently included among its ideological leaders the likes of Tony Benn and Ken Livingstone. Neil Kinnock's recent attempts to recapture the middle ground, or perhaps it should be called the centre left, has come too late for many former Labour supporters. To many Jews, even those who harbour their own reservations about Israeli intransigence, the anti-Zionism rampant in some Labour constituency parties all too easily overlaps with anti-Semitism. There is no doubt that throughout the 1980s, despite the caveats of Foreign Office ministers such as Geoffrey Howe and David Mellor, the Conservative government has been more warmly disposed towards Israel than has the Labour opposition. For many British Jews, support for Israel is an acid test: waverings within the community are regarded as a kind of betrayal, and waverings from a political party are regarded as inimical to Jewish interests. The adoption of a pro-Palestinian resolution by a two-to-one majority at the Labour Party's annual conference in October 1988 can only have weakened further the dwindling support for that party by British Jews. There has also been a radical, and underestimated, change in perception. Israel is no longer perceived by the left as a plucky underdog, just as British Jews can no longer claim to be downtrodden. Israelis, rightly or wrongly, are perceived by many observers, including other Israelis, as oppressors, and British Jews are regarded as prosperous and powerful. Melanie Phillips, assistant editor of the *Guardian*, sees a danger here: 'An undertone to all this is an extremely nasty element which criticism of Israel – which I think is justified – has legitimized: a dislike and a fear of Jews which is rampant now among the modern left in a way that it never used to be.'[3]

During my own extensive spell as a Labour Party *apparatchik* I never witnessed, let alone encountered, anti-Semitism, but Jewish friends in other constituencies had less happy experiences. Many Jewish Labour Party activists left the party for the Social Democratic Party in the early 1980s because they had grown weary of rabid anti-Zionism at grassroots level. Manny Penner recalls how he was shifted from the Tower Hamlets housing committee to the ethnic minorities committee, allegedly because he was better qualified to supervise the latter. The true reason, as he tells it, had to do with attempts to remove council estates from direct political control. Penner objected not to the attempt to manoeuvre him off a committee, but to the fact that his Jewishness was used as a pretext for doing so. Not that views verging on the anti-Semitic are confined to the far left of the Labour Party. Dame Simone Prendergast admitted to me that in districts where the Conservative Party is weak, such as Tower Hamlets, there have been problems with infiltration by neo-Fascist groups. As in the case of the anti-Semitic left, we are talking of a tiny fringe whose importance is inflated by those who wish to make political capital from either circumstance.

Not even her worst enemy could accuse Mrs Thatcher of anti-Semitism. Indeed, she must gain Jewish support from her palpable philo-Semitism, just as comparable proclivities on the part of Harold Wilson during his governments were not taken amiss by the Jewish community. Not only, as has already been mentioned, were prominent ministers then passionately pro-Israel, but Wilson surrounded himself with Jewish cronies and advisers, many of whom he subsequently heaped with honours. Thatcher too feels comfortable among Jews. Her ministers have included Nigel Lawson, Sir Leon Brittan, Malcolm Rifkind, Edwina Currie, David Young, and Michael Howard, and she heeds the views of Stephen Sherbourne, until 1988 one of her foremost political advisers, and the Chief Rabbi, though he is not, contrary to the indignant assertion of his critics, a card-carrying Tory. Of those ministers only Young, Rifkind, and Brittan identify overtly with the Jewish community. Mrs Currie, indeed, became an Anglican when she married. The back-bench MP, Robert Adley, who is of Jewish birth, is highly critical of Israel, and there is no evidence to suggest that Jewish Conservative MPs form any kind of pressure group on behalf of the Israelis or any other Jewish interest. Of back-bench MPs, it is chiefly Ivan Lawrence who takes up the cudgels on issues of concern to Anglo-Jewry, whether it is the plight of Soviet Jews, or proposed modifications to laws governing ritual slaughter, or support for Israel.

On the other side of the House, Greville Janner, a former President of the Board of Deputies, performs the same function from the Labour benches, though he feels a far greater sense of isolation than does Ivan Lawrence. It is significant that the Conservative Friends of Israel has over 200 MPs affiliated to it, whereas Labour Friends of Israel can only count on 54 Labour MPs. Even allowing for the Conservatives' large parliamentary majority, the discrepancy is revealing. Lawrence, a fairly right-wing Conservative, acknowledges that immigrant Jews had sound reasons for supporting Labour earlier this century: 'Wherever they settled, they met with some degree of Establishment resistance, and a high proportion of that was from right-wing governments. But now we've reached the stage where there are second and third generation Jews. They've moved away from the poor areas of London. A high proportion are successful in business as entrepreneurs. As society in Britain has become more prosperous, the freedom which is the essence of Conservatism, the freedom from state interference, has appealed more and more to these generations of Jews, who therefore weaken their traditional ties with the old Labour Party.' Leon Brittan offers a similar analysis and adds: 'But most important of all, the narrow-minded collectivism of the Labour Party is anathema to Jewish individualism.'

Stanley Kalms attempts to link Jewish values and British political values: 'If Judaism had to have a label, it would probably be on the wet side of Toryism ... It is strongly paternalistic, and the ownership and protection of property is a recurring theme. It has strong "get on your bike" attitudes ... It is also strong on moral responsibility in the form of communal obligations.' Although it seems that many Jews fulfil those communal obligations in the form of charitable good works rather than by supporting governmentally directed social welfare provisions, there are still many observers of Anglo-Jewry who insist that, despite the shift to the right, Jews remain attached to collectivist ideals. Ian Mikardo recalls: 'A couple of years ago I was asked to debate with Ivan Lawrence, who's about as far right as you can get in the Tory party, but a lovely man. I debated with him before a Yuppie Jewish audience in the Finchley constituency, no less, the motion that the natural political position for the Jew was on the left. It was carried by a two-thirds majority. I was shattered. And Ivan was more shattered than I was. Nevertheless I think most of them would have voted for Mrs Thatcher.' And Jonathan Miller is convinced that 'a higher proportion of Jewish professionals have left of centre sympathies than you'd find among non-Jews of the same status'.

Even a right-wing historian such as Paul Johnson does not dispute that Jews are natural liberals. He attributes this to the biblical tradition of social criticism, the Talmudic tradition of communal provision, the reluctance, in the light of the supremacy of the Torah and thus of Jewish law, to grant any more than temporary authority to secular powers, to the secular radicalism of a struggling urban proletariat such as immigrant groups, and to the fact that 'the Jewish sense of injustice was never allowed to sleep'.[4] Rabbis Goldberg and Rayner, writing from a more left-wing perspective, boldly declare: 'The modern concept of the Welfare State is in line with biblical tradition.'[5] However, circumstances have changed to such a degree that the accuracy of such sociological assessments has blurred. The Anglo-Jewish proletariat is no more, and what remains of it in Cheetham Hill or Hackney or Stepney is old and moribund. An upwardly mobile middle class is less susceptible to collectivist ideals, especially when self-interest is elevated to the status of a political creed. There is nothing specifically Jewish about this, and there is no reason why Jews should be immune from the political pressures and briberies of Thatcherite Conservatism. By 1987 what had once seemed to be a special link between idealistic Jews and the Labour Party had become a footnote in the history books. In 1966 thirty-eight Jewish MPs were returned to the Commons; by 1987 the figure had dropped to seven. Not that Jewish

would-be politicians had all switched to the Tories, for only sixteen Jewish
Conservative MPs were returned in the same election, and Jewish
representation in Parliament is smaller now than in all the years since
1935.[6]

Leon Brittan is clearly an ideologically committed Conservative, whose
allegiance springs from intellectual conviction rather than from a wish to
endorse a skill for making money. Sir Leon and I have very similar
backgrounds, although he is some years older than me. We both attended
Haberdashers' school and both proceeded to Trinity College, Cambridge. I told Sir Leon that I couldn't recall encountering any Jewish
Tories at Haberdashers', and he admitted that even he had had left-wing
twitches during his schooldays. But not for long. 'There were a number of
events that moved me to the right, but it crystallized on arriving at
Cambridge. At school I was very influenced by Arnold's *Culture and
Anarchy*, which was taught in a very exciting way. I felt some of the
strictures of the Liberal Party in the nineteenth century could be directed
at the left in the twentieth. Then I went for a couple of months to America,
and that seemed to indicate that it was possible to take an aggressive view
of life without supporting socialism. Then there was Suez, when I found
the attitudes of the left really nauseating. There was another thing:
reading Anthony Crosland's *The Future of Socialism*, which seemed to me
devastating in its demolition of the case for classical socialism, and totally
unpersuasive in the attempt to find some other basis for supporting the
Labour Party. It was that combination of events that persuaded me.' He
also believes that the changes within the Conservative Party since the late
1970s have been exaggerated; even in the 1950s, under the benign
influence of Butler and Macleod, it was far from hostile to Jews. He
personally experienced no antagonism from any constituency association during his attempts to enter Parliament. He also pooh-poohed
suggestions that anti-Semitism had played any part in his down-
fall during the Westland affair, even though this seems contrary to
much that one heard and read while those unhappy events were taking
place.

The Jewish community has always striven to maintain contact with
politicians sympathetic to the issues it worries over. Ivan Lawrence clearly
enjoys his dual position as a Conservative back-bencher and Jewish lay
leader. He is a member of the policy planning group of the Institute of
Jewish Affairs, treasurer of Conservative Friends of Israel, secretary of
the all-party Committee for the Release of Soviet Jewry. 'I help to make

sure that the case of Israel is properly and fairly represented, which means I ask questions and make speeches in Parliament defending Israel, because it's very often under attack. I do the same for Soviet Jewry. Also the Conservative government knows of my very close interest in Jewish affairs. If there are problems thrown up at the Board of Deputies, I tell the relevant ministers and ask them to take some speedy action. And if they are upset about anything in the Jewish community, they will tell me and I will see what I can do. *Shechita* is a matter I have raised on several occasions with ministers, and we have managed between us to head off threats to *shechita* when they have been presented by private Members' bills or possible government legislation. If I hadn't taken that action, it is possible that *shechita* would have been abolished or compromised a year or two back. There was great concern that Israel was selling arms to Argentina during the Falklands crisis. I was made aware of the government's feelings in this matter and went to see the Israeli ambassador. He made very strong personal inquiries, satisfied himself of the position, passed it on to me, and I passed it on to the government.'

Clearly Mr Lawrence is a useful figure, both for the Jewish community and for the government he supports. Not being a member of the government, he has more freedom to manoeuvre than would, say, a Cabinet minister, who in his public stance may be able to do little more than radiate general goodwill. David Young is especially adept at this. When in 1987 the Anglo-Jewish Association held its Annual General Meeting at Chatham House, it was Lord Young who was the guest of honour and principal speaker. The Anglo-Jewish Association, founded in 1871, is a curious organization, vaguely educational and cultural in its practical manifestations and very much a cosy network for some of the staider member of the Anglo-Jewish Establishment. In its statement of aims the AJA declares that it is 'open to all British Jews who accept as their guiding principle loyalty to their faith and their country', a curious declaration, since it implies that out there somewhere is a body of disloyal Jews just waiting for the right moment to betray their country. Of course this isn't what the AJA means, but its statement reflects the continuing need of the Jewish Establishment to reiterate that its primary loyalty is to Britain – which, of course, nobody ever doubts. The president is German-born Clemens Nathan. In his mid-fifties, he is a portly man with receding hair and an appealing untidiness; he combines earnestness with a permanently anxious manner. A more typical officer is Sir Peter Lazarus, a civil servant and pillar of the Liberal Synagogue, the perfect

Establishment figure with his three-piece suit, his bald pate, and a mouth so turned down it almost meets his collar.

Lord Young's speech was an unsubtle apologia for Thatcherite policies. There was stuff about 'nobody owes us a living' and 'we can walk tall again', about how benefits have become so generous that people prefer to opt out of the system rather than work. Britain had wiped out its facilities for technical training by getting rid of secondary modern schools – which sounded perilously close to a plea for their restoration. Comprehensive schools, he argued, offered 'academic' training (boo) rather than practical skills (hooray). Education is not supposed to benefit those who work in the field – a reference, I assume, to all those grossly overpaid teachers – but is for the benefit of the children. 'Stalinist' housing estates would be returned to private landlords. He wanted to bring back individual responsibility, 'though we must have care and compassion' for those at the bottom of the heap. Above all, he declared, the Tory Party is a moral party, concerned with 'people standing up for themselves . . . If that isn't morality, I don't know what is.' No, he doesn't know what is.

The response of this very conservative audience to Lord Young's speech was lukewarm, not, I suspected, because the audience disagreed with his views, but because he had insulted their intelligence. The members of the AJA are an educated bunch, highly trained professionals for the most part, and the minister's trite formulations were vapid and unworthy of the occasion. Yet even his cavalier misjudgement was put in the shade by the grovelling vote of thanks moved by Neville Sandelson, a former Labour MP who defected to the Social Democrats, but who on this occasion revealed himself to be 'a non-Tory Thatcherite'. When he added, 'We are all Thatcherites now,' I muttered audibly, I hope, 'Speak for yourself.' I had expected to be hushed and shushed from all sides, but not so. Clemens Nathan, looking on the brink of tears as usual, offered another vote of thanks, and added, as though to remind the minister gently that he hadn't been addressing his party's annual conference, that the nation was still divided between rich and poor.

I left the meeting more inclined to the view that there is a residual liberalism among the more educated elements in Anglo-Jewry, though such things are hard to measure. It is tempting to extrapolate from the presence of Jewish ideologues in the Thatcher camp that they represent a trend somehow inherent in Jewish thought and life but, again, I don't believe that to be so. Ten years ago political theorists such as Keith Joseph and Alfred Sherman were regarded as intellectually weird, and it is only under the patronage of the Prime Minister that their ideas achieved a kind of bizarre respectability. The Conservative rejection of communal responsibility – except for those, as they eloquently put it, at the bottom of the heap or those who fall through the safety net – has been partially endorsed by such influential religious leaders as the Chief Rabbi and Jonathan Sacks. Yet there is no indissoluble link between *laissez-faire* capitalism and Jewish Orthodoxy, even though certain religious leaders may seek to persuade their flock that something along those lines does indeed pertain. Although the ultra-Orthodox community is, on the whole, politically Conservative, one can find a fair sprinkling of socialists among the Orthodox. Arieh Handler told me: 'Socialism is often associated with secularism, so Orthodox people are a little frightened to identify with socialism. I disagree with that. I would say that the spiritual basis of socialism comes from the Bible, from religion. My socialist convictions stem from the fact that I claim the Torah is very much concerned with the way society should be built. For instance, the Torah says that land that has been sold and acquired by other people has to be returned to its original owner after fifty years – a clear indication that the Bible does not want an accumulation of property.' Nevertheless I suspect that more British Jews would identify with Stanley Kalms's 'wet Tory' approach than with Handler's idealistic socialism.

Speculation about Jewish voting preferences is not without its practical consequences. The Jewish Establishment resists talk of a 'Jewish vote'. As usual, the Board displays excessive timidity in this matter, since any electorate is composed of special interests, and those of Jews are no more self-serving than those of local businessmen, pensioners, employees of arms factories, the Irish, or whatever. The concentration of Jewish populations in certain suburbs makes it inevitable that candidates for political office, at local or national level, would be foolish to take no notice of them. Before a general election the *Jewish Echo* publishes a survey of Jewish voters' views on issues of interest to the community, and the candidates no doubt take note. But it would be hard to argue that those views carry any more weight than the opinions of other special interest groups, for the Jewish vote is not monolithic. There is no Jewish consensus on most of the burning issues of the day. A cross-section of Jewish voters' preferences in, say, Ilford on such matters as privatization, the National Health Service, or the introduction of the poll tax would be unlikely to differ greatly from the views of non-Jews in the same district. The effect of the 'Jewish vote', such as it is, is that certain politicians take care to nurture the Jewish electors in their constituencies. Mrs Thatcher, whose Finchley constituency is heavily Jewish, takes great pains to remain on good terms with those voters. In 1987 she 'increased her share of the total poll by 2.8 per cent but her share of the Jewish poll by nearly three times that amount'.[7] And the same is true of all MPs in comparable circumstances. John Marshall, the MP for Hendon South, is staunchly pro-Israel and an ardent supporter of the Jewish community; while that support is doubtless a matter of genuine conviction, it may be boosted by the knowledge that Jewish voters help to sustain his parliamentary majority. Geoffrey Alderman's researches have established that wards with high Jewish population density tend to return Conservative councillors even within boroughs that are overwhelmingly Labour-controlled.

Nor can one legitimately speak of a Jewish lobby in Parliament. In the United States the concentration of millions of Jews in large urban areas with powerful political representation does sustain an effective Jewish lobby with the ability to influence foreign policy. In Britain, however, there is very little evidence to suggest that the majority of Jewish MPs of either party represent Jewish interests. Of course there are exceptions such as Greville Janner and Ivan Lawrence and David Sumberg. Irvine Patnick, a Conservative MP elected in 1987 and a former president of the Sheffield Jewish Representative Council, says: 'I believe in Israel's right to exist, but I am no expert on the Middle East. So I leave it up to others to do the talking on that subject.' Even in times of crisis, Anglo-Jewry cannot assume that Jewish MPs will press the Jewish case. During the Suez crisis of 1956 hardly any Jewish MPs supported the Israeli cause, despite pressure from the community, and in 1973 Sir Keith Joseph and Robert Adley voted in favour of the arms embargo during the Yom Kippur War. The former Liberal MP Clement Freud never affiliated himself to the Jewish community in any discernible way. Nor is there any special warmth of feeling between Jews of opposing parties because of their common religion and heritage. The Conservative Mrs Sally Oppenheim once declared that she felt no 'relationship with Jews on the other side of the House, not even moderates . . . They all make me ashamed. There's no kinship with them. None at all.'[8] Should disaster strike Israel, there is no reason to believe that the presence of Jews in the Cabinet would make a jot of difference to the government's response.

Although there is no reason why British Jews should be any less protective of their material interests than any other section of the community, it is, in my view, a matter for regret that the Jewish radical tradition in this country seems largely extinguished. The Jewish community's perception of its best interests has narrowed. Many Jews, now that they or their parents have clambered up the ladder to the safe platform of middle-class suburban security, have pulled the ladder up behind them, and see no reason to make sentimental common cause with those whose interests they once shared: recent immigrants, the victims of racism, the impoverished, the elderly. The splendid charitable infrastructure within Anglo-Jewry means that most Jews in distress can obtain help from within the community; thus poverty or physical disability have come to be seen as local rather than as national problems. Jews of my generation, who grew up in the '60s, found politics and morality inextricably linked, whichever side we may have taken. In Thatcherite Britain self-interest, whether on a national or personal scale, seems to be the governing principle. The whole notion of a 'social conscience' is now seen as rather quaint. Although organizations such as Jews Against Apartheid are backed by Jews who feel that the kinds of evils inflicted on their parents' and grandparents' generations should not be duplicated in southern Africa, support for them is lukewarm.

When Cyril Harris left St John's Wood United Synagogue to become Chief Rabbi of South Africa in late 1987, all he could say about apartheid was that 'it is horrible and unsatisfactory in moral terms'. He proposed to take 'a long hard look at all the various factors involved before deciding for myself what is best for the general and Jewish communities'.[9] His remarks since his induction as Chief Rabbi have been no less vapid; for instance: 'The wind of change is not blowing strongly enough throughout South Africa.' Of course many South African Jews are vigorous opponents of apartheid, but many of them, just like other South African whites, would find their position considerably less comfortable without it. Rabbi Harris clearly didn't want to antagonize his new congregations before he'd even arrived in South Africa. Nevertheless, if religious leaders refuse to take an unequivocal moral stand on such matters as racial discrimination, how can they urge their congregants to do so? Nor does the lay leadership acquit itself more honourably. The newsletter of the Board of Deputies for April 1987 contains the following nugget: 'Hayim Pinner noted that the Board of Deputies in South Africa has had the courage to condemn the Government for imprisoning children.' A pretty controversial stand, that must have been. And Dr Kopelowitz, referring to his speech to the South African Board of Deputies in 1987, said: 'It's not for me to lambast other communities and tell them what to do, but I did say we must always follow the ethical approach.' In short: be ethical, do nothing.

Rabbi Shlomo Levin is one of the innumerable South African Jews now living outside his native country. He admits he is no political activist: 'I think it's got something to do with backgrounds. We have been a downtrodden people for such a long time that when we finally live in an age where, at least in the Western world, there's a bit of space to breathe, we're only too grateful to get on with the purpose of our creation, which is to be moral people, to study and to learn, and as a result to grow in spirituality. There's much more that the Jew can achieve by strengthening his own inner core than he could achieve by standing outside and shouting a lot, which is something the rest of the world can do as well. But my thinking is not clear on this. I confess to having conflicts. It takes a long time to work these things through.' This is a curiously introspective view, a moral extension of the trickle-down theory of economics: I'm working at being a righteous Jew by studying the Torah, and there's a faint chance that it might to do the rest of you out there some good. If, as Rabbi Levin says, to be 'a moral people' is the Jewish destiny, then morality has to be expressed in deeds and not just by expounding at *shiurim*.

At a meeting to discuss the problems of 'dispirited youth' at Cockfosters United Synagogue a member of the audience declared that the Chief Rabbi's paper on the inner cities had made him feel ashamed: 'When do you hear a United Synagogue rabbi speak out on apartheid? How can youth respond to that kind of leadership?' And Rabbi Michael Rosen, predictably, agreed, saying something along the following lines: 'When it comes to social issues, I feel solitary in the rabbinate. The United Synagogue has become the Tory Party at prayer, and the Church of England has come to occupy a middle position. It's a sad critique. With affluence, we're forgetting the search for social justice that used to be part of Jewish life. Jews today can only respond to their own problems. They have their backs to the wall, perhaps because they've been scarred by the Holocaust. Why should Gentiles help us when we complain of anti-Semitism, when Jews don't come to the aid of blacks and others who suffer from racism? The rabbinate doesn't encourage such views. If a prospective rabbi being interviewed by a community said he opposed the dog-eat-dog attitude and opposed racism – would he get the job?' Rabbi Yisroel Fine, the great conciliator, smoothly countered by saying he was sceptical of those who climb on to the bandwagon of fighting for social issues; he saw this as a kind of play-acting, a way of avoiding local and more immediate matters. Precisely: the Jewish suburbanite has narrowed his vision to the degree that the greatest social evil of the day is perceived as an attempt to alter the *shechita* laws. (Or, as Rabbi Rosen put it on another occasion, in an article relating to Archbishop Tutu's visit to Yakar in late 1987: 'Judaism has more to offer than how to make a cup of tea on Shabbat. A faith that does not address itself to the concerns of the world is an anachronism, a perversion of authentic Judaism.') Dr Kopelowitz once told me: 'It is our task to represent the Jewish community. If it is brought to our attention that a particular group is suffering discrimination and they ask for our support, then we would do it. I would wait for an approach, though. We had a lot of input into the Race Relations Acts of the 1960s and 1970s.' British Jews, wrapped up in their parochial concerns, have come to regard a quest for social justice as a luxury, not as a central part of Jewish consciousness. They are prepared, as Dr Kopelowitz indicates, to act passively but not to take an initiative. In this parochialism they have been abetted by many rabbis.

Fortunately there is an element within Anglo-Jewry that does believe the Jewish community should take a more active role in social and political issues. The Jewish Council for Community Relations pursues inter-faith activities, maintains contacts with other ethnic groups, and campaigns on matters relating to immigration. In December 1987 Yakar sponsored a symposium on relations between Jews and the black community; about 150 people listened to a discussion led by two Labour MPs, Paul Boateng and Diane Abbott. There was a chorus of fully justified indignation when Sir Alfred Sherman, a right-wing ideologue, invited the French National Front leader Jean-Marie Le Pen to address a fringe meeting of the Conservative Party Conference in 1987. By any reckoning, M. Le Pen is a racist, and many Jews expressed their disgust that Sir Alfred was going out of his way to promote such views. Sir Alfred, after much huffing and puffing, eventually backed down. In the spring of 1988, during the debates on Section 28 of the Local Government Bill, which sought to ban the 'promotion' of homosexuality, a group called Jews Against Clause 28 was one of many opposition groups. And five Reform rabbis were among the sixty-four clerics who signed a letter to the Foreign Secretary in April 1988, calling for a freeze on nuclear weapons.

British Jews seem more interested in debate than in power. It would be pleasant to speculate that this is because of some innate Jewish inability to display the ruthlessness on which political success depends, but this clearly isn't so. Many of the early leaders of Soviet Russia, notably Trotsky, were Jews. The murderous thugs who ran Hungary as a police state in the 1950s were almost all Jews. In the United States men such as Henry Kissinger have relished the enormous power they have wielded. Yet in Britain, lack of political ambition seems yet another manifestation of Anglo-Jewish somnolence. Only Disraeli, who of course was baptized out of the faith, achieved not only high office but undisputed political greatness. The Jewish ministers in Harold Wilson's governments were never of great importance, with the possible exception of Harold Lever. Even today, when Jews are very prominent in Mrs Thatcher's Cabinet, only one, David Young, was ever one of her courtiers; the rest are politically marginal, as Edwina Currie discovered in December 1988, when she was forced to resign for tactlessly telling the truth. Leon Brittan paid dearly for what seemed like sycophancy, and his restoration to prime ministerial favour took the form of banishment to Europe rather than return to the Cabinet. Nigel Lawson may be the second most powerful minister in the land, but he is atypical in that he clearly doesn't care desperately about ousting his next-door neighbour. Lawson is notorious for his unwillingness to butter up the rank and file; he is more like a technician who, rather to his own surprise, suddenly gains access to all the controls and is able to conduct some curious experiments with the British economy. He seems deeply engaged in this process, but far less preoccupied with political ambition.

Leon Brittan is doubtful about the idea that British Jews aren't interested in power. 'You might try to derive a thesis that those of Jewish background tend to be interested in ideas and implementing those ideas rather than manipulating people. But then I would regard the implementation of ideas as the exercise of power.' Ivan Lawrence told me that though he tended to support the government on most matters, he was not inhibited from taking a more independent line, especially on legal matters where he claims considerable expertise. 'I remember an occasion when a very senior colleague – I'm sure it wasn't officially directed – said to me that if I ever wanted to be Solicitor General, I shouldn't take a certain stand on a matter of constitutional importance to me as a lawyer. I told him not to hang around! That kind of independence, sticking up for something you believe to be right, does sometimes make the powers that be think that since there are so many fine people to choose from, this awkward cuss can be passed over. Independent, argumentative, imaginative, we Jews do tend to push something and keep on pushing even if it's unpopular or unacceptable to the Establishment. We don't love power more than we love a cause or independence. It may also be, to be fair, that if you're too independent and too flamboyant you may not have the stuff that administrators are made of.'

That seems the essence of the Jewish contribution to politics, and the reason why Jews are not conspicuously successful politicians. Leo Abse was a prime example of a man drawn to politics because he wished to rectify certain injustices. He had influence and often persuaded his fellow MPs to support him, but no prime minister in his right mind would have offered Abse a portfolio. I find this endearing. Of course there are Jewish toadies in politics, but British Jews seem less inclined to toe the party line come what may. The old Anglo-Jewish Establishment always preferred to wield whatever influence it had behind the scenes, and the MPs it dispatched to Parliament tended to be sleepy old gentlemen such as the d'Avigdor-Goldsmids. What need was there for Lionel de Rothschild to speak in Parliament when he had so much power outside it? The descendants of immigrants seem more conscious of their marginality and this in a curious way liberates them from political conformity. British Jews of that generation have never felt as richly integrated into British life as were, say, French Jews, who often achieved great distinction in political life, supplying prime ministers (not, of course, as small a class of individuals in France as in Britain) such as Pierre Mendès-France and, more recently, Laurent Fabius. The situation in Britain may change as smug Jewish suburbanites begin to crowd on to the Conservative benches, and in their ambition they may not differ one jot from their non-Jewish colleagues. In the meantime I prefer to look back with some pride on the gallery of eccentrics, the wilful and principled Jews who enlivened the political scene: Emanuel Shinwell, Sydney Silverman, Keith Joseph, Leo Abse, Ian Mikardo, and even Nigel Lawson. If British Jews have ascended to few of the highest offices in political life, their political contributions to the life of the nation have nonetheless been considerable and often honourable.

Reaching out: Zionism and Soviet Jewry

THE enemies of the Jews have muttered darkly about dual loyalty ever since the establishment of the State of Israel in 1948, as if to suggest that support for Israel somehow undermines devotion to Britain. In fact what many diaspora Jews feel is a joint loyalty: their native country commands their affection, if only for having accepted them or their forebears as refugees, but they are also devoted to the welfare of Israel. Certainly in the case of British Jews, there is no contradiction, since, whatever the stance of British governments towards Israel, it is almost impossible to envisage circumstances in which British Jews would have to make a choice between the two nations. Nevertheless it remains a sensitive point, which is probably why organizations such as the Anglo-Jewish Association keep pledging their loyalty to sovereign and nation even though nobody questions it.

Zionism, of course, has been around for almost as long as Judaism itself. That the Jews will one day return to their land has been an article of faith for millennia. Only there can the Jewish desire to serve God and His commandments be completely fulfilled. Both the Seder services during Passover and the service on Yom Kippur conclude with the fervent wish: 'Next year in Jerusalem . . .' That longing is an ancient one, but it only became a feasible option for the diaspora when the whole idea of nationhood gathered political force in the nineteenth century. That goal of nationhood, which could be put at the service of Jewish aspirations, was also the basis of opposition to Zionism. Among more assimilated Jews and their religious leaders, especially among the stalwarts of the Spanish and Portuguese Congregation, Zionism was seen as a threat to a social position that had long been worked for by Anglo-Jewry. Certain individuals might still experience difficulties or encounter obstacles, but essentially, by the late nineteenth century, British Jews differed from other Britons only in their religious practices. To have adopted Zionism would have laid them open to the accusation that they questioned their future in the country of their birth, that their true loyalties did indeed lie elsewhere. Nothing could have been further from the truth. It was one thing to donate money to support Jewish settlements in Palestine; it was quite another to campaign for a Jewish State.

For the immigrants at the end of the century it was a different matter entirely. For centuries they had wandered through Europe, driven from their villages, never rooted, constantly uneasy, often persecuted. And now, once again in their long history, Jews in their hundreds of thousands were being forced to flee and settle in remote lands. No wonder that their eyes lit up at the prospect that one day the Jews would have a home of their own from which no ruler could ever expel them again. No more pogroms! No more anti-Semitism! The promised land might not flow instantly with milk and honey, but there at least the Jews would be masters of their own fate. Many Jews who remained behind in Poland and Russia to suffer the oppression from which their fellows had had the fortune or resolve to escape, they too were drawn by the hope that Zionism represented. The only question was where this land was to be located. Many early Zionists were by no means committed to the idea that the Jews should settle in Palestine. Anywhere would do, as long as it became a Jewish home. The body that promoted this vague brand of Zionism, the Jewish Territorial Organization, did attract support from some Anglo-Jewish grandees, including the then Lord Rothschild. Nevertheless it was the Palestine-based brand that attracted most popular support, to the alarm of the Establishment, as encapsulated in Edwin Montagu's famous remark to Lloyd George: 'All my life I have been trying to get out of the ghetto. You want to force me back there!'

The protestations were in vain, and the Balfour Declaration, accepting in principle the notion of a Jewish homeland in Palestine, was signed in 1917. The only little problem was its implementation. There was opposition not only from a rump of Anglo-Jewry that still loathed any notion that could lead to accusations of dual loyalty being levelled against them, but from Conservative rabble-rousers on the grounds that doing the Jews a good turn would antagonize Britain's friends in the Arab world. There was also opposition from some of the Orthodox, for whom Zionism was part of the religious fulfilment of the Jews, not a political expedient for the convenience of the diaspora.

But Zionism had its allies too. The Labour Party had always been staunchly Zionist. The left-wing Zionist group, Poale Zion, in at the founding of the party, remains an affiliated organization to this day. According to Leo Abse, the Nonconformist tradition from which Labour drew great strength was often thoroughly sympathetic to Zionism: 'The Welsh have always had a strong commitment to the Holy Land. Indeed, my grandfather used to be invited to go round the chapels in the Welsh valleys. They accepted that a Jew was part of the Chosen People and would be redeemed and go to Zion.' After 1948, despite Bevin's attempts to hinder Jewish settlement in Palestine, a powerful element in the Labour Party remained sympathetic to Israel if only because the kibbutz movement was so resoundingly successful a manifestation of socialism in practice. Poale Zion, though still in existence, has lost all influence, Incompetently organized, it has become little more than a vehicle for Jewish Labour supporters to find their way on to a constituency General Management Committee.

Antagonism to Zionist principles is very much a thing of the past, except for the few bands of Chasidic fanatics who reject the existence of the State of Israel on the grounds that the Messiah has not yet come and that the State as presently constituted is a secular nation inimical to the deepest Jewish aspirations. Marjorie Moos, a founder of the Liberal Synagogue, did confirm that the early Liberals, such as Claude Montefiore and Lily Montagu, were anti-Zionist. 'I still am anti,' she declared robustly. 'I wish there never had been such a place, because I think it's done harm. I think the Jews have to learn to live in the world. But I say thank God for Israel because the harassed Jews from Germany could find a home there. But I don't think they've done what they could have done with their land, and I've been proved right: there's not an inch of safety in Israel.' That is a distinctly confused reaction, combining an outdated ideological opposition with practical reasons why the new nation is doomed to fail.

Miss Moos's own rabbi, David Goldberg, describes himself as a very committed Zionist, despite his personal opposition to much that is going on in Israel today. There are no significant variations in their attachment to Zionist principles among the various synagogal groupings. The Orthodox respond to the idea because it is embedded in their liturgy, inseparable from their religious belief. For Progressive Jews, Zionism was a potential cure for the ills – anti-Semitism and persecution – that had

355

always afflicted the Jewish people. Many left-wing Jews, uneasy about Israel's drift to the political right, have appeased their conscience without compromising their Zionism by assisting organizations striving to bring about equality between Jew and Arab. And most importantly of all, in many ways, Zionism also provided a means of Jewish identification for those who lacked religious belief. After the Holocaust, belief in a loving and righteous God became unsustainable for many Jews, but their sense of fellowship with their co-religionists could be expressed by helping to bring into existence and sustain this marvellous haven, this Jewish homeland. To be a Zionist was a way of being Jewish without being religious, and for many it still is. The Holocaust demonstrated with hideous thoroughness that there is no safety in dispersion. The only solution, it seemed to many, was for Jews to govern themselves in their own land. The existence of Israel provided an incentive for Jews to survive; where there had been devastation there was now creation and growth, and this mesmerized religious and secular Jew alike. The theatrical manager Michael Codron, who doesn't attend synagogue and doesn't go out of his way to mix in Jewish circles, nevertheless makes a point of keeping up with the latest news from Israel. R. B. Kitaj, equally non-observant, is a regular reader of the *Jerusalem Post*: 'As far as Israel is concerned, I don't miss a trick.' Some religious leaders, and not just among the Orthodox, are wary of making any direct association of Jewish nationhood with Jewish survival. David Goldberg and John Rayner give the following warning, which must have a kernel of truth in it: 'To give one's total loyalty to the idea of the State is not only an embarrassing nineteenth-century anachronism but also, by Judaism's ethical standards, a form of idolatry. The survival of the Jewish people, through its many vicissitudes over the centuries, has clearly owed more to fidelity to religious teachings than it has to attachment to a strip of land.'[1]

To some, Zionism became a badge of Jewishness – notably for two of the great Anglo-Jewish clans of this century, the Markses and the Sieffs, who between them founded and managed the Marks and Spencer chain. The Sieff household was not a religious one, though Friday nights and the major festivals were observed. 'They associated davening with poverty,' remarked Anthony Blond, the nephew of Simon Marks. 'Their religion wasn't Judaism at all – it was Zionism.' The family patriarchs were close personal friends of Chaim Weizmann in Manchester; Rebecca Sieff founded WIZO; Teddy Sieff was chairman of the Joint Israel Appeal; and Marcus Sieff and his son David are closely associated with the Weizmann

Institute. Teddy's widow Lois, an American by birth, freely admits that her primary identification with Judaism is through Zionism. She does have an excuse, however. When I met her, she briskly declared: 'My father was Jewish but my mother wasn't, so strictly speaking I'm not Jewish at all. Wanna go home?'

The two clans were a formidable team thirty years ago, but the current generation, with the obvious exception of Marcus Sieff and his family, is far less active in Jewish affairs. The present Lord Marks, for example, does not participate in the Anglo-Jewish community. Dame Simone Prendergast, a Marks by birth, is very conscious of her Jewish identity despite an essentially secular upbringing, and she is active in the Central British Fund for World Jewish Relief. When she married out, she did not scandalize her worldly family, but her uncle Simon Marks did comment: 'We have been such good Zionists that we have forgotten how to be Jewish.' Lord Sieff himself has managed to combine his lengthy career as one of Britain's most successful retailers with a deep involvement in Israeli culture. Yet like so many other Anglo-Jewish grandees, he keeps his distance from the religious and lay establishments, no doubt on the sound principle that he has better things to do with his time. Much of his philanthropy seems to be prompted by a kind of *noblesse oblige*. Referring to Jack Heinz, he revealingly writes: 'Our acquaintance of over fifty years has been celebrated most years by an annual lunch, just the two of us, one frequent topic of discussion being what can be done to help solve the problem of feeding the Third World.'[2]

After 1948, of course, the character of Zionism was bound to change. Logically, Zionism should have self-destructed, since its principal aim had been achieved. But there was more to Zionism than the founding of a Jewish State, as Arieh Handler explains: 'The basic idea of Zionism was not just the establishment of the State, though that was of course an important stage. The final stage is to make sure that the majority of Jews should live in that State, and we are very far away from that. Secondly, if we can't all live in Israel, we should make sure that Zionism in an ideological sense – not just a political or fund-raising sense – should really be the centre of Jewish life throughout the world. What is meant by Zionism is not just partnership, but that Jewish education, Jewish religion, everything connected with Jewish life, should be connected with Israel. This has not yet been achieved. There are still many people who say that the diaspora is as fertile a ground as Israel for the expression of Judaism.'

Now that Israel is forty years old, it is interesting to see how the various

357

religious groups jockey for position when it comes to claiming credit for the realization of Zionist dreams. The fact is that there was intense opposition to Zionism from all camps. Some Orthodox Jews regarded the inevitable secularism of the proposed State with horror. Anglicized Reform Jews, on the other hand, were so dismayed by the prospect of accusations of dual loyalty that they expunged references to the return to Zion from the prayer-books. The strictly Orthodox Rabbi David is especially critical of Reform Jews in this respect: 'Without Orthodox Jews', he insists, with more passion than accuracy, 'you wouldn't have Zionism. Only now is the Reform movement coming round to saying they support Israel. Before that, they had no interest in a Jewish State – they say we are part of the country we live in. Orthodox Jews pray three times a day and our whole aspiration is to go back to the Holy Land. Zionism started about a hundred years ago, and what stirred it? The original Zionists weren't interested in Judaism. They were willing to take Uganda or Argentina. Only we said there is nowhere else besides Israel. And if you look at Israel, you'll see that it's the religious people who are going out there now. The Orthodox are remaining there, building the country, increasing the population. My children are sent to study there, and many stay behind and live in Israel. Whether you say we agree with what the State does or doesn't do, that's a different matter. But we want Eretz Yisroel. For us, not Arabs, for us. We want to live there, because there are *mitzvot* that we can't fulfil outside Israel.'

The rabbi's Jewish chauvinism is not, in my view, very appealing, but he voices a view widely held in Orthodox circles. There are other Orthodox Jews, however, who bitterly oppose the whole notion of the Jewish State. At Yakar one evening, Rabbi Michael Rosen pitted two Orthodox Jews against each other in debate: Rabbi Shimon Felix, an American resident in Israel for fifteen years, and Dr Sifman, a doctor in Golders Green. The rabbi put the case for religious Zionism. In brief, the religious argument is that learned commentators more or less agree that it is a *mitzvah* to live in Israel, though the injunction can be ignored if it would be dangerous to fulfil it. That qualification no longer applies. Moreover, the whole thrust of the Torah is that Jews belong in Israel, where the study of Torah and the keeping of *mitzvot* are more easily fulfilled since working and social life harmonize with religious obligation. Dr Sifman replied that the early Zionists wanted Israel to be a State like any other; Theodore Herzl opposed rabbinical interference in running the proposed State. Thus, for Orthodox Jews to co-operate with Zionism is a desecration, since it puts Jews on a par with any other people. If every action of Israel's secular leaders flouts what religious Jews stand for, then Zionism cannot be a Jewish movement. Thus it is better not to live in an Israel among Jews who teach that the Torah is a legend and that God doesn't exist.

This apocalyptic vision was dismissed by Rabbi Felix as a fantasy. That the Zionist founders were non-religious, he argued, is no disgrace. Nor should it prevent religious Jews from aspiring to build a religious society in Israel. The notion that non-religious people have hijacked the idea of Eretz Yisroel is absurd: 'Let's go to Israel and outvote them! What's more, this strategy is working. There are more *yeshivot* being established all the time. The Orthodox should have the grace to acknowledge that they are now able to live in Israel thanks to the efforts of non-religious Jews. Irreligious Jews can also have a good idea! Jonas Salk was not an Orthodox Jew, but that doesn't lessen our thankfulness for his discoveries.' To which Dr Sifman sniffily replied that Jews are not dependent on the State of Israel for their existence. Rabbi Felix irritated Dr Sifman by making the increasingly plausible point that religious anti-Zionists feel guilty that it was the Zionists who got up and did something by founding the State: 'The jealousy and guilt are awesome! Israel is a secular State because the Orthodox ignored the stage when it was born!' Dr Sifman began to retreat into piety: 'Torah is the only law, Torah is the only path to Jewish survival. Therefore it is unrealistic to think that a secular State and secular education can do any good at all.' The audience groaned. There were Orthodox men and women in the hall, but none supported Sifman, and a rabbi next to me murmured: 'Sifman's argument is unbelievable. It's frightening. It proves that a man can be competent in one sphere and totally immature in another.'

The religious anti-Zionist movement, though still on the fringes of the community, is more potent than it was twenty years ago. A few well-heeled Chasidic groups, such as Satmar, support and finance the anti-Zionists. Organized under the banner of Neturei Karta (the Guardians of the City), the Orthodox anti-Zionists publish and distribute literature that is completely outlandish. They predict imminent doom, for the heresy of Zionism imperils the very survival of Judaism. Only they hold the key, with their unflinching belief in Torah, and their sure knowledge that the return to Zion will only take place once the Messiah has come. Supporters of Neturei Karta can occasionally be seen with a placard outside 10 Downing Street, but their impact on Anglo-Jewry is negligible. Indeed, it would be hard for even a mildly anti-Zionist group to make much impact, since Anglo-Jewish Zionism is so pervasive.

Quite apart from the innumerable political and fund-raising organizations, there is a rarely convened network of influential Jews that takes little active part in the Zionist movement – until Israel is perceived as endangered. This network is no sinister band of conspirators but an often spontaneous coalition of concerned Jews. When in May 1967 President Nasser closed the Strait of Tiran, among the writers who signed a letter of protest to the *Sunday Times* were Harold Pinter, John Gross, Al Alvarez, and Denis Norden, none of whom was a conspicuous figure in the Jewish community. In the two months that followed the Yom Kippur War of 1967, British Jews raised £16 million. A meeting of show business and other celebrities at the Café Royal raised £300,000 in a single hour, much of it from Jews with no formal affiliation to the community. Ten years later Siegmund Warburg, who also stayed aloof from formal Anglo-Jewry, participated, together with Edmund de Rothschild and the ubiquitous Arnold Goodman, in talks to promote peace between Anwar Sadat and Menachem Begin.

In more peaceful times there is no need for such extreme efforts. Fund-raising for Israel is in the thoroughly capable hands of the Joint Israel Appeal (JIA), rather to the irritation of competing domestic charities, which can't help wishing to see more of that largesse devoted to helping the local community. The JIA has established committees within just about every profession in which Jews are well represented: among dentists and jewellers, fur-trade workers and caterers, property developers and market traders. Its honorary officers include Lord Sieff, Gerald Ronson, Trevor Chinn and Cyril Stein, who between them can twist quite a few arms. Other support groups include WIZO, the women's organization founded by Rebecca Sieff more than seventy years ago, and Emunah. Neither is political, and the money raised is earmarked for good works in Israel, such as homes for the handicapped. The forty-four groups that comprise Emunah support religious institutions, mostly for children. These smaller groups are essentially an outlet for good intentions. In terms of Israel's perpetually stricken economy, the British annual donations of £25 million are insignificant.

That there should be dozens of these support groups, all doing their bit to raise a few thousand pounds, is understandable; it appeases any guilt British Jews may feel for not having made the commitment of actually moving to Israel. What is more curious is the existence of a plethora of political Zionist organizations. Mapam is a non-religious socialist group, Mizrachi a religious socialist group, Herut the British arm of the Herut party (the main constituent in Israel's ruling Likud coalition), and Pro-Zion is another religious group except that it is linked to the Progressive synagogues. The leader of British Mizrachi, Arieh Handler, helped me find my way through this maze: 'Twenty-five years ago we used to be divided in this country between the bourgeois religious Zionists and the more socialist religious Zionists. Today it's one movement worldwide. Our task is to be the centre, to make sure that there is no break between the secular and the religious, even if we have different views. Israeli life should be based on Torah but it should not exclude people. The secular should also be part of the nation. There's one other group with a strong ideological force, Herut, who argue against giving up any part of Israel. Then you have groups that call themselves general Zionists or united Zionists, people who say they are non-political – but they still have their party! The Zionist Federation became the institution which represented the Zionists in this country – until 1983, when Herut and Mizrachi walked out. We should reorganize all these little groups because after forty years you can't have exactly the same structure as you had in 1948.' But entrenched Zionist groups have an interest in maintaining the status quo. Participation in the World Zionist Congress and its elections gives Zionist bureaucrats potential access to the considerable resources and patronage of the Jewish Agency.

Such influence and political control are increasingly anachronistic, for as Mr Handler himself admits: 'These Zionist groups haven't had much impact on what happens in Israel. Mizrachi is trying to influence our people in Israel on the issue of dealing with the Arabs and making peace negotiations possible. The other groups push for what they believe in. But when it comes to Anglo-Jewry really giving a lead, it's very weak. You don't hear the voice of Anglo-Jewry in the world councils of Jewish life. One of the reasons is that Anglo-Jewry never had a strong ideological attitude to anything. Anglo-Jewish life is expressed too much in rituals, in going to synagogues. That's also very important, but nothing is done to make the British Jew a little more conscious of his responsibility to our people as a whole.' The Israel-based groups try to foster that sense of responsibility by dispatching Israeli emissaries to countries such as Britain to provide a first-hand link between Israel and diaspora Jews. On their agenda is the wish to persuade diaspora Jews to emigrate, to bolster Israel's population. The structure seems to confirm the old jibe that a

Zionist is someone who collects money to hire somebody else to persuade a third person to settle in Israel.

Since 1948 some 34,000 British Jews have emigrated to Israel. Going on *aliyah* is a mixed blessing: a boon for Israel, but a further weakening of Anglo-Jewry. For some it was an expression of youthful idealism, for others a means of starting a new life in the hope that it might be more satisfactory than the old one. Many couples emigrated on reaching retirement age: a pleasant climate and an inexhaustible supply of bridge partners combined with Zionist ideals drew them to Israel. Since the invasion of Lebanon, *aliyah* has become a less inviting prospect to diaspora Jews, not necessarily because they disapproved of Israeli policies but because they are reminded every day that Israel can be a dangerous place. Economic uncertainties, in particular Israel's high rate of inflation, was a further disincentive. Between 1983 and 1987 the number of British immigrants to Israel halved. The statistics suggest that it is the older people who are staying here, while younger people are continuing to settle in Israel. It is reasonable to suppose that a fair number of the young people who go on *aliyah* are born-again Jews, newly converted to one sect or another.

Those who settle in Israel have established a clear relationship with the Jewish State. Those who choose not to go must work out their own stance *vis-à-vis* Israel. This posed no great problems when, as in 1967, Israel was in peril. Israeli military success in 1967 and 1973 won the country immense admiration. It was easy to be a Zionist then. Since 1982 the relationship between Israel and the diaspora has been more vexed, for there are many Jews whose pride in Israel has diminished, even evaporated, since the invasion of Lebanon. The disturbances in the Occupied Territories in late 1987 and 1988 have put further strains on Zionist sympathies, as we shall see in the chapter that follows.

It is appropriate to mention here the various campaigns on behalf of Soviet Jewry, if only because they too provide a means of identification for Jews who may not be especially religious. The National Council for Soviet Jewry co-ordinates a number of organizations: Exodus, the Reform movement's campaign, the so-called 35s, the Association of Jewish Ex-Servicemen, whose members contact Jewish veterans of the Red Army, and a new group called Refusenik. An All-Party Committee for the Release of Soviet Jewry is active in the House of Commons. From the very beginnings of the campaign, according to Colin Shindler, 'we worked for Soviet Jews rather than for Soviet dissidents. The Jews simply wanted to leave the country and didn't want to change the social system. Just as different nationalities could go and live in their national republics within the multi-republic Soviet Union, Jews could go to their Jewish homeland. The Soviets had accepted this basic idea, since they recognized Israel and also accepted the idea of family reunification. From a tactical point of view, to talk about overthrowing the system was far more dangerous and counter-productive than to call for the simple right to leave the country. It was the right way to proceed, and it did succeed. There were divisions about how one reacted to dissidents. I always took a very liberal line on it, and strongly supported people like Sakharov, who helped a lot of Jews. But there was a policy here at one time to ignore such dissidents totally, because they thought by talking about Sakharov it would make the campaign for Jews to leave much more difficult.'

One of the best-known groups is the 35s, the Women's Campaign for Soviet Jewry, which was founded in May 1971, and has retained the attention of the media by its skill at tactical gimmickry which always guaranteed the presence of cameras and the questions of reporters. The campaign works not only through political and diplomatic and trade-union channels, but by encouraging correspondence between Russian refuseniks and British families. The London offices, behind an unmarked door not far from Golders Green, are amazingly cramped, and half of my conversations were conducted on the stairs. Files and pamphlets are piled up in the corridors, and the tiny rooms are filled with up to five people in each. Posters from campaigns old and current curl from the walls. The co-chairman of the 35s is a remarkably good-humoured – considering the working conditions – and evidently tough woman called Margaret Rigal, who is far from satisfied with the response from the Anglo-Jewish community.

'The Jewish community as a whole is remarkably good at ignoring anything to do with Soviet Jewry. It makes them feel very guilty. We find a tremendous desire to believe everything is all right in the Soviet Union, and a tremendous desire not to feel that they've got to do any work. If you have a group of lectures, you can usually be sure that the one on Soviet Jewry will get the smallest audience. A lot of people, particularly when we started, said that if the Jews in the Soviet Union kept quiet and didn't make a nuisance of themselves they'd be perfectly all right. People suggested it was only the troublemakers who got into trouble. Nowadays that attitude has disappeared. The young are marvellous, from all shades of opinion within Anglo-Jewry and outside it. They've been allowed to go out and shout slogans and picket theatres but they have very good relations with the police. Young people discovered that when they became militant on the subject of Soviet Jewry, they then went to the National Union of Students and received much more respect because they had started to make a noise. But many ex-refugees find it very difficult to work for people whose troubles only slightly resemble their own, and before they can bring themselves to work for Soviet Jewry they have to accept their own past. When we come across people whose roots are in Germany or Austria, we have to tread very carefully because many of them resent any suggestion that other people are suffering as much as they have done.' A colleague added, with some bitterness, that the Establishment kept saying what a great job the 35s and others were doing, but failed to give them more concrete support. Fund-raising is a constant nightmare.

Mrs Rigal admits, unapologetically, that for many supporters of the campaign it has become a primary form of identification with the Jewish community. 'Definitely. It allows all parts of the community to act together. As far as I know, it's the only subject on which rabbis of all opinions usually get together without too much trouble.' Nor does she regret devoting so much energy to so distant a cause: 'I never apologize for working for Soviet Jewry. If everybody focuses on a small patch, they are far more effective than when working over a big field. When any victim of Soviet injustice wants help, they know where to come.' The campaign will not flag because of *glasnost*. According to Soviet Jewry campaigners, rates of emigration have slowed down in recent years and there are no grounds for self-satisfaction. Any slight increase in the number of exit visas granted has been undermined by an increase in Soviet anti-Semitism. The very act of applying for an exit visa inevitably leads to harassment at the workplace and at schools in an attempt to crush the morale of applicants. The campaign must battle against Soviet resistance to losing more of their best scientists and technicians. Colin Shindler admits that some of the activists in the Soviet Jewry organization may be motivated by guilt, but he doesn't think that this vitiates the cause: 'To some people the campaign is a psychological reaction to the failure to save Jews during the Holocaust. Now they perceive a concrete problem, they want to act. I don't think that's unworthy.'

– 27 –

Opinion and silence: responding to Israel

T
o assess the reaction of the Anglo-Jewish Establishment to Israel's response to the uprisings on the West Bank and in Gaza, I sat in on the January 1988 meeting of the Board of Deputies at which the situation was to be discussed for the first time. Dr Kopelowitz made a statement deploring the loss of life in Israel, where dozens (soon to be hundreds) of Palestinian demonstrators had been shot by Israeli troops. He pointed to Israeli efforts to improve the lot of refugees in the camps despite obstacles put in its way. Some deputies attacked Mrs June Jacobs, who chairs the Board's Foreign Affairs Committee, for co-signing a letter published in the *Independent* critical of Israeli tactics, and describing in a radio interview the events on the West Bank as 'quite appalling and absolutely horrific'. She was rapped over the knuckles by Dr Kopelowitz on the grounds that her statements were contrary to Board policy – even though the Board had no policy, or if it had, nobody knew what it was.

Mrs Jacobs made a brief speech defending her right to speak out as an individual and to criticize what she perceived as 'an erosion of rights' within Israel. Dr Kopelowitz declared the matter closed, but some deputies kept it open for a while longer. Michael Fidler, a former Conservative MP and former president of the Board, suggested Mrs Jacobs should resign and attacked remarks critical of Israel made by the Bishop of Dudley on a radio interview that morning. Since the BBC had broadcast a measured rebuttal of the bishop's remarks by Greville Janner immediately afterwards, there didn't appear to be strong grounds for complaint. Fidler then attacked David Mellor, the Foreign Office minister who had expressed indignation at army tactics to an Israeli officer.

Television cameras had been rolling as Mr Mellor spoke out, and the incident seemed set to become a *cause célèbre*. Fidler maintained that it was Israel's primary duty to restore law and order, and that critical remarks from British ministers were out of place. It was, said Fidler, important for Anglo-Jewry to be united in its support for Israel. Another deputy, Michael Goldblatt from Finchley, attacked Board members (presumably Mrs Jacobs) who irresponsibly 'undermined the elected government of Israel from a safe distance'.

Colin Shindler pointed out that Mr Mellor had at least provoked the Board into discussing the situation in Israel. It appeared that the Board was more interested in public relations than realities, and he opposed any witch-hunts led by Michael Fidler. Shindler's remarks were greeted with only tepid applause. Mrs Hilary Curtis, a deputy from Oxford, supported Shindler and argued that as Israel's friends it was our duty to voice our legitimate concerns. It was wrong to use guns in response to stones. Another deputy attacked Mrs Jacobs, saying that Greville Janner's dictum should be followed: 'Criticize in private, support in public.' Other deputies echoed this view. A Mr Lewin added a melodramatic touch: 'All our enemies have risen against us!' He defended the enlarged frontiers of Israel as a halachic conception: 'Give away Gaza and the West Bank, and you may as well give away Jerusalem!' This was greeted with a mixture of applause and laughter. A Cockfosters deputy supported Mr Lewin and compared the situation to Munich in 1938, though the nature of the analogy was unclear. A Mr Feinbaum stated that the British press and government didn't back Israel – as though they were under some obligation to do so. Consequently British Jews must stand behind the Israeli government and stand up for themselves.

The respected solicitor Aubrey Rose added a new note when he applauded Colin Shindler and Hilary Curtis for adhering to Jewish values. But he also stressed the concern for Jewish security, and agreed that the British media were biased against Israel. As he was speaking I was flicking through that day's edition of the *Sunday Times*, which printed opposite its leader page a lengthy article by the Israeli ambassador, which struck me as a curious way of expressing bias. Greville Janner told his fellow deputies that they couldn't duck the fact that forty unarmed people had been killed by Israeli troops, nor that the camps, for whatever reasons, are wretched places. 'If we fail to express our concern about these matters, we'll get no sympathy from those among whom we live. We have enough enemies as it is, without going out of our way to make more. We must try in every way we can to influence the media not to give Israel's case but to give a fair presentation of the case.' The debate was concluded by the head of the Israel Committee, Mr Klausner, who attacked Colin Shindler for being 'negative' and added that 'we have to recognize our enemies'.

So. There was a clear divergence of views, but only a small minority of deputies expressed criticisms of Israeli policy. Two other views appeared to prevail. First, that we had no business telling the Israelis how to deal with their internal problems, and that they had a duty to restore law and order, just as any other country would in similar circumstances. Second, that there was disquiet about what was happening, but it was inadvisable to voice that concern in public. Presiding over this jockeying of different views was Dr Kopelowitz, who never wavered in his view that Anglo-Jewry must present a united front and express no open criticism of Israel. My own view, which there is no point disguising, is that since Israel itself is deeply divided on such issues as how to deal with riots and whether or not to negotiate with the Palestinians – and, if so, which Palestinians – I see no reason why diaspora Jews should labour to express a non-existent unified view. Some provincial leaders were voicing profound unease and virulent criticism of Mr Shamir and Mr Rabin, but it was clear that Dr Kopelowitz and his fellow officers were determined to suppress such views if at all possible. Three months after this meeting, the President was contributing the following sunny sentence to the Board's newsletter: 'The pressures upon Israel at the moment are intense, but I have no doubt that the future will be bright and that Israel will reflect the spiritual and moral values of Judaism at their best, which have been our strength and support through the Dispersion.'

Of course the Don't Criticize Israel brigade does have a case, though it usually makes it ineptly. It was expressed in its most aggressive form to me by Stanley Kalms. 'Compared to other countries such as South Africa, what's happening in Israel is nothing, but it gets a disproportionate amount of criticism, because we're the most civilized people in the Middle East. Why should Jews behave better than anybody else? England fought against Israel in 1948, and it has no right to have an attitude like this towards Israel, but it does. That's not to say that those of us in England aren't very concerned. Being a Western liberal society, we are very concerned about Gaza. Of course we are. But do we have a view? We protest against the bad treatment, but we have no view of how to deal with the situation. No one would argue if constructive views could be put forth, but unfortunately no one has a constructive view. There is no solution.

367

Time, maybe, or a permanent conflict, like Northern Ireland. So by criticizing, all you do is weaken Israel's resolve. Writing to the non-Jewish press doesn't add one iota to the solution. The diaspora has to be 100 per cent solid.'

I asked Kalms how he could reconcile his view that the diaspora had to be solid in its support with the fact that even the Israeli government is split down the middle. To which he replied: 'Ah, but that's Israel's style, its extrovert, rather unpleasant, Byzantine political system expressing itself.' (Funny, I thought Israel was a democracy.) 'Go there! Then you'll see there's a unity there, a lot of people all running in different directions but all ending up in the same place. In forty years, Israel's done more than England in 400 bloody years.' I enjoyed the rhetoric, but it offered no argument. Nor could I find much intellectual meat in the passionate defence of Israel presented by George Weidenfeld, who defined himself to me as a tribalist rather than a nationalist Jew, and whose loyalty to Israel remains unwavering. In his view, the Israelis are reacting and not acting: 'I have nothing but admiration for the self-restraint of the Israelis. Their record is exemplary. Jews abroad must bless the consensus and not take sides in the electoral process in Israel.' The consensus? Ivan Lawrence, however, attempted a more reasoned defence: 'Israel was surprised by the strength of the uprising, and therefore was not militarily prepared. Unforgivable, but understandable. Anybody in any country in those circumstances would have behaved in exactly the same way and it's hypocritical of countries to pretend that they wouldn't. One of the things that makes me so staunchly pro-Israel – not necessarily pro-government – is that we want to get rid of the hypocrisy, we want to tell people the facts, that Israel has rehoused 10,000 families from Gaza with its poor re-sources. The world has got to convince the Arabs that continued enmity with Israel is just completely unacceptable. When that message gets home the Arabs will make peace with Israel.' He lamented the lack of moderate Palestinian leaders with whom Israel could negotiate, a line of argument sadly reminiscent of the South Africa government's view that they will negotiate with any black leaders except the ones favoured by the blacks themselves.

Time and again the response of the Anglo-Jewish Establishment is to focus on the Arabs' failure to respond to the plight of the refugees in their camps; the unacceptability of the PLO as a negotiating body; Israel's need to restore law and order; the distortions of the situation as portrayed in the news media; the intractability of the problem – hence the Northern

Ireland analogy – which somehow justifies abandoning any attempt to find a political solution; the hypocrisy of Israel's critics who excoriate Israel for the slightest violation of human rights while turning a blind eye to the wholesale violations of such rights in most Arab countries; a resentment of British criticism of Israel in the light of British behaviour in Palestine before 1948. There is a desperate, and entirely understandable, desire on the part of Anglo-Jewry to give every benefit of every doubt to Israel. To concede that the Israeli government has pursued unacceptable policies undermines not only Israel but the delicate and intimate relationship between the diaspora and Israel, as though a trust had been betrayed. Naturally, the Israelis, through the ambassador and other emissaries stationed in London, cuddle up to the Anglo-Jewish Establishment to the greatest possible extent. By sending British dignitaries on 'fact-finding tours' to Israel and allowing them to meet Israeli ministers and public figures, they bolster the domestic reputation of those dignitaries. It's pleasant for an officer of the Board or the JIA to be able to say, 'As I was saying to Shimon Peres last week . . .' It's no bad thing that Anglo-Jewish leaders should be well informed about political developments in Israel, but the cosiness of the relationship makes it very difficult for those leaders to deviate from the official Israeli position.

During the bitter debates of 1988 Dr Kopelowitz continued to pretend that there was no significant dissension. The president of the United Synagogue, Sidney Frosh, declared in April 1988: 'The United Synagogue is supporting Israel every inch of the way.'[1] Consensus had become a form of deafness and blindness. In a bewilderingly opaque remark, Dr Kopelowitz told me: 'You try to make a consensus when you can. If you can't, then you can't speak out too openly. I've had to try, and I think reasonably successfully, to keep the community together. The community hasn't broken apart. There have been strong views here and there, but up till now the thing hasn't come to pieces.' The best reading of such complacent remarks is that he has been so busy papering over the cracks that he hasn't noticed that the walls are falling down. As Chaim Bermant incisively remarked some years ago, and it is truer than ever, 'In recent years [the diaspora] has been used merely as a claque to cheer on every turn and twist of Israeli policy and every caprice, no matter how unreasonable or extreme, and as such it has harmed both the Jewish State and the Jewish people.'[2] The long silence of the Board, followed by its repeated refusal to criticize any aspect of Israeli policy, contrasted with the reactions of American-Jewish organizations. In January Rabbi Alexander

Schindler, president of the Union of American Hebrew Congregations (Reform), described Yitzhak Rabin's justification of beatings as 'morally wrong and practically unavailing', and Ruth Popkin, the president of Hadassah, the largest Jewish women's movement, said she was 'appalled' by the policy.[3] Rabbi Arthur Hertzberg, a vice-president of the World Jewish Congress, said, to the fury of Michael Fidler, that diaspora support for Israeli policies was 'counter-productive, disastrous and insane'.[4] He has also written that all 'recent studies of the attitudes of American Jews toward Israel have shown that a majority by at least two to one reject the hard-line policies of the Likud'.[5] Meanwhile, in Britain the phoney consensus continued to stifle dissenting voices. The Anglo-Jewish leadership chose not to lead but to tag along in Mr Shamir's wake.

To see how consensus was coming along, I attended the opening session of the Zionist Federation conference one evening in late March 1988, when the Palestinian uprising was at its height. The first thing that surprised me was the low attendance. There couldn't have been more than a hundred people in the hall, even though the session was to be addressed by the Israeli ambassador. The elderly gentlemen who comprise the honorary officers of the Federation ranged themselves on the platform above a banner that, poignantly, read: WE STAND BY ISRAEL, as though 'Israel' were still some ideal that all Jews could subscribe too, as though its own government weren't bitterly divided between a Likud prime minister and a Labour foreign secretary. Dr Stephen Roth, the chairman of the Federation, set the tone by referring in his opening address to Israel as 'attacked, criticized, misunderstood' – though he added: 'internally torn apart in a search for the right path'. The ambassador announced, in defiance of all the facts: 'The situation has exploded on us unanticipated.' The riots had been organized by the PLO and Islamic fundamentalists. He deplored the presence of the largest foreign press corps in the world, which offered potential rioters an unmissable series of photo opportunities. Israel gained the Territories, he insisted, not by conquest but by repelling Arab aggression. Occupation follows war and lasts until there is peace, but – with the exception of Egypt – there is no peace because Israel has no partners in peace.

Dr Roth then mentioned that the Federation had decided to open this session to the public because of the widespread interest in the topic throughout the community. 'It is preferable to express those views here than in the letter columns of the *Guardian*.' He didn't want to exclude constructive criticism, but he attacked those who criticized from outside the Zionist movement. He then called on four honorary officers of the ZF in a row to make their speeches. The veteran Zionist Dr S. S. Levenberg, a man who commands great respect but who gives very boring speeches, voiced support for the plan initiated by American Secretary of State George Shultz, which was about to come to nothing. The plan was at least an attempt to bring the parties concerned to a negotiating table, and it is to the credit of the ZF that it eventually stuck its neck out to the extent of supporting Shultz, whose efforts were being backed by almost every Western government.

The irrepressible Dr Kopelowitz spoke of Anglo-Jewry's 'unimpaired support for Israel. There is no weakening of support among the deputies' – thus demonstrating yet again his refusal to see what he doesn't like. 'Israel has faced many crises, but we must have confidence in the justice of Israel's case and must speak out on every occasion.' Pressed to give an opinion on the Shultz plan, the President of the Board told us he couldn't do so 'because I haven't got all the facts' (which hadn't prevented the Israeli foreign secretary and the Chief Rabbi from supporting it). Ninety minutes after the meeting began, the public were at last allowed to express their views. Predictably, they varied from unflinching support for Mr Shamir to the more radical views of Dr Barry Shenker, the chairman of Mapam. He pointed out that just as Jews wish to determine their fate free from external pressures in the State of Israel, so the Palestinians wish to do the same, and until we recognize this, we'll get nowhere. A former chairman of British Friends of Peace Now, Pauline Levis, asked how Jews would respond after twenty years of occupation. There's no point just castigating Palestinians as enemies, she argued, since the whole point of a peace process is that you seek an accommodation with your enemies, not with your friends.

The Israeli ambassador's embittered remarks about misrepresentation in the media echoed a view that obsesses many British Jews. To blame the messenger for the bad news is not a new stratagem for coping with unwelcome information. Nevertheless a substantial section of Anglo-Jewry seems utterly convinced that the newspapers and the BBC and probably the tea-ladies at Thames Television are engaged in a conspiracy, aided by Arab propaganda and Arab money, to present Israel in the worst possible light. Every week the *Jewish Chronicle* runs a column by Philip Kleinman, who spends his days scanning the newspapers and his evenings glued to the television set on the lookout for any sign of bias or imbalance.

To the unsleeping eyes of Mr Kleinman, the bias is constant, the imbalance as fixed as a street trader's scales. The vigilantes of the media seem perpetually astonished that the press should take so keen an interest in Israel. It has become inconvenient to recall that since its founding Israel has, with every justification, called attention to its achievements, its transformation of desert into orchard, its preservation of democracy. Now the news from Israel is no longer so good, there is resentment that the journalists haven't packed their bags and gone off to report on the comings and goings of swallows in Italy. Because diaspora Jews in particular have benefited vicariously from Israel's good image – especially during the heady days of Israel's brilliant military victories – they feel personally unsettled by the obvious deterioration of that image. Although a politician such as Ivan Lawrence is wise enough to insist: 'I don't think the image of Jewry is anything like as important as a settlement of the Arab-Israeli conflict' – he went on to say: 'Israel suffers from distortion of image. Some of it is accidental and some of it is deliberate. The deliberate distortion is done by those who are fanatically pro-Arab or because they have some personal reason why they hate Jews.'

Mr Kleinman is paid to be a watchdog of the press and can't resist sinking his teeth into the flanks of passing newsmen and television producers. What is more reprehensible is the tendency to maintain a constant barrage of criticism against the press as a way of avoiding discussion of the issues. Hayim Pinner attacked Channel 4 for showing Victor Schonfeld's film about Israel, *Shattered Dreams*, a deeply thoughtful look at changes within Israeli society. Not good enough for Mr Pinner, who denounced the film as 'yet another in a series of programmes about the Middle East which is one-sided and reflects badly on Israel,' which is an absurd distortion of Mr Schonfeld's film. Henry Guterman remarked to me, as did many other Jewish leaders, that Israel hasn't presented its case well, as though the principal problem was one of public relations. Dr Kopelowitz, at the Zionist Federation conference, actually declared: 'The most sinister evil – I repeat, the most sinister evil – is television.' Of course he doesn't mean that exactly. What he probably means is that television is being put to evil ends when it shows images he finds disturbing. At the same conference, Martin Savitt, who sits on almost every Anglo-Jewish committee you can think of, deplored the fact that the media are allowed to roam freely and interview rioters. Cameras, he insisted, are an incitement to violence, an argument identical to the South African government's insistence that disorders in the African townships can be prevented if nobody is allowed to report on them. Nor, I imagine, would Mr Savitt reject the comparison, for he advocated banning cameramen from sensitive areas, presumably on the same grounds as the ultra-Orthodox *Jewish Tribune*, which wrote in an editorial in April 1988: 'With no photographs and luridly anti-Israeli news stories on the front pages and on the screens, the rioting would have died down at a very early stage and life would have returned to normal.'

Organizations such as the ZF, the Board, the Union of Jewish Students, and BIPAC (Britain-Israel Public Affairs Committee) have formed an *ad hoc* committee to counter media bias. Readers and viewers are encouraged to flood the switchboards with complaints at the first whiff of bias. And they do. I must confess that I myself was taken aback when listening to the London radio station, LBC, one night in April 1988. I had tuned in because Dr Elizabeth Maxwell, the organizer of the conference on the Holocaust held in July 1988, was to be interviewed. It was a chat-show, and the presenter, Mark Smith, in discussing the disturbances in Israel with a caller, said that 'Zionism was an extreme form of Judaism'. He also had no idea who Martin Gilbert was, and at one point described Israel as a State that has laws that involve beating Palestinians with rocks. Mark Smith is no anti-Semite, and his remarks betrayed not so much bias as appalling ignorance. If some reporters and news editors are as ill informed and as eager to sound off on subjects they admit they know nothing about as is Mark Smith, then the Jewish community has some reason to feel concerned.

The critics of the media do have one sound point to make. News reports tend to convey what is happening in the present without examining the causes of the situation. The difficulty surely is that the media cannot append a lengthy historical essay to every news report. Moreover, the 'background' is often itself open to a variety of interpretations. Most Anglo-Jewish critics of Israeli policies do not lack an understanding of the historical roots of the situation. Perhaps the Establishment's desperate attempts to play down the unappetizing news from Israel is connected with a desire to minimize the damage that such reports may do to Anglo-Jewry in general. This certainly worries Sir Sidney Hamburger, though he was not blaming the media as such: 'We must have suffered enormously in our relationship with the non-Jewish community. I think that they see us now as the ruling class and the poor Arabs as the downtrodden people. On the other hand there are a number of people who, knowing the history of the whole creation of the State of Israel, are prepared not to excuse but at least to understand why these things have happened. What I am worried about is the effect that all this has had on the moral fibre of the Jewish community over here. I find many people who were always good Zionists who have become more lukewarm in their Zionism. People who were giving money have expressed some doubts and anxiety as to what is happening over there and whether what they are doing is right. While I can understand all these things, I feel that as a people we have to resist the danger of judging ourselves even more severely and more harshly than people outside want to. The world wants to have double standards in judging us. They want us to be constantly on moral heights that they themselves never attain.' That may well be true, but an observation of George Steiner's on the fortieth anniversary of the foundation of Israel can serve as an extension of the argument: 'The world at large may, indeed, have no right whatever to apply a double standard of ethical, political exaction to the Jew. The Jew must apply it to himself.'[6]

An unsavoury aspect of the Anglo-Jewish Establishment's defensiveness regarding criticism of Israel is that attempts are made to smear those critics as consumed with Jewish self-hatred, or with ignorance, or as playing into the hands of our enemies. Yet the criticism is coming not only from the Jewish Socialist Group, which openly sympathizes with the Palestinian cause, but from some of the most respected voices in the community. It is impossible to deny, unless you're an Anglo-Jewish leader, that the community is deeply divided on the issue. Arnold Goodman told me: 'A Jew who isn't a Zionist has something missing. But that doesn't mean that one defers to the worst voices and the most stupid precepts of people who are Zionists. I deeply deplore the present government in Israel. It appears to me to be set on a disaster course. One hopes and prays that they can be diverted. One can have great sympathy with Peres; you can't have any sympathy at all with Prime Minister Shamir. But that doesn't mean one ceases to be a Zionist. It means one remains a critical Zionist.' Sir Isaiah Berlin echoed the sentiments when he described what was happening in the Occupied Territories as stupid and criminal. Sir Monty Finniston says: 'The present impasse between Jews and Arabs on the West Bank is terrible, terrible. We've got to come to some accommodation with them.'

Ian Mikardo told me how in the 1970s when Yitzhak Rabin was prime minister, Rabin asked him what Israel should do about the Occupied Territories. 'I said: "I would give six months' notice of unilateral evacuation of 85–90 per cent of it, except for Jerusalem and a few places near the border for security. I'd say anyone as wants can have it, provided it's demilitarized. If it stops being demilitarized, we come back. I'd allow a customs corridor between the West Bank and Gaza and free port facilities." Of course that's no longer possible, but it was then. Rabin said: "Why do you say this?" And I said: "Because all history goes to show that territory which a country holds against the will of its inhabitants is not an asset, it's a hideous liability." But the biggest price that's being paid is the fact that there are hundreds and thousands of young Israelis leaving Israel. I have two Israeli grandsons. They're not in Israel. They're in Los Angeles.' William Frankel, the former editor of the *Jewish Chronicle*, also told me of prophetic conversations he'd had with Israeli leaders. 'The last time I saw Ben Gurion, who was an old friend, was about a year before he died [in 1973]. He'd always said we must return the Territories. He became very despondent about it all and said to me on that visit: "I don't have very much longer to live, and I know that I shall die in Israel. But I'm not sure that my son is going to die in Israel." He had his doubts about the future, and I have my doubts. On the whole I force myself to believe it's going to work, and that something will happen in spite of all the evidence to the contrary. But if you look at it calmly and rationally, you're bound to feel very concerned.'

Ever since the Likud government came to power in Israel, more liberal-minded Jews, in the diaspora and in Israel, have felt cause for concern. A deeper unease set in with the invasion of Lebanon in 1982, and with what appeared to be Israeli complicity in the massacres that took place inside the Palestinian camps at Sabra and Shatila. Colin Shindler recalls how troubled he was not only by Israeli government actions at that time but by official attempts to manipulate public opinion in the diaspora. 'There were tens of thousands of people demonstrating every Saturday night in Israel, but the PR machine suggested that there was a consensus where none existed either in Israel or in the diaspora. It propagated unsophisticated material designed for the non-Jewish world as part of the war of words in the public domain, but the same material was also sent to the Jews. So what was propaganda for the non-Jews was so-called information for the Jews, and this process had been taking place for a long time before Lebanon. So it's no wonder that when it came to the 1982 war, a lot of Jewish supporters of Israel were totally confused, if not devastated. There was certainly press bias which needed to be countered, but it should be recognized that it was also a mechanism for many Jews to avoid confronting the issues – it was far easier to bash the anti-Zionists. I went to a lot of meetings at that time, and basically we just sat around holding our heads. What could we do? After Sabra and Shatila there was a Peace Now meeting in London. The place was packed out. The meeting gave voice to a great sense of unease within the community which no communal leader or organization had been willing to face. Then as now, I believe that rational criticism of the bad policies of an Israeli government is actually a sign of your commitment to the State of Israel and not a manifestation of self-hatred or disengagement. We are told that we are part of the international Jewish people, and if we do not contribute our views to the debate, then effectively we disenfranchise ourselves. You can't have it both ways. We don't have the ultimate political weapon of a vote in Israel – but we are still Jews and we have a right to express our views within the Jewish world. If there's no consensus in Israel, then why shouldn't Jews in this country reflect different views, and why shouldn't those views be represented?

'I firmly believe in the old-fashioned idea that Israel – meaning the Jewish people – should be a light unto the nations. It's part of our history, our heritage, our experience. The founding fathers of the State wished to build a new society based on the vision of the prophets as well as create a haven for persecuted Jews. Ahad Ha-am said we should build a Jewish State rather than a State of Jews. Since 1967 this approach has been debased, mainly because of the influence of Likud, which doesn't care about the world outside. In 1967 the victory in the Six Day War was an uplifting experience for Jews everywhere. The emigration movement in the Soviet Union started as a direct result of this. Yet something happened between 1967 and 1973, and there was both shortsightedness and political arrogance in not coming to terms with the occupation of the West Bank. Unfortunately we are now paying for it. It's the corrosive effect on the Jewish population that is weakening Israeli society and creating schisms in the diaspora.'

Not all Zionists would agree with Shindler that Israel should be excessively concerned about ethics in a world governed by *realpolitik*. Certainly Stanley Kalms and Ivan Lawrence don't believe that Israel has a duty to behave with any special regard for ethical values, though of course they are not arguing that Israel ought to behave amorally either. My own view is that because of the peculiar circumstances of its creation, Israel does have a responsibility to behave according to the finest Jewish ethical traditions. Israel was created to put right a most terrible wrong; its very foundation was a moral act, even though it entailed to some degree a displacement of other peoples which was in itself morally questionable. Strip Israel of its ethical foundations, and its right to exist becomes open to challenge once again. Israel should attempt to be a light unto nations – even though the difficult circumstances in which the country has always found itself may mean that the attempt may not always be successful – since every act that betrays contempt for Jewish values strikes at the self-respect of Jews everywhere.

Sir Siegmund Warburg, who was so infuriated by Begin's intransigence that he refused to go to Israel while Begin held power, wrote to a friend in February 1980: 'I think that the policy of colonizing the West Bank is contrary to the interests of Israel, as not only does it expose her to great danger, but it also damages the great founding cause of Israel, that of an exemplary community built on Justice and Humanity.'[7] Anthony Blond, so passionate a Zionist that in 1967 he tried to go to Israel to fight ('although I'm a conscientious objector – that's a very typical Jewish reaction'), takes a similar view: 'I'm horrified by what's happening now. I think it's a great sadness that we formed a State which became just like any other, only more so.' Leon Brittan, with whom I discussed this difficult matter, was able, since he has at least one foot planted in the world of *realpolitik*, to summarize the dilemma most delicately: 'If you mean would I like Israel to behave better than other countries, the answer is yes. If you ask whether it would be in Israel's interests to do so, the answer is again yes, because whether we like it or not Israel will be judged differently. If you ask whether you can reasonably expect Israel to behave better than other countries – that, I think, is more questionable.'

There are more disenchanted voices too within the Jewish community. Evelyn de Rothschild diplomatically described himself as feeling 'fairly aghast' at what is happening in Israel, but added that Israeli policy was contrary to everything Jews had learnt from their parents or grandparents, who used to tell of the days when they had received beatings at the hands of their oppressors. Rothschild pointed to the irony that whenever Jews constitute a minority, they are understandably sensitive to any hostility towards them, but once they are in a majority they appear to behave in a very different manner. While supporting Israel, he also criticized the country for its 'macho arrogance'. The novelist Eva Figes told me: 'I've never been a Zionist. I've never felt any curiosity about Israel. Obviously in the 1967 War I supported Israel. But when I watch the news now I have to keep reminding myself that this is Israel and not South Africa. It always seemed to me a logically impossible position. You've got this little strip of land which firstly really belongs to somebody else, and then secondly, you want however many million Jews there are in the world to come and settle there. It's against all the ideas I associate with Jewish enlightenment. It's retrogressive in the sense that it's bringing out Jewish fundamentalism, which I find just as appalling as Arab fundamentalism.'

Jonathan Miller clearly felt some impatience at having his proclaimed indifference to Israel ruffled by events. 'I don't feel Jews are "my people". The whole idea of a people is totally repulsive to me. I only feel reluctantly that I'm English, reluctantly as any fastidious intellectual must feel at the end of the twentieth century, when you rather flinchingly attach yourself to any identity. I have no interest in Israel at all. I mean I'm interested in not seeing it obliterated, not because of the Jews, but because I don't want to see any civilized country go by the board. On the other hand I wish it were a little bit more civilized. I feel disquiet, but I don't feel "my people" are behaving badly. I sometimes feel misgivings when Jews do behave badly in Israel because I think it just brings trouble on to our own heads. When I went there, the only place where I felt any affinity was at some of the old atheistic kibbutzim. I felt, "Hey, this is rather nice, I'd feel at home here." Then I said to my wife, "Why do I feel at home here?" and she looked around and said, "Well, it's like Bedales." It's simply a place where progressive intellectuals were at work.'

Many non-Zionist Jews are uncertain about whether they have the right to criticize Israeli policies. Israel and the diaspora are interdependent – Israel is nothing without Jewishness, and Jewishness has (arguably) been enriched by the existence of a Jewish State – but what rights does that give diaspora Jews who have no personal stake in Israel? The standard Zionist view is that such Jews had better keep their thoughts to themselves. Arieh Handler put it like this: 'Israel can only exist if it feels that it is the expression of what the Jewish people really want. A person who does not see Israel as the centre of his ideal cannot and should not say what Israel should do. But a Zionist, for whom Israel is the centre of Jewish life, should be able to express his views on the society to which he wants to belong. I feel a Jewish State should be something different from any other State. If today there were no Israel, the revival in Jewish life we have today in the diaspora would not exist. And the other way round. The moment Israel loses its contact with the Jews in the diaspora, it is doomed. We cannot from here decide whether Mr Rabin should have said that the police should use beatings. On the other hand, with the whole question of what type of society we should build in Israel – should it be a purely materialistic society or not – there a Jew is entitled to say something. We in the diaspora, even if we are not living there, are entitled to demand of Israel to give Jewish feeling a lead, to unite our people. We should be a light unto the nations.'

Being entitled to say something is one thing, but who you say it to is another. 'My view', said Mr Handler, 'and that of the majority in the community, is in what I said to June Jacobs: "To express the view in letters to the Israeli ambassador and to the Jewish press that ways must be found to act differently – yes. But to write to newspapers and show that the Jewish community is divided, there's no purpose in it." She gave me a good answer. She said: "We did it because we wanted to show the non-Jewish world that there are Jews who think otherwise." I said: "Granted. At the same time, if this were done by just anybody in the community, all right. But you are part of the leadership of the community."' Greville Janner concurs: 'Beating our breast in public helps nobody, least of all the Jewish people. If you want influence in Israel, the way to get it is by having it, as I have it, behind the scenes.' Yes, but what do you do if Mr Peres doesn't return your calls? Only a handful of Anglo-Jewish leaders have the kind of access that Greville Janner presumably enjoys.

William Frankel takes a different view: 'I see no reason why Jews individually or as institutions shouldn't express their opinions publicly about Israel. It's really something of the ghetto mentality to say: But what will the *goyim* think? I think Jews in England are sufficiently well established to be able to feel free. As for their relationship with Israel, I don't think that Israelis can speak out of both sides of their mouths. We are supposed to be partners in the great experiment and although it's right that they should make their decisions because they're going to have to live or die for them, it's equally right that we should have our own input into the process. It's part of our responsibility. That Israelis are on the front line doesn't make the opinions of people in Chicago or London irresponsible or useless.'

I asked Dr Kopelowitz whether we, as diaspora Jews, had the right to speak out on the Israeli government's handling of the uprisings. He reminded me that he couldn't speak in a personal capacity – it would be too confusing if he continually had to remind people whether he was speaking as President of the Board or as a private individual. However, I

379

suspect that his public declarations of support for Israel are a sincere reflection of his private views. What is astonishing is that he justifies his public stance on the grounds that he doesn't really know what's going on: 'People have attacked me in recent months because I haven't taken an anti-Israel stance. I've always condemned all forms of loss of life, all forms of violence. Having said that, nobody must base his views on what he sees on television after only a few edited shots. One has to look at the wider issue, the genesis of the violence. It's not for me, or for any other Jewish community, to tell the government of Israel how to go about its business. Certainly not in public. I can tell them in private, which I have done. Because unless you have access to all the papers and all the information which the government has access to, you're not able to compete in the debate on equal terms.'

'Then nobody', I interrupted, 'could ever debate with any government about anything!' (Ponder, too, the logical implications of Dr Kopelowitz's definitive statement of this theory: 'What's important is that people discuss issues on the basis of solid facts, not on the basis of instincts. I don't know if they have the facts. Only the Government of Israel has all the facts.')[8]

To which he replied with the *non sequitur*: 'But we have the right to debate with our government because we pay rates and taxes.'

'You still may not have the papers and the information.'

'But we have the right to turn the government out. We don't have that right in the Knesset.'

Since, I asked the President, Jewish individuals and organizations in Britain have been very generous to Israel and Zionist bodies, what rights does that give these benefactors?

'They should voice a general view that Israel should enrich the Jewish way of life and be a guardian of Jewish ethical values. But I don't believe that we are in a position to talk about whether you should do what the Chief Rabbi calls trading land for peace. If I was to come out firmly and say Mr Shamir's policy is absolutely wrong, governments could use that against him in the international arena and say you haven't even got the support of world Jewry in what you are doing, and therefore I could weaken his position in negotiation. That's not for me to do. That's one of the reasons I've held back. Secondly, I sometimes fear, perhaps wrongly, that if the President of the Board was to be openly critical of Israel, the fund-raisers might have difficulty with some of their appeals. You have to live with the consequences of any policy you take up.'

He has a point. By speaking out, he could contribute to sabotaging whatever policy, other than obstinacy, the Israeli government may have for solving this long-standing conflict. Rather than lay himself open to such an accusation, Kopelowitz and many other Anglo-Jewish leaders will keep silent even if it means that, in their heart of hearts, they know that Israel is sinking ever more deeply into a quagmire from which it may not emerge. Such leaders have accepted their impotence, which seems to me one of the greatest ironies of all. For millennia Jews have been powerless, subject to the whims of tyrants, the dogmas of churches, the prejudices of the masses, the murderousness of Cossacks and Nazis. Today, Jews have temporal power for the first time in 2,000 years. Now that we are in a position to influence, however slightly, the destiny of our people, we are enjoined, begged, urged not to use it. We must, we are told, remain silent, at least within the public forum, while Israeli soldiers, even if they are a totally unrepresentative handful of delinquents, bury Arabs in the sand. By December 1988 even the normally acquiescent delegates to the Board of Deputies had wearied of their leaders' unimaginative flaccidity. When the chairman of the Israel Committee, Menny Klausner, appeared to support Mr Shamir's refusal to be swayed in the slightest by Yasser Arafat's overtures, many deputies, including such stalwarts of the Establishment as Ivan Lawrence and Greville Janner, attacked such obduracy with great vehemence.

Diaspora Jews have few illusions as to their influence. They do not make the policies of a separate sovereign nation, and nor should they. But they can and should warn if they feel compelled to do so. As George Steiner told me: 'We must speak up, because our identity is being besmirched.' Chaim Bermant, whose humour often masks his essential moral seriousness, has stated the case clearly: 'The real damage to Israel, of course, lies not in what is being said by its critics, but in what is being done by its politicians, and I regard my criticisms of Israel as part of my commitment to it.'[9]

– 28 –

On guard: anti-Semitism in Britain

I s there anti-Semitism in Britain? Yes and no – that's the unsatisfactory answer. For if one wants to know whether anti-Semitic incidents
still take place in Britain, then the answer has to be yes. But if one asks
whether there is a deep and rooted layer of anti-Semitic feeling here, then
the answer, most observers would agree, has to be no. An anti-Semitic
ideology has never taken hold of the British imagination in the way it did
in, say, Poland or Germany. To be sure, there were unsavoury anti-
Semitic theoreticians such as Houston Chamberlain, who had a considerable influence on Adolf Hitler, and paranoid Catholic anti-Semites such
as Hilaire Belloc. They were marginal figures, fortunately. Unlike Germany in the late nineteenth century, there were no political parties in
Britain that included prejudice against Jews as part of their manifesto.
Recent polls in Austria show that a sizeable proportion of the population
still admits to harbouring anti-Semitic views even though Austrian Jews
are now almost an extinct species and despite all the revelations of
Austrian complicity in some of the worst Nazi atrocities. Such a situation
is inconceivable in Britain, despite the excesses of Mosley's Blackshirts
in the 1930s and the equally reprehensible fellow-travelling of Nazi
sympathizers among the upper classes.

What does persist in Britain is a snobbish attitude towards Jews, on the
grounds, it would appear, that they lack class and breeding – they just
aren't 'one of us'. There is also an undercurrent of yobbish anti-
Semitism, based on mindless antagonism towards anything unfamiliar
and distinctive. This stems from the same mentality that has given us in
the 1970s and 1980s Paki-bashing and queer-bashing and other exuber-
ances of working-class thuggery. Since snobbish clubmen tend not to

patronize pubs in Poplar, and since Bermondsey skinheads are not usually granted admittance to grand country houses, these two threads never overlap, and should be regarded as separate phenomena rather than as twin expressions of a single impulse.

The last serious outbreak of anti-Semitic feeling took place in 1947. Three Irgun terrorists who had liberated a prison in Acre had been tried and hanged – whereupon Menachem Begin, one of Irgun's leaders, hanged two British sergeants in retaliation. Since the sergeants had been taken prisoner with the sole intention of stringing them up if the Irgun men were hanged, the British people certainly had very strong justification for regarding Begin and his followers as brutal murderers. There was rioting in Britain, and if one defines anti-Semitism as hostility towards Jews, then those riots were, at least in part, anti-Semitic. Of course many Jews felt the same revulsion as the rest of the British people at the incident. The bad feeling between Zionists and the British in Palestine during the last years of the Mandate has left a residual unease. Many British Jews are convinced that the Foreign Office is largely staffed by anti-Semites, though there is little evidence to support this view. No doubt there are thoughtless Jews who would accuse the former Foreign Office minister David Mellor of anti-Semitism, although all the evidence points in the opposite direction, despite Mr Mellor's lack of delicacy in expressing himself.

The Christian anti-Semitism that inspired the conspiracy theories of Hilaire Belloc and other Catholic intellectuals ran out of steam some time ago. Pope John XXIII put an end to the Catholic Church's accusation that the Jews were responsible for the murder of Jesus Christ, the Son of God, and such views had never played a significant part in Anglican theology. That in certain cultures there is still a strong link between Catholic belief and anti-Semitism is unquestionable. I have already cited the case of Austria, and much the same could be said of Poland. On the other hand, a richly Catholic country such as Italy has rarely been given to anti-Semitic excesses.

What is more difficult to assess is the amount of institutionalized discrimination against Jews that persists in England. There are very few Jews in senior positions in the five clearing banks; some golf clubs may still exclude Jews or admit one or two simply as token members to justify excluding the rest. One or two of the St James's clubs appear not to admit Jews. Maurice Miller, a retired Labour MP from Glasgow, recalls the time when it was almost impossible for a Jew to be appointed to a chair at a

Scottish university – but those days are long over. And Emanuel Litvinoff, recalling his youth in London and referring to his attempts to find a job in commerce, wrote: 'Some people were frank enough to tell me that it was their policy not to employ people of the Jewish faith, others preferred ambiguity . . . This was how I made the dismal discovery that I was not quite British enough even to empty the waste-paper baskets in the civil service. Without British-born parents, I learned, they would have nothing to do with you as a postman, a policeman, a naval rating, a customs and excise officer, a government cipher clerk or a weights and measures inspector.'[1]

I can sympathize wth Litvinoff, for in the late 1960s I found myself blocked by similar regulations. After my graduation from university, I thought it might be fun, for want of anything better to do, to apply to enter the Diplomatic Service. No way. My parents were foreign-born and that ruled me out. The fact that my parents had arrived as penniless refugees in their late teens proved neither here nor there. I was British-born, British-educated, but not sufficiently British to represent my country. I found the assumption distinctly insulting, especially in view of the record of such true Brits as Guy Burgess, Kim Philby, and Donald Maclean. Moreover, not only did the United States not discriminate against citizens with foreign-born parents, but foreign-born citizens themselves, such as Henry Kissinger and Zbigniew Brzezinksi, had been among the most powerful shapers of American foreign policy. Twenty years on, the regulations have only been slightly modified. The Civil Service Commission renders ineligible any candidates for posts in the Cabinet Office or Ministry of Defence whose parents were not both born in the Commonwealth – except 'by special permission of the minister responsible for the department concerned'. Nowadays to be admitted to the Diplomatic Service, at least one parent must have been a Commonwealth citizen for at least thirty years before your appointment. Of course these regulations are not anti-Semitic but they are xenophobic, especially since the Prime Minister is at perfect liberty to appoint a Member of Parliament with foreign-born parents to be Foreign Secretary.

There are still those who believe that anti-Semitism lingers in certain City circles. Some banks and stockbroking firms never seem to have got round to appointing a Jewish partner, but, again, this may not be anti-Semitism so much as an instinctive preference for your fag at Harrow. Nor has the Guinness scandal generated a pogrom. Anti-Semitic reaction appears to have been restricted to a nudge and a wink at the wine bar. There is no Kosher Nostra, no Jewish Mafia – most successful Jewish businessmen spend more time at each other's throats than kissing in the corner – though it's entirely possible that a business-man would rather phone up a co-religionist than a total stranger when he wants a favour. The same clubbiness would be as true, and probably as insignificant, of Old Wykehamists and mates from the same polo team.

The City will discriminate against Jews – when it's to its financial advantage to do so, as the Arab boycotts have demonstrated. In 1963 the Norwich Union Insurance Society – which was actually based in Norwich, thus demonstrating that such foolishness is not restricted to the City of London – was approached by the Arab Boycott Office, an anti-Israeli pressure group. Norwich Union was requested not only to desist from issuing policies to Israeli concerns but to give the push to one of its directors, Lord Mancroft, who happened to be Jewish. When Mancroft was told that his fellow directors were in this quandary, he saved them from having to cave in to blackmail by resigning. Word got out. There were rebukes from the Prime Minister and resignations of various Norwich Union directors, including the chairman. Although there was great indignation that Norwich Union had agreed to be pushed around by the Arabs in this unseemly and offensive way, there was also some amusement at the whole affair, for the company had behaved with astonishing stupidity and naivety, and it was refreshing to know that in an increasingly slick and organized age, men were still capable of making complete idiots of themselves.

The boycotts, or attempts at boycotts, continued, and pressure was exerted in the 1970s on the business establishment to sever financial connections with Jewish banks. Siegmund Warburg had the unpleasant experience of finding that former associates were suddenly unwilling to support his ventures or to invite him to support theirs. His biographer writes: 'The Foreign Office, to which Siegmund turned, like the Bank of England, acted as though they saw nothing, or did not move – anyway not enough for him . . . Siegmund had already experienced something similar forty years earlier, and this time he was determined not to give in.' He didn't hesitate to sever his connections with financial institutions whose directors had given in to Arab pressure.[2] Warburg was a man of great power and influence, but the boycott also affected those less well equipped to fight back. In 1981 a London solicitor, Anthony Simmons, was dismissed from a senior position in suspicious circumstances. He had sufficient evidence, he believed, to prove that the real reason for his dismissal was related to the fact that his company had extensive dealings with a Kuwaiti company which had threatened to take its custom elsewhere if the British company continued to employ the Jew. Simmons took his case to an industrial tribunal, if only because the vague circumstances of his dismissal would hinder his chances of finding work of comparable seniority elsewhere. He was out of work for a year, and the legal proceedings cost him over £10,000 – but he won.

One might imagine that the Jewish community, so sensitive to the slightest thrust of anti-Semitism, so well armed with its Defence Committees and freelance vigilantes, would have been up in arms about the Arab boycott. There was certainly verbal condemnation, but in Simmons's experience the indignant words weren't followed by persuasive action. He claims to have received virtually no support from the Jewish Establishment. The Chief Rabbi's office let it be known that they would rather he did not pursue the matter and urged him to accept a settlement – which he refused to do. Nor was the Trades Advisory Council, a body that concerns itself with, among other matters, fighting discrimination in the workplace, much interested in his case. The company from which he had been dismissed had among its directors some very well connected people, and Simmons had the impression that the Anglo-Jewish leaders didn't want to provoke any bad feeling between themselves and some pillars of the British Establishment. Simmons's case was the last one to have come to light in recent years. The boycott has always affected trade more than finance, and is not usually directed at individuals. Where individuals are affected, it is often very difficult to prove that a dismissal was a direct result of Arab pressure; no company in the 1980s would be as candid as Norwich Union was in the 1960s. In 1988 the Arab-British Chamber of Commerce did try to persuade the Association of British Travel Agents not to hold its annual convention in 'Israeli-occupied Jerusalem', but the attempt failed.

The Jewish Establishment's cool refusal to become too worked up about the boycott persists. Sidney Bloch, a Lloyd's underwriter, told me: 'People say that Lloyd's became very anti-Semitic in the last ten, fifteen years. They didn't. What they found, frankly, was that Arab business was very profitable and the Arabs said: "Look, you're doing business with Israel, then don't do business with us." Well, they were no more pro-Arab than pro-apartheid. God knows how many organizations in this country are still doing business in South Africa, and if you ask their board if they agree with beating up blacks, they'd be horrified. I think the same thing applies. Also Israeli insurance business was damned unprofitable, and a lot of the Arab insurance business was very profitable. I think it's pretty grim, but against that it's commercial considerations, not Jewish considerations. There's a big difference between people who are prepared to sacrifice anything for profit, and those who are anti-Semitic. There are no morals in business.'

A most curious argument. If a British company, in order to preserve a relationship with an important client, is prepared, openly or covertly, to dismiss employees on a purely racial basis, then it is behaving immorally and ought to be condemned, especially by those who claim to be so stout in their defence of the interests of the Jewish community. The reluctance not only to condemn those who succumbed to the blackmail of the boycott but also to support its victims is merely another symptom of the Anglo-Jewish tendency not to make waves. At the same time the leaders of Anglo-Jewry are sick with worry that events such as the Guinness scandal, whatever its outcome, will reflect badly on the community. And woe betide any newspaper that refers to someone as a 'Jewish businessman' – the Defence Committee will be down on it like a ton of bricks. Sir Claus Moser of Rothschild's admits the contradiction: 'I do bristle when I see a newspaper reference to a "Jewish businessman", and yet I'm very proud of belonging to a Jewish bank. I can't defend the contradiction. Nothing that Lyons and Ronson and the others may have done has anything to do with being Jewish, but I dread the fuel it gives to the flames.' To the surprise of many British Jews, there is no reason to believe that the Guinness scandal has fuelled anti-Semitism; the same has been true of the Boesky scandal in the United States. As William Frankel points out: 'It seems that the majority of the non-Jewish population doesn't even know that some of those accused in the scandal are Jews, and if they do they don't care.'

The Anglo-Jewish Establishment also rarely managed to emit more than a thin bleat on the subject of school quotas. It was no secret that many public schools operated, and for all I know some still do, a quota system, on the grounds that, since the schools were church foundations, to admit a substantial proportion of non-Christians would fundamentally alter the schools' character. There's an argument there, of course, though since Christianity is these days very much a minority pursuit, I can't take it terribly seriously myself except in the case of overtly denominational schools. In 1957 I sailed through the entrance examination for St Paul's and did well enough, I thought, at the interview. Yet I was rejected by the school. I was dumbfounded, since I knew there was no academic justification for my failure. It was not until a year or so later that the headmaster of my prep school told me I'd been axed by the quota, which required 85 per cent of the intake to be 'Christian'. Four boys from the school, all Jews, of whom I had been one, had satisfied all the requirements for admission. St Paul's, however, could admit only three of us. I drew the short straw. I can't prove the story, but since St Paul's never denied that it operated a quota system, it sounds probable enough. Isaiah Berlin, an Old Pauline, fought against the quota some time after it excluded me. He too was politely asked to shut up by the Jewish Establishment. He was asked whether hypocrisy, in the form of secret or unverifiable quotas, was preferable to the brazenness of the quotas operated by St Paul's. To which Sir Isaiah replied: Yes, it is, since brazenness validates overt discrimination and sets a precedent. He objected to quotas on the grounds that Jews, or other groups affected by it, are not competing in an open market, but must fight among themselves for a limited number of places – which had been, of course, precisely my situation.

I also suspect that the guff spouted about maintaining the integrity of church foundations is humbug. Haberdashers' was vaguely ecclesiastical in its structure – an Anglican chaplain intoned prayers each morning – but the school is geared to academic success and admits hundreds of Jews these days. I'm not disposed to believe that those schools that maintain a quota that discriminates against Jews are fundamentally anti-Semitic. I suspect there's a flattering fear that if admission were to be decided solely on merit, then the situation could arise in which Jewish pupils could dominate a so-called Christian foundation. But the problem appears to have evaporated. Hayim Pinner can't even recall a complaint about quotas in recent years. St Paul's, the object of all the controversy in the early 1970s, has abolished its quota. Gratifyingly, few Jews who attended overwhelmingly non-Jewish public schools can recall being the victims of anti-Semitism. In 1941 there were nine Jews at Eton, and one of them, Anthony Blond, says he experienced no anti-Semitism. Nor did my cousins, who attended Westminster. Frederic Raphael, on the other hand, suffered considerably from anti-Semitism at Charterhouse.

If the Jewish Establishment has been relatively unconcerned by Arab boycotts and school quotas, there's nothing like a newspaper article to get it steamed up. Hayim Pinner told me: 'We monitor the media very very carefully, and there's no doubt that in the light of the City scandals, the debate about *shechita*, the animal welfare lobby, the Middle East and

Israel, Waldheim – there's no doubt that the media seem more inclined than they have been for a long time to publish things which we may regard as anti-Semitic.' The week we spoke he had objected to no fewer than three articles in the *Sunday Telegraph*, in one of which Sir John Colville argued that it was time the Jews regarded the Holocaust merely 'as a crime against all humanity . . . We lose our sense of proportion if we devote too much energy to muckraking the past'.[3] The article was grotesque, and Sir John was recalled by his Maker the following week, a divine rebuttal of sorts. Pinner 'didn't phone up the editor and object, but I took objection. Then we had an *Evening Standard* article which claimed that Mayfair was a favoured location for Jewish property developers. [The complaint against the *Evening Standard* was upheld by the Press Council.] We had a case with the BBC, where they announced that the man who was standing bail for Ronson was a Jewish millionaire. We asked them what was the relevance of the fact that he was Jewish in this case, and they said none at all and broadcast an apology. We're getting more and more of that. Some people are anxious to highlight whatever Jewish connections there are in different scandals. A journalist has to show a relevance. If he is claiming that the Jews have got together as Jews and conspired to defraud, then that's very relevant, much as I wouldn't like it. But if it's just the case that some of them were born of Jewish mothers, then it's not relevant at all to the scandal. A journalist has to make out a case, otherwise he's showing prejudice, or pointing out that they're Jewish in order to create a prejudice. In these cases we take appropriate action, though we're not paranoid, we don't react hysterically, we haven't shouted that Peregrine Worsthorne is an anti-Semite.'

Journalists or newspaper editors may on occasion be too casual and thoughtless in their inclusion of an irrelevant 'Jewish factor', but very few would argue that such slips reflect a deep-seated national anti-Semitism. British politics is admirably free of it. The prejudice of certain Conservative associations – not only against Jews, of course, but against women and Catholics, too – is a thing of the past, and the only anti-Semitism to be encountered in the Labour Party would be here and there on the anti-Zionist extreme left. Extreme right-wing racism is a negligible force, confined to fragmented fringe parties the names of which change every few years and to a few malodorous corners of the Conservative Party. When John Stokes remarked during the Westland affair that the replacement for Leon Brittan at the Department of Trade and Industry should be a 'red-blooded, red-faced Englishman', the anti-Semitic nuance was lost on nobody. The fact that Jews are so prominent in the higher reaches of Conservative politics worries some of their co-religionists, who, for reasons that I do not understand, fear that such public exposure of Jews could backfire. There have certainly been whispering campaigns mounted against Lord Young which may have had anti-Semitic over-tones, for there is a good deal of envy at the way he has achieved great political power entirely through the patronage of the Prime Minister. Greville Janner, however, insists: 'Anti-Semites cause anti-Semitism, not Jews. I have the biggest filth mail of any MP outside those who deal in Ireland, and I don't think it makes the slightest difference what I say. It's not all crank mail – some of it's dangerous. Anti-Semitism is a very considerable force – within the woodwork – but it is no force at all at high levels of power in either party.'

Political anti-Semitism lurks in some student unions, where life can be very uncomfortable for Jewish university students; they must fight off innumerable hostile resolutions from Arab students, who often outnum-ber them. Some of these resolutions seek to 'remove Zionist elements from the union' or to ban the sale of Israeli produce.[4] Michael Rosin, a former Jewish chaplain at many provincial universities, is convinced that anti-Zionist groups on campuses receive lavish outside funding, es-pecially from Libya.[5] It could also be argued that Israel's trigger-happy policy in the Occupied Territories has given anti-Zionist students vast quantities of free ammunition. It would be foolish to equate anti-Zionism with anti-Semitism, but certainly the dividing line between the two is blurred, and it is hardly surprising that many British Jews often find the distinction hard to make. Rightly or wrongly, some Jews believe that anti-Semitism is on the increase in Britain, though there is no evidence to support the view. Although the Board monitors the incidence of anti-Semitic outrages, very little serious research has been done to assess the extent of the problem. When some years ago Tony Lerman wrote an article in the *Jewish Quarterly* questioning the extent of anti-Semitism in Britain, there was a tremendous row. 'It's still a highly sensitive issue and not really discussed openly. The word anti-Semitism is used incredibly loosely, so that today it's lost a good deal of its force, especially when it's used by Israelis to deflect any criticism.'

There cannot be a Jew in the land who has never overheard or been at the receiving end of an anti-Semitic jibe. Whether such remarks consti-tute anti-Semitism is a moot point. Clearly many British Jews think so. Alan Greenbat comments: 'Twenty years ago Christopher Mayhew thought it important enough to take court action because somebody called him an anti-Semite. Today nobody would think that was important enough. You can be an anti-Semite and respectable. I don't think you could twenty years ago, and definitely not forty years ago. I remember when I was in the army, we had a chef who had come from the camps, and he said to us: "You British Jews don't know how lucky you are, because in England you've got the best anti-Semites in the world." That was how he saw his world. As we've become more and more assimilated, so I believe that people have taken to being more open in their anti-Semitism. There is a sense in which educated opinion formers in this country feel that it's no longer necessary to hold back on anti-Semitism.' And the evidence? 'I've heard that if you could sit in the hotel bars in the provinces where commercial travellers gather, the jokes that are told are anti-Semitic and vicious.' On a cruise one year, he recalls the guides informing the passengers that when the ships docked, the shop-owners dispensed with their siesta and kept the shops open. Greenbat overheard someone say: 'So the Jews have got here, have they?'

When I suggest to Anglo-Jewish leaders that such hypersensitivity smacks of paranoia, I often receive replies such as that from Jonathan Lew: 'Of course we're paranoid. Our children are under enormous pressure on campus with millions of pounds of Arab money being poured in to deal with our kids as harshly as they possibly can. They're being told Zionism is racism, Judaism is racism, Jews should be shut out of this or that – yes, we're paranoid. My son, who left Cambridge two years ago, won't agree with you that anti-Semitism isn't a factor. He works in the City now, and he still won't agree with you. I spent seventeen years in advertising, which is a pretty free and easy industry, and I can tell you it certainly was not on the surface, but it was pretty close underneath. People say, "Oh, there's something else you don't eat, is there?" Or my wife was told at an office party: "Is that also part of your religion, not drinking gin and tonic?" – because she only wanted a tonic water. There are still many organizations and companies in this country where Jews can only reach a certain level. It may be xenophobia, but we don't perceive it that way. It may not all be anti-Semitism pure and simple, but if it's not its brother, it's a cousin.' Or Stanley Kalms: 'I don't think you can ever be over-sensitive. We have every right to be sensitive. We are always at the verge of being persecuted. I believe it's a fallacy to think we've permanently found a home in the diaspora away from persecution. Why should 2,000 years disappear in one particular century? These things can be revived, and they take a different form. Jews are still excluded from a whole range of activities, quietly. But then Jews choose to be excluded. We still live in our own closed society. There's still a very narrow range of mixing, though there are Jews in high places today.'

The sensitivity and defensiveness of which Kalms speaks were amply demonstrated when in January 1987 Jim Allen's play *Perdition* was scheduled for performance at the Royal Court Theatre. The play argued that Zionist leaders in Hungary collaborated with the Nazis in 1944 in order to secure a Jewish homeland after the war, with the consequence that half a million Hungarian Jews were exterminated. The thesis, which most historians deride, naturally caused considerable offence among the Jewish community, and the ensuing protests and a report commissioned from the historians David Cesarani and Martin Gilbert persuaded the Royal Court to cancel the performances forty-eight hours before the first preview. At this there was much indignation on the part of the author. But as Hugo Gryn shrewdly observed, Allen criticizes Hungarian Jews for passivity and collusion, and then protests when British Jews defend their interests. The play, in a much revised version, was then given a few performances at Conway Hall in London in May 1988. The Union of Jewish Students was dispatched to mount a small demonstration outside the hall, but the performances were not disrupted. I haven't read the play and I am no historian, but it seems dangerous to assume that any play or article critical of individual Jews is automatically anti-Semitic, an assumption certainly made by some Jews in the case of Mr Allen. As Robin Lustig observed in an article printed after the Conway Hall performances, a play presenting similar arguments had been performed in Israel without adverse comment, so it seems likely that the fact that Mr Allen is not Jewish himself contributed to the umbrage taken.[6] Even if the play repellently seeks to shift blame for atrocities from persecutors to victims, little, it seems to me, is achieved by the Jewish community seeking to ban a play that doesn't meet with its approval.

The argument for banning offensive material is far stronger in the case of such publications as *Holocaust News*, an openly anti-Semitic sheet published by extreme right-wing racist organizations. The paper alleges that the Holocaust never took place and is 'an evil hoax'. Thirty thousand copies were distributed throughout Britain by pushing them through letter boxes in streets with a large Jewish population. Prosecution was urged on the grounds that the sheet incited racial hatred, but the Director of Public Prosecutions, Allan Green, concluded that there were no grounds for prosecution, which suggests that whatever laws Britain has on the statute book to deal with racial hatred are ineffectual. Under French or German law, the publishers of *Holocaust News* could certainly be prosecuted.

Manny Penner reports that you can still hear East Enders talking about 'Jewboys'. 'To jew' is still used as a verb, and Lois Sieff recalls being told by a friend that a shop in Kensington was 'a bit Jewy'. Sir Sidney Hamburger believes that much anti-Semitism is merely a generalization from the particular: 'If one Jew happens to be aggressive in his politics or unkempt in his social habits, then the whole community suffers because of what they don't like about that Jew. But I couldn't say widespread anti-Semitism exists. But I'm not blind enough to believe that if the economic situation in this country were to deteriorate, it couldn't recur. Some of the comments I've heard in recent weeks about Jews trying to hijack the media make me realize that the veneer is very very thin.'

Most anti-Semitism in Britain takes two forms: the yobbish and the snobbish. When I was about fourteen I had to put up with a great deal of anti-Semitic barracking from my schoolmates, who enjoyed sitting in the back row and chanting 'Yid, yid' or 'Wog, wog' simply to provoke a response from the few Jews and the sole Indian in the class. Yet such racist jibes seemed merely one more weapon employed in the sustained warfare of school life. Although it was irritating and unpleasant to be on the receiving end, I never recalled feeling that the anti-Semitism was in any way profound. Indeed, in later years I became moderately friendly with some of my former persecutors, who had by then grown out of their mindless phase.

Some of these yobs never forsake such crude forms of self-expression. Each year there are reports of swastikas and foul anti-Semitic slogans daubed on synagogue walls or gravestones, abusive telephone calls to the *Jewish Chronicle*, windows broken at Jewish community centres, unprovoked verbal abuse, and so forth. Yobbish humour is freely expressed on such items as Hitler T-shirts and neo-Nazi regalia, all of which are available at tawdry Carnaby Street shops in central London. Football matches provide a context for anti-Semitic jibes, especially when Arsenal-supporting opponents of Tottenham Hotspur turn up to jeer at the 'Tottenham Yids' and to sing the jolly lines: 'I never felt more like gassing the Jews, when Arsenal win and Tottenham lose.' Such infantile viciousness is so clearly the recreation of a tiny degenerate minority that to get overexcited about its general significance is to give it a weight it does not merit. Sometimes too there are physical assaults. A rabbi told me how one evening in Hendon, a group of yobs chanting anti-Semitic abuse got rather too close to a band of ultra-Orthodox young men walking home from a restaurant; the *yeshiva* lads defended themselves with great success, and the yobs were routed.

Such working-class anti-Semitism has its parallels in upper-class circles too, where it takes very different forms. At university, I sat in hall one evening opposite a bishop's son, an intimate of the heir to the throne, who was sitting nearby. The bishop's son made a disparaging remark about Jews, which earned him, to his surprise, a rebuke from me. I don't suppose he had ever formulated any clear attitudes towards Jews as such; it was merely commonplace in the circles in which he moved to sneer at Jews from time to time. Jonathan Miller, who claims he has never experienced anti-Semitism, explains such offensive remarks as 'just part and parcel of English racism and snobbery. Anti-Semitism in Britain is a very weak factor. There is a sort of faint fringe of contemptuous disparagement, but it's much more snobbery than racism, and "that nasty little Jewboy" is a view of English upper-middle-class Gentiles who've always had a view of the Jew as a grubby person, with grubby appetites and grubby motives – and that's snobbery.' I mentioned to Miller the occasion on which, at a smart Chelsea dinner party, I had mentioned to my neighbour a clever idea I'd had which I wanted to have patented and franchised; having no business expertise whatsoever, I didn't know how to go about it. 'Oh,' he replied, 'the first thing you need to do is get yourself a good Jew lawyer.' I bristled, but was puzzled because the disparagement seemed to have a complimentary tinge to it, in that a Jewish lawyer would serve my purposes better than a non-Jewish one. Jonathan Miller pinned down precisely what was offensive about the remark: 'It's that use of the word "Jew" rather than "Jewish". It's a view of the Jew as a fairly squalid figure who, when you need squalid initiatives, is the one to do it. Again, that's part of that tradition of snobbery.'

As a lawyer himself, Leo Abse believed that being a Jewish lawyer in a non-Jewish town probably worked to his advantage. Since people were predisposed to believe that a Jewish solicitor would be clever, they flocked to his practice, which thrived. He recalled being taken by his wife-to-be to meet her mother, a staunch Welsh lady, for the first time. She looked him up and down and then said: 'Well, it could have been worse. He could have been English.' Anti-Semitic? Snobbish, surely. For George Steiner, that such disparagement of Jews has a firm place in certain layers of

British society is deplorable, but may also function as a kind of jester's licence, a safety valve. 'Britain harbours much stronger feelings against Catholics than against Jews. There's no Guy Fawkes night here for Jews.'

Allied to the snobbish view that Jews are 'not one of us' is the slightly cruder formulation that Jews are, somehow, foreigners. Greville Janner recalls sitting in the House of Commons beside a colleague. '"Oh look," said the colleague, "your ambassador's sitting in the gallery." He was referring to the Israeli ambassador.' The remark was in no way disparaging, but there was clearly a subconscious conviction in his mind that because Israelis tend to be Jews, that Jews must therefore be Israelis – or at any rate, not British. Almost every British Jew has experience either of the slighting remark or, as in Janner's anecdote, of the nuance that, although not hostile, confirms that Jews may be splendid chaps but are not fully paid up Brits. Brazenly anti-Semitic remarks are rarely encountered. It is not often that a public figure goes into print with a remark such as the following, made by Roald Dahl to a *New Statesman* interviewer: 'There is a trait in the Jewish character that does provoke animosity.' Britain's trash press, which routinely abuses Krauts and Wops, has not yet got round to maligning the Yids, nor is it likely to happen.

Most Jews are resigned to the fact that on occasion a disparaging remark may come their way. Lord Goodman observes: 'Occasionally at a dinner party somebody mistakenly fails to observe what is self-evident, that I'm Jewish, and makes an anti-Semitic remark, but that isn't an important symptom. There are lots of people who are much more conscious of it because in a way they attract it. Of course anti-Semitism exists, but it exists in a tolerable form. You have to adopt a Nelson touch and not see it. It isn't a terrible deprivation that you can't get elected to certain St James's clubs; it isn't a terrible deprivation that apparently the clerks in some banks aren't Jewish – since I've never had either ambition. It shouldn't be worrying. People who have a sense of inferiority enjoy asserting a spurious superiority over others. It makes insignificant people feel bigger.' The former MP Maurice Miller notes that 'no minority community can maintain its identity without paying a price for it. It's a different story if people act on their dislike and attack people physically. But some xenophobia is unavoidable.'

It is the younger generation of Jews who feel strongly that there is nothing to be ashamed of in parading their differences from the majority. Sikhs wear their turbans, Indian women their saris – so why, the argument goes, shouldn't Jews wear *kippot* or Chasidic garb? Why not, indeed?

Rabbi Jeffrey Cohen of Stanmore United synagogue urged his congregation to wear hats rather than *kippot* in the streets; but as Rabbi Alan Plancey remarked, 'If they are going to come after you, they'll get you no matter what you are wearing.'[7] Other Jews worry about the flaunting of wealth indulged in by vulgar Yuppies who attract critical comments after moving into suburbs where Jews are not widely settled. Worrying about faulty image protection is futile, for anti-Semitism has nothing to do with how Jews behave. In Vienna some Jews suffered anti-Semitism because they were too rich, while others suffered because they were too poor and thus were perceived as a threat to working-class livelihoods. No wonder that Jews, with their history, should worry over such things. For a persecuted group to exhibit some signs of paranoia – and, as Anthony Blond remarks, 'Jews are tops at paranoia' – is understandable.

Yet any dispassionate observer has to conclude that British Jews have remarkably little to worry about. Anthony Blond, indeed, claims that for him philo-Semitism is far more of a problem than anti-Semitism: 'I'm always being expected to take the Jewish line. I go to grand country houses and bang on like mad. I've been lucky enough to have seen the attitude to Jews change quite dramatically – through the bayonets of the Israeli army. I think it's lamented, and not only by me, that the skill of Einstein, the rhapsodies of Horowitz and Menuhin, haven't affected the Christian view as much as the bullets and the gutsiness of the Israelis.' Tony Lerman is right to distinguish between the kind of anti-Semitism that leads to persecution and, ultimately, genocide, and the occasional jibe to be heard in the streets of North London or at Belgravia dinner tables. 'When people accuse others of being anti-Semites, they're implying that the kinds of attitudes that they are putting forward are the same kinds that could or did lead to a Holocaust. I don't think that's so. This is a distinction that most people dealing with anti-Semitism on a communal level in this country don't recognize at all.'

I have heard even so distinguished a historian as Hyam Maccoby talking at a Mapam seminar about how anti-Semitism is ingrained in the English language, how the media like to diabolize Israel, and how Christianity preserves the image of the Jew as the Christ-killer. This is complete rubbish. Despite the trivial anti-Semitism I and most other Jews have, on rare occasions, experienced, all the evidence suggests that the great majority of Britons are simply indifferent to Jews. They don't give us a thought. Jews will count up the numbers of heads of Oxbridge colleges who are of Jewish birth, but how many non-Jews would find the exercise of any interest? Excessive vigilance against the slightest manifestation of anything that could conceivably be labelled anti-Semitic is, at root, an unhealthy response in a society that, in general, is benign and tolerant. It strikes me as excessively defensive, and for once I agree with the Chief Rabbi, who told me: 'I myself often caution against over-reaction. That in itself can be counter-productive. Nor should the Holocaust be over-invoked, as certain leaders in Israel did, notably Begin. I seek to strike a balance here. Some people are overly preoccupied with anti-Semitism at the expense of other more positive concerns that ought to exercise the Jewish community. There's a disproportionate emphasis on fighting against things – anti-Semitism, Arab propaganda, Soviet oppression – instead of fighting for things that we ought to stand for, such as moral values with which Jews ought to be identified.'

I would also be more sympathetic to Anglo-Jewry's hypersensitivity if I discerned a corresponding sympathy with the far more aggressive racism endured by other immigrant groups, notably Asians. Indeed, one of the reasons why anti-Semitism is so negligible a factor in modern British life is that other groups have, so to speak, stepped into the front line. Blacks and Asians provide more obvious scapegoats than Jews, and it is they who bear the brunt of intolerance. Sadly, most Jews are indifferent to racism except when it is directed against themselves. Festivals and other events organized by local authorities in London to promote anti-racism rarely receive formal support from Jewish bodies. Crusading individuals, such as Gerry Gable, the editor of the anti-Fascist monthly *Searchlight*, are rare exceptions. As Rabbi Michael Rosen put it: 'There must be some reciprocity. You can't ask the Gentile world to support our fight against anti-Semitism if by the same token Jews are not prepared to be involved in fighting other forms of racism.' The Chief Rabbi endorses this attitude in a somewhat guarded way: 'That in principle our concerns should transcend our own confines is something that I for one certainly keep on stressing. Our Board of Deputies is very much involved in anti-racism and in helping the black communities. I give every possible encouragement to that. We have a very special commitment to share the travails and agonies of other oppressed minorities by making common cause with them.'

It was Isaiah Berlin who pointed out that in certain countries – France, Russia, Austria – it would be reasonable to assume that a Jew could encounter hostility. There are other countries, such as Denmark or Italy, where one can make the opposite assumption: that there is no predisposition to anti-Semitism on the part of the population. Britain too, for all its snobbery and xenophobia and penchant for hooliganism from upper as well as lower classes, falls into this second category. While it is understandable that Jews should remain on guard against complacency, there appear to be no grounds for British Jews to feel any deep anxiety on this score. There is no likelihood of pogroms in Edgware. British Jews should perhaps adopt the stance of the narrator of M. Ageyev's *Novel with Cocaine*, who declares: 'Anti-Semitism is far from frightening; it is merely repulsive, pitiful and stupid: repulsive because it is directed against the tribe rather than the individual, pitiful because it is envious where it would appear to be derisive, stupid because it consolidates what it purports to destroy.'

– 29 –

Settling down: the refugees

I T should already be clear that a major contribution to British artistic and intellectual life in this century has been made not so much by established Anglo-Jewry as by the refugees from Nazi Europe who found a new home in Britain before the outbreak of war. Since I myself am the son of refugees, I have been acutely aware of this generation of refugees as a social group quite separate from the rest of Anglo-Jewry. Although like any generalization this one is inaccurate, there is still an extraordinary cohesiveness within refugee circles, even though almost all the surviving refugees have by now spent two-thirds or more of their lives in Britain. In part it is a cultural attachment. While many British Jews of more rooted ancestry retained some of the ghetto mentality, German Jews were always extremely Germanic, while Austrian Jews oozed *Gemütlichkeit*. (Or, as Weizmann put it in a famous formulation: 'Ah, the German Jews. All the charm of the Germans, and all the modesty of the Jews.') The novelist Elaine Feinstein, who grew up in Leicester, recalls that her parents – of Russian and German descent – took in a Hungarian refugee who astonished them by her reluctance to relinquish the German language. Many English Jews, according to Feinstein, felt it was wrong for central Europeans to associate so closely with the host culture, believing that excessive assimilation had been partly responsible for the disaster that befell them – an argument that is hard to support. Nevertheless, many refugees earned a reputation for 'uppityness' which was not always undeserved.

Erich Fried, the Austrian poet, came to London from Vienna in 1938 at the age of seventeen. His parents had been arrested after an indiscreet conversation had been reported to the Gestapo by a waiter. His father died from the beatings he received from the Gestapo, but Fried was able to get himself and then his mother out of Austria. Until his death in 1988 he still wrote mostly in German because, as he said, he wouldn't let Hitler deprive him of his language. In his untidy house in Kilburn he surrounded himself with objects, some precious, others junk, because they acted as bulwarks against his earlier impoverishment, as 'ramparts against despair.' Acclaimed as one of the greatest poets writing in the German language, he was virtually unknown in the country where he lived for half a century. Almost deliberately, he refused to settle in: he wrote in the language of his birth, and his anti-Zionism – on the grounds that Israel is racist in conception – won him few friends in Anglo-Jewish circles.

Many refugees, like Fried, are happy to remain on the margin or even outside the Anglo-Jewish community. Others congregate among the broad if confined group of the Belsize Square synagogue. Others – notably the Chief Rabbi and Rabbi Hugo Gryn – are prominent religious leaders. And quite a few have gone to considerable lengths to conceal their Jewishness. There is no standard pattern of response to deracination. If there is a common factor among refugees, it is demographic: that they are an ageing community. Almost by definition, there are no refugees from Nazi Europe who are younger than fifty-five. Those who came from Germany or Czechoslovakia have received reparations in the form of pensions that help to sustain them as they drift into old age. Those who had the bad luck to come from Austria have received nothing or very little, for (as is explained at some length in my book *The Double Eagle*) Austria has been allowed to claim the status of a victim of Nazism rather than an accomplice, and thus feels no obligation to make amends for atrocities and thefts committed after the Anschluss. Austria may be right on a technicality; morally, its position is indefensible. Austria's niggardliness has certainly contributed to the poverty of many elderly refugees. Nor were successive British governments much help, since until 1987 the United Kingdom was the last country in Europe to tax such pensions at 50 per cent. There is also considerable loneliness, for many refugees lack a network of extended families. To compensate for this, there is a closeness of relationships within refugee circles. Friendships formed in times of stress, shortly before the war or in the army, have frequently endured for half a century or more.

There were at one time some 70,000 refugees from Nazism living in Britain. Some died young, others emigrated to the United States or Israel. Nobody knows how many remain. The Association of Jewish Refugees, which was founded in 1941, has 4,000 members worldwide, most of whom live in north-west London. Thousands more either no longer associate formally with the refugee community or have gone to the extreme of denying they ever were refugees. While the membership of the AJR is gradually shrinking as older refugees die off, the demands for the Association's services have trebled in the past five years. The AJR has established a day centre in West Hampstead, an area richly populated by elderly refugees. There was considerable criticism when this centre was opened, on the grounds that there was no need for separate facilities for refugees.

How wrong they were. My grandmother, who died in 1981 shortly before her eighty-fourth birthday, was a Hungarian, and typical, in an extreme form, of refugees of her generation. She lived in West Hampstead in a cramped little flat, stacked high with her possessions, a miniaturized version of the orderly world she had inhabited in Budapest and Vienna. As a child I occasionally had to share her bed, and I can recall the experience of near suffocation beneath a mountainous heap of feather bedding and cumbersome eiderdowns. Her cooking revelled in roast duck and potato pancakes and stuffed peppers and goulash. Her poppy-seed strudels, one of which used to accompany me to Cambridge at the beginning of each term, were hugely admired by my friends, who had never tasted anything like them. She had a middle-European respect for culture, but no real interest in it.

She was snobbish to a quite fantastic degree. Mrs Lassman, the director of the AJR, admits that one of the reasons they founded the West Hampstead day centre was because of the refugees' snobbishness. She must have had my grandmother in mind. With her thick accent, she used to pour scorn on Harold Wilson, a prime minister who had augmented her pension more than any of his predecessors, on the grounds that he was 'common'. My grandmother was in those days earning a meagre living as a cashier in a food supermarket, but that never diminished her sense of social worth. Since half the refugees in London shopped there, she was on nodding terms with thousands of them. To whom had she not given change in her time? Yet she had a tremendous capacity for writing people off. She hated Germans, and with good reason. She loathed Austrians, and with good reason. She loathed Hungarians, for less well-defined reasons. There wasn't much left to like. There was no way my grandmother would have wanted to mix socially with her Anglo-Jewish counterparts. What on earth would she have had to say to them? She had nothing against the British, whom she hardly ever encountered. She inhabited the tiniest world imaginable, though my aunt often took her on holidays to those parts of Europe my grandmother didn't actively disapprove of. Her idea of an outing was to walk to one of the Finchley Road restaurants or coffee-houses – Cosmo's in particular – frequented by her clones. There we would eat schnitzel and/or strudel before returning to her flat.

Like most central-European refugees, she was not religious, though she exhibited piety when it suited her. The only aspect of my girlfriends that interested her was whether or not they were Jewish. Devoted to me, she was astonishingly indifferent to others. Worried about failing eyesight, she moved into an old people's home. There, grudgingly, she admitted to her presence one or two of the old ladies who also inhabited the home, most of whom were far better educated than she was. She was imperious but ungenerous, except to me. She was a prude. She lacked curiosity. She was, indeed, a perfect product of her time and place: a wine merchant's daughter, and then the wife of a prosperous cattle-dealer. She had been a person of substance in Vienna: I still use her engraved silverware and the lovely embroidered linen that formed her dowry seventy years ago. Her life was dedicated to the domestic virtues, at which she excelled. When she and my mother left Vienna in 1938, they took employment in rural England as domestic servants. But in her own mind she was always a lady. She chugged steadily through her life, unyielding to the last, and died of inertia.

My grandmother was, I hope, an extreme case. She was over forty when she came to England. She had the psychological resources to adapt sufficiently to her new situation but had no interest in assimilation. Everything she needed – her recipe books, her playing cards, her heirlooms – was contained within the walls of her little flat, and she felt no need to explore the strange environment known as Britain. In contrast, many more sophisticated refugees from Nazism assimilated with extraordinary speed and success. Almost as soon as the war had ended, the careers of publishers such as André Deutsch and George Weidenfeld and Paul Hamlyn were well under way. The descendants of the Russian immigrants had become anglicized, but they also remained tightly within their suburban enclaves, their narrowness of cultural interest in great contrast to the ravenous cultural appetites of the refugees, their social and even economic cautiousness a pale shadow of the daring of the bolder refugees. Many middle-class British Jews still talk of the *goyim* and perceive non-Jews as alien beings, an attitude rarely found among the refugees, who mostly came from more worldly backgrounds. I remember attending a party given by Anglo-Jewish neighbours when I was in my early teens. The grown-ups were dancing a hideous and raucous number known as the 'hokey-cokey'. No refugee would have participated as a free agent in such vulgarity. One reason, Mrs Lassman told me, why elderly refugees prefer the West Hampstead Centre to, say, the Michael Sobell Day Centre in Golders Green, is that it is less noisy. They like to read or listen to Brahms on the gramophone, not practise handicrafts or learn Yiddish.

The AJR will soon self-destruct. In twenty-five years time very few of the refugees will still be alive. As the population ages, problems such as survivor syndrome loom larger. More generalized problems of anxiety and paranoia are common in this segment of the community. Refugees who have spoken English for fifty years revert to German again. Refugees who are not camp survivors can experience piercing guilt as, in old age, their solitariness reminds them that they, once perhaps part of a large extended family, have become the sole relic, a consequence of luck rather than merit. It affects their children too. As long suppressed memories begin to surface once more, the children, in the words of a psychoanalyst who has dealt with the syndrome, must pick up a heavy parcel that has never been unwrapped and examined.

Yet despite the sadness of many individual cases, most refugees coped very well. They often came from middle-class backgrounds; for those with professional skills or business experience it was not too difficult to build new careers. Many others came as children, and so their education and training was conventionally British. Sir Claus Moser, who came here as a boy, still marvels at the Britishness of his life, which he himself describes as 'an Establishment career with all its trappings'. Brought up in a rich household in Berlin, where famous artists and musicians were regular visitors, he has memories of a very happy childhood. Although by now thoroughly rooted in England and unwilling to live anywhere else, he still admits to feeling at home in Germany. His childhood memories have also prompted a revival in middle age of a personal interest in his religion: 'My parents were very much part of the leading cultured Reform Jewish community in Germany, and so I think of my past in Germany as a Jewish past. Although ours was not a religious family, the fact that I was a Jewish boy ranks highest almost in my memories of childhood – partly because the last two years were the Hitler years, when being Jewish marked one out as part of a despised little minority. What one has to do

403

as one grows old is try without prejudice to get the different parts of one's background into proportion, not to deny that any of them existed, to decide what role they played in one's ultimate balance. In my case what is dominant is that I'm a Middle-European Jew, and that's what I will remain until I die. But I think that anybody who has more than a single background, either of religion or nationality, is bloody lucky. It's a protection against parochialism.'

Despite Moser's British education, there were to be constant reminders that he would in some respects always be seen as an outsider. While studying at the London School of Economics, he tried to spend a year at the Central Statistical Office, but for 'security' reasons this was not allowed. It was gratifying when in 1967 Harold Wilson appointed him to head the Office and brushed aside the objections that had barred him from junior membership all those years earlier. While head of the CSO, Moser recalls lunching with another permanent secretary of the Civil Service. 'We drank a certain amount and let our hair down, and eventually he said to me: "It really says a great deal for this country that somebody with your background can become head of a government department." That was a reminder that one is always an outsider. Even this year somebody very high up said to me, "What's it like working here as a German?" I said: "I have actually been British for forty years."'

For other German-Jewish children the transition was more painful. The novelist Eva Figes came to England when she was seven. Schooldays were difficult, since she only dimly understood the circumstances that had brought her to this foreign environment. 'Children are very cruel. They pick on anyone who's a bit different. There's a class difference too. I came from a very wealthy upper-middle-class family, and I was suddenly in a working-class suburb, and that was a bigger difference almost than the difference of language and country. It was wartime and I had to sink or swim by myself. It was made quite clear from day one that we had to adapt. We spoke no German at home, only English, right from the beginning. I had no religious upbringing whatsoever. This is something I almost resent these days, as I feel I should have been told I was Jewish and known why we were here. I had to find out by myself little by little. I could have coped better with the battering I quite often got at school if I had known why I was here and who I was. Once I went on to grammar school, it was okay, as by that time my English was fluent. I didn't really have a strong feeling of being Jewish until I found out what was happening in the concentration camps. That was my strong moment of identification.'

A school friend of mine, obviously Jewish, was in fact brought up as a churchgoer, and as a boy would tell the inquisitive: 'I'm not Jewish but my parents used to be.' Many years went by before the absurdity of this attempt to resign from the club sank in, and when that happened he began to explore his Jewishness with intense diligence. I also knew the daughter of a Viennese psychoanalyst who strenuously denied as a child that she was Jewish. Even today she remains an occasional churchgoer, though less, I suspect, out of religious conviction than out of a zeal for all things English. Curiously, she made no attempt to disguise her foreign background, while at the same time she and presumably her parents had gone to great efforts to discount its significance. Such denials, which were not uncommon though hard to quantify according to the degree to which they were successful, were one response to deracination. For others, establishing an identity proved difficult in other ways. Many German-Jewish refugees found that once in England their Germanness counted for more than their Jewishness, and to be German in 1940 was a most undesirable thing. To be unalterably German was the last thing many of them wanted to be. A friend of mine tells of a patient of his who registered under the name of George Evans. Evans, however, had a thick European accent. He had come from Czechoslovakia in the 1930s and settled in, of all places, Pontypridd. Encumbered with a long German name and aware that all his neighbours 'were called Yones or Yenkins', he changed his name to Evans. Somehow he and his wife still weren't fully accepted, so they learnt Welsh and became highly proficient at it. 'And still ze buggers von't accept me!'

A psychoanalyst of German birth confessed to a different puzzlement: she doesn't feel German, she doesn't feel English, but she does feel Jewish. She feels at home everywhere but not truly at home anywhere. This is not, in her view, necessarily a bad thing: she relishes being on the margins, and even the element of unease enables her, as a psychologist, to make links between ideas and cultures that assist her work. This is made easier because she operates in an international profession, and the same reason was given to me by George Weidenfeld. He feels at home in Britain, and grateful to Britain, but prefers to see himself as a patron of the wider Western world. Like many refugees, he made a conscious decision after the war to put the past behind him without severing his connection with it. His life peerage anchors him even more firmly in Britain, yet his loyalties are complicated, though not undermined, by his unflinching Zionism.

405

The majority of refugees made a kind of pact with their new country. While devotedly loyal to Britain, many of them retain an unbreakable attachment to their native culture. Food, mealtimes, a dislike of hard liquor, the arrangement of furniture, social habits – all these essentially European Jewish characteristics remained unchanged. When I was a teenager, my father would be most annoyed if I went to town – say, to an exhibition at the Tate – without putting on a tie. Since he was working at his office while I was at the gallery, I could never understand why it mattered to him. It was, I think, a legacy of Germanic correctness. To be properly dressed for the occasion was a cultural value of his generation, though not of mine. To this day I like to sneak tieless into stuffy restaurants. Although the refugees lacked the ghetto mentality of many native-born British Jews, they retain a sense of separateness. I once attended a lecture at Mapam in London at which many refugees were present. Time and again, in the course of the discussion, they would refer to 'the English'. Even after fifty years, they couldn't think of themselves as 'English' – 'British' perhaps, with its more impersonal overtones of mere nationhood, but not 'English', which implies a cultural inheritance to which they couldn't, and possibly wouldn't have wanted to, lay claim. They argued fiercely over the extent to which successful Jewish refugees, such as Robert Maxwell, are 'accepted', a preoccupation that, I would guess, rarely troubles that gentleman. Many refugees still suffer from a residual insecurity and a frustrating inability to feel truly at home.

Curiously, this unease has been inherited by some children of immigrants. I knew of the existence of the Association of Jewish Refugees, but had no idea until recently that there was also an Association for the Children of Jewish Refugees. Children of refugees do have an altered perspective. This is inevitable. In my own case, my parents went out of their way to give me the broadest possible rearing, to ensure that their burdens wouldn't become mine too. When I was a child, they employed German au pair girls, and I spent long summer holidays in Germany with the girls and their families. That was an atypical strategy for most refugees from Nazism, who were disinclined even to have Germans in the house, let alone entrust part of the care of their children to them. I was given a fairly basic Jewish education, but no attempt was made to restrict my social life to Jewish circles. I grew up feeling English and still feel English, though not in any chauvinistic sense. Yet at the same time I feel genuinely cosmopolitan.

Any tension that existed between my ancestry and my own identity came into focus at Cambridge, where I first encountered the cream, allegedly, of British society. There was a tremendous social self-confidence among the gangs of Old Etonians and Wykehamists, but with a few delightful exceptions their vision was narrow. Any envy I felt for their social eminence and sure-footedness was undercut by my disdain for their essential philistinism. I could never aspire to join their ranks, but this did not bother me. My closest friends were oddballs – a scruffy philosopher who smoked Havanas and kept his trousers up with string, an Anglo-Indian brother and sister, a stupendously lazy old Etonian, a manic poet given to frequent suicide attempts – and far more interesting than the smart set, with their predictable enthusiasms. I realized that those who came from clearly defined social backgrounds had a self-confidence I couldn't match, but they also had their lives mapped out for them. Some would be lawyers, others politicians, other bankers. I hadn't the faintest idea what I was going to do with my life. There was no pattern which I could follow. If this uncertainty was daunting, it was also immensely liberating. No estates to inherit! No family motto to sustain! No path to tread! I was lucky. Having feet in different camps never scared me. Lacking in social privileges, I had the far greater privilege of *carte blanche*.

Other acquaintances from similar backgrounds report a variety of responses and strategies. I spent an afternoon discussing such questions of identity with Tony and Marion, a married couple of my age, both the children of refugees. Tony began by admitting: 'I feel slightly stateless. I'm very proud to be English but I'm not part of it. I don't know whether that's being a Jew or whether that's being the child of refugees.' Marion had given it more thought: 'The difference it's made to me is that I'm very aware that you can lose absolutely everything – property, money, anything, can disappear just like that. Because that's what happened to our parents. It's very important to me, for example, that our son has as good a formal education as we can possibly give him, because he's never going to lose that.' Tony pondered aloud: 'I don't feel insecure, though I probably am. I feel very different. I don't feel the same necessarily as other Jews. My father used to announce to everybody – it was terribly embarrassing – who he was. We were coming down from the Lake District by train and there were two old ladies sitting there knitting. He suddenly stood up and said: "My name is Godfrey, and I am a German-Jewish refugee of Nazi oppression." He didn't quite give his inside leg measurement, but almost.

This was his standard introduction. I know why he said it. It was because of his accent. He wanted people to know his situation.'

Marion added: 'They felt a terrible loss of status as well, because they'd had a certain standing in the community in Germany, and they came over here on a domestic permit when they'd never even seen the inside of a kitchen. It was a terrible come-down.'

'Yes, my mother was thirty-nine when she came here, and she'd never cooked in her life. She became a cook, and my father a butler. Of course English cooking was easy in those days. You took something and you put it in boiling water, or if it was meat you stuck it in an oven. One day my father was serving, and the head of the household said, "Vinegar, please, Fritz," so my father removed some of the potatoes from the plate. "No, Fritz, vinegar." So he removed some of the fish. "I said vinegar." So he took off some peas. He thought the man was saying "*Wehniger*", which in German means less.'

'One day,' chimed in Marion,' 'my mother was presented with a list of things to do. At the top of the list it said: CLEAN AGA. She didn't know what an Aga was, so she looked for the dog.' If parents can cope with their own ineptitude in such circumstances, it can be more difficult for their children to handle the social unease. 'For half of my life,' says Marion, 'I had this feeling of being very different and hated it, kicked against it. Even my other Jewish friends felt there was something strange about me because my parents spoke with a funny accent, because we ate different foods. My dream has always remained a Shippam's fish-paste sandwich. Destroy the illusion: tell me it's not good. It was very important when we went on half-term shopping expeditions that I was correctly dressed. Even to pop down to Marks and Spencer in Marble Arch was a big occasion. It was part of the camouflage. It's also a Teutonic streak, this desire for correctness, and I've inherited some of it.'

'So have I,' nodded Tony. 'The refugee thing is so strong. We're born here and we're still terribly conscious of it. When there's a mixed marriage of English Jew and Continental Jew, there's often a huge clash.'

'Continental' – there's a word that took me back decades. I'd forgotten that this is how refugees define themselves – 'refugee' itself being considered slightly demeaning, especially if you own a £2-million house in Hampstead. I was to hear it again at a 'social' organized by the Association for the Children of Jewish Refugees. Tony and Marion were very much aware of being refugees' children and equally aware that this gave them a special perspective and possibly a few problems in relating to the mysterious 'English' Jews. But I doubt that they would have felt the need for a support group such as the ACJR. I found the 'social' a depressing occasion, with participants showing an over-earnest absorption in their own social unease. Most members are of German or Austro-Hungarian parentage, though a few had Polish or Russian backgrounds. In most cases both parents were refugees; in a few only one was foreign-born. Some members lived in Home Counties towns, such as Watford, where the Jewish community is small, and felt a need to mix with other Jews from a similar background. It was the common assumptions within the group that created the bond between the members. They were all 'Continentals' and almost all found it difficult to communicate with British-born Jews, whom they consider too materialistic in their preoccupations. Moreover, few of the Continentals were religious and they disliked the selective but socially excluding Orthodoxy of much of Anglo-Jewry, just as I had been discomfited in childhood by grillings to establish whether my parents kept a kosher home. For many this awareness of their 'Continental' background had come relatively late: their parents had often been reluctant to talk about their past, and the children had grown up dimly aware of this turbulent and often tragic background, yet unable to come to grips with it themselves. Increasingly obsessed by the circumstances that had led to the deracination, they had found their parents – if they were still alive – unwilling or unable to enlighten them, and were turning to their peers in order to express freely their need to understand the past. Indeed, according to some members, only after their parents had died did they feel 'permitted' to explore their background.

I understood the need but didn't share it. Neither do Tony and Marion, who had made quite a speciality of sending up the Continentals. One evening I attended my aunt's birthday party. Most of her friends were fellow refugees. They had all, as my Texan friends say, 'done good' and most of the guests could lay claim to a jewel or a cigar or a fur, or all three. Tony and Marion, joined by my cousin and his wife (the daughter of refugees) who were also present, entertained the crowd after supper by presenting a cabaret. Mimicking the thick German and Austrian accents of their audience, they pretended to be two typical Continental couples fussing about as they tried to organize a trip to the theatre or a holiday abroad. The essence of the humour was malapropism. As the refugees improved their English, their German grew rusty, and sometimes the two languages fused. My mother, whose English was very good, would gabble away at me in German in an attempt to teach me the language, but

409

whenever she was stuck for a word she'd throw in the English one instead. I knew exactly what she was talking about, but an eavesdropper would have been mystified if he'd heard her say, *'Mach' schnell! Der* postman *kommt bald!'* or whatever. The cabaret team mined this rich vein, and came up with such undoubtedly authentic linguistic fusions as: *'Ach, nein!* This bill is *horrendig!'* and the malapropisms: 'You can't find ze car keys? So vy don't you look in the glove department?' Or, an old favourite in refugee circles: 'They're British now. They've been nationalized.' And a *Brewer*-full of new proverbs and phrases came pouring out: 'Deaf as a bat . . . I wouldn't touch him with a lamp-post . . . If there's one thing drives me crazy, it's a backside driver . . . I can't find my cough-links . . . He's a chip off the old brick.'

The audience took it pretty well, especially when you consider that there was scarcely a single member of it who hadn't committed one of these clangers at some time or other. After the show, I was standing by the front door chatting to Tony when an old dragon, Mrs Potlitzer by name, came up to give the whippersnapper her review of the cabaret. *'Na ja,'* she conceded, 'it vas kvite amusing. But it vas too long!' Tony shrugged and smiled. 'Anyvay,' she continued, 'it's out of date. Ve don't have eksents any more.' And she stomped off. Tony, despite the V-sign he presented to her departing back, said there were always a few old dears who were offended by the show, and nothing offended them more than the stigmatizing accents. Others were astonished by the rich Germanic rumbles for a different reason. Marion told me how she overheard one old lady saying to another: 'It's amazing. Zey vere born here, but zey still speak viz an eksent!'

Much as I enjoyed the show, it also surprised me that any immigrant group would so readily, despite the Mrs Potlitzers in the audience, appreciate and clearly enjoy being parodied by their own children. Tony, of course, had an explanation for that too: 'Jews are good at laughing at themselves. They're self-deprecating. But the truth is they never think it's them we're mimicking. They think it must be Mrs Balzheimer down the road "who spiks rilly bedly".'

Legs and roots: Anglo-Jewish identity

IN the early years of this century the non-religious Zionist thinker Ahad Ha-am wrote in 'Zionism and Jewish Culture': 'The complete, or almost complete, sterility of Hebrew culture dates only from the modern period of assimilation and emancipation; and it does not mean that we have suddenly lost our original creative faculty. It is due simply to the development of a tendency to sink our national individuality in the pursuit of assimilation. We have voluntarily and of set purpose tried to cease being original and become merely imitators; and as a natural consequence the most gifted Jews have found no scope for their talents in Jewish life, and have deserted it for other fields of activity.'[1] This passage strikes me as astonishingly prophetic. Although its general truth applies to all diaspora communities, it seems especially true of lacklustre Anglo-Jewry. British Jews have lost out in two ways adumbrated by Ahad Ha-am: philistinism and intolerance within the fold have persuaded countless gifted Jews to direct their energies away from their community; and British Jews loyal to their religious and cultural tradition have always sought to adopt the lowest possible profile. It is certainly respectable to be Jewish in Britain, but it's neither exciting nor chic. To express your Jewishness is even perceived as embarrassing. When Maureen Lipman, although Jewish herself, made a series of advertisements in which she depicted, with the gentlest of humour, an anxious Jewish grandmother, there was a fair amount of outrage from within the community. It was ridiculous to claim, though some did, that her impersonation was tantamount to anti-Semitic stereotyping. The real reason for the outrage was embarrassment: it isn't done in Britain to proclaim your Jewishness, even in tranquil and humorous ways.

After a lengthy presence as a British sub-culture, Anglo-Jewry does not wish to be regarded as an ethnic minority; hence any portrayal that plays on ethnic characteristics can be seen as threatening. Colin Shindler deplores the tendency of British Jews to 'anglicize ourselves to the point of non-existence, to become as far as possible like the people we're living amongst'. He points out that when the next national census is taken, the government proposes that members of ethnic minorities should identify themselves. This seems sensible enough, if only as an aid to combating racism, and most immigrant groups have not objected. British Jews have opposed the proposal. To admit to being an ethnic minority would somehow align Anglo-Jewry with Bangladeshis and Greek-Cypriots, whereas the Jewish Establishment wants its primary identity to be British. That's an understandable position, but the price that has to be paid is a repression of Jewish culture and values, or at least an insistence on keeping them well confined within the community. Chaim Bermant prefers to see the assimilationist process in a more favourable light: 'If English society is exclusive, English culture is hospitable, and if the sons and the grandsons of the immigrants rushed to seize everything it offered, it wasn't out of the desire to forsake their own heritage, but because of the overwhelming attractions of the English one.'[2]

Anglo-Jewry has always been self-effacing. With the exception of the Chief Rabbi, who never misses an occasion or pretext to laud Jewish values (or his idea of Jewish values) in the context of British society as a whole, Anglo-Jewry is remarkably silent on issues not of direct and immediate concern to itself. As an editorial in the *Jewish Quarterly* put it: 'Perhaps the most unsavoury aspect [of the deliberate policy of acculturation] has been the tendency, with few exceptions, to opt out of national debates, in which Jewish thought and experience could make a valuable contribution, and to participate only on questions of vested Jewish interest.'[3] Self-effacement leads to timidity, the bedfellow of mediocrity. The intellectual barrenness of Anglo-Jewry is depressing, and the only consolation is that the host society isn't much of an improvement. George Weidenfeld speculates that the mediocrity of Anglo-Jewry may be related to the fact that new entrants into British society weren't required to innovate in the way that immigrants to countries such as the United States were obliged to do. Those who came to Britain found a fully formed society, not the malformed chunks of nationhood and national identity that immigrants to America encountered. In mitigation of the Anglo-Jewish experience, Lord Weidenfeld observes: 'You can't fill a gap that isn't there.'

Others are less kindly in their appraisal. Leo Abse views Anglo-Jewry with a kind of sadness: 'I think we have a very poor Jewish community in Britain. We have our intellectuals and professionals, but the main contribution that has come from Jews is in the distributive trades. We are glorified shopkeepers. Nevertheless there are certain quite distinctive features. Most of the poor Jews who came over in the late nineteenth century saw the hardships and hazards of artisan work. But they also came out of communities where above everything else there was respect for learning. When they first arrived they expressed this in a secular form. They couldn't make their sons rabbis, but they could push them into the professions. It was done for security, for they were poor and living in times when depressions could hit hard, but the professions offered more than security. The Jews took pride in learning. But now they've become debauched and corrupted. The bulk of the Jewish community are *gefilte fish* Jews. They haven't had the enrichment I had from my grandfather, because most of them around now, their fathers knew nothing, they never had that background, they had no spiritual capital. Neither did they have the background of knowing their history and knowing about what I call the alternative tradition. They lived in a vacuum, and latter-day capitalism and its values were able to fill that vacuum.'

Abse's is a gloomy and censorious view, but there is an element of truth in it. Even though attempts are being made to revive what Abse calls the alternative tradition, it is hard to envisage a generation of Jewish intellectuals that could restore the cultural vitality of the community – and I'm not talking about Israeli dancing and baking Purim cakes. Scan the cultural pages of the *Jewish Chronicle*, and weep. The standard of critical writing is, for the most part, abysmal. The arguments raging within Anglo-Jewry are well aired by the paper, but it rarely peeks at the world outside. As George Steiner remarked, 'The great philosophical debates pass us by. Of course, not everyone can be Spinoza, but it's arguable that we are the only nation of dumb Jews.'

Even though there is only a minimal amount of Anglo-Jewish culture worthy of the name, British Jews are desperately anxious that what there is of it should be transmitted to their children. Scared rigid by nightmares of out-marriage and demographic decline, a tremendous emotional investment has been made in Jewish youth, whose sense of identity has had to be nurtured, bolstered, sustained. During those post-barmitzvah days when many teenagers drift away from communal identification, youth groups,

413

whether synagogal or Zionist, do their best to recruit new members. Most of those who attend such clubs pay little heed to the ideological content of their chosen organization, and regard it, sensibly enough, as a social club where they can meet their peers in a relaxed setting. Jewish student groups have been equally unsuccessful in persuading a majority of Jewish students that they have anything to offer them. Out of all the Jewish students in Britain, probably no more than 10 per cent have joined Jewish student groups. As has already been mentioned, not even the expansion of Jewish education seems to have had any effect on the strength of Jewish commitment among the graduates of the system.

Teenagers, of course, resist being organized, especially on Saturday night. Bored suburban kids with plenty of cash in their pockets and rejoicing under the collective title of Becks descend on Edgware Station or various Hendon bagel shops every Saturday night during clement weather. On Thursday nights up to 400 kids congregate on the streets of Hampstead, where certain pizzerias and coffee-houses and pubs have become favourite hangouts for Jewish teenagers. The girls tend to have frizzy hair, plenty of make-up, and are quite smartly dressed, though some, like the boys, prefer to wear stone-washed jeans. The gatherings of the Becks are widely perceived as a blight on the community, though the teenagers seem perfectly well behaved and only occasionally boisterous. The anxiety tells us more about the paranoia of the parents than the deficiencies of the children. All teenagers hang out if given half a chance, especially those marooned in the London suburbs, and Jewish teenagers are no exception. Many have spent summers in Israel where street life is part of the culture. There is a slight danger that the occasional drug-pusher might relieve them of a few fivers in their wallets, but there is no reason why young Jews should be exempt from the fashionable if danger-ous temptations of the age. There is also concern that anti-social behaviour by the teenagers themselves, especially in annoying local residents late at night by making too much noise, could harm relations with the non-Jewish community.

It does appear that what worries parents most is not the illicit vodka and tonic or joint of marijuana, but the possibility that dozens or hundreds of massed young Jews on the streets could damage the image of the community. Having watched parents, dressed to the nines and heading for an evening out, drive up to the forecourt of Edgware Station in a very large BMW and there disgorge their pampered kids, it seems to me that parents are as much to blame as their children for any social embarrassment that might ensue. As Alan Greenbat of the Association for Jewish Youth remarked: 'It's bad to be conspicuous, and we don't know what we'll bring upon ourselves. I don't know why we have this insecurity, but I don't think we serve our own best interests by living in perpetual fear.' If the Becks are smoking dope and eating too many bagels, at least they're doing it in the company of other Jews, which should come as a relief to parents who live in terror of the greatest disgrace of all: out-marriage. What's more, Becks are rather discouragingly conventional. The girls' hearts seem set on a detached house in Stanmore and an apartment in Marbella, the boys' on a career as an accountant or estate agent. Becks don't shave their heads or rape grannies or go on CND marches, and those anxious parents should consider themselves lucky.

That the so-called crisis among Jewish youth is mostly a confusion in the minds of their parents and other assorted elders became transparently clear in the course of yet another barometric meeting at the Cockfosters United synagogue, where, under the beaming chairmanship of Rabbi Fine, the formidable pair of Dr Lionel Kopelowitz and Rabbi Michael Rosen had been invited to address an audience on the subject of 'dispirited youth'. Rabbi Fine, in his introductory remarks, used fighting words: the pressure is on, he told us, and Jewish youth is threatened by missionary activities (i.e. crazed Christian evangelists who are turned on by telling Jews about Jesus) and drugs. But we should take heart, since the community is fighting back with its secret weapon: day schools. Rabbi Rosen was prepared to recognize the vast parental anxiety over the weekly Jewish invasion of Edgware Station, but confessed he had no obvious solution. If Mickey Rosen has no solution, that's a sure sign there's no problem in the first place. A member of the audience had a suggestion, though: more youth centres with wholesome Jewish entertainments. At which point a youth, present in person at the meeting instead of stuffing his face with bagels in Hendon, said that he and his pals at Edgware Station were perfectly happy and couldn't think of anything they wanted less than to be marched off to a youth centre for the evening.

Dr Kopelowitz, endearingly, totally misunderstood the topic under discussion. Gazing avuncularly at the handful of teenagers in the audience, he declared that they didn't look dispirited at all! He patronized them hugely, and they knew it, rewarding his booming condescensions with silence. The only possible reason why kids could be dispirited, Dr Kopelowitz apparently believed, was that other kids had been saying beastly things about Israel to them. Hands up those who have suffered

415

unfriendly comments about Israel, commanded the President of the Board. No hands. Unhappy with the result – not a single dispirited child! – he pressed them hard. Don't be shy! Eventually two children raised their hands, more, it seems likely, to get the elderly doctor off their backs than because their suffering had been intense. It didn't seem to have occurred to Dr Kopelowitz that the children present probably attended Jewish schools, safe from anti-Zionist menaces. Indeed, we later learnt that the two children who had raised their hands were both pupils at Hasmonean, which either confirms my theory or tells us something rather peculiar about that school. On the slender statistical evidence before him, Dr Kopelowitz stuck to his guns and declared that the reason kids were dispirited was that they couldn't put across to their critics the historical context of what was happening in Israel. At least he was now on familiar territory, could dispense with the topic supposedly under discussion, and treated us to a school-prizegiving speech about how it's tougher to be a good Jew in good times than in bad times, and how parents need to learn along with their children. Stressing the dangers of assimilation, he urged the children, who continued to look perfectly cheerful, not to be dispirited after all.

It was a splendidly pointless evening. Nobody had the faintest idea whether the premise of the discussion was true, and if it was, to which of an infinite number of causes, depending on which hobby-horse you fancied riding, it should be attributed. It is obvious that dispirited youth is less of a problem within the community than faltering and unimaginative leadership. The community at large must believe, despite all the evidence to the contrary, that the amiable Dr Kopelowitz is its best possible leader, since he was reelected unopposed to the presidency of the Board in 1988. He'll pat 'Jewish youth' on the head but discourages moves to alter the rules of the Board to give Jewish youth, dispirited or ebullient, a greater say in the community. Representation of those under thirty-five years old among the deputies is negligible. Dr Kopelowitz is happy with the status quo: 'If young people want to get themselves elected, the opportunities are there. It's up to them to take them but nobody's going to run with a spoon and feed them into it. If people don't want to challenge, they can't then argue they don't have a chance.' Fair enough, but Jewish respect for the elderly makes it far more probable that a synagogue, the most likely electoral body, will elect a deputy as a kind of long-service medal rather than elect a relatively youthful member. In the meantime, if the leaders of the various Jewish youth movements are to be believed, they are becoming increasingly fed up with a communal leadership that constantly pays lip service to our wonderful youth but refuses to consult them or give them any say in communal affairs. Melanie Sobell, the national secretary of the Reform Netzer movement, once remarked that communal leaders were so uninspiring that young people couldn't even bring themselves to rebel against them.[4]

Not that the Board is a crucial forum when it comes to determining the future of the Anglo-Jewish community. Far more important are factors such as religious polarization and the demographic decline of the community. That decline gives a licence to many younger Jews to become more assertive in declaring their Jewish identity. Curiously, notions of Jewish identity are simultaneously being narrowed – by the Orthodox establishment – and broadened. To be Jewish is no more than an inheritance, a combination of genetics and legalism. To feel Jewish is entirely different. To cease to be Jewish is virtually impossible. A new element has been added with the establishment of the State of Israel. Before 1948, it was easy to tuck into one's sense of Jewishness vague Zionist aspirations. Today, however, the Jews have a nation State. A degree of loyalty is expected among diaspora Jews to that State, for few Jews regard Israel as a nation State like any other; indeed, many Jews argue that Jewish survival itself is to a large extent bound up with the survival of Israel. Hence the tremendous sensitivity of Establishment Jews in the diaspora to criticisms voiced within the community against Israeli policies or attitudes. Perhaps too, though this is pure speculation, some leaders of diaspora Jewry feel guilt that they, for all their fine words, have never chosen to move to Israel themselves, and now feel that the least they can do is stick by Israel through thick and thin.

For the non-religious and the non-Zionist, it is still possible to feel Jewish. Mike Anderson, growing up in Sheffield, found himself in this position. 'I was brought up to believe that there were only two ways you could be Jewish. One was to be a Zionist, and one was to be religious. I was neither and didn't see how I could be Jewish. Until I was about thirty, when I began to realize there was a history and a culture and lots of other positive things there. Now it's up to each Jew to define for him or herself whether they are Jewish and you should never let anybody do it for you.' Some Jews, however, feel that they have allowed others to define their Judaism around them. The writer Brian Glanville has remarked: 'One is and remains Jewish, partly because the roots are much more profound, partly because one's temperamental inheritance and early determining experience are Jewish, partly because it was made so clear to one in a Gentile society that one *was* Jewish.'[5] Despite the anxieties of some community leaders that conspicuous behaviour on the part of Jews can lead to increasing anti-Semitism, most Jews recognize that how Jews act or appear is not in itself a cause of anti-Semitism. Paul Johnson has quoted the remark of the Austrian writer Arthur Schnitzler, who observed: 'You had the choice of being insensitive, obtuse or cheeky, or of being oversensitive, timid and suffering from feelings of persecution.'[6] What was true of turn-of-the-century Vienna is still true today, although in a more muted form. The poet Dannie Abse insists that the ancient fear felt by the Jew in a hostile environment is still with us: 'Why is it that every Jew over-reacts, however much he feels himself to be delivered from a ghetto mentality, when a Jewish figure like Peter Rachman features villainously in some contemporary scandal? The fact is, I don't believe any Jew in the diaspora, however much he proclaims the contrary, is other than a Ghetto Jew, in the deepest sense – and this is, above all, because of the wartime destruction of the Jew in Europe.'[7]

The 'Ghetto Jew' is a negative formulation of that sense of alienation, of not fully belonging, that is common among the first wave of immigrants, for reasons that are hardly obscure. That sense of being an outsider in British society persists, and not only among refugees, though there are many Jews who have not experienced it at all. Greville Janner states that he is 'totally immersed in both societies. My father used to say that British Jews were the most fortunate people in the world, because you have one foot in one great culture and the other foot in another. His other view, which I accept entirely, is that you don't become a better Briton by becoming a worse Jew.' Lord Goodman has also never felt marginalized, 'but I don't think I'd feel on the margins of any society. If I arrive somewhere, I feel happily that I belong until someone expels me. It's a matter of temperament. Lots of people feel uneasy in society who are not Jewish. If you look around, you'll find that the first generations – from Greece, Italy, wherever – have varying degrees of confidence, good humour, satisfaction, stability. Some are happy and assimilated from the moment they arrive. Others never become happy and assimilated.'

But to Sir Isaiah Berlin, social unease is characteristic of Jews. He himself feels perfectly at ease sunk into an armchair at the Athenaeum, but when he chats to his fellow clubmen he knows he's not one of them. Anthony Blond also registers a sense of alienation: 'I feel slightly alien when I go to very grand houses. Not ill at ease, but I feel it's not me at all.

I'm not in that bloodstream. The Jew is the permanent alien. That's why I've never lived in a Jewish neighbourhood. I like the alienation. It gives me a little tingle, an awareness, an extra sensitivity on the skin.' Ian Mikardo is resigned to being perceived as different, though he feels no alienation: 'It's not because of what you feel, but because of what other people feel about you. There are people who think a Jew has a foot in another camp. To some extent, how you are perceived is what you are. But I haven't felt any great difference. All my closest associates in politics have been *goyim*, and I haven't felt any different from them.' Jonathan Miller feels his Jewishness only in response to the perception of others: 'I remain uninterested in being Jewish. It doesn't have any influence or effect on my life. People sometimes say, "Oh, you wouldn't think the way you do if you weren't Jewish," as if there were some genetic thing, but I don't think there's any genetic way of thinking. I'm a Jew for anti-Semites, and some people would say I'm an anti-Semite for Jews. I'm only a Jew if someone wants to make an issue out of it. If someone wants to say, "You're a dirty Jew," I'll say, "Yes, yes, I am."'

For George Steiner, characteristically, the very question has little meaning: 'I'm at home wherever there is a typewriter. Give me a station waiting-room and a typewriter, and I'm as happy as I'd be at All Souls. My home is in time. Since Auschwitz we cannot speak of having a home. Trees have roots, but we have legs – that's a marvellous advantage for us. For Jews life is never boring, we can enjoy the *mitzvah* of never being bored – except perhaps in England!' Frederic Raphael is wary of making a cult of rootlessness: 'One can't actually spend one's life, and Jews don't have the temperament to do so, with one's bags packed. I don't think any virtue comes out of any such form of waiting.'

Although many Jews continue to feel like outsiders, that sense of alienation, whether slight or profound, does seem to be diminishing, which is a sign of health. Rabbi Vogel of Lubavitch, which spearheads the new assertiveness among British Jews, feels that Jews have been humble too long. A combination of factors – notably, fear of persecution and gratitude for refuges such as Britain – has persuaded Jews that they should present the lowest possible profile. 'While I'm the first to recognize the humaneness of the Western societies who accepted Jewish people, nonetheless that attitude is evaporating for a number of reasons. First, it has cost the Jewish people enormously, in the sense that they have never felt able to assert themselves, they've had to disguise their Judaism, in the office and in the street. This has caused a dilution and eventually disintegration of Jewish family life. Secondly, the open society in which we live today not only tolerates a pluralistic society and an independent point of view, it expects it. The Gentiles have come to expect the Jewish people to set standards and lead the way, not in an arrogant or even assertive way, but definitely by example, to re-establish values which can be of value to the country in which we live. It is axiomatic that a better Jew must be a better citizen. A person who is not loyal to his own traditions is suspect in his adoption of loyalty to new traditions.' This view of the Jews as moral standard-bearers is reassuring to those who proclaim it, but carries with it the dangers of smugness and hypocrisy, for it would be deeply dangerous to assert that Jews, because of their religious and ethical beliefs, are intrinsically 'better' than their fellow citizens. Moreover, non-religious Jews will proclaim values, based on the same ethical teachings, that are at odds with those of the Orthodox.

The revival of Jewish assertiveness has been aided by the arrival in Britain of other immigrant groups who have taken the spotlight off the Jews. Moreover, in Thatcherite Britain, as Frederic Raphael remarks, 'assertiveness has now become a licensed form of behaviour, and Jews, having got the licence, have no intention of not using it'. It has also been stimulated by a unique factor, the recent memory of the Holocaust. When the deportations to the death camps began, it made no difference to the Nazis whether you were an assimilated Jew or a pious *shtetl* Jew. Your destination was the same. Heredity not behaviour sealed the fate of those who were murdered. One lesson many Jews draw from this is that since your enemies don't discriminate between Jews, there is no point in adopting the low profile that used to be, and to some extent still is, the hallmark of Anglo-Jewry.

Another lesson is that it is the primary duty of the Jewish people simply to survive, so that never again shall murderous anti-Semitism be given an opportunity to eradicate Jewry. Dow Marmur laments that contemporary Judaism 'seems unable to offer a positive reason for staying Jewish but at the same time is neurotically preoccupied with the danger of ceasing to be Jewish . . . A faith that is only expressed when the enemy attacks, and not when God calls man to prayer and atonement, is a faith forged by foes. There is much to suggest that the survival syndrome, which so strongly dominates contemporary Jewish life, is based on such faith.'[8] That such an emphasis on survival has taken root is understandable. But, as Rabbi Marmur implies, there are dangers too. Whether one regards the Holocaust as a unique event in world history, unforeseeable and probably unrepeatable, or whether one regards it as the culmination of a series of persecutions directed at the Jews for countless centuries, it could be unhealthy if the community dwelt obsessively on its unfathomable cruelties.

In recent years a number of events have sought to bring the reality of the Holocaust more forcibly to the consciousness of Britons, Jews and non-Jews. There was the television screening of Claude Lanzmann's harrowing but unsensational epic documentary *Shoah*, and in 1988 a conference on the theme of 'Remembering for the Future' was organized by Dr Elizabeth Maxwell. Some observers, such as George Steiner, feel that Britons are simply indifferent to the Holocaust. 'In Britain the Shoah has no reality, not even to the Jews. Those who speak and write about it, and raise the crucial questions of how Auschwitz has altered our perceptions, our theology, are considered bombastic. Leading literary figures – Kingsley Amis, Philip Larkin – have written as though unaware that the Holocaust had ever taken place. Out of all the countries in the world with a sizeable Jewish population, Britain alone, out of the whole diaspora of remembrance, is oblivious of the Shoah. Britain behaves as though the nineteenth-century contract with rationality and meliorism were still intact. The experience of our own century seems to have had no effect. The Jewish Establishment will never remonstrate, it will never rock the boat. Did it speak up in the 1940s when unspeakable things were being done to those who had survived the Holocaust? No. Consequently we live in an oasis of unreality. Yet it is a miracle that the Jews of Britain were spared the horrors of Europe. Only twenty miles of salt sea separated them from extinction.' Rodney Mariner has a contrary impression. 'The thing I found most interesting about the Anglo-Jewish community was the part the Holocaust played. In Australia, where I lived until a few years ago, the Holocaust was an embarrassment, like being related to a rape victim.' And Frederic Raphael makes the pertinent point that 'the British won. They don't regard the Holocaust as their problem. It really isn't very surprising. Your bad foot is not my bad foot. I may be sympathetic, I may give you a hand across the street, but I don't limp.'

Yet Britain has seemed slow to take cognizance of the monstrousness of the Holocaust. I was watching *Shoah* on television in Austria, of all places, one whole year before the film was shown in Britain. But I do not see why writers are under any obligation to reflect the Holocaust in their work. It is not a theme that is, or should be, lightly tackled or incorporated. After Dr Maxwell's conference had taken place, her husband, the publisher Robert

421

Maxwell, corroborating Steiner's theme, fumed that it had been given virtually no press coverage. I certainly read press accounts of the conference, and that same week watched a television documentary about artists who had depicted life in the concentration camps. After reading those accounts I remained unclear what purpose was served by the conference itself. The main outcome was a plea for further research into the Holocaust to establish, in as much detail as possible, what exactly happened, the whens and the hows if not the whys, both to counter the obscene allegations that the Holocaust never took place and to ensure that by publicizing the full horror of it one does everything humanly possible to prevent its recurrence, not only to Jews but to any group. In its final document, the conference called on national and international agencies 'to devise early-warning systems to ensure effective action against the danger of genocide', which sounds fairly meaningless to me. A prophylactic aim may be a worthy one, but do conferences of this kind further it? Dr Maxwell declared: 'It is our sacred duty as teachers to amass stark facts, to read and publish diaries and survivors' accounts, to interest ourselves in details concerning the death of the Jews.'[9] Is it? Of all teachers? Jewish teachers? What purpose is served by Dr Maxwell's gross oversimplification: 'The unbearable catastrophe was perpetrated by baptized Christians, on Christian soil, among Christian people who kept their silence'?[10] Guilt cannot be backdated. Such statements explain nothing.

Anglo-Jewry's less publicized efforts to commemorate the Holocaust seem, in their different ways, equally unsatisfactory. Each year in April, on the day known as Yom Hashoa, a brief ceremony is held at the Holocaust Memorial in Hyde Park. In 1988 many hundreds of people, including schoolchildren, gathered and listened as the Chief Rabbi read from the Bible and Stephen Robins of Edgware Synagogue chanted, very beautifully, a prayer for the dead. There the ceremony should have ended, but no. Ruth Rosen, who has made something of a speciality of this kind of reading, declaimed the passage from Elie Wiesel's *Night* describing his arrival at Auschwitz as a boy. I do not care for Mr Wiesel's rhetorical style and prefer the restraint of a Primo Levi, who writes of the same terrible happenings with greater delicacy and penetration. I care even less for Ruth Rosen's hectoring. She pitched the emotion at maximum voltage, piling horror upon horror, as though stridency were the only way to move an audience. After her long declamation, six survivors lit memorial candles and then the crowd recited the *Kaddish* in unison. The ceremony raised the question of how a community can memorialize so shattering an event in a satisfactory way. Myself, I would have restricted the ceremony to the Hebrew prayers. Those who take the trouble to gather in the park on a cool spring morning surely don't need to be reminded why they are there.

A few days later a few hundred Jews gathered at a London theatre to commemorate the forty-fifth anniversary of the Warsaw Ghetto Uprising. That the commemoration was laid out like a vaudeville programme was not encouraging. It opened with a twenty-minute medley of songs performed by a children's choir, and a poetry reading in Yiddish. The chairman of the Polish-Jewish Ex-Servicemen's Association, Leon Feit, gave a long address about Polish attitudes towards the Jews. Speaker after speaker referred to 'martyrs', a fundamental misunderstanding of the Holocaust and a sign of how automated our responses can become when they are routinely summoned up. Martyrs choose to die rather than abandon their beliefs. Jews, for the most part, did not choose to die; they were murdered. To describe them as martyrs is to heighten the emotion, but to diminish the tragedy.

The principal address was given by the Speaker of the House of Commons, Bernard Weatherill. It began with the extraordinary admission, for a man of his years, that until the previous week he hadn't actually known about the destruction of the Warsaw ghetto – which made me wonder why we should be required to listen to his reflections on the matter. He referred, dismayingly, to the uprising as a symbol of Jewish experience, and praised those who had fought to preserve freedom in Poland, another misreading of that desperate situation. Mr Weatherill's final gesture was, literally, to salute the audience. In his reply to the Speaker, Martin Savitt, a pillar of Anglo-Jewry, used the occasion to sound off on his favourite themes: anti-Semitic literature and the defence of Israel in a time of crisis. After a brief ceremony by ex-servicemen parading flags and children lighting memorial candles, the event concluded with Emanuel Freilich's chanting of a memorial prayer, the only moving part of this inept and incoherent commemoration.

I asked Dr Kopelowitz why he considered Holocaust commemorations important, and he told me that 'young people should be aware of the depths to which human beings can descend on occasions, and know that certain peoples have in previous generations acted with crass inhumanity. This should be a guide to them to put all this behind them for the future.' A confused thought if ever I encountered one, for how does one put something behind one by dwelling on it exhaustively? The Holocaust is not an event, surely, that can be studied like an item on a curriculum, ticked off, and 'put behind one'. For Jews and others, holding conferences or adding to the thousand courses already taught on the subject at American colleges does not help them come to terms with the near destruction of European Jewry a mere forty-five years ago. And it certainly isn't aided by such events as the Holocaust concert at Covent Garden organized in conjunction with the Maxwell conference. The concert consisted of three lugubrious pieces of music, preceded by the blowing of the ram's horn and a minute's silence. What response did the organizers hope for from the audience as they sat through two hours of gloomy music? Tears? Images of bone-filled crematoria? Such events, for all the good intentions of Dr Maxwell and her co-organizers, can be little more than an emotional self-indulgence.

Other responses to the Holocaust are plainly exploitative. The ultra-Orthodox often justify their zest for procreation with the claim that they are doing no more than replenishing the stock which Hitler eradicated. Israeli politicians, notably Menachem Begin, have invoked the Holocaust as an all-purpose riposte to criticism, as though such suffering had given the Jews a kind of impunity and as though the guilt of non-Jews disqualified them from passing any judgements on Israeli politicians. Such manipulations are, of course, obscene. The experience and memory of the Holocaust should be turned, if at all possible, to practical purposes. The Council of Christian and Jews, which was founded in 1942 as the Nazi extermination programme was getting into high gear, has helped Christians to acknowledge those elements in Christian theology that have been used to justify anti-Semitic feelings and acts. This awareness has led to changes in Christian theology and dogma. Moreover, inter-faith work that will broaden mutual understanding among religious groups, Muslim as well as Christian and Jewish, can only be a good thing. The memory of the Holocaust should also make Jews especially sensitive to other genocidal outrages. Jews were indeed prominent among those who expressed horror and organized relief after the Khmer Rouge killed about a third of the Cambodian people in the late 1970s, but one often senses that the Jewish attunement to injustice is all too often confined to its own sufferings.

Mike Anderson expresses a disquiet felt by many: 'You can't base a viable culture on those awful happenings. You simply have to find a way of moving away from it. To bring up children with constant reminders of the Holocaust can have awfully negative repercussions. What is the image of the Jew that the concentration camp evokes? I don't know what that does to a twelve-year-old. It does frighten me that a classful of kids is being brought up with the Holocaust being a central feature of Jewish experience. I don't know what relationships one builds with people thinking that there might be another Hitler.' Chaim Bermant has voiced a similar wariness: 'Excessive concern with the Holocaust can also have a pernicious effect on Jewish attitudes to the outside world. It intensifies paranoia and the sense of isolation.'[11] And so has the Chief Rabbi: 'I have some doubts about the sanctification of the Holocaust as a cardinal doctrine in contemporary Jewish thought.' The obligation to the living, he remarked, should be greater than the obligation to the dead.[12] I fear that the time may be approaching when the thoughts expressed by a character in Frederic Raphael's novel *After the War* may become all too apt: 'In the end, the camps'll be yet another thing they'll be saying gives us an unfair advantage. Auschwitz will be one more Jewish racket. An old school tie we won't let anyone else wear.'[13]

Astonishingly, in a century during which six million Jews were systematically murdered, the guardians of the faith seem more intent on throwing Jews out of the fold than in keeping them in. The Progressives take a more accommodating attitude and welcome conversions from non-Jewish spouses as a way of keeping that family, and its possible offspring, within the fold. Should a child marry out, it is not uncommon for Orthodox families to go through the formal process of mourning, as though there had been a death in the family. Nor is the horror restricted to Orthodox families. William Frankel observes: 'It's a curious phenomenon. You've got Jewish parents, who don't believe anything, who don't observe anything, but when one of their children wants to marry out of the faith, they go berserk. It's a primeval desire to perpetuate the tribe.' Sometimes parental antagonism to out-marriage moderates once a grandchild is born, but not always. The politician Edwina Currie married a non-Jew and since that time never saw her father again, nor did he ever see her children.

Hostility to out-marriage comes not only from Jews who are anxious that their descendants should be born into the faith, but from non-religious Jews who deplore any act that further depletes the strength of the Jewish population. George Steiner, no Orthodox Jew, told me: 'Being Jewish is not something one ought to want to give up. That's why I am unhappy about intermarriage. Being Jewish is not a card to throw aside.'

Nonetheless, there is no way in which a minority culture such as Anglo-Jewry can ever prevent defections of this sort. They can be, and are, discouraged, but they can never be banned. For the sanctions against out-marriage to be successful, there has to be a consensus of opinion that the primary duty of the Jew is to perpetuate his or her Jewishness. That is not a stance that all Jews would wish to adopt, though the Chief Rabbi heartily endorses it: 'Those who dishonour the Jewish people by doing the ultimate damage to us, which is to marry out and break a link in the continuity of Jewish existence, should not be honoured by the Jewish community.' The language is revealing: 'ultimate damage' and 'dishonour' – harsh terms to throw at people who may feel that their happiness is more bound up with marrying the person of their choice, regardless of religious affiliation, rather than dutifully ensuring the perpetuation of the Jewish people, desirable though that aim may be.

Lord Jakobovits goes further, for he wishes to impose social ostracism on those who marry out: 'It is incompatible, I think, with their own free choice to opt out of the full identification with the perpetuation of our ideals, that we should be seen publicly to give tacit recognition to such acts of religious betrayal by doing public honour to them. Since we no longer have the sanctions that were available to us in the Middle Ages, when we could virtually excommunicate people, the least we can do is to draw a line somewhere and indicate public disapproval by not going out of our way to bestow communal honours.' Does this mean, I asked the Chief Rabbi, that the primary duty of the Jew is to maintain continuity? 'The primary task of the Jew,' he replied, 'is to perpetuate his Jewishness. Of course. There can be no Judaism without Jews. And we are here in order to ensure as the eternal people that Judaism will prevail not by conquering the world but by always being there. If we voluntarily opt out and complete Hitler's work, nothing could be more horrendous to the Jewish destiny.'

I imagine many Jews who have married out might be offended by the Hitlerian comparison, nor is it encouraging to have to deduce that Jewish continuity can only be maintained by applying sanctions; there seems to be something wistful in the Chief Rabbi's evocation of the times when excommunication was still possible. There is also, it seems to me, a distasteful small-mindedness in the Chief Rabbi's attitude, which is widely shared. Jewish synagogues and organizations should not, in his view, 'endorse' out-marriage by inviting along as guest-speakers Jews who have married out. To do so would be to 'honour' an act of 'religious betrayal'. Thus, according to Lord Jakobovits, Harold Pinter, Britain's finest contemporary playwright, should never be invited to address a Jewish audience, since he has married out. If a Jew won a Nobel Prize for science but happened to have married a non-Jew, a sizeable proportion of the Anglo-Jewish community, if it heeds its religious leader, wouldn't want to know. A distinguished Jewish writer told me of being at the receiving end of discourtesies whenever he is invited to Jewish events such as book weeks. 'None of my books is available. I'm forced to wear a *kippah*. It's a way of saying, You think you're a big fella but we'll cut you down to size. It's a very uninteresting approach, to say the least.' No wonder, then, since it is so eager to close ranks, that Anglo-Jewry is as philistine and intellectually somnolent as it is. Nor am I comfortable with the suggestion that Jews have a mission, as expressed by Anthony Blond: 'We have a mission to circulate among the *goyim* and spread the light. I think we were definitely put in the world to improve it. We have a mission, a responsibility.' I prefer Isaiah Berlin's formulation: 'Jews have no mission, any more than Danes do.'

Jews are individualists; they do not, with sheepish exceptions, take kindly to being dragooned and disciplined. The fumings and banishings of rabbis won't change that. Jews are not, by and large, happy within corporate structures. They are pitiful sports players. Jews are better at games that involve single combat, such as boxing or tennis, but generally hopeless at team sports that involve concepts such as 'pulling your weight' and 'team spirit', all utterly alien to the self-respecting Jew. The boxer Jack 'Kid' Berg won the world welterweight title in 1930; and Angela Buxton won the women's doubles, or half of them, at Wimbledon in 1956. In general, however, Jews prefer to manage teams than be members of them. Thus many old-time boxing managers, such as Mickey Duff and the late Harry Levene, are Jews, and so is the football team manager David Pleat of Leicester City, and formerly of Luton and Tottenham Hotspurs.

Nor do some Jews like to be robbed of their identity by a small-minded Establishment. So-called unaffiliated Jews are just as Jewish as properly signed-up Jews. I cannot be disinherited from my culture and my history because I choose, however unsportingly, not to join a synagogue or support Zionist organizations. Since the Establishment's notion of Jewish identity is so narrowly defined, it is not surprising that many Jews feel more comfortable asserting their Jewish identity outside the formal community than within it. The Establishment may obstruct such expressions of Jewishness by refusing to validate those who operate outside its structures, but that scarcely matters. A fierce article by the historian David Cesarani puts this view even more harshly: the established community, he writes, 'has the cultural aspirations of assimilated nineteenth-century Anglo-Jewry and the paranoia of the *shtetl*. These are the sources of its self-image and its self-esteem. The Jewish community defines itself according to religious and racial characteristics . . . It does not include Marxists, Trotskyists, pacifists, anti-Zionists, critics, nuclear disarmers, homosexuals, lesbians, readers of the *Guardian* (and the *Jewish Quarterly*), the Reform and Progressive movement (or maybe just about, grudgingly). The Jewish community has a system of discourses which marginalize and de-judaize these groups: they are dissidents, intellectuals . . . they are "lost and searching for an identity", they are self-hating, they are well-meaning but confused, they don't belong to synagogues and therefore can't be Jews.'[14]

Dr Cesarani estimates that there are almost 100,000 Jews, a third of the community, who are not affiliated to a synagogue or major Jewish organization. Many are loosely associated through their participation in groups such as adult education classes, Jewish film festivals, the British Friends of Peace Now, Jews Organized for a Nuclear Arms Halt (JONAH), Jews Against Apartheid, or support groups. Others have immersed themselves in Jewish history. Others feel unequivocally Jewish but may have been excluded from the community after marrying out; others are the children of mixed marriages. Some of those active in the 'alternative community' may also, like Colin Shindler, participate in synagogal life or the Board of Deputies, but most will not, for lack of Jewish education or any religious feeling. Within the alternative community, nobody will ask to see your mother's birth certificate and nobody will laugh if you can't read Hebrew. Attempts are being made to organize this loose coalition of the unaffiliated into a more structured body, and a conference in Leeds in May 1988 established a group calling itself Ruach, the Alternative Jewish Network, but it is too early to say whether or not it will succeed. If it does, it will have to do so without any aid from Establishment organizations, which were approached but refused to contribute. One founder of Ruach described the mainstream community as 'very money-oriented, very anti-intellectual, complacent on the surface and fear-ridden underneath, which has nothing to offer me, either spiritually or intellectually . . . Orthodoxy is unbearably sexist and Reform feels like a church.'[15] A correspondent to the *Jewish Chronicle* wrote off Ruach as appealing to those who support nuclear disarmament and are 'partial to sexual perversions', and predicted that the network would be 'a breeding ground for anti-Semitism'[16], which gives one some idea of what unaffiliated Jews are up against.

Perhaps British Jews simply worry too much. The Establishment worries about the inexorable demographic decline of the community, and endures paroxysms of anxiety whenever prominent Jews fail to toe the party line. Jews who cannot identify with the synagogues or formal organizations probably expend too much energy railing against those who seek to exclude them and hold a pillow against their mouths. Excessive anxiety about Jewish survival and dwindling support for Israeli policies has made the argument more raucous, positions more extreme. There is no doubt that the Anglo-Jewish community does have a future. What kind of future that is likely to be we shall examine in the next chapter.

– 31 –

The year 2000

H ow to deal with the spectacle of one's own demographic decline is the problem that worries almost all sections of the Anglo-Jewish community. With an ageing population and a governmental retreat from the welfare state, greater demands are being made on Jewish charities at the same time that the number of those who support those charities continues to dwindle. The number of British Jews is no higher than it was fifty years ago, a statistic that reflects not a static community but a declining one. Britain's cluster of about 330,000 Jews constitutes less than one third of all western European Jews, who number about 1,250,000. A mere 130,000 Jews live in eastern Europe, reminding us with a jolt of the sheer thoroughness of the Holocaust. The total Jewish population today is some 13,500,000 but before the Second World War the number stood at 18,000,000. So it is hardly surprising that ardent Jews are deeply worried about the future of their communities. To the prewar British figure of 350,000 one must add over 100,000 to account for the influx of refugees not only from Europe but, in the postwar years, from the Middle East. A healthy community enjoying an average birth rate should have increased its numbers to about 750,000 by now, but this has not happened. Instead, between the period 1965–9 and 1975–9, the net loss within the Jewish community amounted to 14.6 per cent, an alarmingly high figure. Many respond to these signs of decline with deep gloom. A Manchester rabbi, citing these figures, asked rhetorically: 'Where have the others gone? The answer has to be assimilation, and that means that one whole half of the community has assimilated. The Orthodox community claims to be saving the community by bringing people back to Judaism, but it's too late. The assimilation has already taken place. Just

430

look at Manchester. People move out from Jewish districts to certain suburbs for professional reasons or because of property prices. They may retain their synagogue membership for burial rights, but they now live far away and hardly ever attend. The children of these families are almost certain to marry out. We face a very gloomy future.'

Tony Lerman of the Institute of Jewish Affairs predicts greater fragmentation among religious Jews 'because of unresolved conflicts that are bound to come out into the open eventually and because of what's happening in Israel. Israel has exerted a powerful influence here and it's been an influence for unity. It's always been possible when Israel has been under threat for appeals to be made to Jewish unity. That situation is going to deteriorate. The control over the community that the Zionist Establishment has had over the years is bound to break up as things get worse in Israel. The old certainties that held in the community maintained, for good and bad, a certain structure. I think they are slipping, and what exactly is going to come in their place I don't really know. If the Liberals and Reform were recruiting people much more quickly to their synagogues than they are – their portion is remaining fairly static – then we might see big changes, but that just isn't happening. I wish I could also see a radical flowering of alternative views, but I don't necessarily think that's going to happen either.'

The consensus view of the Anglo-Jewish Establishment is, however, less despondent. It can be summarized as the belief that Anglo-Jewry by the year 2000 will be smaller but somehow better. Simon Caplan of the Jewish Educational Development Trust accepts this view: 'There's a picture of demographic decline, and decline in synagogue attendance and religious marriage. The only thing that seems to be going up is the burials statistics. So it seems depressing. Yet I live in Hendon and we see every day another kosher restaurant or delicatessen opening up, another adult education course or institute, more students coming to Jews' College, publications such as *L'Eylah*, Israelis based here who are not classic New York taxi drivers but ideologically committed people making a contribution to the community, and many new schools. It seems to me, observing day by day, that this a boom time for Judaism – at least in this section of the community, which is not insubstantial. So there's a dissonance between all the statistics and the reality of the streets of north-west London. Basically we are measuring different things.

'By 2000 the community will have declined to below 300,000 and the rate of civil marriage will be on the increase. At the same time the very pertinent and unmeasured statistic is that the number of Jewish eighteen-year-olds who are leaving school and spending long periods in Israel will increase yet further. The number of adults who spend some proportion of their weeks studying Judaism will have increased dramatically. The type of rabbi and educator coming into the community will have improved dramatically, the number of Jews attending day schools will have increased. What we're going to get is quality versus quantity. United Synagogue general membership and attendance is on the decline, but in the last three or four years I can't even count how many new bases have opened up catering for all kinds of individual needs. There's the Ner Yisroel congregation, Yakar, a faster service, a slower service, more singing, less singing, study in the middle of the service, whatever it might be. People are breaking out and doing their own thing. It's very refreshing. Fortunately we're finding the learning and commitment coming from people who are also modern and outward-looking and not trying to return to the ghetto.'

Jonathan Sacks foresees a growth in peripheral organizations and adds that 'the synagogue service, for so long the central event of Anglo-Jewish life, may become only one of an increasing variety of contexts for Jewish affirmation.'[1] Others, such as Jonathan Lew of the United Synagogue, are cheered by what they see as a return to stricter observance: 'My children have had a better integrated Jewish education than I had, and probably they will ensure that their children have an education that's better still. I'm heartened to a certain extent when I listen to my own children talk about the numbers of their friends who wish to keep a kosher home, who are conscious of dietary laws when they go out – I find that encouraging. I'm encouraged by the number of young men and women who are participating in the adult education programmes that are in existence. It's not enough, I accept that, but I still think it's a larger proportion than it was.' Nor is Dr Kopelowitz unduly worried: 'There is now more Jewish learning at every level in this community than at any time in history. Therefore in that sense the outlook is fairly good. I don't see that we have a great deal to fear, provided we keep ourselves educated and knowledgeable on the matters which concern Jews.'

Stanley Kalms is almost rhapsodic about the possibilities, though he expressed his positive view in typically eccentric fashion. 'People are marrying out at a very fast rate, particularly in the provinces. The provinces are dying. On the other hand there's a greater intensity coming. You win some, you lose some. I don't see the next twenty years making a major difference to our community. Yes, it will be smaller, but it'll be in a very good state, I'd imagine. There's a great move now towards establishing the faith of traditional Judaism, a serious philosophy of being middle of the road. That's not something to be ashamed of. It is something to express positively: the ability to live in a secular world and still keep your Jewish traditions and have deep feelings for them. Judaism now has confidence. It's Torah-based, and yet we can still enjoy Shakespeare, university, and cinema and television, to name but some. If we miss a couple of the rules, there are 613 in all. If you observe 124 that's good too. I'm giving a lay view – a rabbi couldn't actually say that.' No, not quite in those words.

For Sidney Bloch, it's largely a matter of packaging. By 2000 Judaism could be entering a period of revival or disintegration. 'Fresh thinking could produce the former. Current attitudes may lead to the latter. There is no problem with the products but many, unfamiliar with their enduring values, find the packaging unattractive and the marketing uninspiring. Might one propose a *small select group* of the most able, rather than the most willing, to prepare a sales campaign for meaningful and lasting Judaism.'[2] It's not clear how Mr Bloch envisages this campaign for New Improved Judaism, or whom he would designate as the most able Jews, but presumably he would approve of the kind of initiative recently announced by the Central Council for Jewish Social Service, which he chairs, and the Joint Israel Appeal. The idea is to recruit and train a highly motivated and skilled band of potential lay leaders for the Anglo-Jewish community. Candidates, who will pay a fee, will enrol in courses that will supposedly develop their skills as managers as well as refresh their acquaintance with Jewish history and belief. Successful trainees will be rewarded with a diploma, and then – well, what then? One can hardly dispute that the community desperately needs more inspiring leadership than it is offered at present, but it seems doubtful whether leaders, as opposed to administrators, can be trained in this way. While such a scheme, and another new scheme to improve the training of teachers at Jewish schools, is bound to make some difference, it is unlikely that men and women of vision are created by diploma courses.

There is, it seems to me, a certain unseemly smugness inherent in the 'small but more Jewishly active' school of thought. As a prediction, it seems accurate enough, but it also assumes that the community will simply, for all Stanley Kalms's welcome talk of 'inclusivism', have to write off those British Jews who, in its religiously based view, don't come up to scratch. Rabbi Michael Rosen has remarked that he takes no comfort from the fact that by the year 2000 the Jewish community will be smaller but more committed. His interest, as his work at Yakar demonstrates, is in the uncommitted. It seems clear from the Establishment views I solicited that there will still be no, or very little, room within the Anglo-Jewish community for the unaffiliated or for those who prefer to express their Jewishness in 'alternative' ways. Any further reform of the Board of Deputies will be resisted, and it will continue to express meaningless consensus rather than judicious debate. As Tony Lerman suggests, disquiet over Israeli policies – unless there are radical changes in the decade ahead, which seems unlikely – will, however much the Establishment tries to gloss over the dissatisfaction, lead to a weakening of the Zionist groups and, for many Jews, a weakening of their identification, hitherto expressed more through loyalty to Israel than synagogue membership.

I am in no position to predict the future development of the community. There are too many imponderables: the extent to which ultra-Orthodoxy will continue to strengthen its forces through *teshuvah* and fecundity; the ability of the Reform movement to sustain its modest growth; the response of the mainstream United Synagogue to what will almost certainly be further polarization; the relation of Anglo-Jewry to Israel; the extent to which the community, aided by a growing Jewish educational network, begins to close in on itself; the extent to which the ideal of Simon Caplan, Stanley Kalms, and Rabbi Jonathan Sacks of Jews expressing their Orthodoxy without lessening their determination to live in the modern world will remain the norm; the identity of the Chief Rabbi's successor and the views he will express; the dissatisfaction of women; the alienation of a youth that feels patronized by its elders – all these factors, jumbled and moving in contrary directions, are, to me at least, inscrutable. It would be comforting to look forward to an Anglo-Jewish community in the next century that is not only viable and contented in its diversity, but that exhibits a fraction of the independence and intellectual and artistic vitality of its American counterpart, but that seems an unlikely prospect. For the Jewish Establishment in Britain is not only mediocre in itself, but revels in its mediocrity, shallowness, and philistinism, and as long as such attitudes prevail, Anglo-Jewry may survive, may even be more intensely Jewish, but it will never thrive and enrich the nation as a whole. In North America, Jews, whether religious or not, relish their Jewishness because they feel no self-imposed stigma of inferior status because they belong to a minority.

Indeed, there are times when it is easy to feel that American culture and Jewish culture, whether in the form of Hollywood epics or the novels of New Yorkers such as Heller and Roth and Mailer, are almost indistinguishable. In Britain, by contrast, Jews marginalize themselves and thereby relegate themselves to obscurity. Very few Jews of distinction take an active role within Anglo-Jewry. Unless the Anglo-Jewish leadership is prepared to cast off its cautious diffidence and widen its embrace, the community, whatever its size or state of health by 2000, will never do more than cool its heels on the sidelines of British life.

Notes

A BRIEF HISTORY

1. Laying the foundations
[1] V. D. Lipman, *The Social History of the Jews in England*, pp 77–8.

THE RELIGIOUS COMMUNITY

4. Holier than thou: the ultra-Orthodox
[1] Eimer, 'Ground Rules for Dialogue'.
[2] *Jewish Chronicle*, 27 May 1988.
[3] Gubbay and Levy, *The Ages of Man*, p 33.
[4] Marmur, *Beyond Survival*, pp 11–12.

5. The Lubavitch movement
[1] Article by Jack Shamash in *Jewish Herald*, 12 November 1987.
[2] *Challenge*, pp 176 ff.
[3] Ibid, p 208.
[4] Ibid, p 237.
[5] *Lubavitch News*, December 1987.
[6] Woody Allen, 'Hassidic Tales', in *Getting Even*.
[7] *Lubavitch News*, December 1987.

6. The burgeoning of ultra-Orthodoxy
[1] Maybaum, 'The Rise of Modern Jewish Theology', pp 90–1.
[2] Marmur, *Beyond Survival*, pp 11–12, 67.
[3] Jacobs, 'Fundamental Questions'.
[4] *Jewish Chronicle*, 15 January 1988.

7. The United Synagogue
[1] Bermant, *On the Other Hand*, p 28.
[2] *Jewish Chronicle*, January 1988.

9. Reform Judaism

[1] Maybaum, 'The Rise of Modern Jewish Theology', p 79.
[2] Eimer, 'Ground Rules for Dialogue'.
[3] Goldberg and Rayner, *Jewish People*, pp 19–20.
[4] Maybaum, 'The Rise of Modern Jewish Theology', pp 79–80.
[5] Rayner, 'Towards a Modern Halachah', pp 113–127.
[6] Marmur, *Beyond Survival*, p 47.
[7] Ibid, p 13.

10. Liberal Judaism

[1] Brichto, 'Halacha with Humility'.
[2] *Jewish Chronicle*, 17 June 1988.

12. Battle lines: a polarized community

[1] Brichto, 'Halacha with Humility'.
[2] Jakobovits, 'Preserving the Oneness of the Jewish People', p 19.
[3] Berkovits, 'Coming to Terms'.
[4] Letter from Mervyn S. Kersh, *Jewish Chronicle*, August 1987.
[5] Berkovits, 'Coming to Terms'.
[6] 'The New Chief Rabbi', *Jewish Chronicle*, 14 January 1988.
[7] *Jewish Chronicle*, 19 February 1988.
[8] Ibid.

13. Being Jewish

[1] Charles, 'I Believe', pp 79–80.
[2] Mankowitz, 'I have a very Strong Sense of Origin', pp 82–3.
[3] Bermant, *Coming Home*, p 166.
[4] Miller, 'Among Chickens', p 146.

14. Know your place: the role of women

[1] Goldberg and Rayner, *Jewish People*, p 323.
[2] Rayner, 'Women's Status in Judaism', pp 205–11.
[3] *Challenge*, pp 218–20.
[4] *Jewish Chronicle*, 12 February 1988.
[5] *L'Eylah* 23.
[6] Ibid.
[7] Bermant, *On the Other Hand*, p 37.

THE ESTABLISHMENT

15. The Chief Rabbi

[1] Alderman, 'London Jews in the 1983 General Election'.
[2] *Jewish Chronicle*, 5 February 1988.

16. The Board of Deputies
[1] Alderman, *Jewish Community in British Politics*, p 121.
[2] *Jewish Chronicle*, 1 July 1988.

17. Passing the baton: education
[1] Kalms, Speech to Cambridge University Jewish Society.
[2] Marmur, *Beyond Survival*, p 126.
[3] *Jewish Chronicle*, 1 January 1988.
[4] *Jewish Chronicle*, 26 February 1988.
[5] *L'Eylah*, April 1988, p 30.
[6] *Jewish Chronicle*, 31 July 1987.
[7] *Jewish Chronicle*, 15 July 1988.

18. The charity network
[1] Bermant, *Coming Home*, p 45.
[2] Aris, *Jews in Business*, p 216.
[3] *Jewish Chronicle*, 11 March 1988.
[4] Article by Lee Levitt in *Jewish Chronicle*, 19 February 1988.

THREE COMMUNITIES

19. Fading away: the East End
[1] Gould and Esh, *Jewish Life*, p 64.

21. Glasgow
[1] Benski, 'The Edge of Friendliness'.
[2] Bermant, *Coming Home*, p 49.
[3] Benski, 'The Edge of Friendliness'.

22. The provinces
[1] *Jewish Chronicle*, 27 May 1988.
[2] *Jewish Chronicle*, 25 March 1988.
[3] Paul, Address to St John's Wood synagogue.

JEWS AS BRITONS

23. Making a living
[1] Aris, *Jews in Business*, pp 112–122.
[2] Krausz, 'Economic and Social Structure'.
[3] Quoted in Attali, *Siegmund Warburg*, p 215.
[4] Aris, *Jews in Business*, pp 18–21.
[5] Kalms, Address to Cambridge University Jewish Society.
[6] Article by Nick Kochan, *Sunday Times*, 13 March 1988.
[7] Gordon, *Two Tycoons*.
[8] Aris, *Jews in Business*, p 137.

[9] Article by David Nathan, *Jewish Chronicle*, 25 December 1987.
[10] Kalms, Address to Cambridge University Jewish Society.
[11] *L'Eylah*, September 1987.
[12] *Jewish Chronicle*, 15 July 1988.
[13] Kalms, Address to Cambridge University Jewish Society.
[14] Bermant, *On the Other Hand*, pp 18–20.
[15] *Sunday Times*, 17 April 1988.
[16] *Jewish Chronicle*, 1 July 1988.
[17] Krausz, 'Economic and Social Structure', p 28.

24. Art and intellect

[1] *Jewish Chronicle*, 4 March 1988.
[2] Mankowitz, 'I have a very Strong Sense of Origin', p 81.
[3] Raphael, 'Something to be Serious About', pp 76–7.
[4] Bermant, *What's the Joke?*, p 185.
[5] Kitaj and Hyman, 'A Return to London', p 43.
[6] Paul, Address to St John's Wood synagogue.
[7] Lipman, *Social History*, p 82.
[8] Koestler, *The Invisible Writing*, p 426.
[9] Quoted in Olsover, *Jewish Communities of North-east England*, p 165.

25. Eyes right: Jews in politics

[1] Alderman, *Jewish Community in British Politics*, pp 52–4.
[2] Kadish, 'Jewish Bolshevism', p 18.
[3] *Jewish Quarterly*, Vol. 34, No. 2, 1988.
[4] Johnson, *History*, pp 354–7.
[5] Goldberg and Rayner, *Jewish People*, p 309.
[6] Alderman, 'London Jews and the 1987 General Election'.
[7] Ibid.
[8] Quoted in Alderman, *Jewish Community in British Politics*, pp 151–3.
[9] *Jewish Chronicle*, 15 January 1988.

26. Reaching out: Zionism and Soviet Jewry

[1] Goldberg and Rayner, *Jewish People*, p 190.
[2] Sieff, *Don't Ask the Price*, p 28.

27. Opinion and silence: responding to Israel

[1] *Jewish Chronicle*, 29 April 1988.
[2] Bermant, *On the Other Hand*, p 57.
[3] *Jewish Chronicle*, 29 January 1988.
[4] *Jewish Chronicle*, 19 February 1988.
[5] Hertzberg, 'The Illusion of Jewish Unity'.
[6] Steiner, 'Why a Jew can only Grieve'.
[7] Quoted in Attali, *Siegmund Warburg*, pp 296–300.

[8] *Jewish Chronicle*, 24 June 1988.
[9] Bermant, *On the Other Hand*, p 11.

28. On guard: anti-Semitism in Britain
[1] Litvinoff, 'A Jewish Writer', pp 95–6.
[2] Attali, *Siegmund Warburg*, pp 281–2.
[3] *Sunday Telegraph*, 15 November 1987.
[4] *Jewish Chronicle*, 4 March 1988.
[5] *Jewish Chronicle*, 12 February 1988.
[6] *Observer*, 8 May 1988.
[7] *Jewish Chronicle*, 15 April 1988.

30. Legs and roots: Anglo-Jewish identity
[1] Ahad Ha-am, *Essays*, p 85.
[2] Bermant, *What's the Joke*, p 189.
[3] *Jewish Quarterly*, Vol. 34, No. 4, 1987, p 2.
[4] *Jewish Chronicle*, 26 February 1988.
[5] Glanville, 'At a deeper level', p 73.
[6] Johnson, *History*, p 394.
[7] Abse, 'Jews are bound to each other', p 86.
[8] Marmur, *Beyond Survival*, pp 29–31.
[9] *Jewish Chronicle*, 1 April 1988.
[10] *Jewish Chronicle*, 15 July 1988.
[11] Bermant, *On the Other Hand*, p 123.
[12] *Observer*, 17 July 1988.
[13] Raphael, *After the War*, p 185.
[14] Cesarani, 'Alternative Jewish Community', pp 51–4.
[15] *Jewish Chronicle*, 27 May 1988.
[16] *Jewish Chronicle*, 8 July 1988.

31. The year 2000
[1] Sacks, 'Towards 2000', *L'Eylah* 23, p 27.
[2] Bloch, 'Anglo-Judaism in Crisis?', *L'Eylah* 23, p 19.

Glossary

Aggadah: rabbinic lore

Aliyah: 'going up', either to read from the Torah in synagogue, or emigrating to Israel

Ashkenazim: Jews of north European origin

Barmitzvah: religious ceremony by which males take on the responsibilities of Jewish observance

Batmitzvah: barmitzvah-style ceremony adapted for girls in Reform and Liberal synagogues

Beth Din: rabbinical court

Bima: elevated platform with reading desks in a synagogue

Bnot chayil: United Synagogue version of batmitzvah

Cabbalah: Jewish mysticism

Chanukah: festival that commemorates the rededication of the Temple in Jerusalem by the Maccabees

Chasidism: eastern European movement of very pious Jews under charismatic rabbinical leadership

Chazan: cantor

Cheder: religion school

Chupah: wedding canopy

Daven: the act of prayer, often accompanied with swaying and other movements

Dayan (pl. *Dayanim*): judge in a rabbinical court

Erev: eve (of Sabbath or a festival)

Frum (Yiddish): religious

Gaon: head of rabbinic academy

Gedolim: the sages, great ones

Gemara: Commentary on the Mishnah; the two together form the Talmud, but the name Talmud is often applied to Gemara alone

Goyim: Gentiles

Haftorah: Sabbath reading from the Prophetic books

Haggadah: prayer-book containing the Passover eve liturgy
Halachah: religious law
Haskalah: enlightenment
Havdalah: the ceremony which ends the Sabbath week
Kaddish: mourner's prayer
Kashrut: dietary laws
Kelal Israel: the Jewish community
Kiddush: ceremony to usher in the Sabbath or a festival
Kippah (plural: *Kippot*): skullcap. Also known as *Yarmulke*
Kollel: a postgraduate institution in which married men and ordained rabbis
   engage in higher Talmudic studies
Kosher: suitable for consumption by religious Jews
Ma'ariv: evening service
Maskil: 'Enlightened one', educated and willing to question Jewish tradition
Menorah: seven-branched candelabrum
Mezuzah: small tube containing religious texts attached to a doorpost
Midrash: scriptural interpretation
Mikveh: ritual bath used by women after menstruation
Minchah: afternoon service
Minhag: custom
Minyan: quorum of 10 adult males
Mishnah: earliest codification of Jewish law by Rabbi Judah Ha-Nasi in the
   second century
Mitnaggedim: traditionalist opponents of the Chasidic movement
Mitzvah: religious commandment or obligation
Musaf: additional Sabbath service
Neturei Karta: religious Anti-Zionists
Rebbetzin: rabbi's wife
Seder: meal and ceremony on Passover eve
Sefer Torah: Scroll of the Law
Sephardim: Jews of North African and Iberian origin
Shabbat (or Shabbos): Sabbath
Shechita: religiously approved animal slaughter
Sheitl: wig
Shiur (p. *shiurim*): study session based on verses of scripture
Shiva: period of mourning
Shofar: ram's horn
Shtiebel (pl. *shtieblach*): 'Small house', a secondary synagogue
Shul: synagogue
Shulchan Aruch: sixteenth-century code of Jewish law
Sidrah: portion of the Torah read during Sabbath service
Tallis (*tallit*): prayer shawl

Talmud: cumulative rabbinic commentaries on Scripture and Jewish law

Tefillin: leather boxes containing passages from the Torah. Bound by leather strips to the left arm and to the forehead, and worn during the morning service except on Sabbath and scriptural festivals

Teshuvah: repentance, return

Torah: teaching; the Pentateuch

Trefah: unfit to be eaten

Tzaddik: Chasidic leader

Yeshiva: academy for rabbinic studies

Yishuv: the Jewish community in the Holy Land

Yomtov: Jewish festival

Select bibliography

AHAD HA-AM, *Essays, Letters, Memoirs*, translated by Leon Simon, Oxford: East and West Library, 1946

ALDERMAN, GEOFFREY, *The Jewish Community in British Politics*, Oxford: Clarendon Press, 1983

ALLEN, WOODY, 'Hassidic Tales', in *Getting Even*, New York: Warner Paperback Library, 1972

ARIS, STEPHEN, *The Jews in Business*, London: Jonathan Cape, 1970

ARONOVITCH, BELLA, *Give it Time*, London: Deutsch, 1975

ATTALI, JACQUES, *A Man of Influence: Sir Siegmund Warburg*, translated by Barbara Ellis, London: Weidenfeld & Nicolson, 1986

BERGHAHN, MARION, *German-Jewish Refugees in England*, London: Macmillan, 1984

BERMANT, CHAIM, *Coming Home*, London: George Allen & Unwin, 1976

—, *The Cousinhood*, London: Eyre & Spottiswoode, 1971

—, *London's East End: Point of Arrival*, New York: Macmillan, 1975

—, *On the Other Hand*, London: Robson, 1982

—, *What's the Joke?: A Study of Jewish Humour Through the Ages*, London: Weidenfeld & Nicolson, 1986

COLLINS, KENNETH E., *Aspects of Scottish Jewry*, Glasgow: Jewish Representative Council, 1987

FIGES, EVA, *Little Eden*, London: Faber & Faber, 1978

GABBAY, LUCIEN, and LEVY, ABRAHAM, *The Ages of Man*, London: Darton Longman & Todd, 1985

GOLDBERG, DAVID J., and RAYNER, JOHN D., *The Jewish People: Their History and Their Religion*, London: Viking, 1987

GORDON, CHARLES, *The Two Tycoons*, London: Hamish Hamilton, 1984

GOULD, JULIUS, and ESH, SHAUL, *Jewish Life in Modern Britain*, London: Routledge & Kegan Paul, 1964

JACOBS, LOUIS, *Hasidic Prayer*, New York: Schocken, 1973

KATZ, STEVEN T., *Jewish Ideas and Concepts*, New York: Schocken, 1977

KOCHAN, LIONEL, *The Jew and his History*, New York: Schocken, 1977

KOESTLER, ARTHUR, *The Invisible Writing*, London, 1954

LEVIN, BERNARD, *The Pendulum Years: Britain in the Sixties.* London: Jonathan Cape, 1970

LIPMAN, V. D., *Social History of the Jews in England 1850–1950*, London: Watts, 1954

LUBAVITCH FOUNDATION, *Challenge: An Encounter With Lubavitch-Chabad*, London: Lubavitch Foundation, 1970

MARMUR, DOW, *Beyond Survival: Reflections on the Future of Judaism*, London: Darton, Longman & Todd, 1982

MARMUR, DOW (ed.), *Reform Judaism: Essays on Reform Judaism in Britain*, London: Reform Synagogues of Great Britain, 1973

OLSOVER, LEWIS, *The Jewish Communities of North-east England*, Gateshead: Ashley Mark Publishing Co., 1980

SEBAG-MONTEFIORE, RUTH, *A Family Patchwork*, London: Weidenfeld & Nicolson, 1987

SICHER, EFRAIM, *Beyond Marginality: Anglo-Jewish Literature after the Holocaust*, New York: State University of New York Press, 1985

SIEFF, MARCUS, *Don't Ask the Price*, London: Weidenfeld & Nicolson, 1986

SONNTAG, JACOB (ed.), *Jewish Perspectives: 25 Years of Modern Jewish Writing*, *Jewish Quarterly* Anthology, London: Secker & Warburg, 1980

STEVENS, AUSTIN, *The Dispossessed*, London: Barrie & Jenkins, 1975

WILLIAMS, BILL, *Manchester Jewry: A Pictorial History 1788–1988*, Manchester: Archive Publications, 1988

Articles and Pamphlets

ABSE, DANNIE, 'Jews are Bound to each Other . . .' in Sonntag, *Jewish Perspectives*, 1980

ALDERMAN, GEOFFREY, 'London Jews and the 1987 General Election', in the *Jewish Quarterly* Vol. 34, No. 3, 1987

BARON, ALEXANDER, 'Jewish Preoccupations . . .' in Sonntag, *Jewish Perspectives*, 1980

BENSKI, TOVA, 'The Edge of Friendliness', in the *Jewish Echo*, 24.9.76

BERG, CHARLES, 'Revelation, Halachah and Mitsvah', in *Reform Judaism*, 1973

BERKOVITS, BEREL, 'Coming to terms', in the *Jewish Chronicle*, 18.9.87

BORTS, BARBARA (ed.), 'Women and Tallit', London: Reform Synagogues of Great Britain, 1987

BRICHTO, SIDNEY, 'Halacha with Humility' in the *Jewish Chronicle*, 2.10.87

BROTMAN, ADOLPH G., 'Jewish Communal Organization', in Gould and Esh, *Jewish Life in Modern Britain*, 1964

CESARANI, DAVID, 'The Alternative Jewish Community', *European Judaism*, '82: 2, '86: 1

CHARLES, GERDA, 'I Believe', in Sonntag, *Jewish Perspectives*, 1980

COHEN, MARLENE, 'Children & Family Break-up in Anglo-Jewry', London: West-Central, 1984

COHEN, NORMAN, 'Trends in Anglo-Jewish Religious Life', in Gould and Esh, *Jewish Life in Modern Britain*, 1964

CORNEY, HYAM, 'Lubavitch on the March', in the *Jewish Chronicle*, 4.9.87

CURTIS, MICHAEL, 'The Beth Din of the Reform Synagogues of Great Britain', in *Reform Judaism*, 1973

DAICHES, DAVID, 'Some Aspects of Anglo-American Jewish Fiction', in Sonntag, *Jewish Perspectives*, 1980

EIMER, RABBI COLIN, 'Ground Rules for Dialogue', in the *Jewish Chronicle*, 1.1.88

GLANVILLE, BRIAN, 'At A Deeper Level One is and Remains Jewish', in Sonntag, *Jewish Perspectives*, 1980

GOULSTON, MICHAEL J., 'The Theology of Reform Judaism in Great Britain: a Survey', in *Reform Judaism*, 1973

HERTZBERG, ARTHUR, 'The Illusion of Jewish Unity', *New York Review of Books*, 16.6.88

Inform: Newsletter of the Reform Synagogues of Great Britain

JACOBS, LOUIS, 'Fundamental Questions', in the *Jewish Chronicle*, 10.6.88

JAKOBOVITS, IMMANUEL, 'AIDS – Jewish Perspectives', London: Office of the Chief Rabbi, 1987

—, 'From Doom to Hope', London: Office of the Chief Rabbi, 1986

—, 'Human Fertilisation and Embryology – A Jewish View', London: Office of the Chief Rabbi, 1984

—, Preserving the Oneness of the Jewish People', lecture to Jewish Marriage Council, 14.12.87, London: Office of the Chief Rabbi, 1988

KADISH, SHARMAN, 'Jewish Bolshevism and the "Red Scare" in Britain', in the *Jewish Quarterly*, Vol. 34, No. 4, 1987

KITAJ, R. B., and HYMAN, TIMOTHY, 'A Return to London', in *Kitaj: Paintings, Drawings, Pastels*, London: Thames and Hudson, and Washington, D.C.: Smithsonian Institute, 1981

KOSMIN, BARRY A., 'Divorce in Anglo-Jewry 1970–1980', London: West-Central, 1982

KOSMIN, BARRY A., and LEVY, CAREN, 'Jewish Identity in an Anglo-Jewish Community', London: Research Unit, Board of Deputies, 1983

—, 'Synagogue Membership in the United Kingdom 1983', London: Research Unit, Board of Deputies, 1983

—, 'The Work and Employment of Suburban Jews', London: Research Unit, Board of Deputies, 1981

KOSMIN, BARRY A., LEVY, CAREN and WIGODSKY, PETER, 'The Social Demography of Redbridge Jewry', London: Research Unit, Board of Deputies, 1979

KRAUSZ, ERNEST, 'The Economic and Social Structure of Anglo-Jewry', in Gould and Esh, *Jewish Life in Modern Britain*, 1964

LEIGH, MICHAEL, 'Reform Judaism in Britain (1840–1970)', in *Reform Judaism*, 1973

LERMAN, ANTONY, '"Diaspora Blues": Real or Imagined?' in the *Jewish Quarterly*, Vol. 34, No. 4, 1987

L'Eylah, London: Jews' College Publications

LITVINOFF, EMANUEL, 'A Jewish Writer in England', in Sonntag, *Jewish Perspectives*, 1980

MANKOWITZ, WOLF, 'I Have a Very Strong Sense of Origin', in Sonntag, *Jewish Perspectives*, 1980

Manna: the Journal of the Sternberg Centre for Judaism, London

MAYBAUM, IGNAZ, 'The Rise of Modern Jewish Theology', in *Reform Judaism*, 1973

MILLER, JONATHAN, 'Among Chickens', *Granta 23*, Spring 1988, pp 141–8

NATHAN, DAVID, 'Profile of Stanley Kalms', in the *Jewish Chronicle*, 25.12.87

RAPHAEL, FREDERIC, 'Something to be Serious About . . .' in Sonntag, *Jewish Perspectives*, 1980

RAYNER, JOHN D., 'Towards a Modern Halachah', in *Reform Judaism*, 1973

—, 'Woman's Status in Judaism', in *Reform Judaism*, 1973

ROTH, CECIL, 'The Anglo-Jewish Community in the Context of World Jewry', in Gould and Esh, *Jewish Life in Modern Britain*, 1964

SPENCER, CHARLES, 'Towards a Definition of Jewish Art', in Sonntag, *Jewish Perspectives*, 1980

STEINER, GEORGE, 'Why a Jew Can Only Grieve', *The Times*, 14.5.88

WATERMAN, STANLEY, and KOSMIN, BARRY, *British Jewry in the Eighties*, Board of Deputies of British Jews, 1986

Unpublished

KALMS, STANLEY, Address to Cambridge University Jewish Society, 13.2.87

KALMS, STANLEY, Address to United Synagogue, 15.2.88

PAUL, GEOFFREY D., Address to St John's Wood United synagogue, 14.6.88

Index

449

450

Hill, 6, 257, 263; Golders Green,
36, 66, 88, 126, 146, 246, 251–3, 268,
323, 358, 363–4, 403; Hackney, 36,
77–8, 250, 342; Hampstead, 31, 36,
135, 139, 241, 314, 323, 408, 414;
Harrow, 230; Hatch End, 126, 294;
Hendon, 36, 57, 83–4, 88, 126, 189,
219, 229, 269, 347, 394, 414–5, 431;
Highgate, 258; Holland Park, 143;
Houndsditch, 18; Ilford, 36, 146, 149,
229, 257, 316, 346; Kenton, 229;
Kilburn, 31, 262, 400; Maida Vale,
144, 233; Mile End, 23, 27, 258;
Pinner, 294; Redbridge, 36, 257, 316;
St John's Wood, 36, 135, 149, 199;
Southgate, 36, 252; Spitalfields, 21,
24, 257, 258; Stamford Hill, 47,
49–52, 57, 60–1, 64, 70, 77, 82, 108,
128, 143, 151, 159, 264, 268, 283;
Stepney, 23, 250, 259, 342; Swiss
Cottage, 31, 36, 139; Tower
Hamlets, 199, 259, 264, 338, 340;
Waltham Forest, 316; Wanstead,
257; West End, 18, 21, 117, 304, 327;
West Hampstead, 401, 403;
Whitechapel, 21, 24, 26, 27, 199;
Willesden, 229–31
Lubavitch movement, 52, 53, 54, 57, 59,
61, 68–76, 79, 101, 102, 159, 162,
169, 184–6, 209–10, 234, 258, 268,
283, 285, 294, 304, 318, 419–20
Lustig, Robin, 392
Lyons, Sir Jack, 306, 387

Maccabi, 274
Maccoby, Hyam, 396
Macmull, Rabbi Yitzhak, 260–1
Magonet, Rabbi Jonathan, 46, 120, 122,
124, 126, 136–8, 157, 159, 160, 180,
207, 219–20, 242, 307
Mail on Sunday, 306
Mailer, Norman, 435
Maimonides, 174, 189, 234
Manchester, 17, 19, 21, 26, 31, 69, 107,
112–3, 114, 118, 130, 143, 148, 161–2,
167, 228, 242, 248–9, 265–78, 279,

281, 282, 287, 288, 291, 292, 311,
322, 335, 356, 430–1; Broughton
Park, 268–9, 273, 276, 277, 283;
Bury, 273, 174; Cheadle, 268, 274,
277; Cheetham Hill, 26–27, 267, 269,
279, 342; Didsbury, 268; Gatley, 268;
North Manchester, 270–1; Sale,
268, 277; Salford, 271; South
Manchester, 268, 270–1, 275;
Withington, 268
Manchester Gazette, 274, 275–6
Manchester Jewish Blind Society, 274
Manchester Jewish Museum, 269
Manchester Jewish Representative
Council, 265, 270, 271
Manchester Jewish Social Services,
238–9, 248, 254, 271, 273–4
Manchester Shechita Board, 270
Manchester Telegraph, 275–6
Manchester Zionist Central Council,
274, 277
Mancroft, Lord, 385
Mankowitz, Wolf, 175, 324
Manna, 201
Manor House (Sternberg Centre for
Judaism), 126, 128, 181, 229, 235,
242
Mapam, 274, 361, 371, 396, 406
Mappah, 79–80
Margulies, Ephraim, 54, 300, 306
Mariner, Rabbi Rodney, 62, 76, 138–41,
150, 167, 172, 421
Markova, Dame Alicia, 325
Marks and Spencer, 356
Marks family, 19, 268, 322, 356–7
Marks, Alfred, 325
Marks, Laurence, 326
Marks, Lord, 357
Marks, Simon, 356–7
Marmur, Rabbi Dow, 61, 86, 124, 127,
228, 420
Marshall, John, 347
Marx, Karl, 319
Masorti, *see* Conservative Judaism
Mattuck, Dr, 129
Maxwell, Dr Elizabeth, 373, 421–2, 424